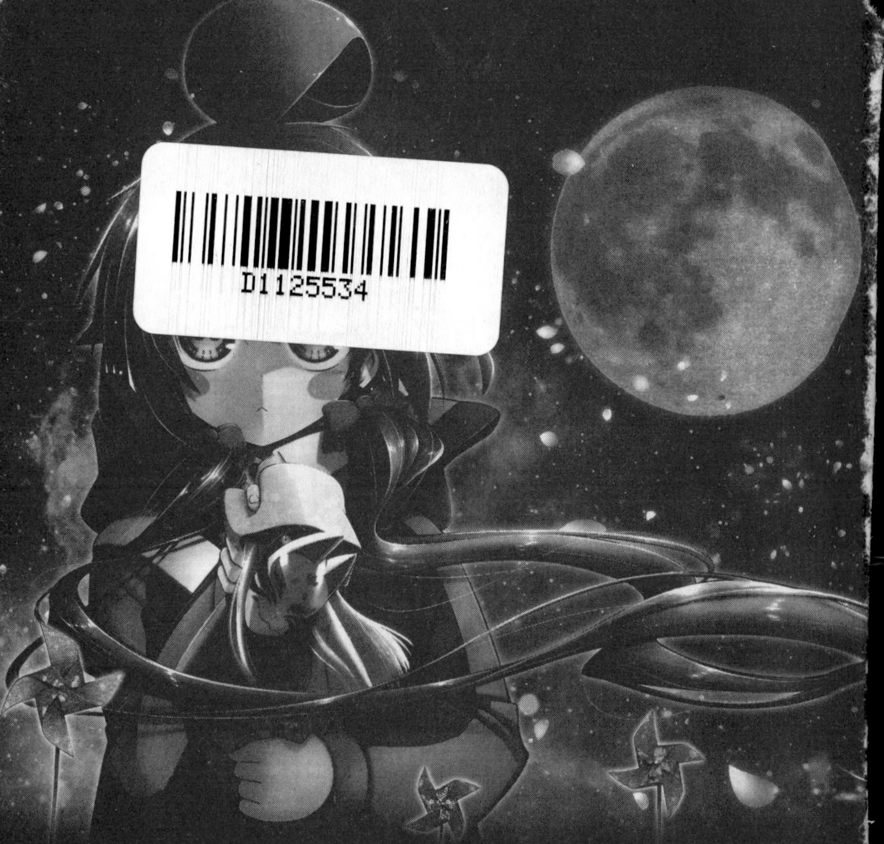

DARK GATHERING

1

Story and Art by

Kenichi Kondo

contents

DARK GATHERING 1

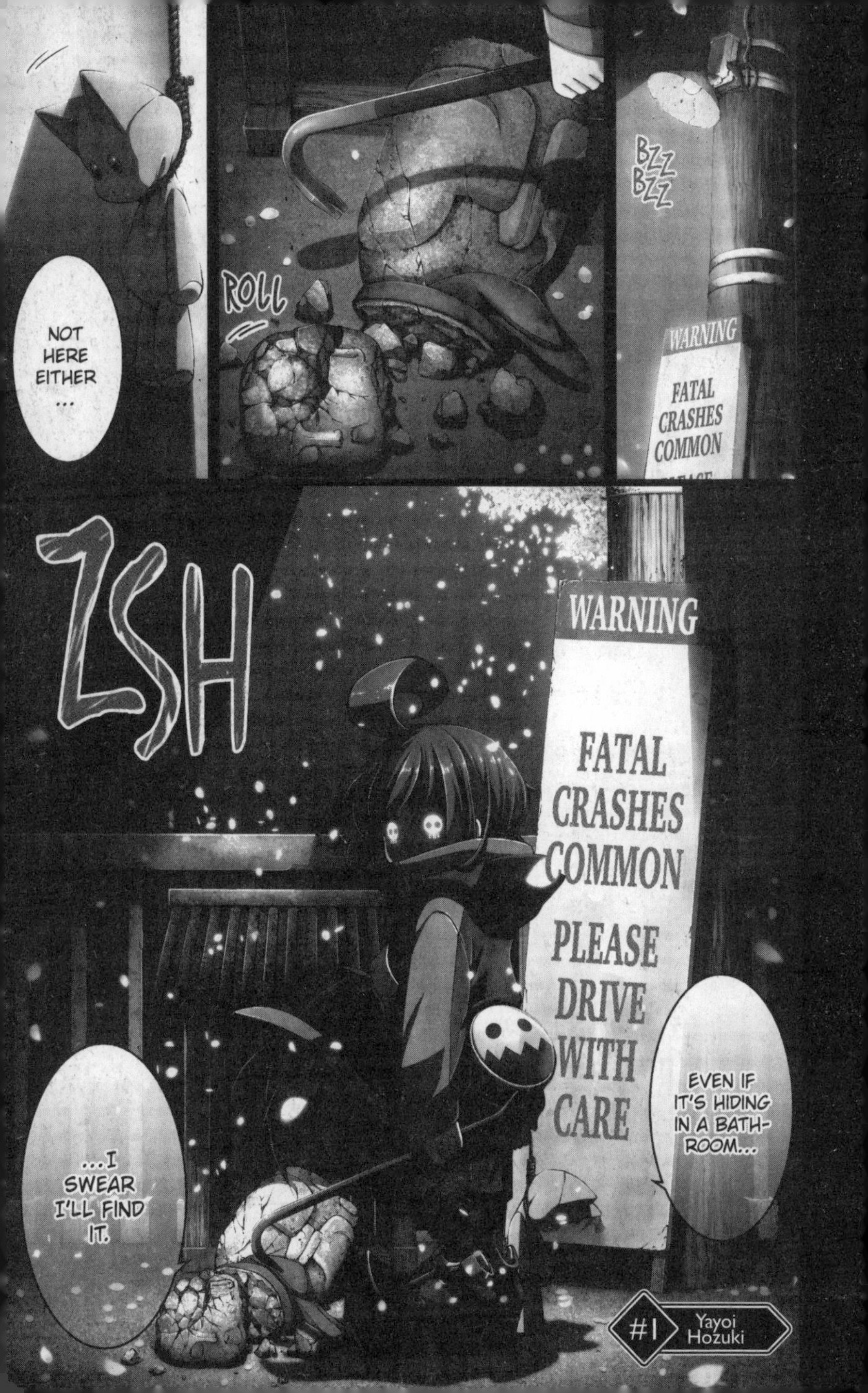
BZZ BZZ
WARNING
FATAL CRASHES COMMON
ROLL
NOT HERE EITHER ...
ZSH
WARNING
FATAL CRASHES COMMON
PLEASE DRIVE WITH CARE
EVEN IF IT'S HIDING IN A BATH-ROOM...
...I SWEAR I'LL FIND IT.
#1 Yayoi Hozuki

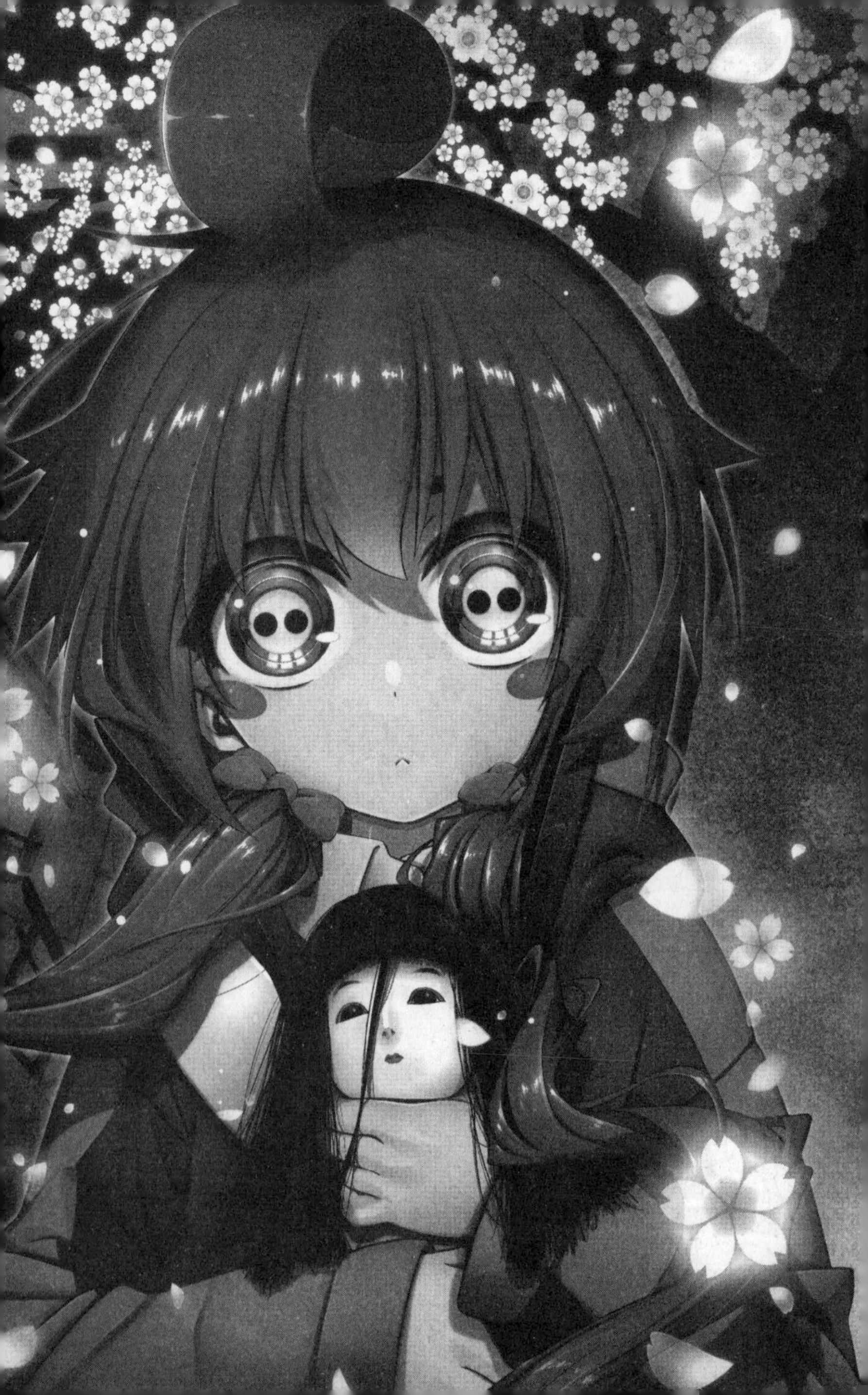

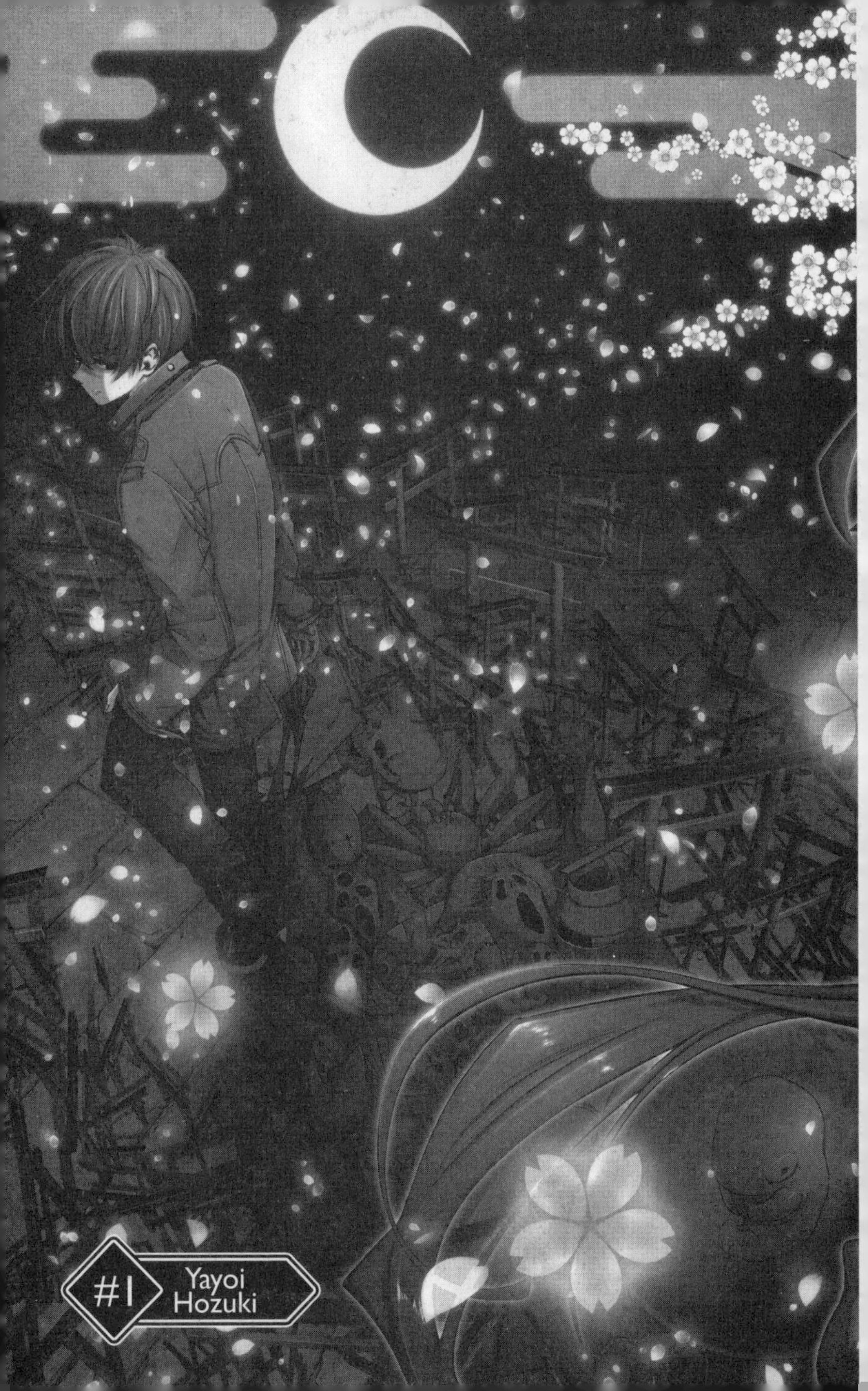
#1
Yayoi Hozuki

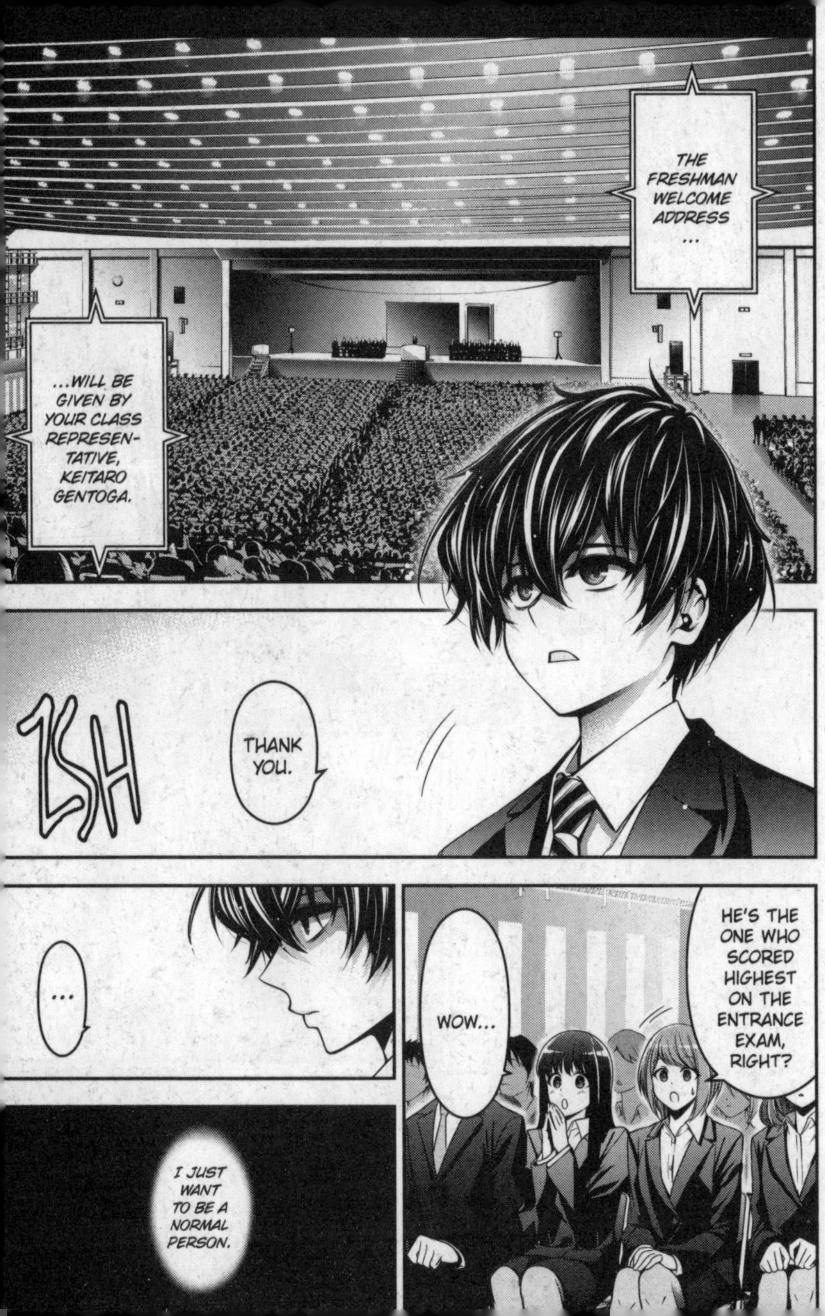
THE FRESHMAN WELCOME ADDRESS ...
...WILL BE GIVEN BY YOUR CLASS REPRESEN-TATIVE, KEITARO GENTOGA.
THANK YOU.
TSH
HE'S THE ONE WHO SCORED HIGHEST ON THE ENTRANCE EXAM, RIGHT?
WOW...
...
I JUST WANT TO BE A NORMAL PERSON.

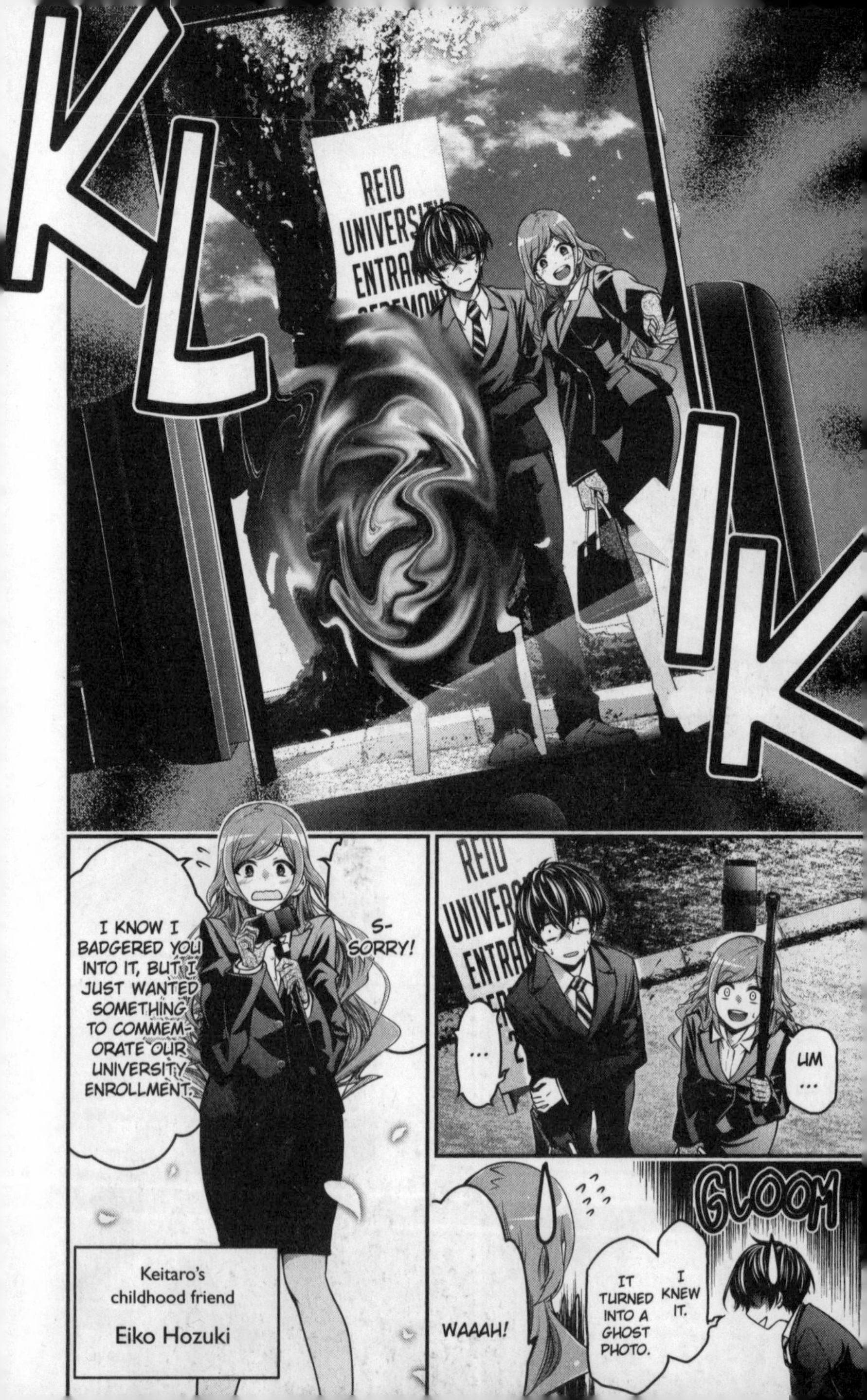
KLIK
REIO
UM ...
...
GLOOM
I KNEW IT.
IT TURNED INTO A GHOST PHOTO.
WAAAH!
S-SORRY!
I KNOW I BADGERED YOU INTO IT, BUT I JUST WANTED SOMETHING TO COMMEMORATE OUR UNIVERSITY ENROLLMENT.
Keitaro's childhood friend
Eiko Hozuki

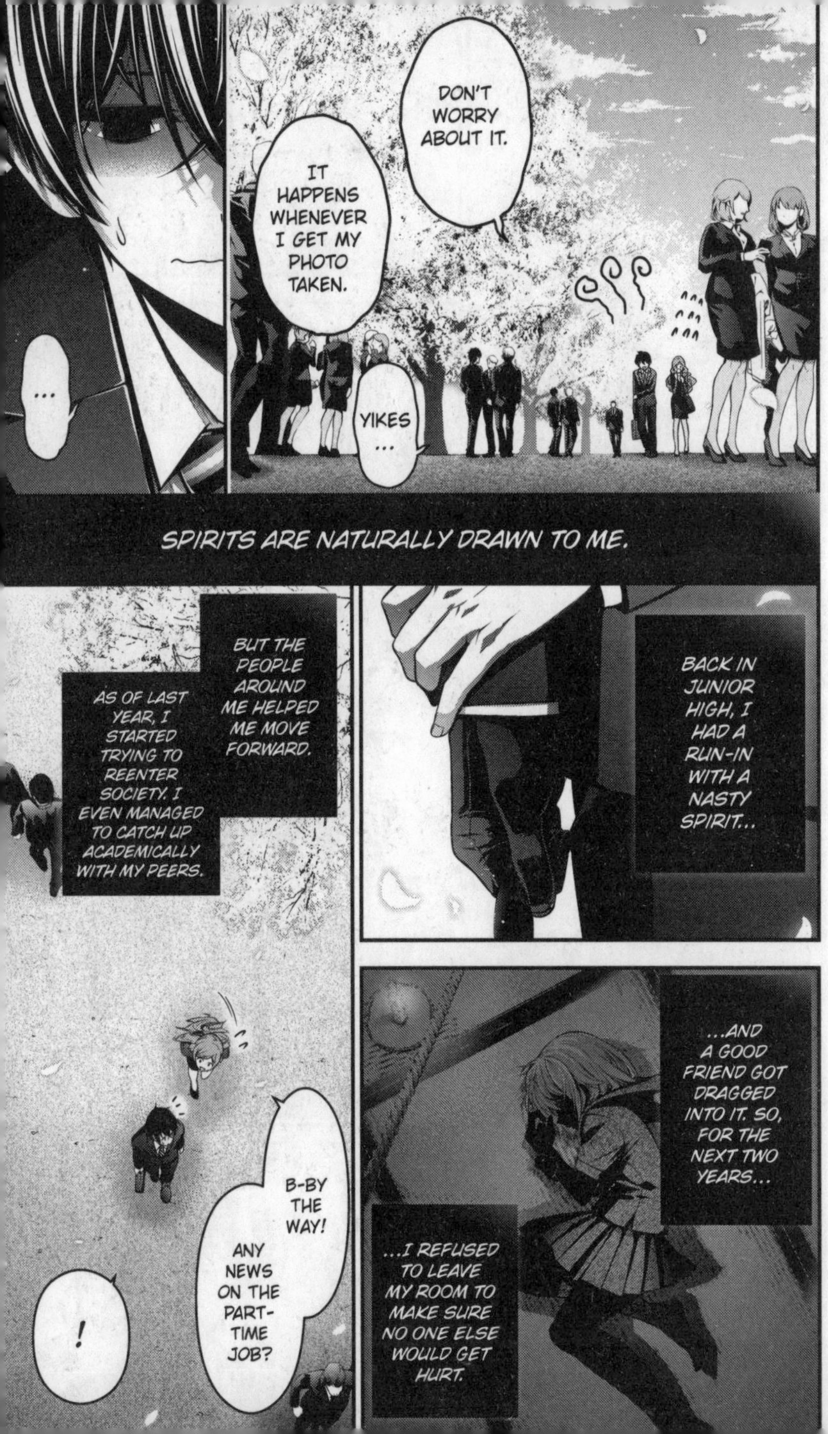
DON'T WORRY ABOUT IT.
IT HAPPENS WHENEVER I GET MY PHOTO TAKEN.
YIKES...
...
SPIRITS ARE NATURALLY DRAWN TO ME.
BACK IN JUNIOR HIGH, I HAD A RUN-IN WITH A NASTY SPIRIT...
...AND A GOOD FRIEND GOT DRAGGED INTO IT. SO, FOR THE NEXT TWO YEARS...
...I REFUSED TO LEAVE MY ROOM TO MAKE SURE NO ONE ELSE WOULD GET HURT.
BUT THE PEOPLE AROUND ME HELPED ME MOVE FORWARD.
AS OF LAST YEAR, I STARTED TRYING TO REENTER SOCIETY. I EVEN MANAGED TO CATCH UP ACADEMICALLY WITH MY PEERS.
B-BY THE WAY!
ANY NEWS ON THE PART-TIME JOB?
!

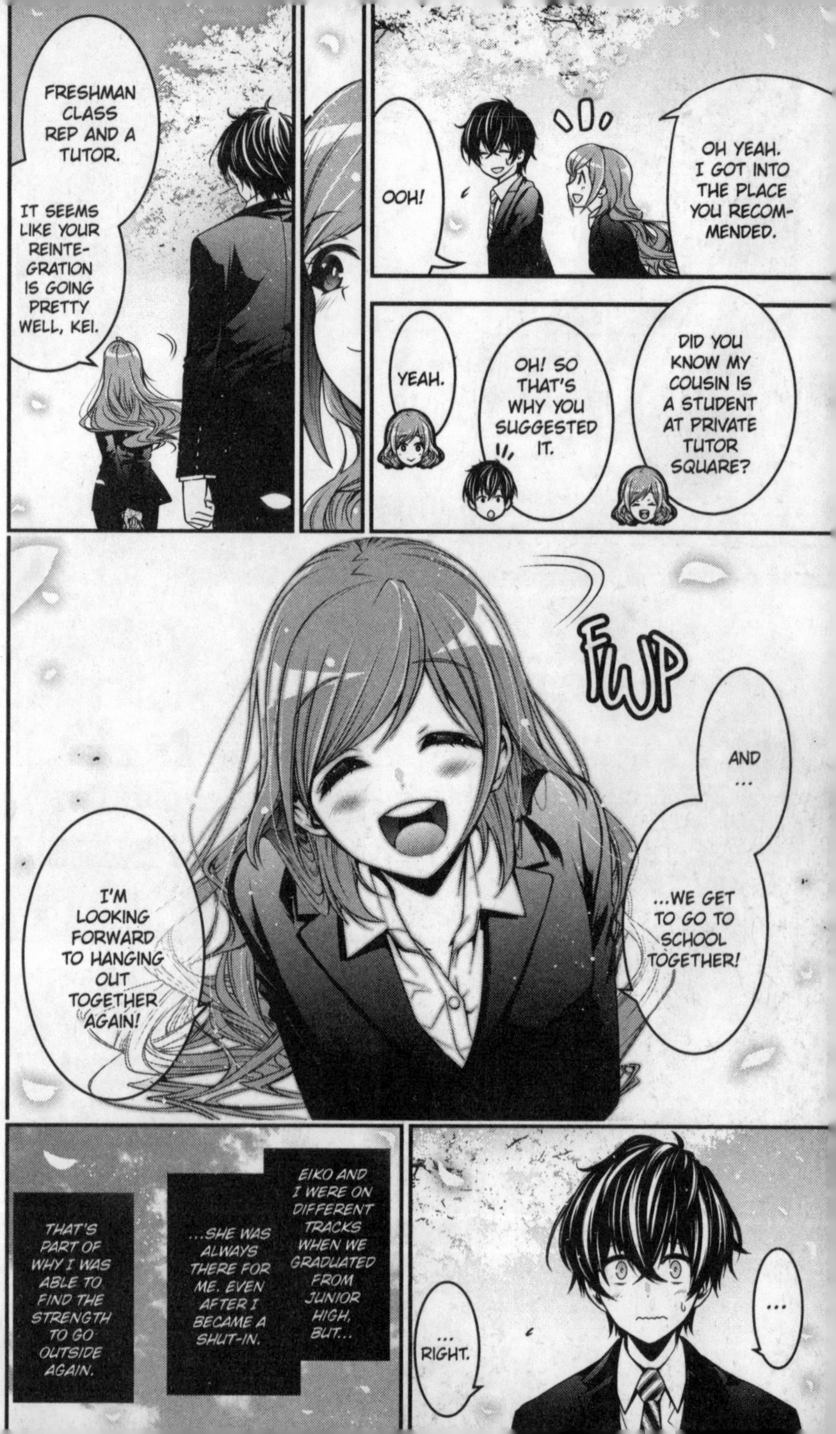
OH YEAH. I GOT INTO THE PLACE YOU RECOMMENDED.
OOH!
DID YOU KNOW MY COUSIN IS A STUDENT AT PRIVATE TUTOR SQUARE?
OH! SO THAT'S WHY YOU SUGGESTED IT.
YEAH.
FRESHMAN CLASS REP AND A TUTOR.
IT SEEMS LIKE YOUR REINTEGRATION IS GOING PRETTY WELL, KEI.
FWP
AND ...
...WE GET TO GO TO SCHOOL TOGETHER!
I'M LOOKING FORWARD TO HANGING OUT TOGETHER AGAIN!
...
...RIGHT.
EIKO AND I WERE ON DIFFERENT TRACKS WHEN WE GRADUATED FROM JUNIOR HIGH, BUT...
...SHE WAS ALWAYS THERE FOR ME. EVEN AFTER I BECAME A SHUT-IN.
THAT'S PART OF WHY I WAS ABLE TO FIND THE STRENGTH TO GO OUTSIDE AGAIN.

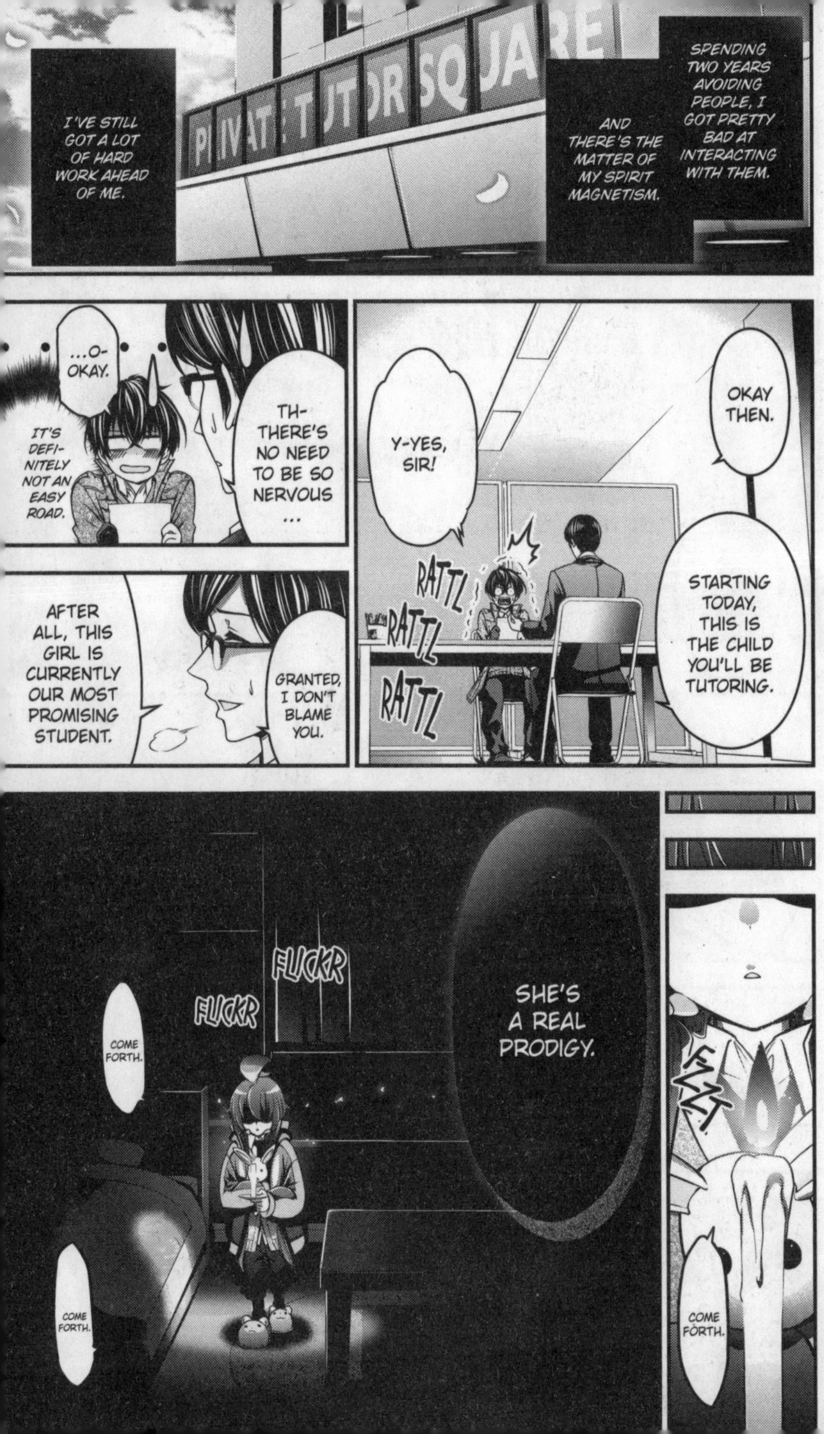
SPENDING TWO YEARS AVOIDING PEOPLE, I GOT PRETTY BAD AT INTERACTING WITH THEM.
AND THERE'S THE MATTER OF MY SPIRIT MAGNETISM.
I'VE STILL GOT A LOT OF HARD WORK AHEAD OF ME.
OKAY THEN.
STARTING TODAY, THIS IS THE CHILD YOU'LL BE TUTORING.
Y-YES, SIR!
RATTL
RATTL
RATTL
TH- THERE'S NO NEED TO BE SO NERVOUS ...
...O- OKAY.
IT'S DEFINITELY NOT AN EASY ROAD.
GRANTED, I DON'T BLAME YOU.
AFTER ALL, THIS GIRL IS CURRENTLY OUR MOST PROMISING STUDENT.
FZZT
COME FORTH.
SHE'S A REAL PRODIGY.
FLICKR
FLICKR
COME FORTH.
COME FORTH.

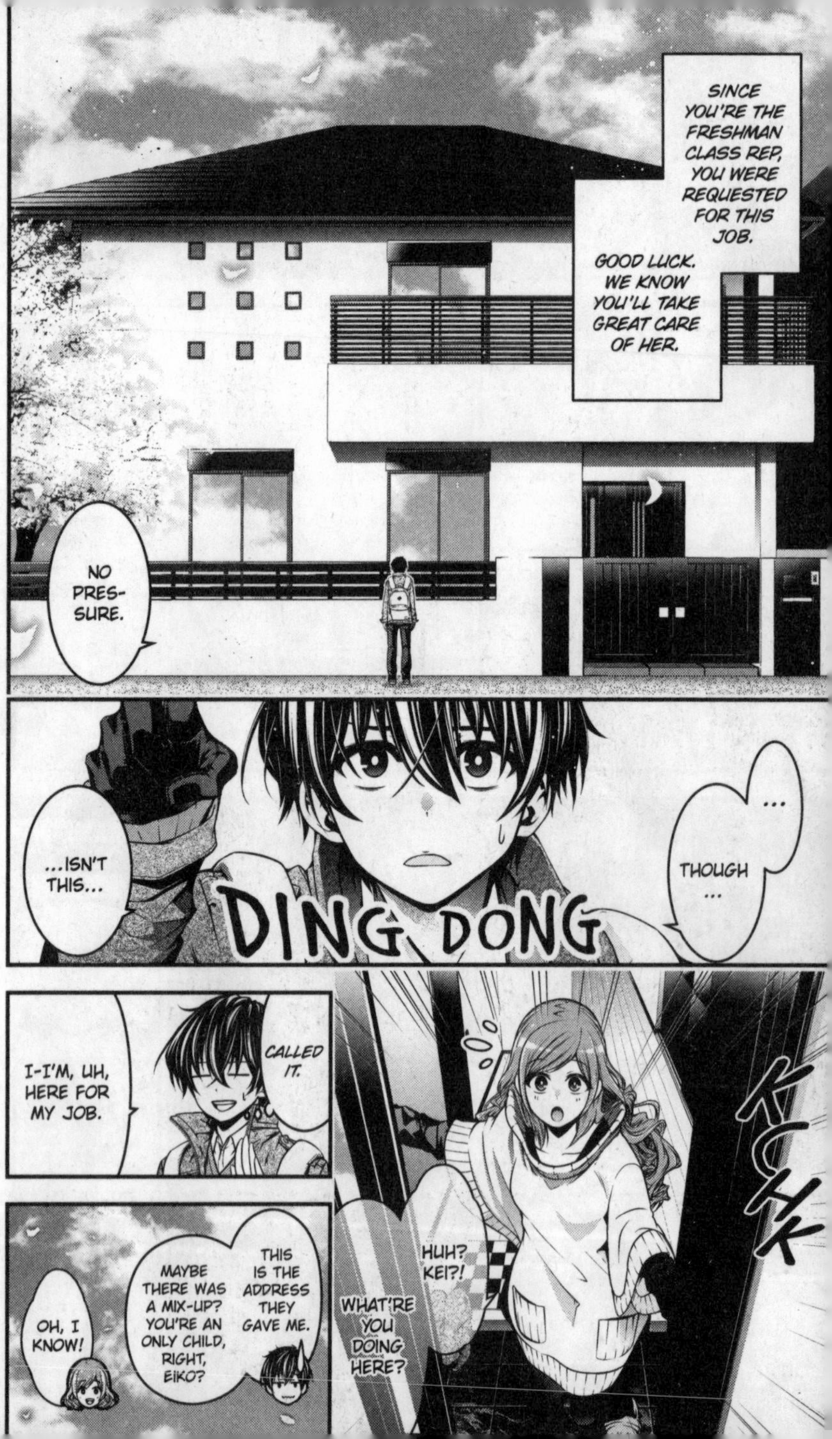
SINCE YOU'RE THE FRESHMAN CLASS REP, YOU WERE REQUESTED FOR THIS JOB.
GOOD LUCK. WE KNOW YOU'LL TAKE GREAT CARE OF HER.
NO PRES-SURE.
... THOUGH ...
DING DONG
...ISN'T THIS...
KCHK
HUH? KEI?!
WHAT'RE YOU DOING HERE?
CALLED IT.
I-I'M, UH, HERE FOR MY JOB.
THIS IS THE ADDRESS THEY GAVE ME.
MAYBE THERE WAS A MIX-UP? YOU'RE AN ONLY CHILD, RIGHT, EIKO?
OH, I KNOW!

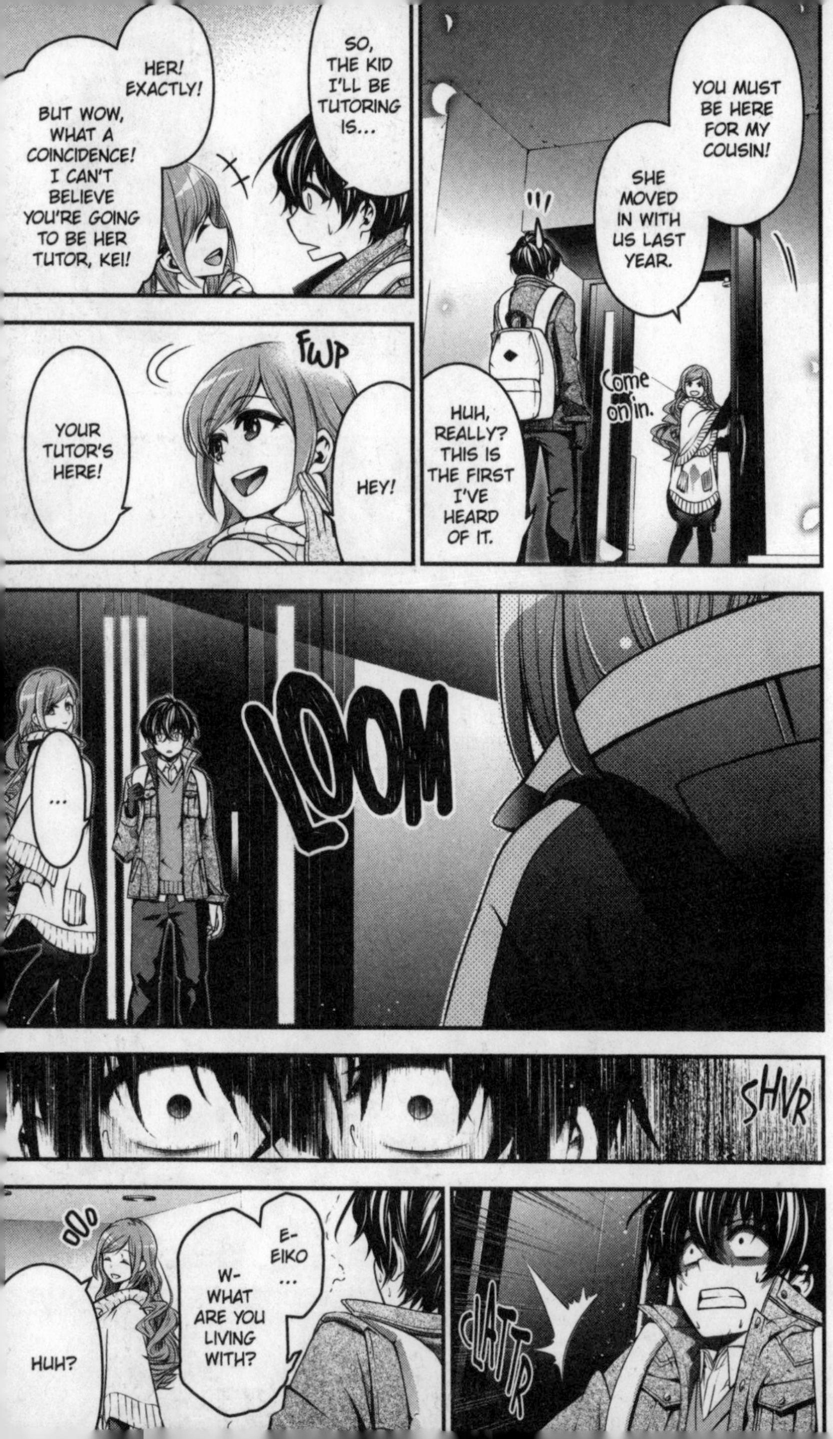
YOU MUST BE HERE FOR MY COUSIN!
SHE MOVED IN WITH US LAST YEAR.
Come on in.
HUH, REALLY? THIS IS THE FIRST I'VE HEARD OF IT.
SO, THE KID I'LL BE TUTORING IS...
HER! EXACTLY!
BUT WOW, WHAT A COINCIDENCE! I CAN'T BELIEVE YOU'RE GOING TO BE HER TUTOR, KEI!
FWP
HEY!
YOUR TUTOR'S HERE!
LOOM
...
SHVR
CLATTR
E- EIKO...
W-WHAT ARE YOU LIVING WITH?
OOO
HUH?

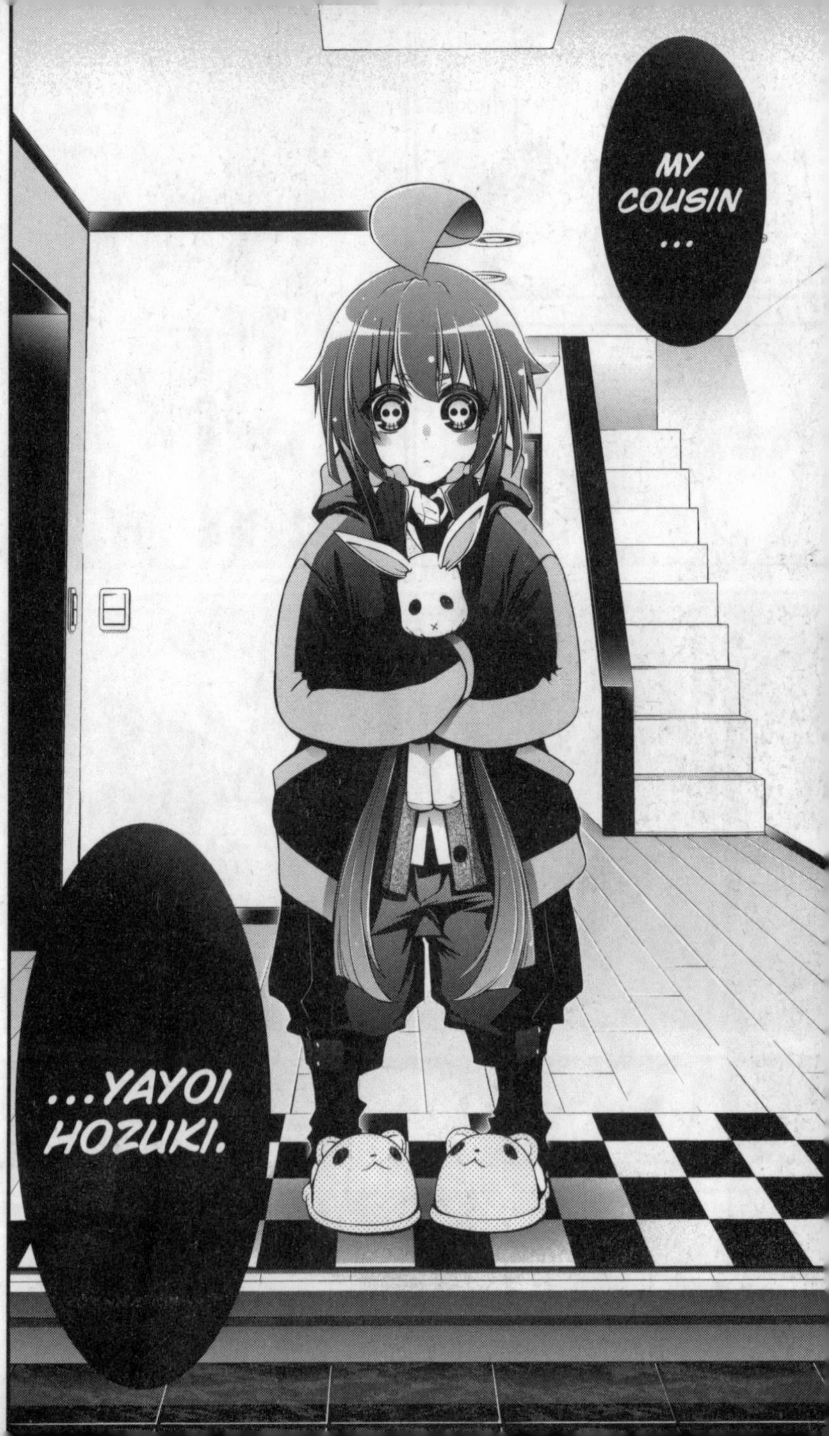
MY COUSIN ...
...YAYOI HOZUKI.

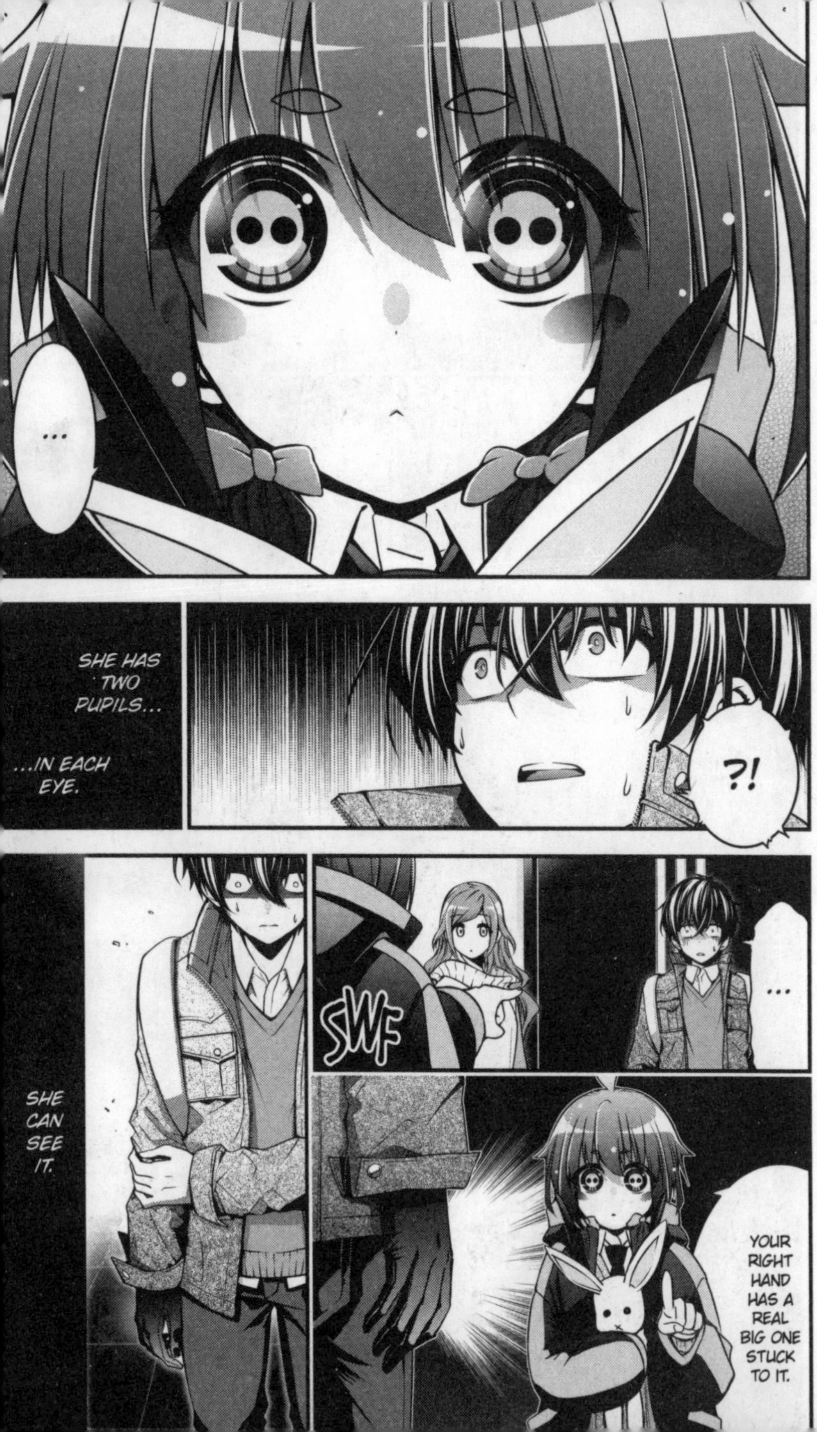
...
?!
SHE HAS TWO PUPILS...
...IN EACH EYE.
...
SWF
YOUR RIGHT HAND HAS A REAL BIG ONE STUCK TO IT.
SHE CAN SEE IT.

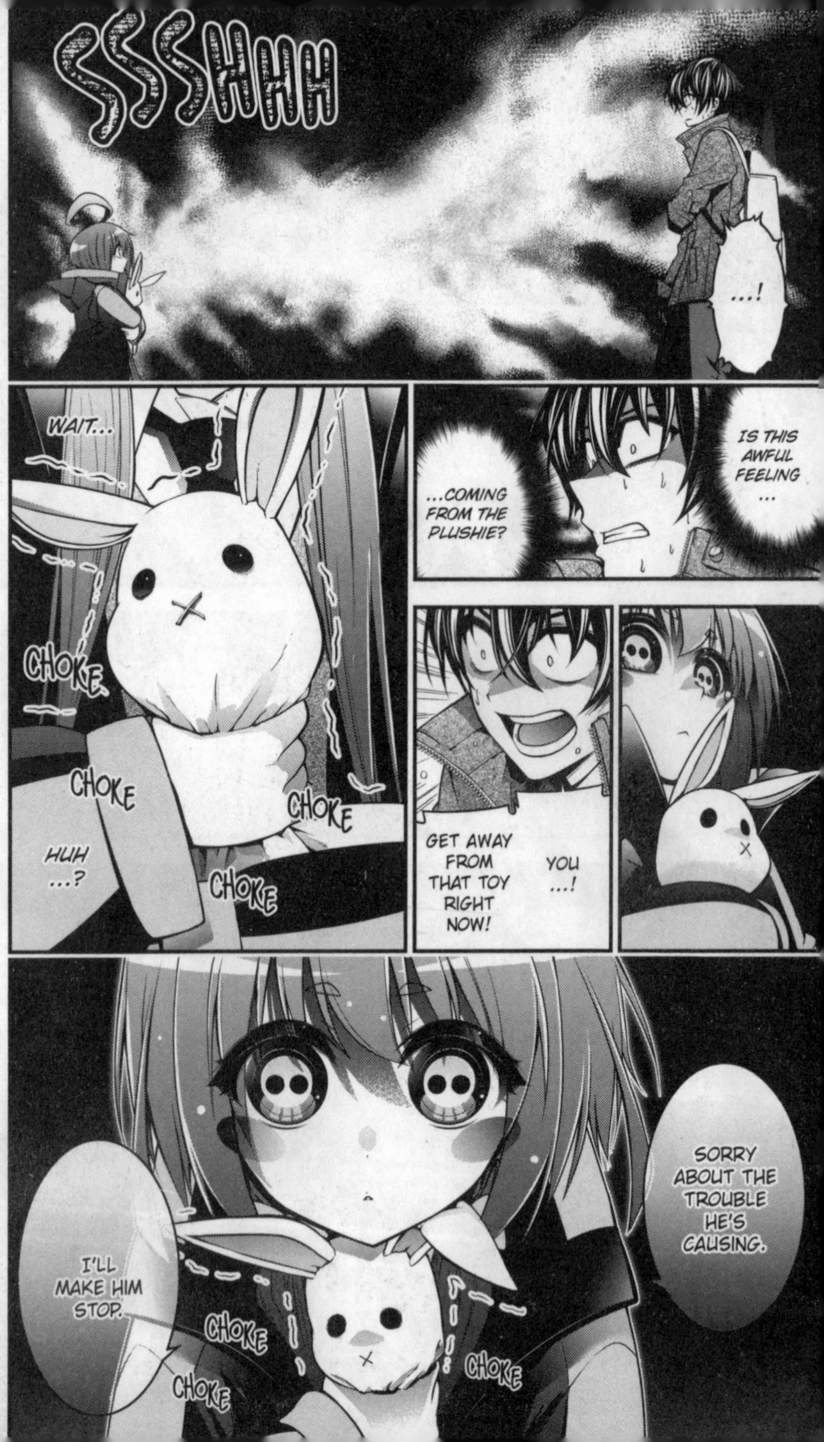
SSSHHH
...!
IS THIS AWFUL FEELING ...
...COMING FROM THE PLUSHIE?
YOU ...!
GET AWAY FROM THAT TOY RIGHT NOW!
WAIT...
CHOKE
CHOKE
CHOKE
HUH ...?
CHOKE
SORRY ABOUT THE TROUBLE HE'S CAUSING.
I'LL MAKE HIM STOP.
CHOKE
CHOKE
CHOKE

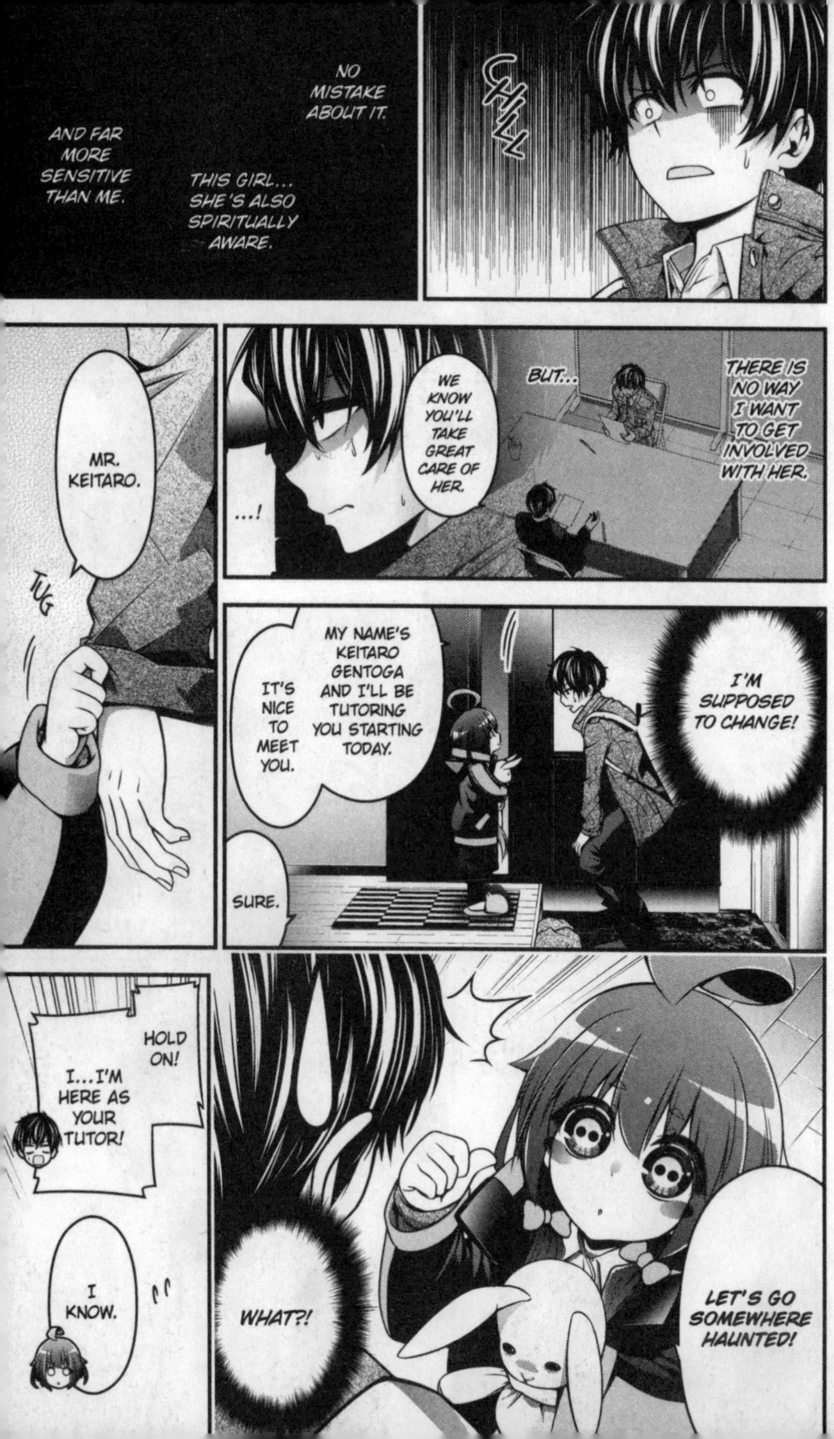
CHILL
NO MISTAKE ABOUT IT.
THIS GIRL... SHE'S ALSO SPIRITUALLY AWARE.
AND FAR MORE SENSITIVE THAN ME.
THERE IS NO WAY I WANT TO GET INVOLVED WITH HER.
BUT...
WE KNOW YOU'LL TAKE GREAT CARE OF HER.
...!
I'M SUPPOSED TO CHANGE!
MY NAME'S KEITARO GENTOGA AND I'LL BE TUTORING YOU STARTING TODAY.
IT'S NICE TO MEET YOU.
SURE.
MR. KEITARO.
TUG
LET'S GO SOMEWHERE HAUNTED!
WHAT?!
HOLD ON!
I...I'M HERE AS YOUR TUTOR!
I KNOW.

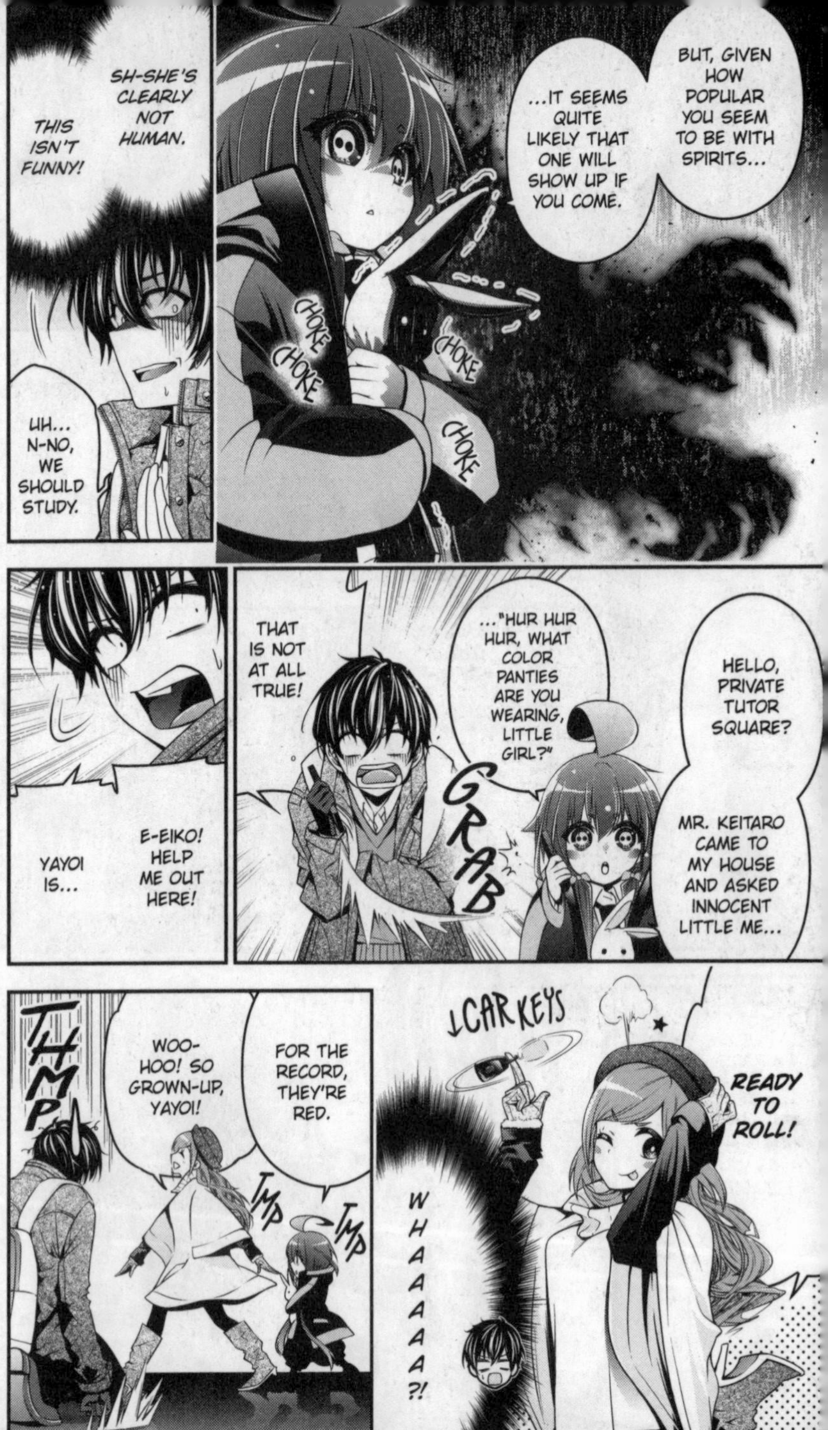
BUT, GIVEN HOW POPULAR YOU SEEM TO BE WITH SPIRITS...
...IT SEEMS QUITE LIKELY THAT ONE WILL SHOW UP IF YOU COME.
CHOKE
CHOKE
CHOKE
CHOKE
SH-SHE'S CLEARLY NOT HUMAN.
THIS ISN'T FUNNY!
UH... N-NO, WE SHOULD STUDY.
HELLO, PRIVATE TUTOR SQUARE?
MR. KEITARO CAME TO MY HOUSE AND ASKED INNOCENT LITTLE ME...
..."HUR HUR HUR, WHAT COLOR PANTIES ARE YOU WEARING, LITTLE GIRL?"
GRAB
THAT IS NOT AT ALL TRUE!
E-EIKO! HELP ME OUT HERE!
YAYOI IS...
READY TO ROLL!
↓CAR KEYS
WHAAAAAAA?!
FOR THE RECORD, THEY'RE RED.
TMP
TMP
WOO-HOO! SO GROWN-UP, YAYOI!
THMP

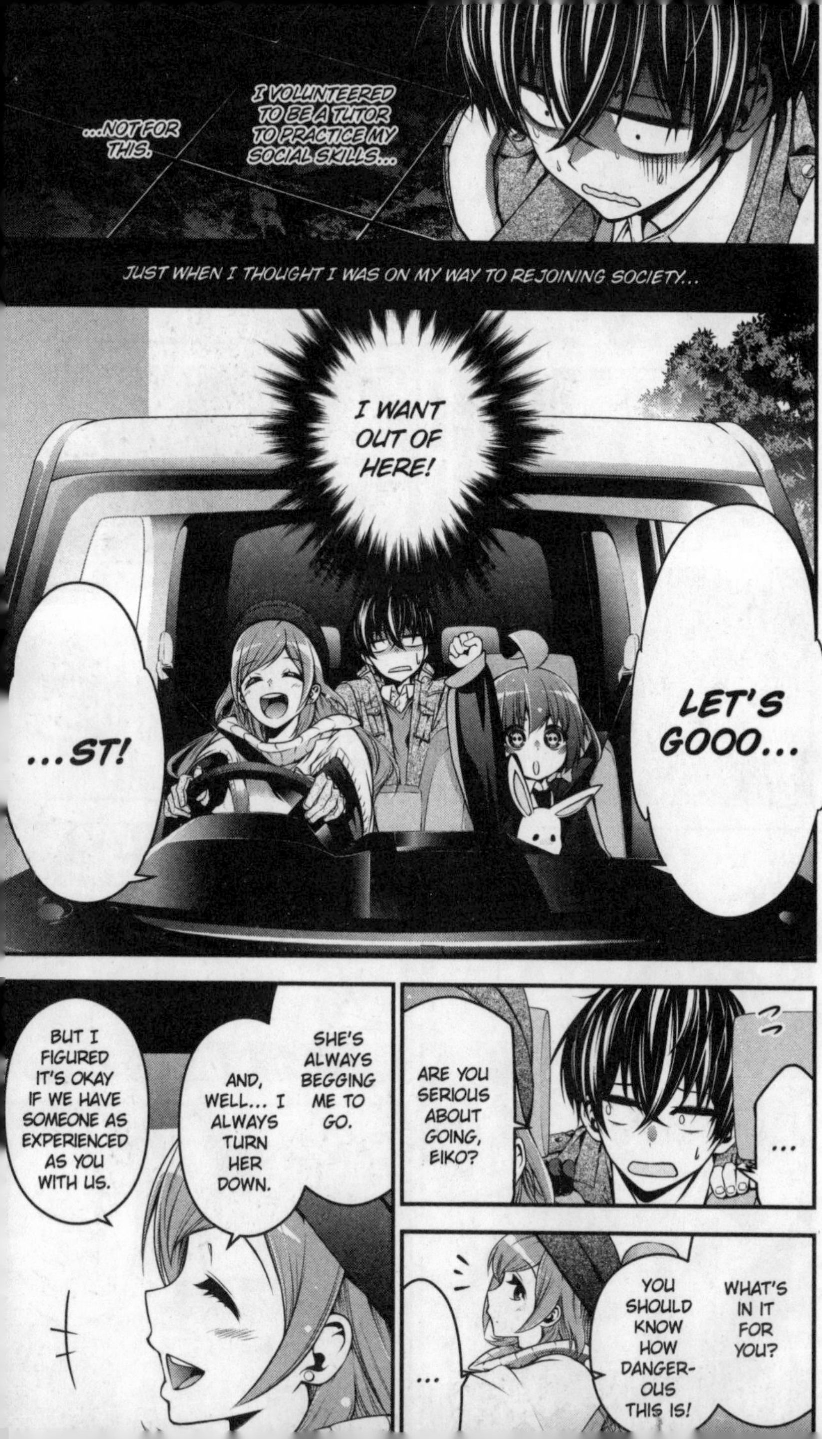
I VOLUNTEERED TO BE A TUTOR TO PRACTICE MY SOCIAL SKILLS...
...NOT FOR THIS.
JUST WHEN I THOUGHT I WAS ON MY WAY TO REJOINING SOCIETY...
I WANT OUT OF HERE!
LET'S GOOO...
...ST!
...
ARE YOU SERIOUS ABOUT GOING, EIKO?
WHAT'S IN IT FOR YOU?
YOU SHOULD KNOW HOW DANGER-OUS THIS IS!
...
SHE'S ALWAYS BEGGING ME TO GO.
AND, WELL... I ALWAYS TURN HER DOWN.
BUT I FIGURED IT'S OKAY IF WE HAVE SOMEONE AS EXPERIENCED AS YOU WITH US.

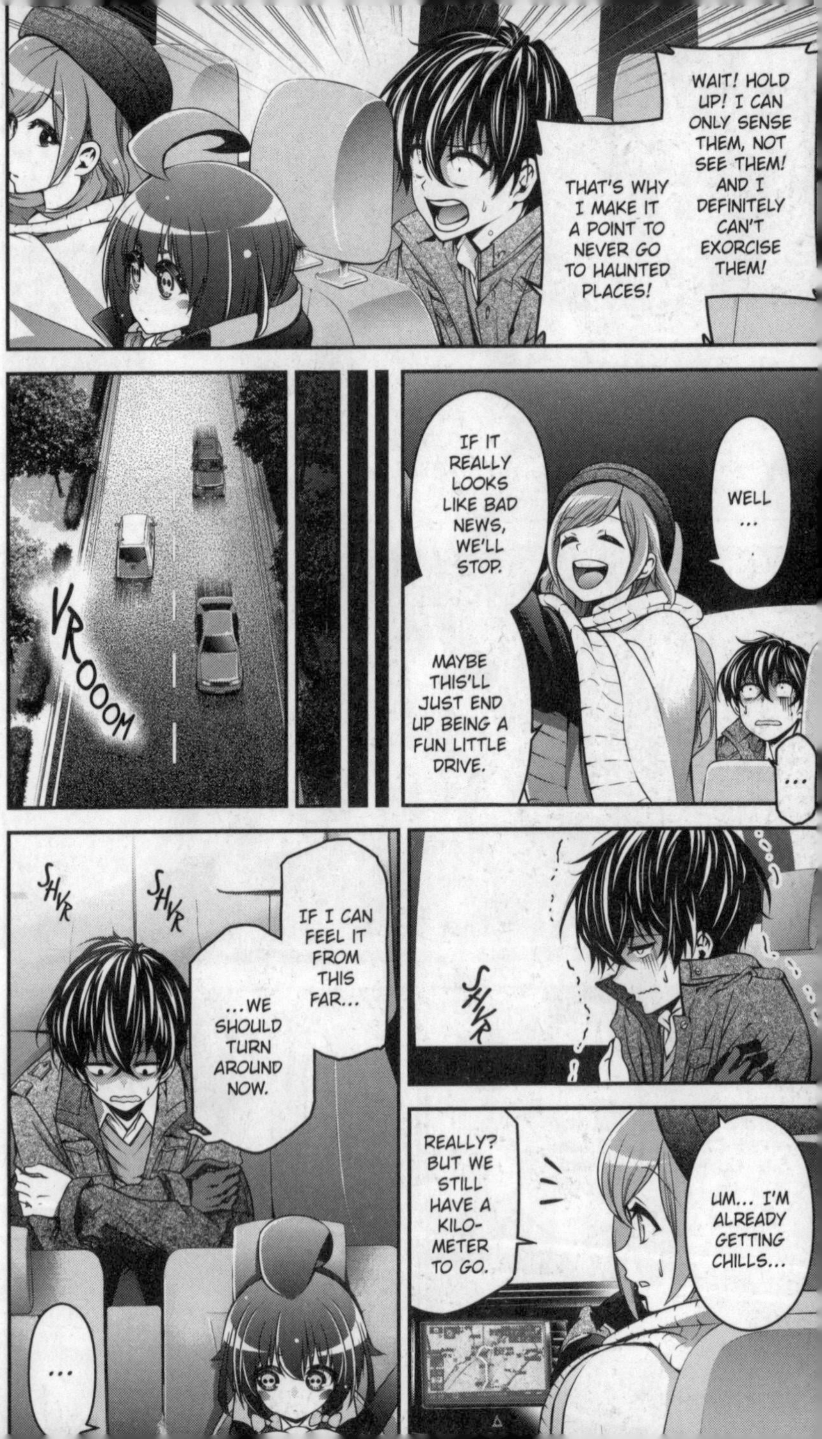
WAIT! HOLD UP! I CAN ONLY SENSE THEM, NOT SEE THEM! AND I DEFINITELY CAN'T EXORCISE THEM!
THAT'S WHY I MAKE IT A POINT TO NEVER GO TO HAUNTED PLACES!
WELL ... .
IF IT REALLY LOOKS LIKE BAD NEWS, WE'LL STOP.
MAYBE THIS'LL JUST END UP BEING A FUN LITTLE DRIVE.
...
VROOOM
SHVR
UM... I'M ALREADY GETTING CHILLS...
REALLY? BUT WE STILL HAVE A KILO-METER TO GO.
SHVR
SHVR
IF I CAN FEEL IT FROM THIS FAR...
...WE SHOULD TURN AROUND NOW.
...

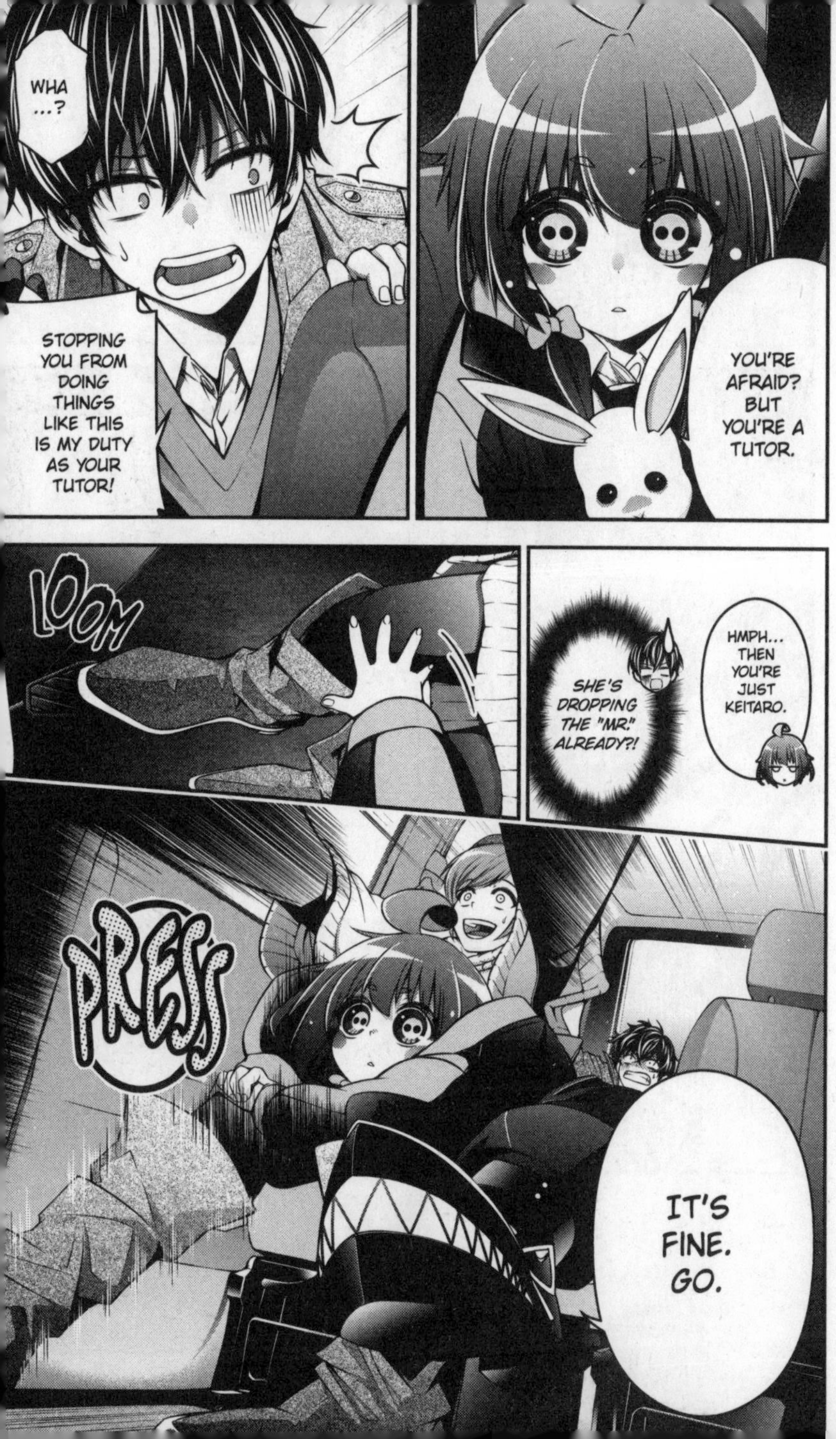
YOU'RE AFRAID? BUT YOU'RE A TUTOR.
WHA ...?
STOPPING YOU FROM DOING THINGS LIKE THIS IS MY DUTY AS YOUR TUTOR!
HMPH... THEN YOU'RE JUST KEITARO.
SHE'S DROPPING THE "MR." ALREADY?!
LOOM
PRESS
IT'S FINE. GO.

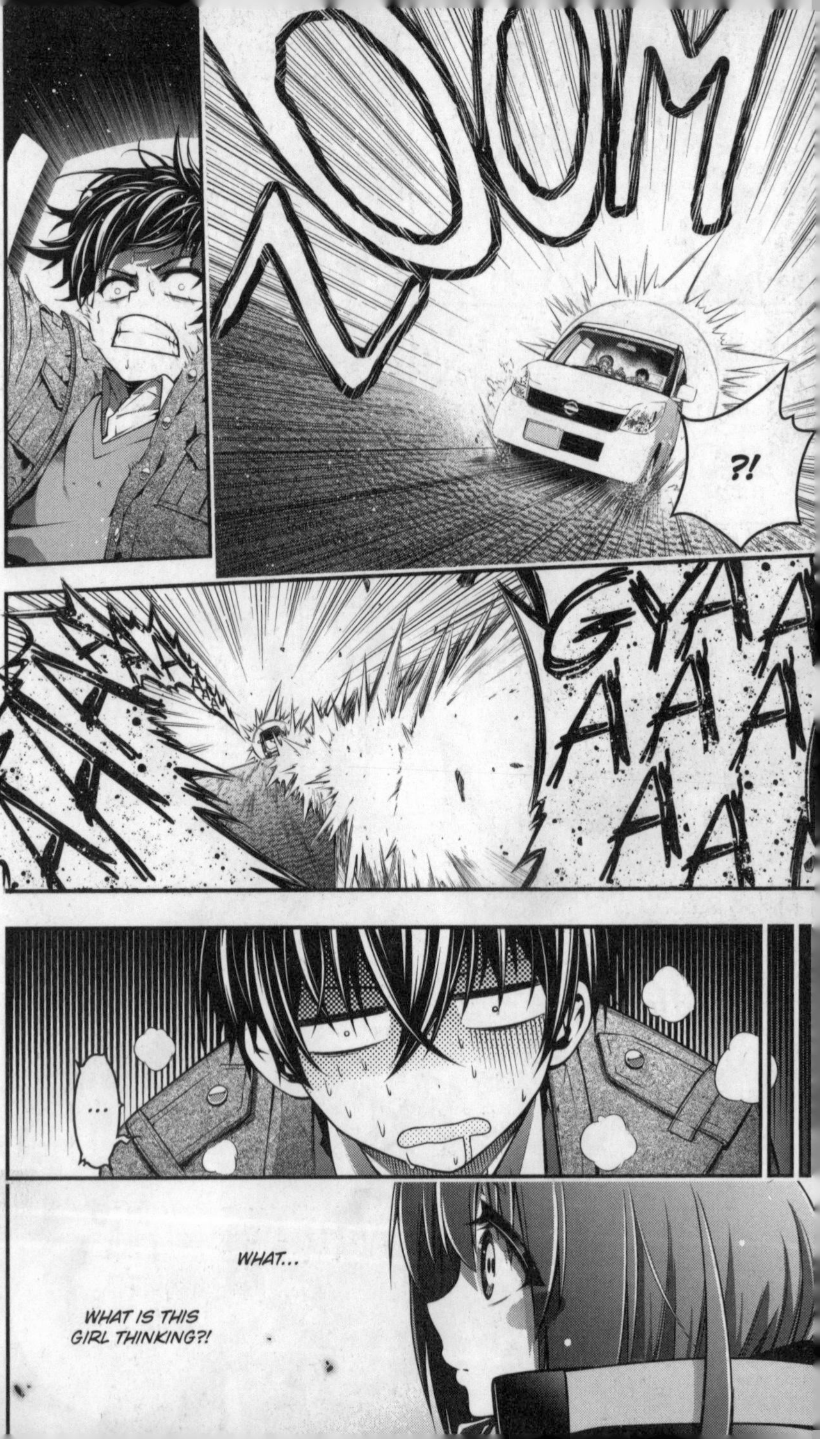
VROOM
?!
GYAAAAAAA
BAM
...
WHAT...
WHAT IS THIS GIRL THINKING?!

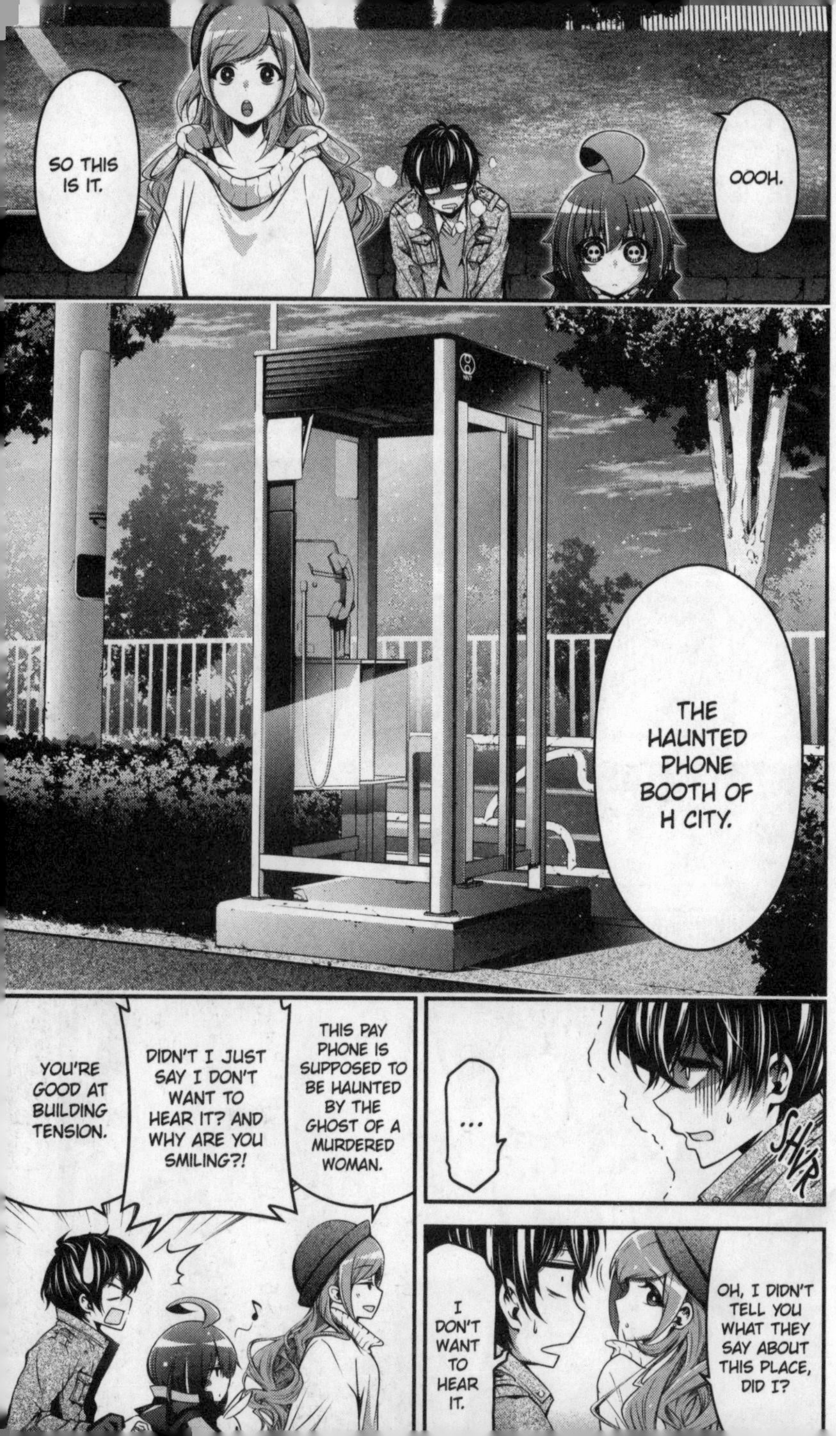
OOOH.
SO THIS IS IT.
THE HAUNTED PHONE BOOTH OF H CITY.
...
SHIVR
OH, I DIDN'T TELL YOU WHAT THEY SAY ABOUT THIS PLACE, DID I?
I DON'T WANT TO HEAR IT.
THIS PAY PHONE IS SUPPOSED TO BE HAUNTED BY THE GHOST OF A MURDERED WOMAN.
DIDN'T I JUST SAY I DON'T WANT TO HEAR IT? AND WHY ARE YOU SMILING?!
YOU'RE GOOD AT BUILDING TENSION.

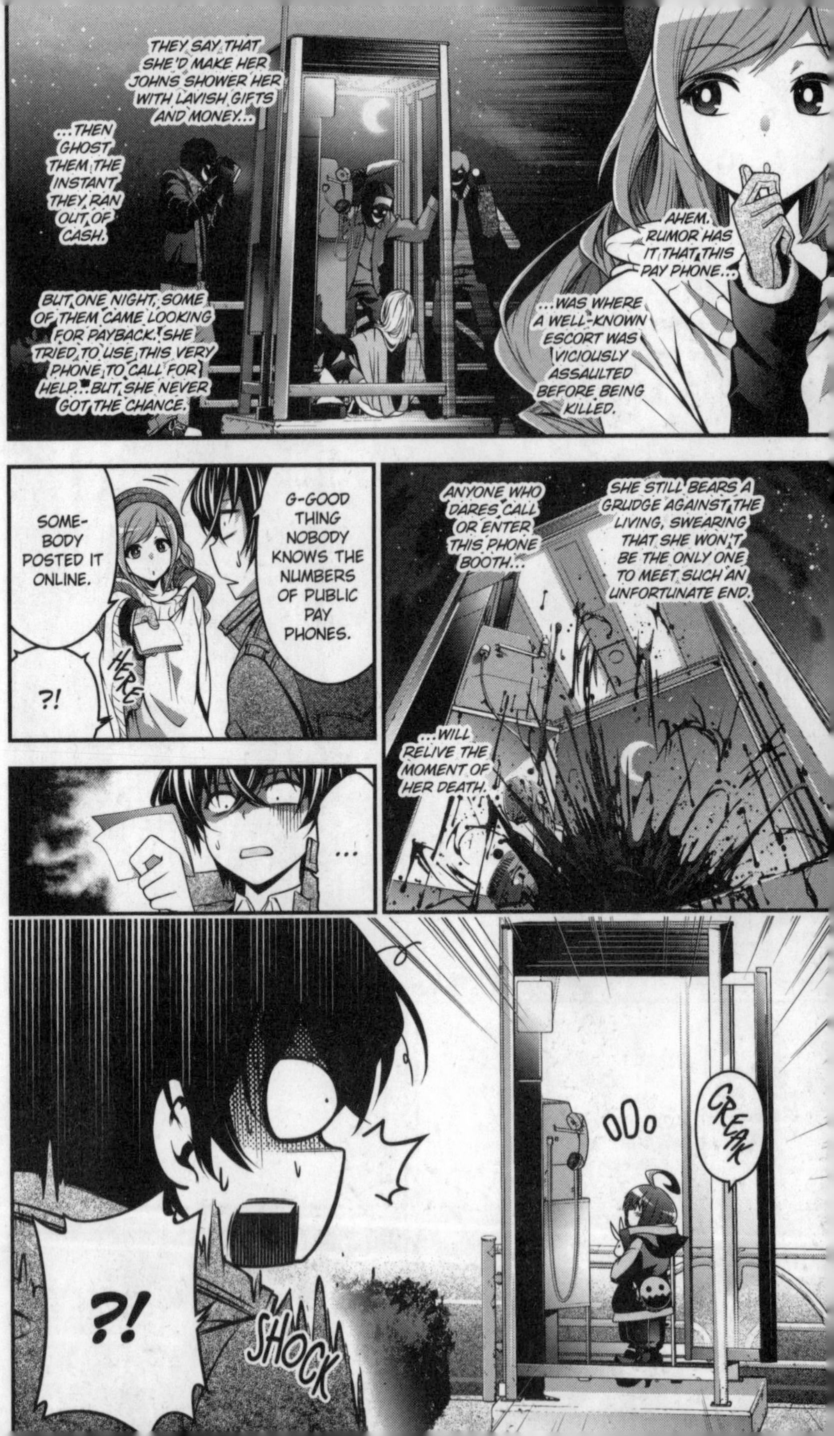
AHEM. RUMOR HAS IT THAT THIS PAY PHONE...
...WAS WHERE A WELL-KNOWN ESCORT WAS VICIOUSLY ASSAULTED BEFORE BEING KILLED.
THEY SAY THAT SHE'D MAKE HER JOHNS SHOWER HER WITH LAVISH GIFTS AND MONEY...
...THEN GHOST THEM THE INSTANT THEY RAN OUT OF CASH.
BUT ONE NIGHT, SOME OF THEM CAME LOOKING FOR PAYBACK. SHE TRIED TO USE THIS VERY PHONE TO CALL FOR HELP... BUT SHE NEVER GOT THE CHANCE.
SHE STILL BEARS A GRUDGE AGAINST THE LIVING, SWEARING THAT SHE WON'T BE THE ONLY ONE TO MEET SUCH AN UNFORTUNATE END.
ANYONE WHO DARES CALL OR ENTER THIS PHONE BOOTH...
...WILL RELIVE THE MOMENT OF HER DEATH.
G-GOOD THING NOBODY KNOWS THE NUMBERS OF PUBLIC PAY PHONES.
SOME-BODY POSTED IT ONLINE.
HERE
?!
...
CREAK
?!
SHOCK

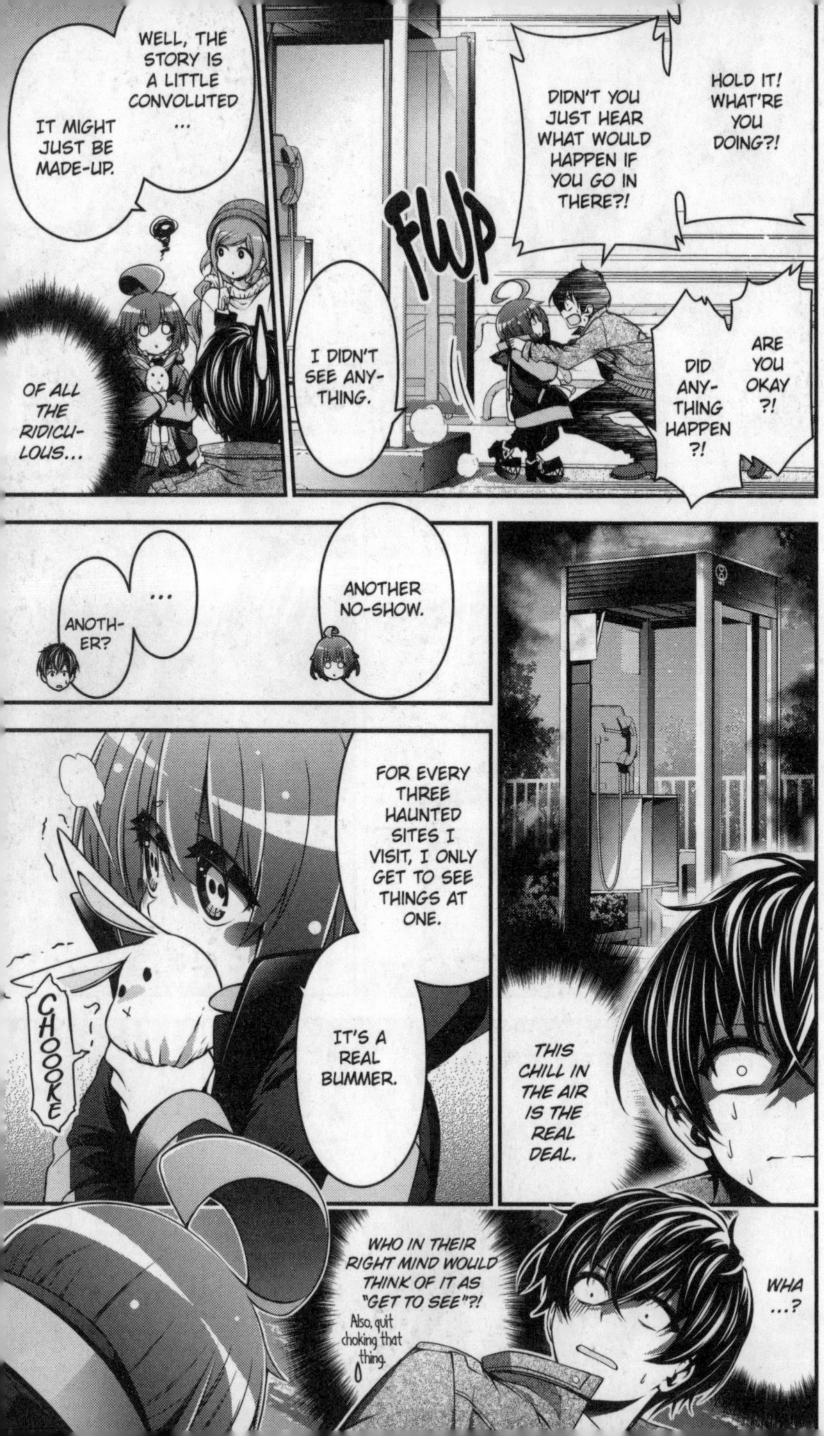
HOLD IT! WHAT'RE YOU DOING?!
DIDN'T YOU JUST HEAR WHAT WOULD HAPPEN IF YOU GO IN THERE?!
FWP
ARE YOU OKAY ?!
DID ANY-THING HAPPEN ?!
I DIDN'T SEE ANY-THING.
WELL, THE STORY IS A LITTLE CONVOLUTED ...
IT MIGHT JUST BE MADE-UP.
OF ALL THE RIDICULOUS...
THIS CHILL IN THE AIR IS THE REAL DEAL.
ANOTHER NO-SHOW.
...
ANOTHER?
FOR EVERY THREE HAUNTED SITES I VISIT, I ONLY GET TO SEE THINGS AT ONE.
IT'S A REAL BUMMER.
CHOOOKE
WHA ...?
WHO IN THEIR RIGHT MIND WOULD THINK OF IT AS "GET TO SEE"?!
Also, quit choking that thing.

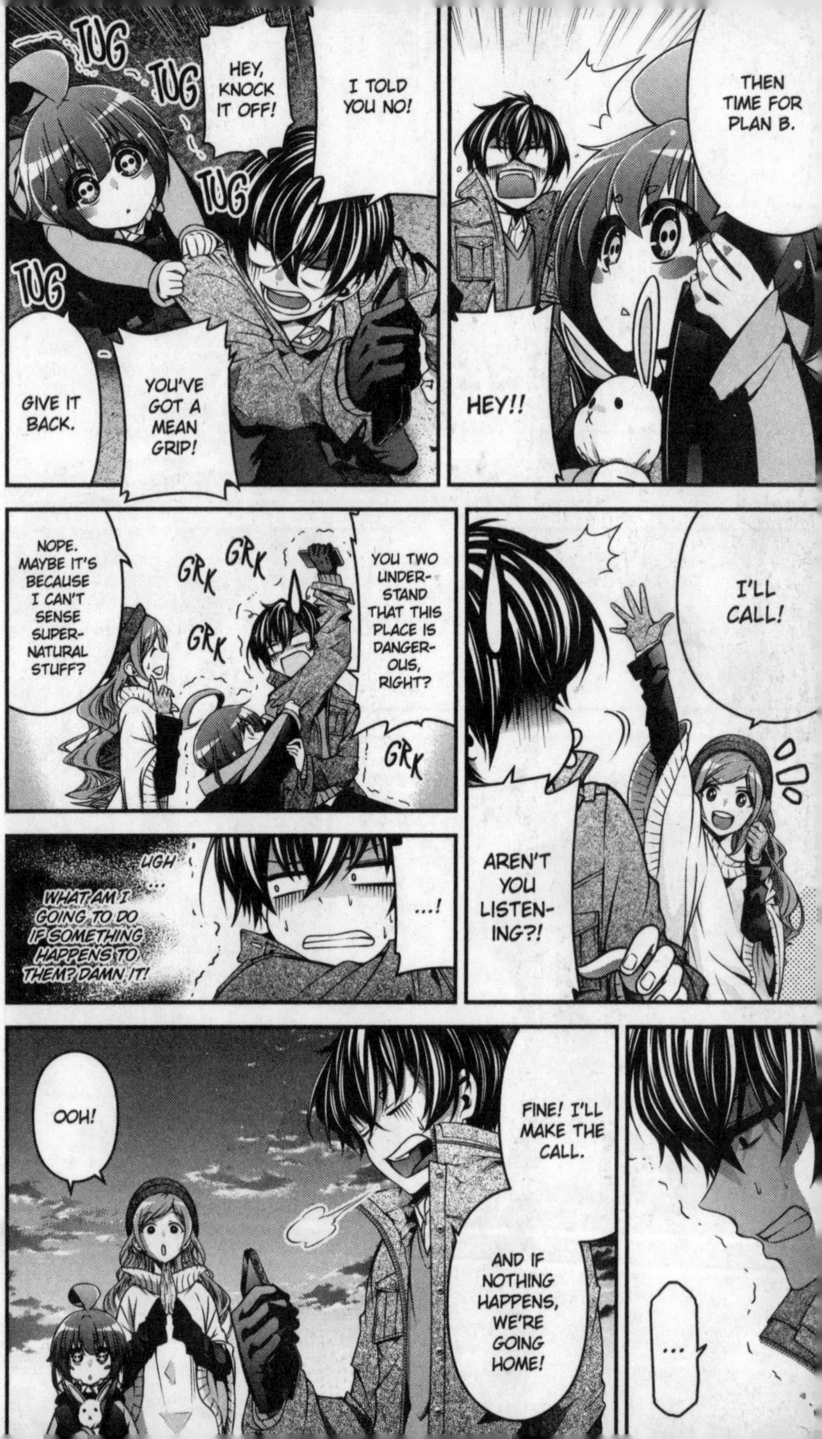
THEN TIME FOR PLAN B.
HEY!!
I TOLD YOU NO!
HEY, KNOCK IT OFF!
TUG
TUG
TUG
TUG
YOU'VE GOT A MEAN GRIP!
GIVE IT BACK.
I'LL CALL!
AREN'T YOU LISTENING?!
YOU TWO UNDERSTAND THAT THIS PLACE IS DANGEROUS, RIGHT?
GRK
GRK
GRK
GRK
NOPE. MAYBE IT'S BECAUSE I CAN'T SENSE SUPERNATURAL STUFF?
...!
UGH... WHAT AM I GOING TO DO IF SOMETHING HAPPENS TO THEM? DAMN IT!
...
FINE! I'LL MAKE THE CALL.
AND IF NOTHING HAPPENS, WE'RE GOING HOME!
OOH!

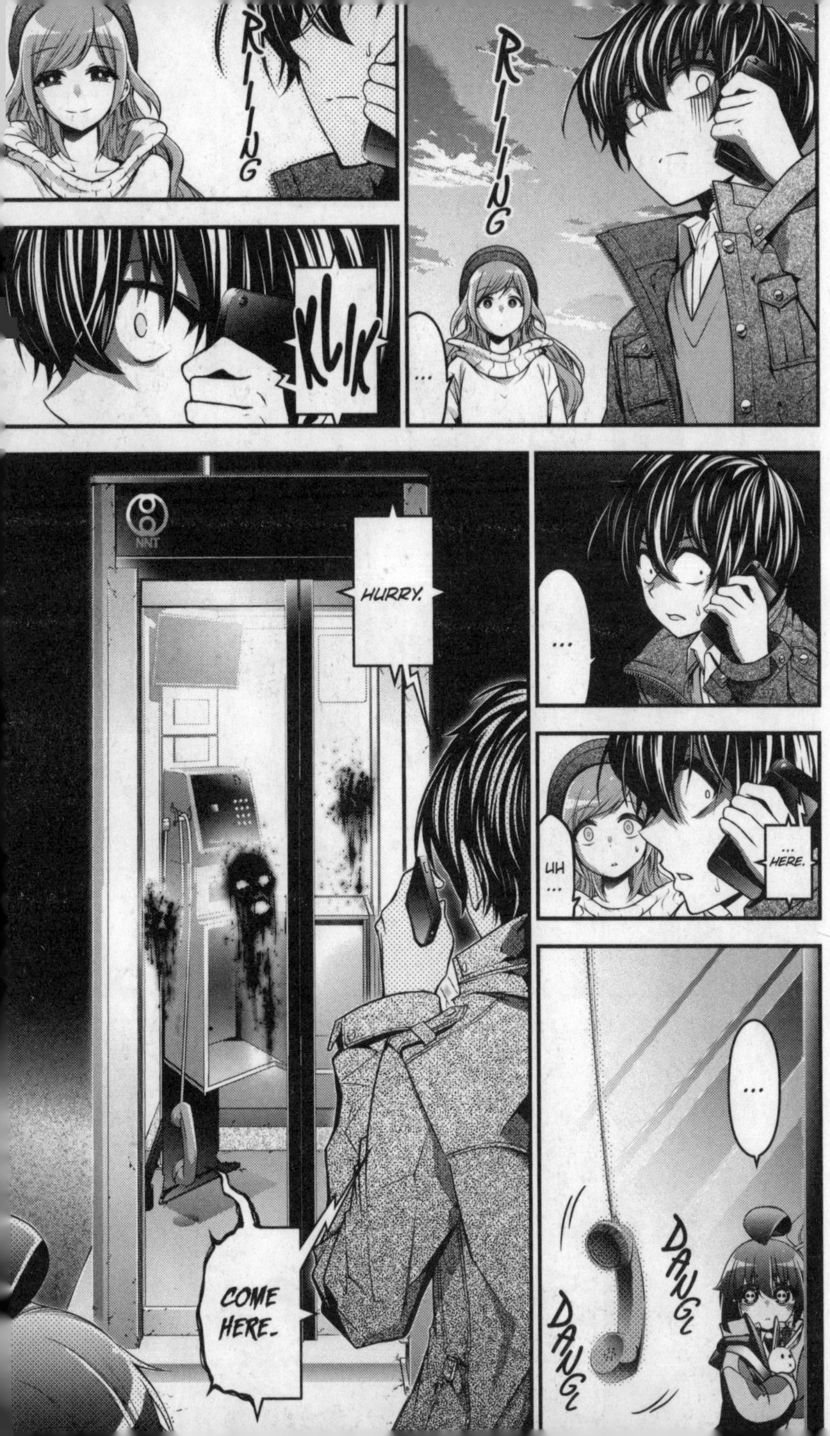
RIIIING
...
RIIING
KLIK
...
... HERE.
UH ...
...
DANG!
DANG!
HURRY.
COME HERE.

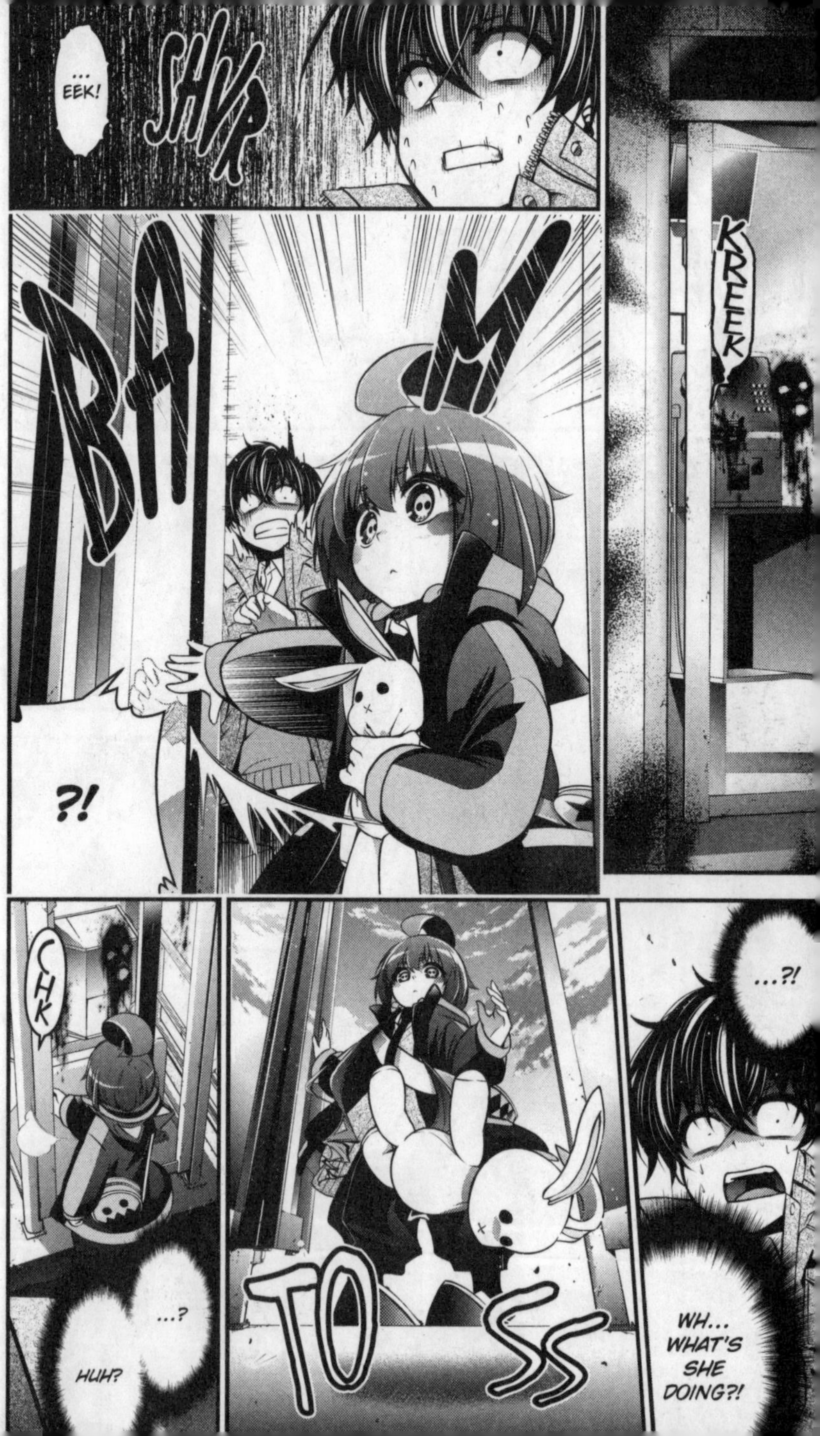
KREEK
SHVP
...EEK!
BAM
?!
...?!
WH... WHAT'S SHE DOING?!
TOSS
CHK
...?
HUH?

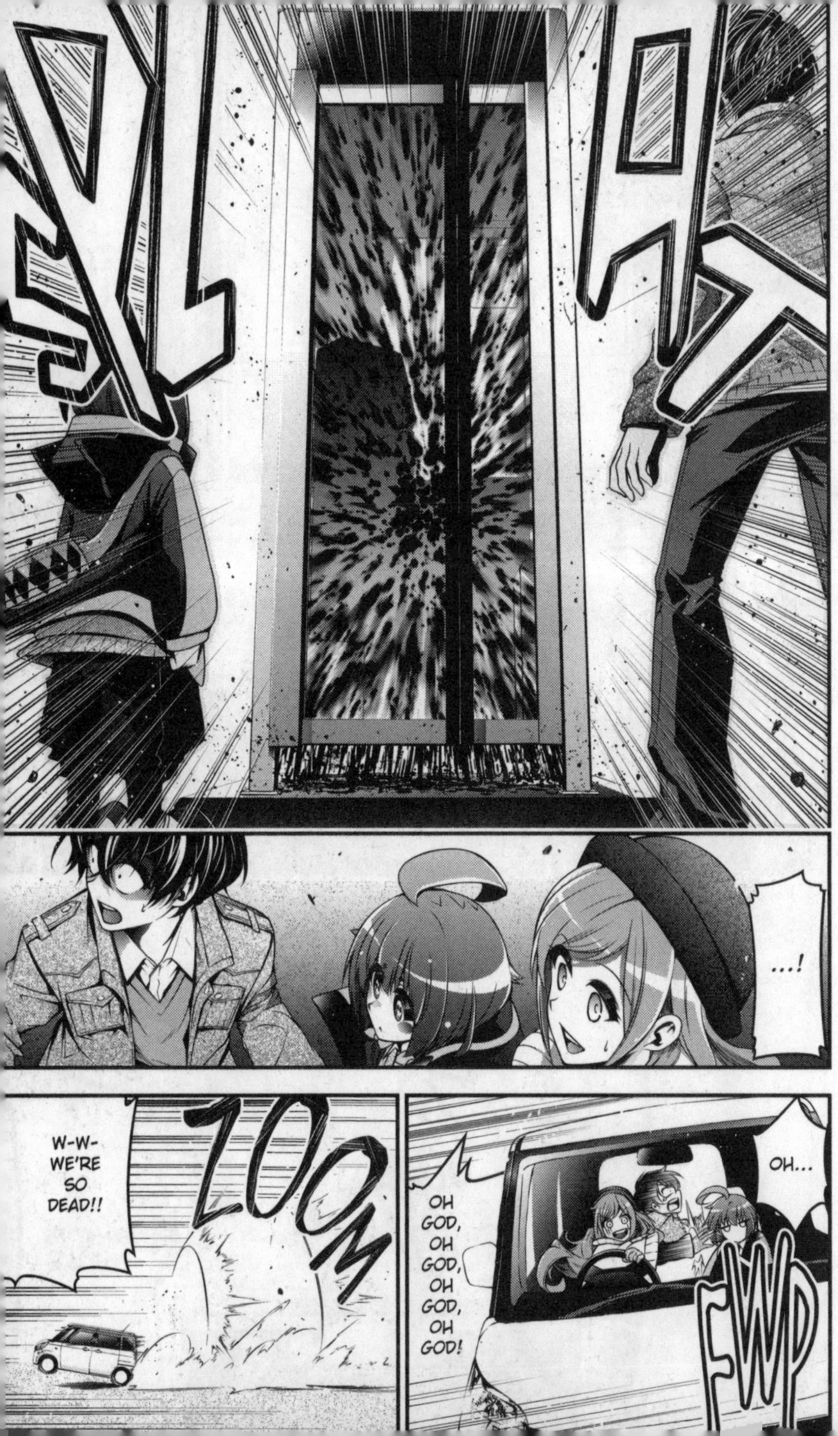
...!
OH...
OH GOD, OH GOD, OH GOD, OH GOD!
FWP
ZOOM
W-W-WE'RE SO DEAD!!

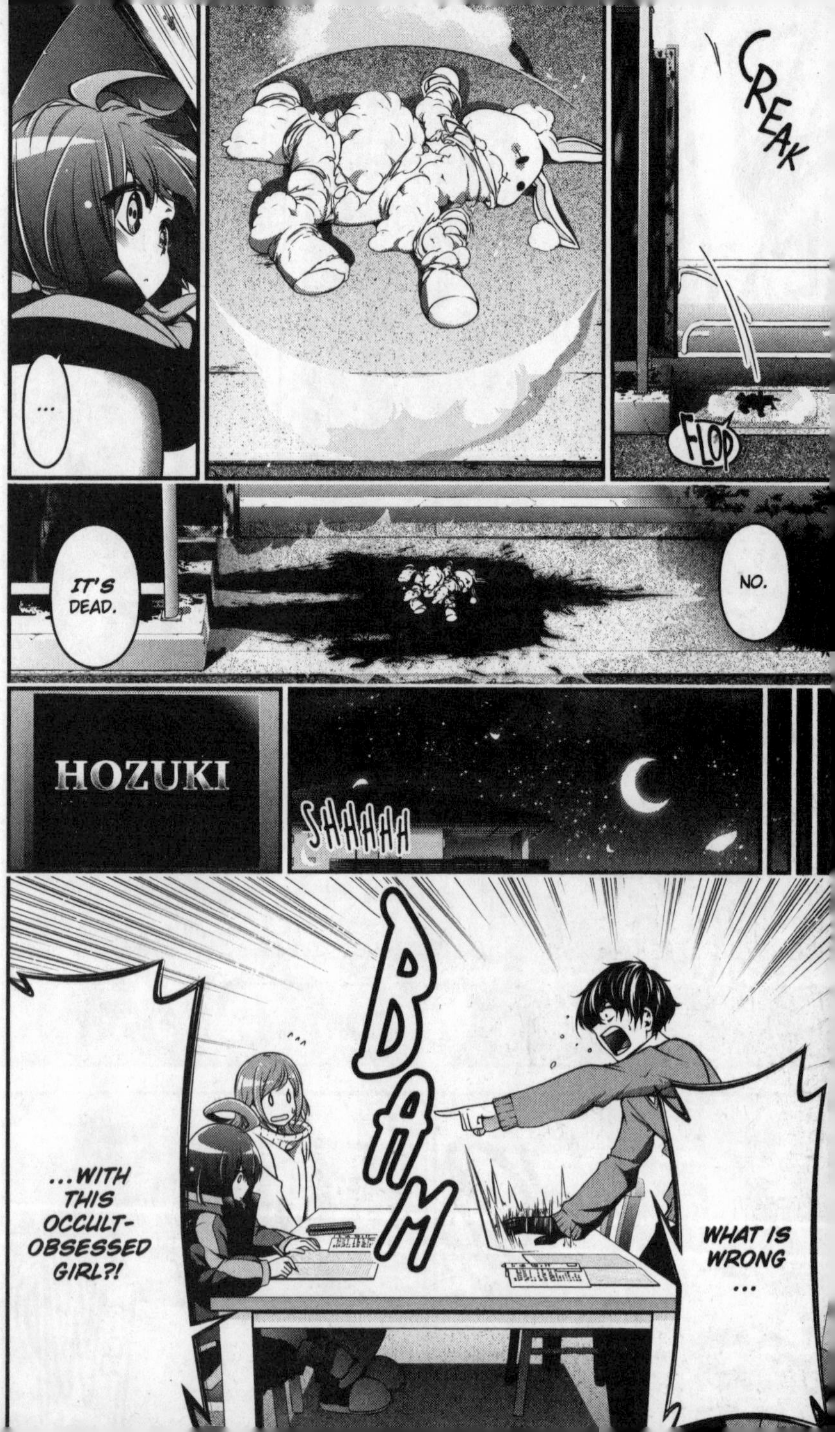
CREAK
FLOP
...
NO.
IT'S DEAD.
SHAAAAH
HOZUKI
WHAT IS WRONG ...
BAM
...WITH THIS OCCULT-OBSESSED GIRL?!

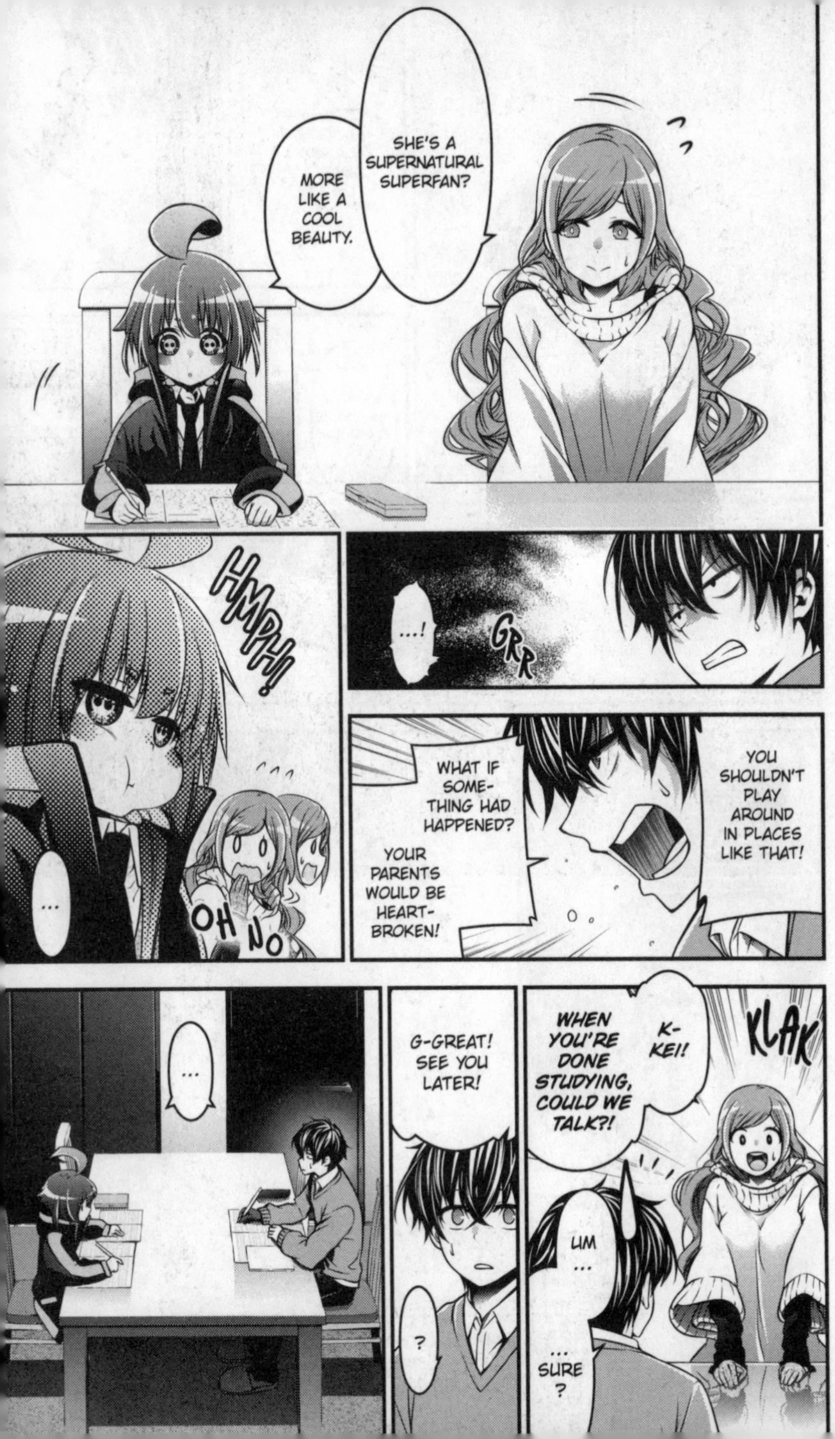
SHE'S A SUPERNATURAL SUPERFAN?
MORE LIKE A COOL BEAUTY.
GRR
...!
YOU SHOULDN'T PLAY AROUND IN PLACES LIKE THAT!
WHAT IF SOME-THING HAD HAPPENED?
YOUR PARENTS WOULD BE HEART-BROKEN!
HMPH!
OH NO
...
KLAK
K-KEI!
WHEN YOU'RE DONE STUDYING, COULD WE TALK?!
UM ...
... SURE ?
G-GREAT! SEE YOU LATER!
?
...

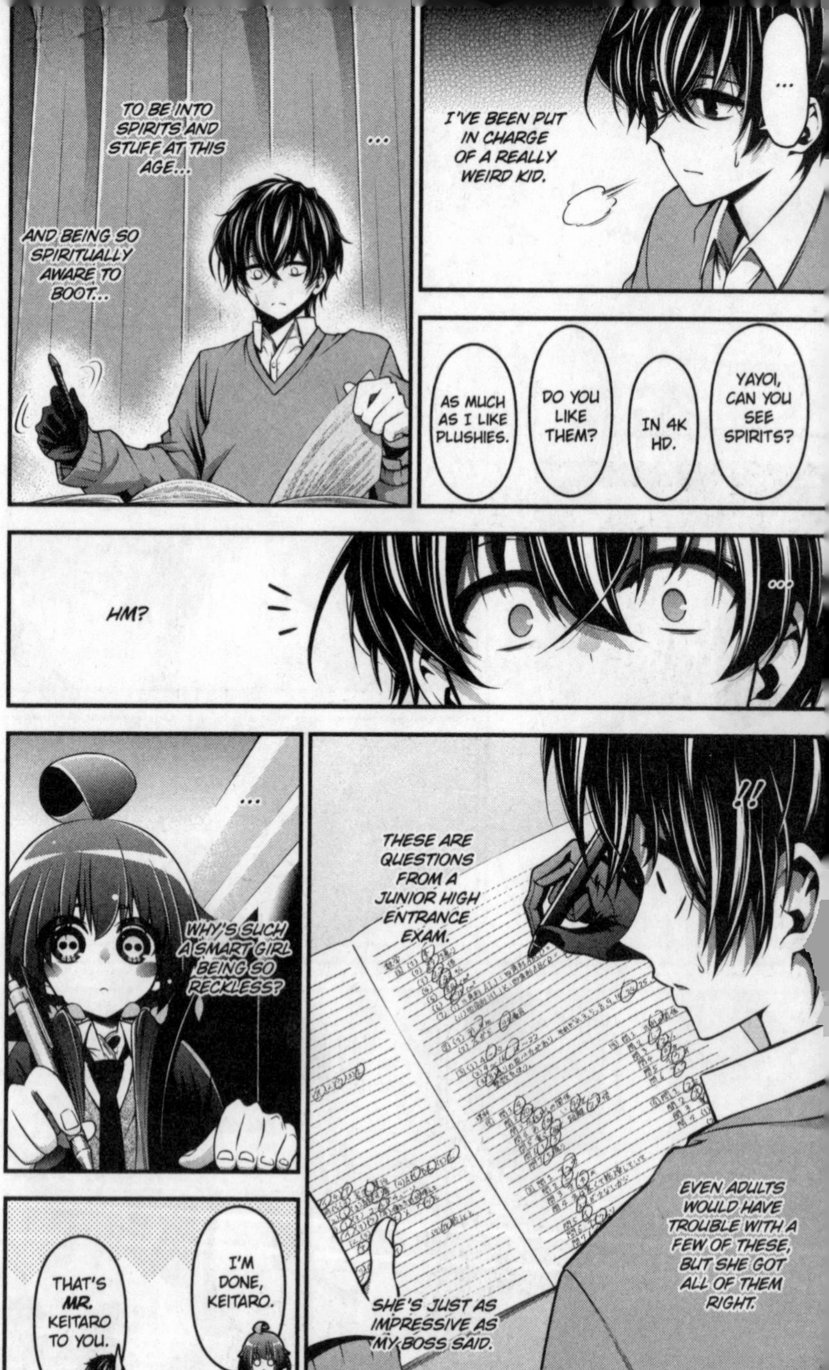
...
I'VE BEEN PUT IN CHARGE OF A REALLY WEIRD KID.
YAYOI, CAN YOU SEE SPIRITS?
IN 4K HD.
DO YOU LIKE THEM?
AS MUCH AS I LIKE PLUSHIES.
TO BE INTO SPIRITS AND STUFF AT THIS AGE...
...
AND BEING SO SPIRITUALLY AWARE TO BOOT...
...
HM?
!!
THESE ARE QUESTIONS FROM A JUNIOR HIGH ENTRANCE EXAM.
EVEN ADULTS WOULD HAVE TROUBLE WITH A FEW OF THESE, BUT SHE GOT ALL OF THEM RIGHT.
SHE'S JUST AS IMPRESSIVE AS MY BOSS SAID.
...
WHY'S SUCH A SMART GIRL BEING SO RECKLESS?
I'M DONE, KEITARO.
THAT'S **MR.** KEITARO TO YOU.

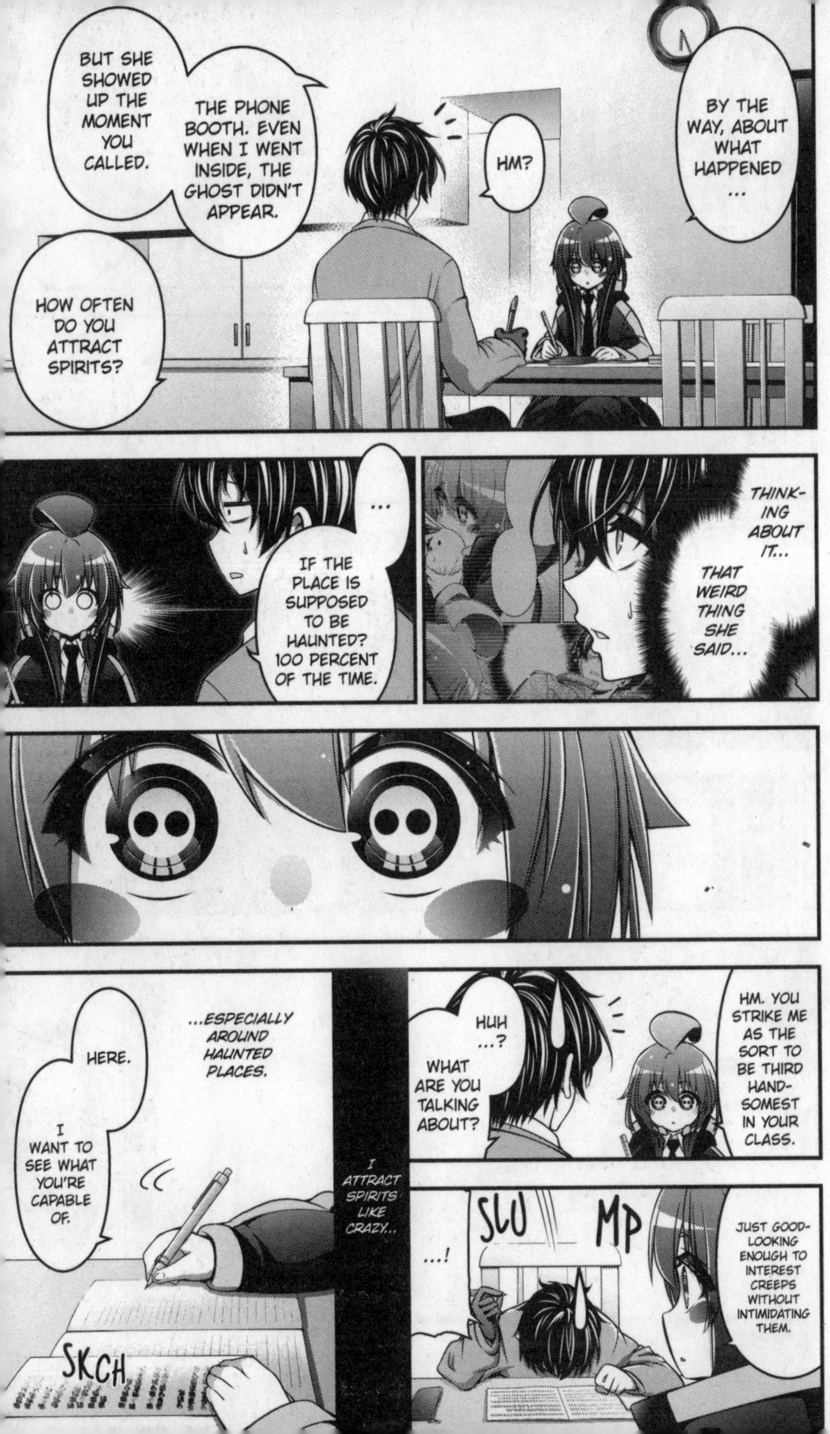
BY THE WAY, ABOUT WHAT HAPPENED ...
HM?
THE PHONE BOOTH. EVEN WHEN I WENT INSIDE, THE GHOST DIDN'T APPEAR.
BUT SHE SHOWED UP THE MOMENT YOU CALLED.
HOW OFTEN DO YOU ATTRACT SPIRITS?
THINKING ABOUT IT...
THAT WEIRD THING SHE SAID...
...
IF THE PLACE IS SUPPOSED TO BE HAUNTED? 100 PERCENT OF THE TIME.
HM. YOU STRIKE ME AS THE SORT TO BE THIRD HANDSOMEST IN YOUR CLASS.
HUH ...?
WHAT ARE YOU TALKING ABOUT?
JUST GOOD-LOOKING ENOUGH TO INTEREST CREEPS WITHOUT INTIMIDATING THEM.
SLUMP
...!
I ATTRACT SPIRITS LIKE CRAZY...
...ESPECIALLY AROUND HAUNTED PLACES.
HERE.
I WANT TO SEE WHAT YOU'RE CAPABLE OF.
SKCH

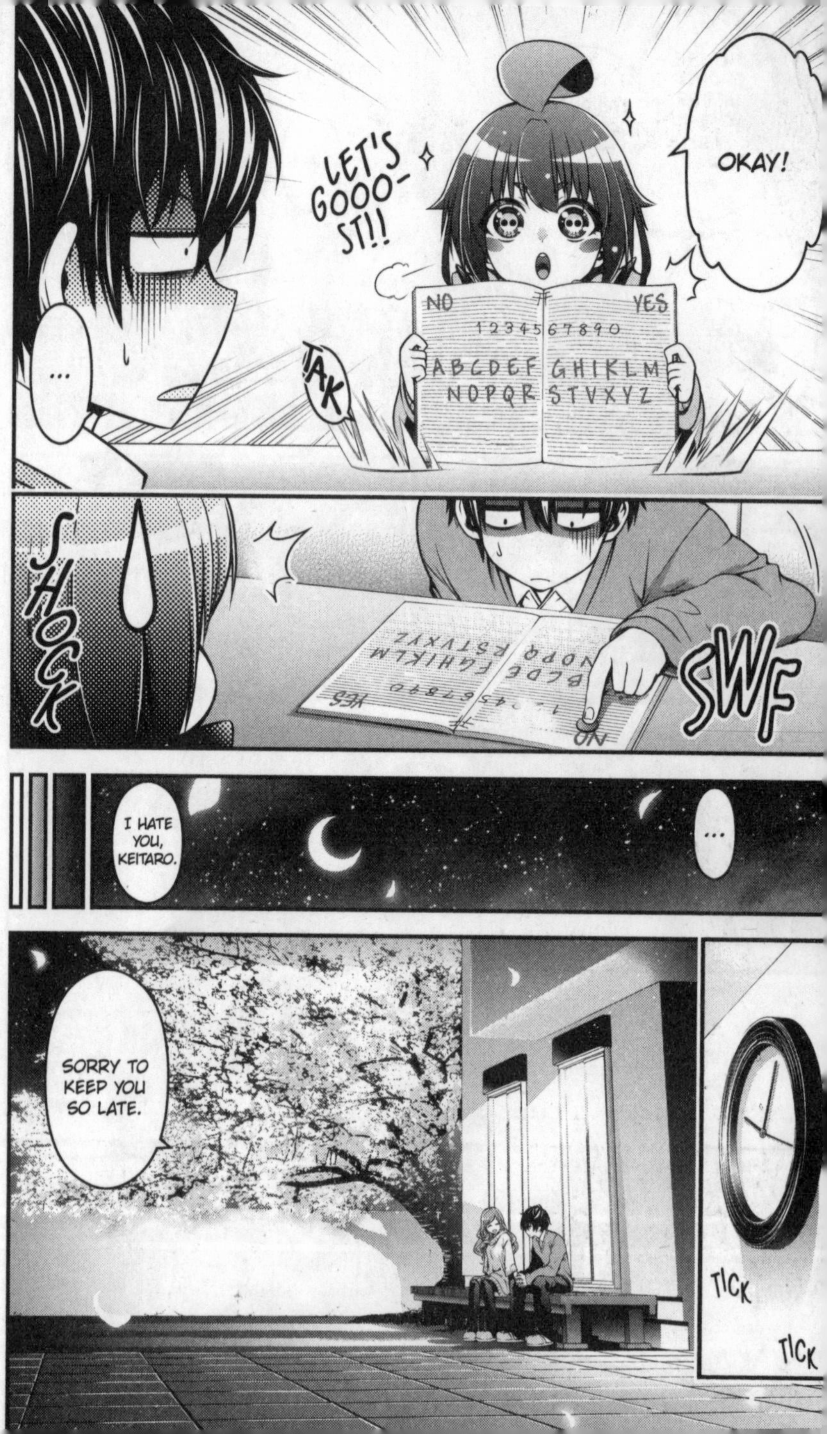

OKAY!
LET'S GOOO-ST!!
NO YES
1234567890
ABCDEF GHIKLM
NOPQR STVXYZ
TAK
...
SWF
SHOCK
...
I HATE YOU, KEITARO.
TICK
TICK
SORRY TO KEEP YOU SO LATE.

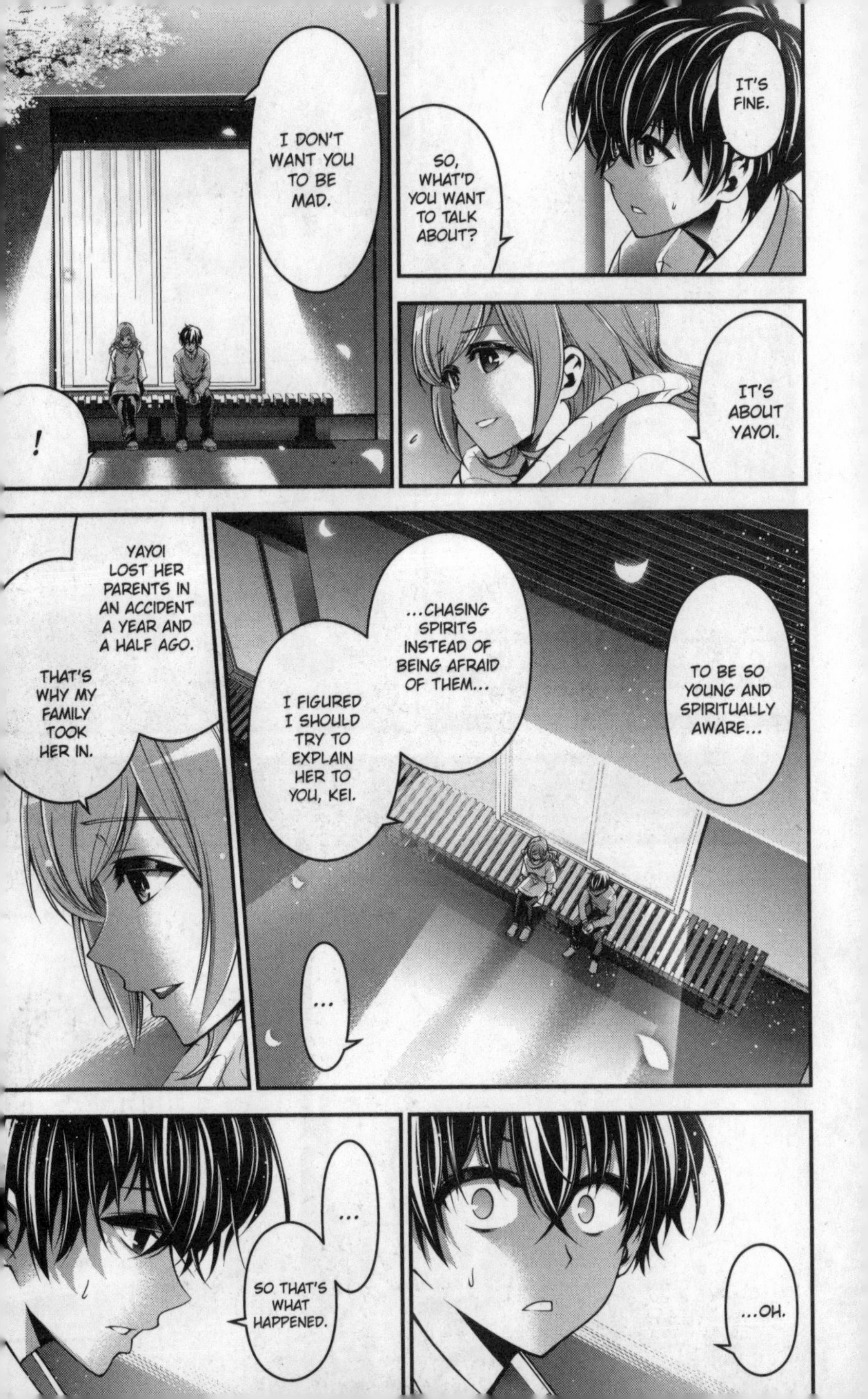
IT'S FINE.
SO, WHAT'D YOU WANT TO TALK ABOUT?
IT'S ABOUT YAYOI.
I DON'T WANT YOU TO BE MAD.
!
TO BE SO YOUNG AND SPIRITUALLY AWARE...
...CHASING SPIRITS INSTEAD OF BEING AFRAID OF THEM...
I FIGURED I SHOULD TRY TO EXPLAIN HER TO YOU, KEI.
...
YAYOI LOST HER PARENTS IN AN ACCIDENT A YEAR AND A HALF AGO.
THAT'S WHY MY FAMILY TOOK HER IN.
...OH.
...
SO THAT'S WHAT HAPPENED.

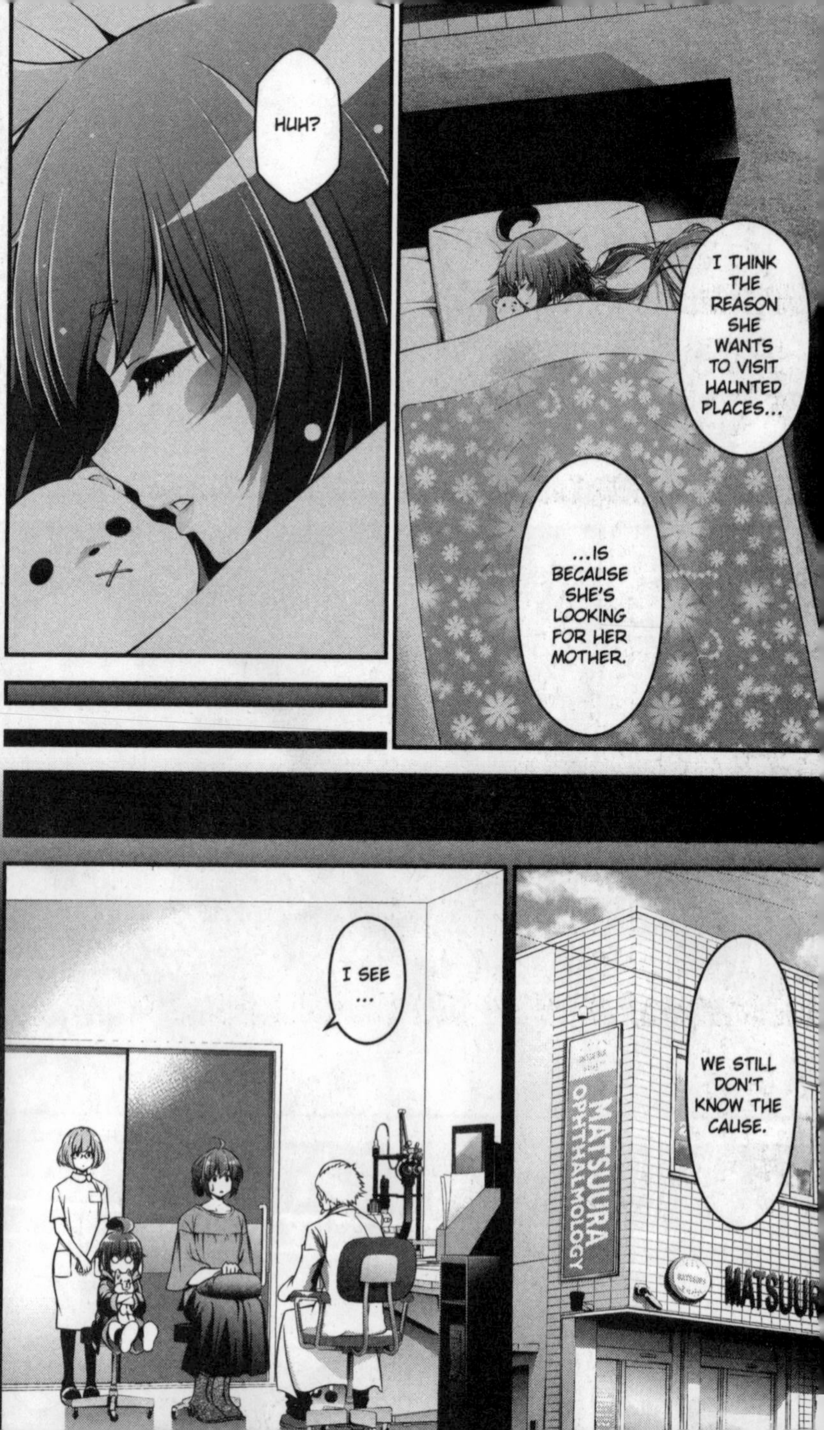
I THINK THE REASON SHE WANTS TO VISIT HAUNTED PLACES...
...IS BECAUSE SHE'S LOOKING FOR HER MOTHER.
HUH?
WE STILL DON'T KNOW THE CAUSE.
MATSUURA OPHTHALMOLOGY
MATSUUR
I SEE ...

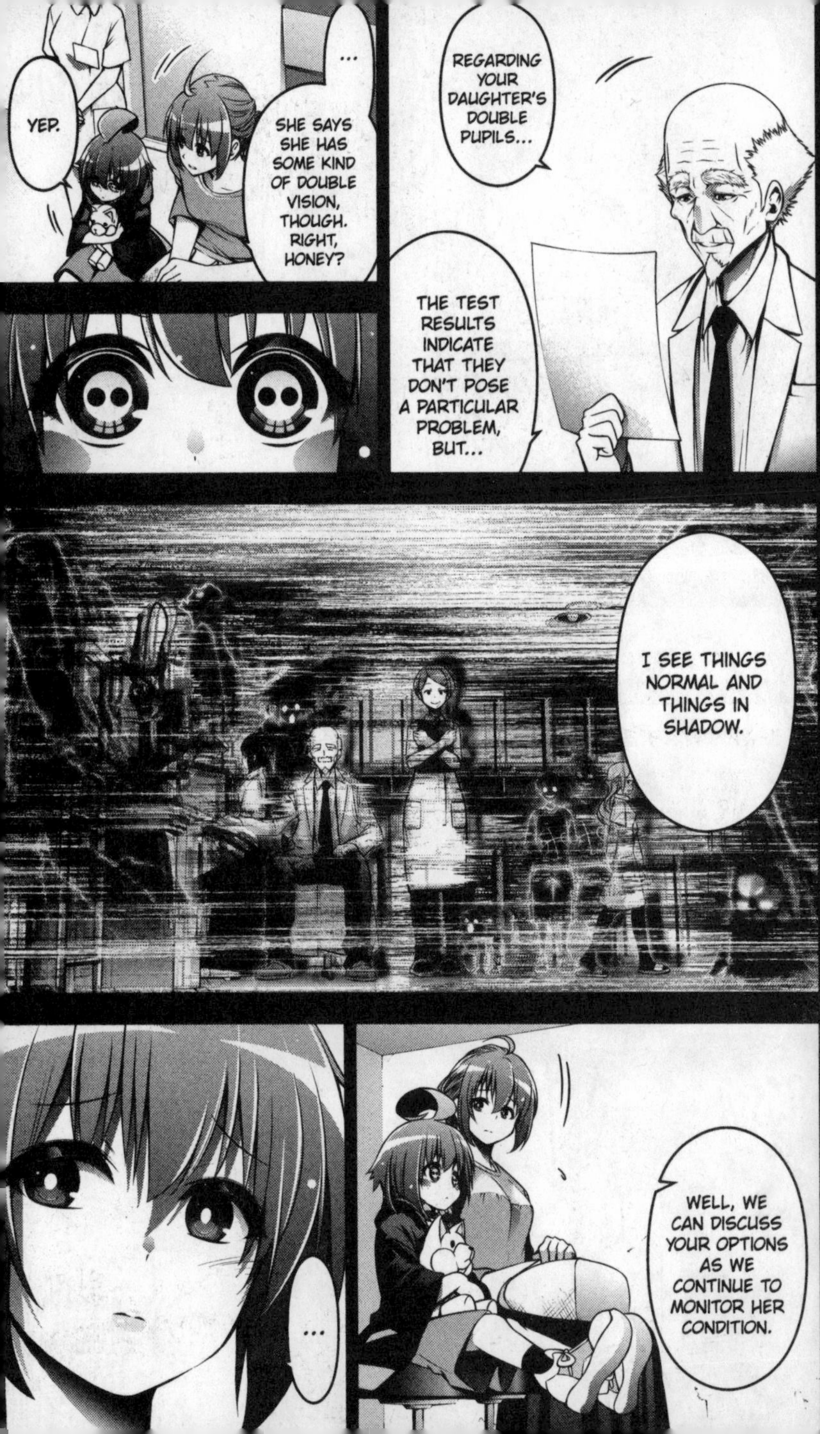
REGARDING YOUR DAUGHTER'S DOUBLE PUPILS...
THE TEST RESULTS INDICATE THAT THEY DON'T POSE A PARTICULAR PROBLEM, BUT...
...
SHE SAYS SHE HAS SOME KIND OF DOUBLE VISION, THOUGH. RIGHT, HONEY?
YEP.
I SEE THINGS NORMAL AND THINGS IN SHADOW.
WELL, WE CAN DISCUSS YOUR OPTIONS AS WE CONTINUE TO MONITOR HER CONDITION.
...

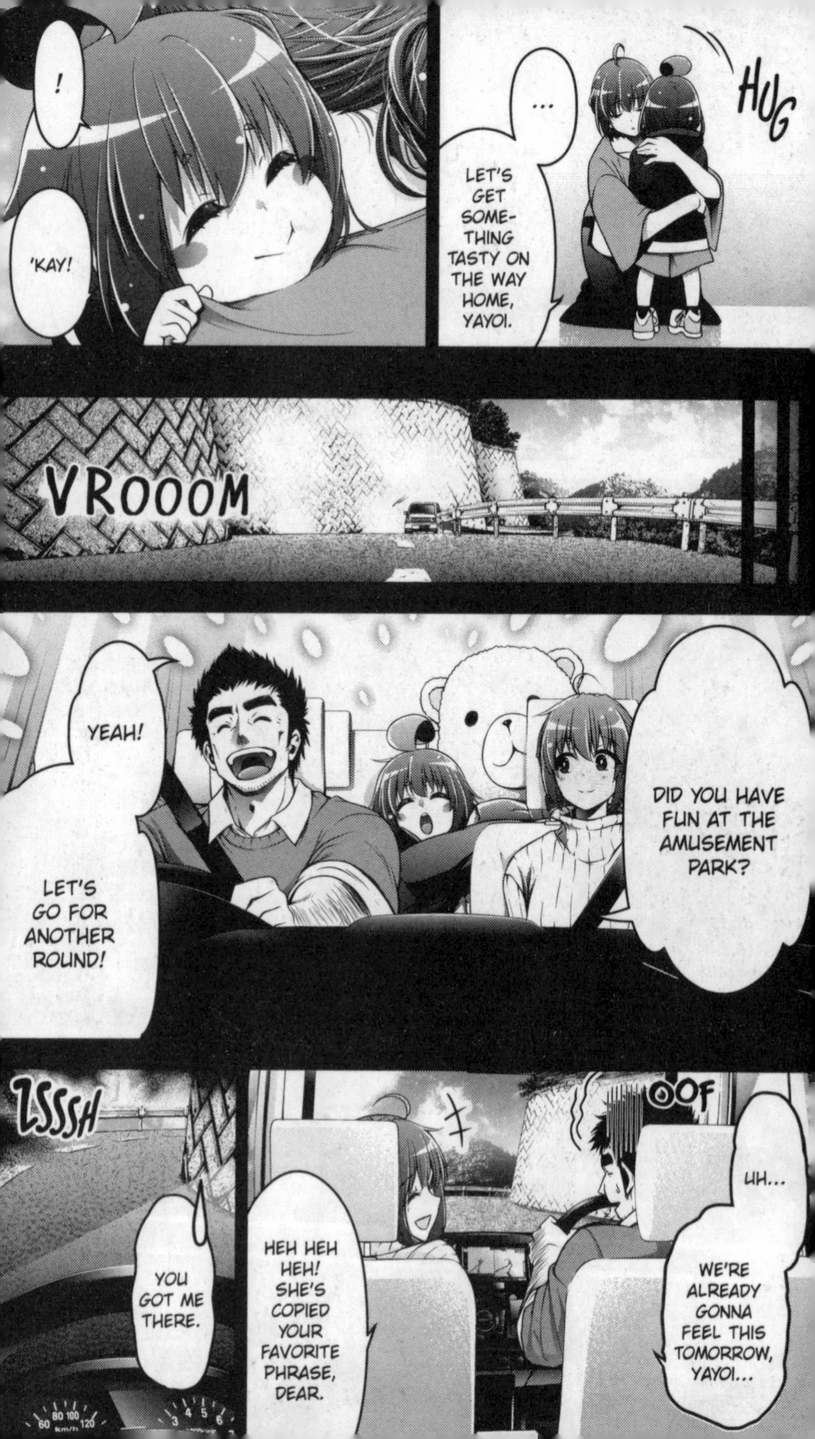
...
LET'S GET SOME-THING TASTY ON THE WAY HOME, YAYOI.
HUG
!
'KAY!
VROOOM
DID YOU HAVE FUN AT THE AMUSEMENT PARK?
YEAH!
LET'S GO FOR ANOTHER ROUND!
OOF
UH...
WE'RE ALREADY GONNA FEEL THIS TOMORROW, YAYOI...
HEH HEH HEH! SHE'S COPIED YOUR FAVORITE PHRASE, DEAR.
ZSSSH
YOU GOT ME THERE.

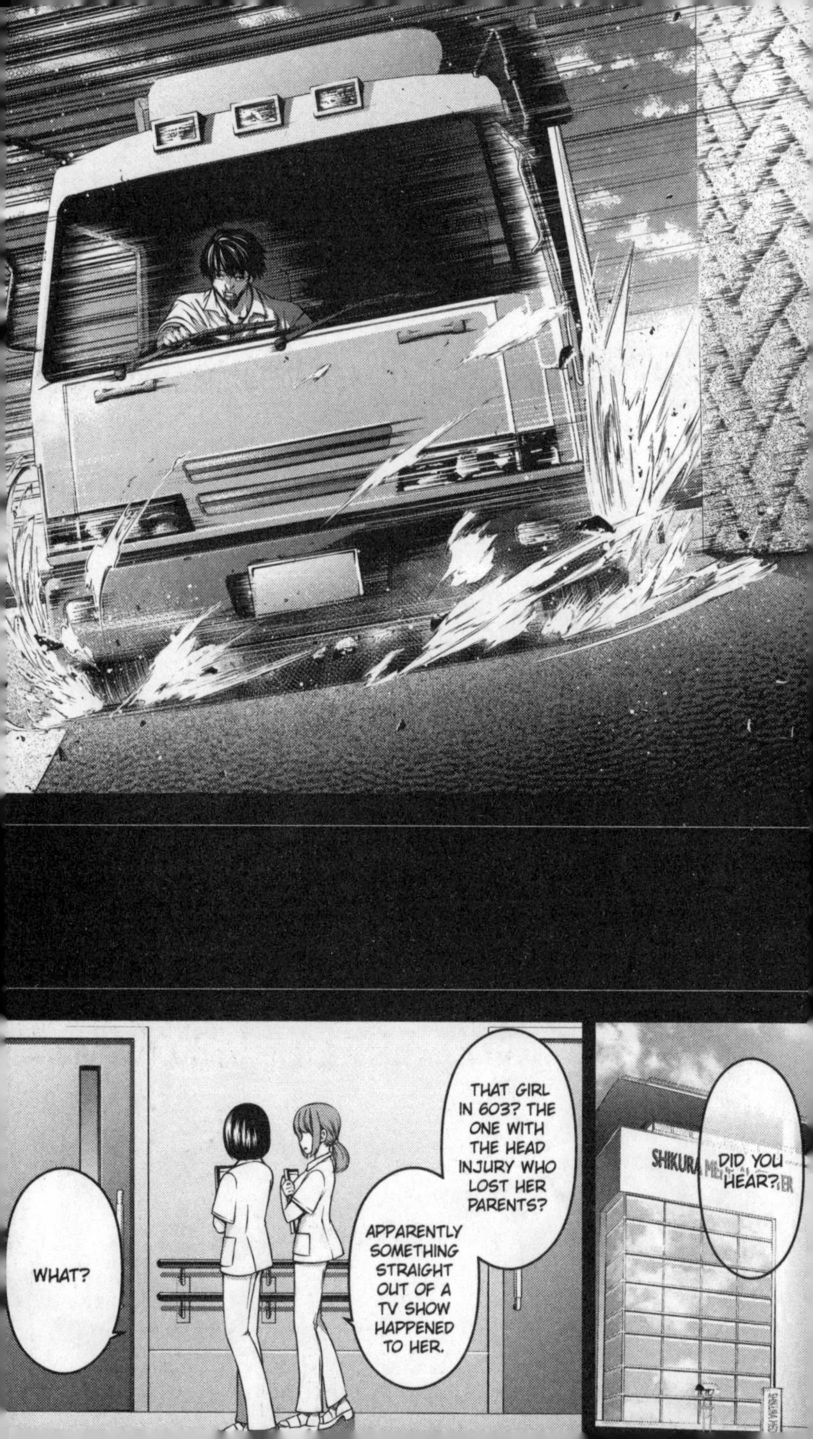
DID YOU HEAR?
THAT GIRL IN 603? THE ONE WITH THE HEAD INJURY WHO LOST HER PARENTS?
APPARENTLY SOMETHING STRAIGHT OUT OF A TV SHOW HAPPENED TO HER.
WHAT?

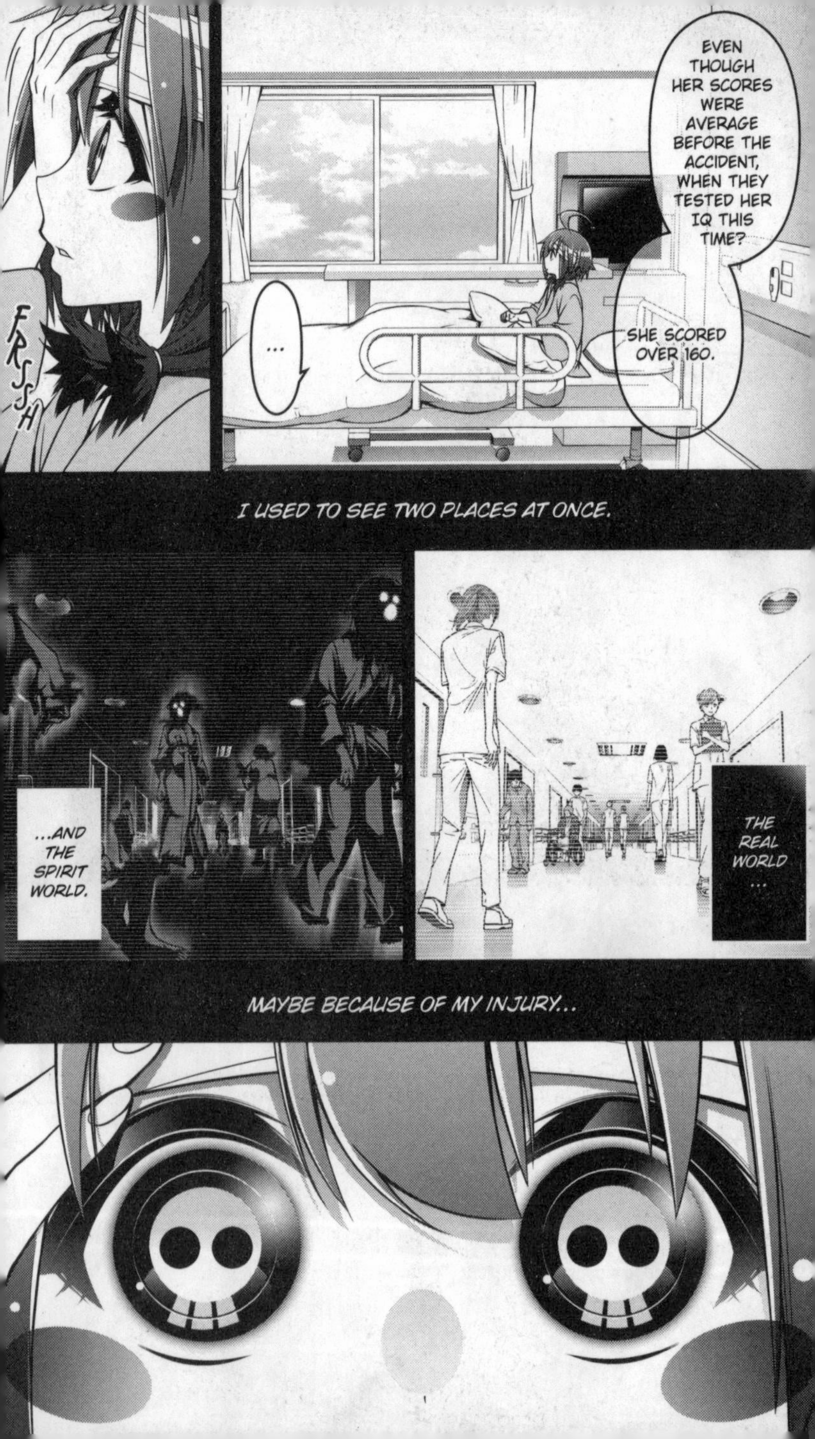
EVEN THOUGH HER SCORES WERE AVERAGE BEFORE THE ACCIDENT, WHEN THEY TESTED HER IQ THIS TIME?
SHE SCORED OVER 160.
...
FRSSH
I USED TO SEE TWO PLACES AT ONCE.
THE REAL WORLD ...
...AND THE SPIRIT WORLD.
MAYBE BECAUSE OF MY INJURY...

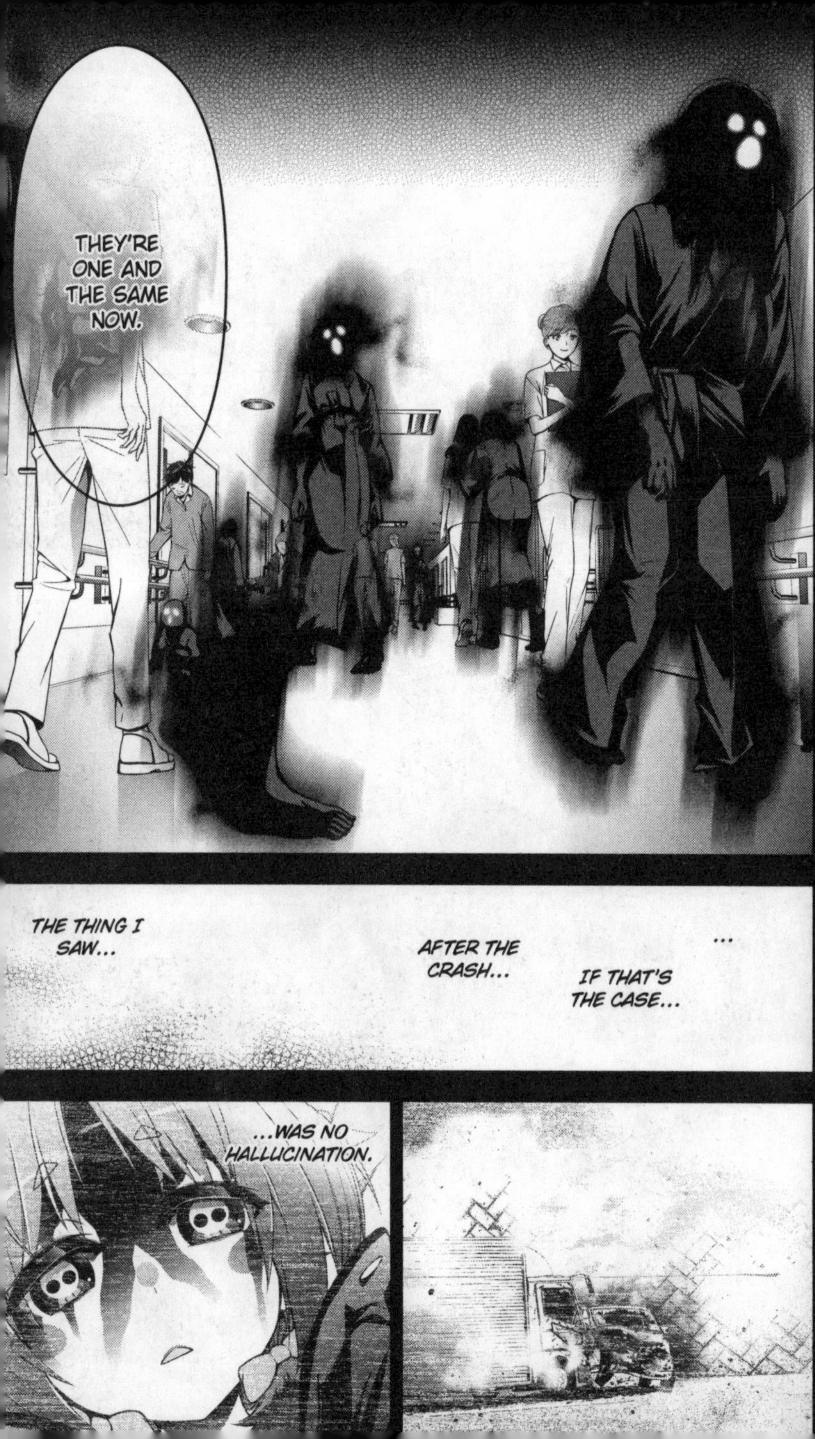
THEY'RE ONE AND THE SAME NOW.
...
IF THAT'S THE CASE...
AFTER THE CRASH...
THE THING I SAW...
...WAS NO HALLUCINATION.

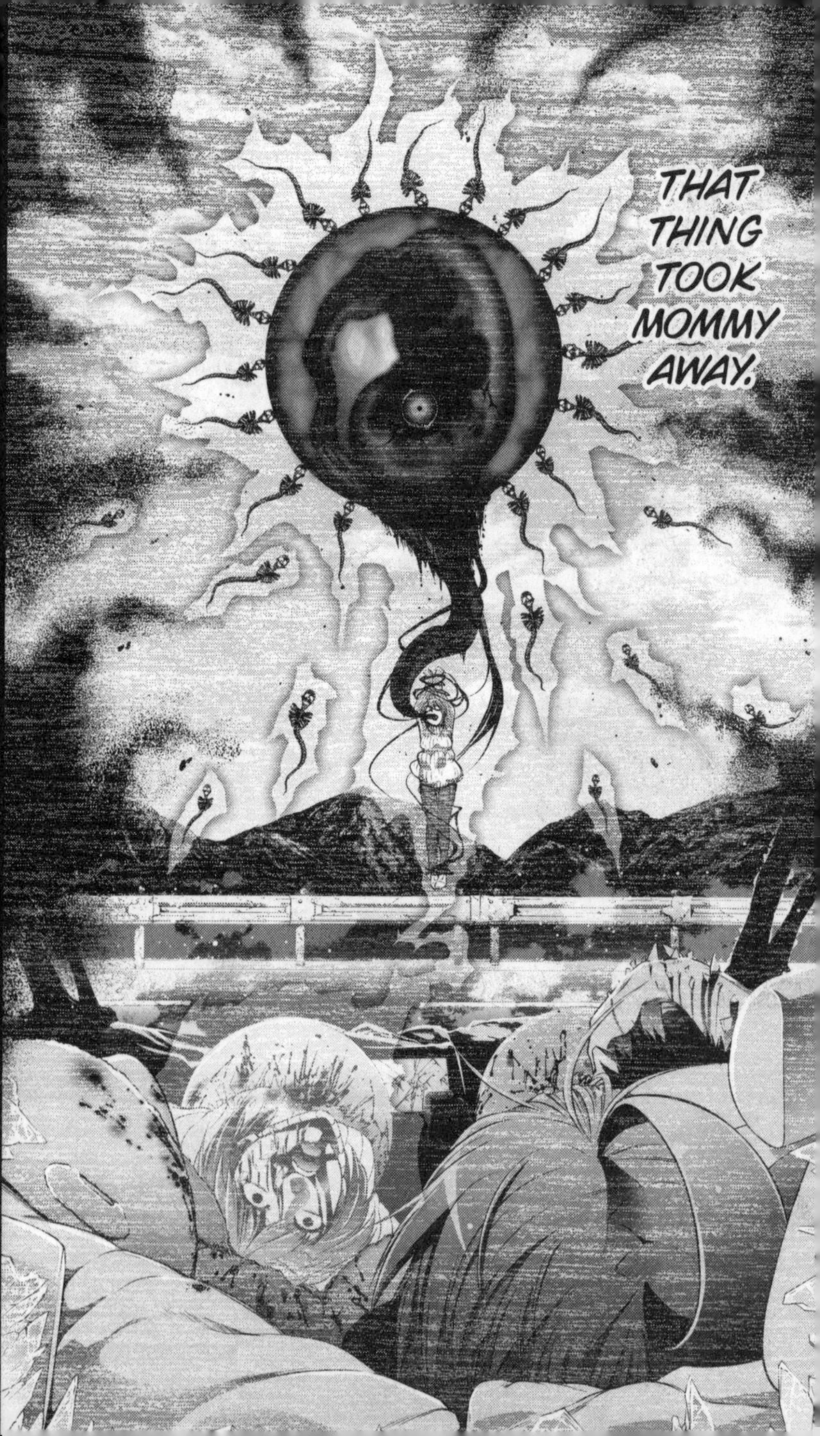
THAT THING TOOK MOMMY AWAY.

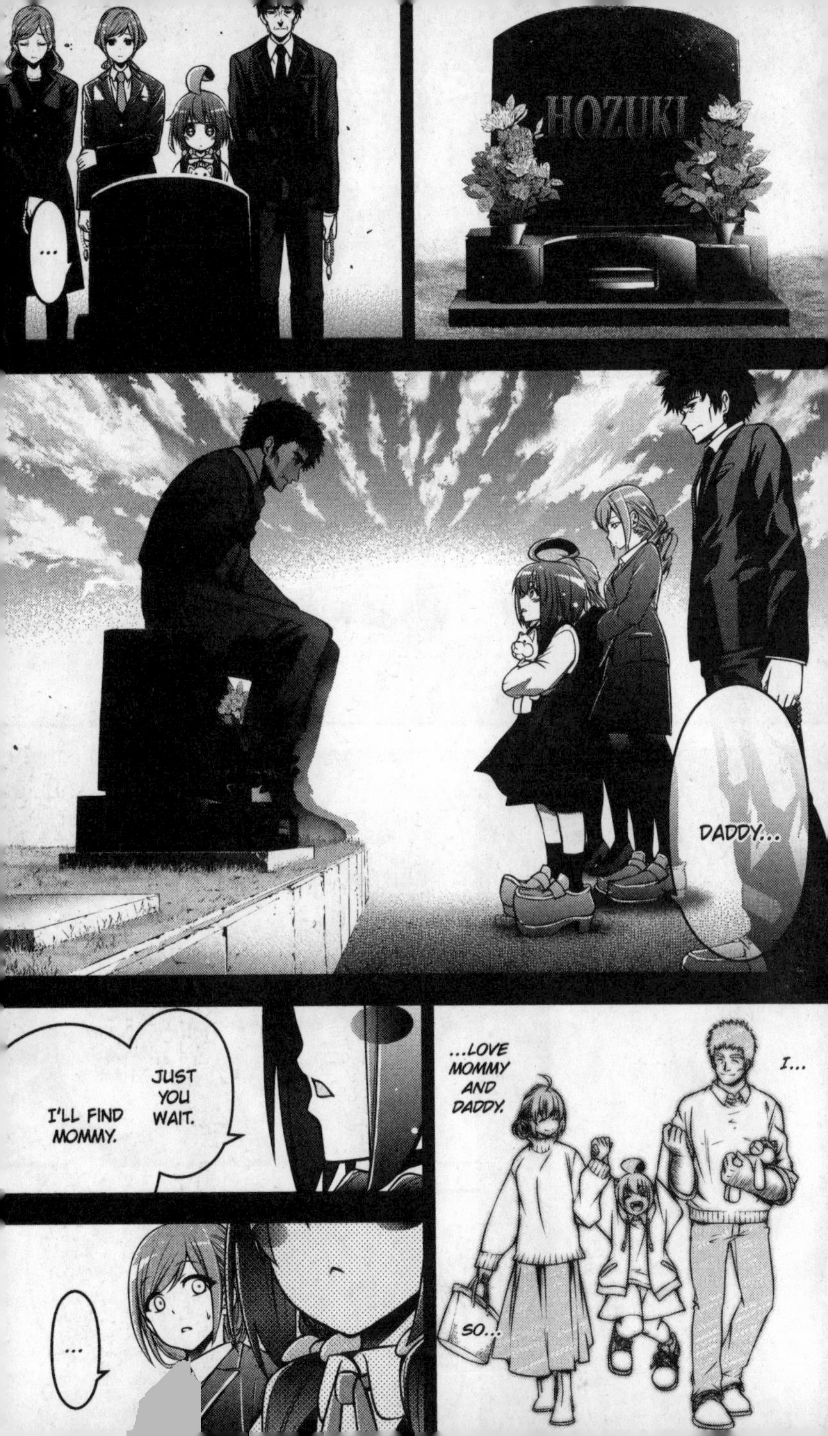
HOZUKI
...
DADDY...
I...
...LOVE MOMMY AND DADDY.
SO...
JUST YOU WAIT.
I'LL FIND MOMMY.
...

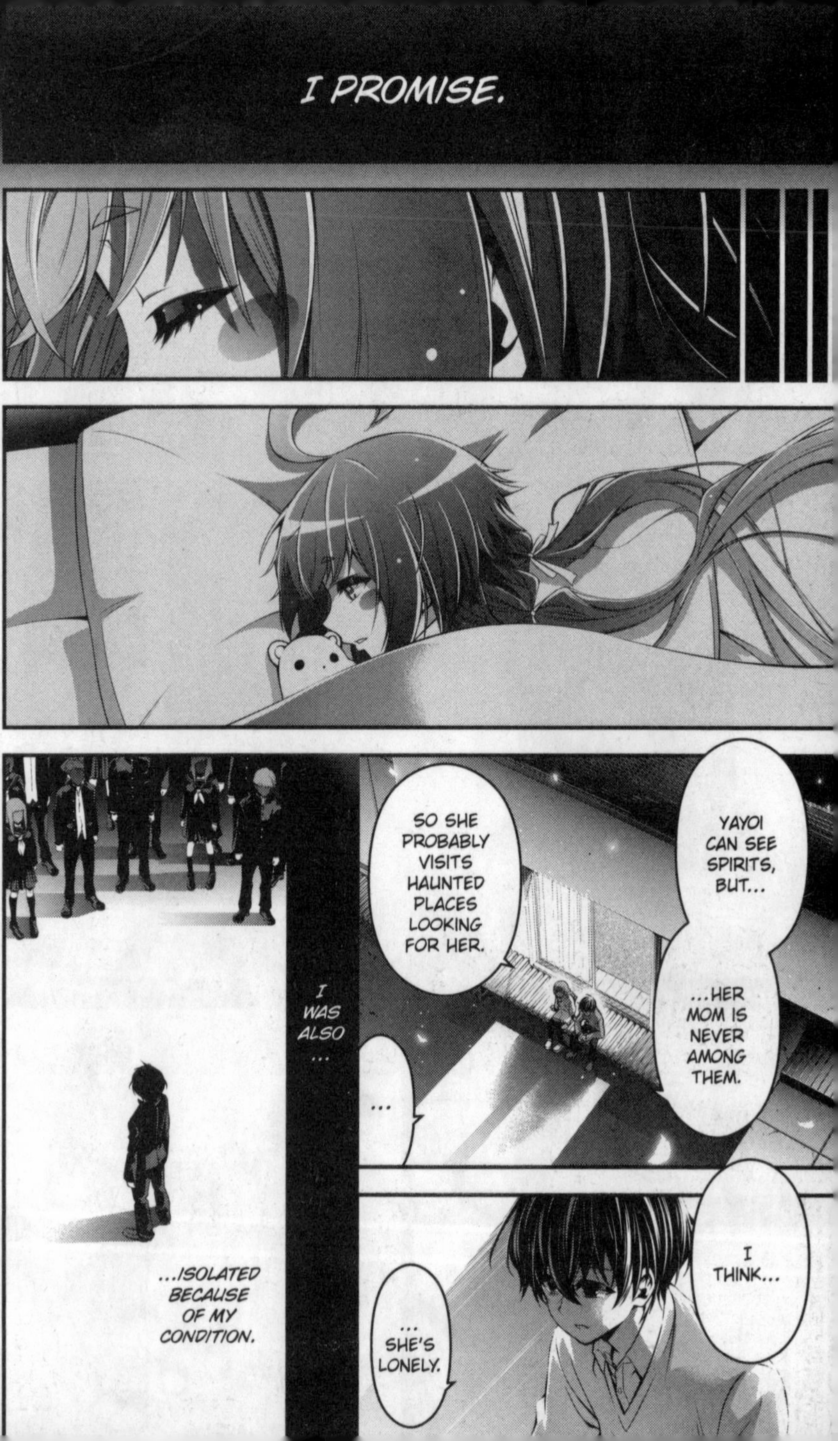
I PROMISE.
YAYOI CAN SEE SPIRITS, BUT...
...HER MOM IS NEVER AMONG THEM.
SO SHE PROBABLY VISITS HAUNTED PLACES LOOKING FOR HER.
...
I THINK...
...SHE'S LONELY.
I WAS ALSO...
...ISOLATED BECAUSE OF MY CONDITION.

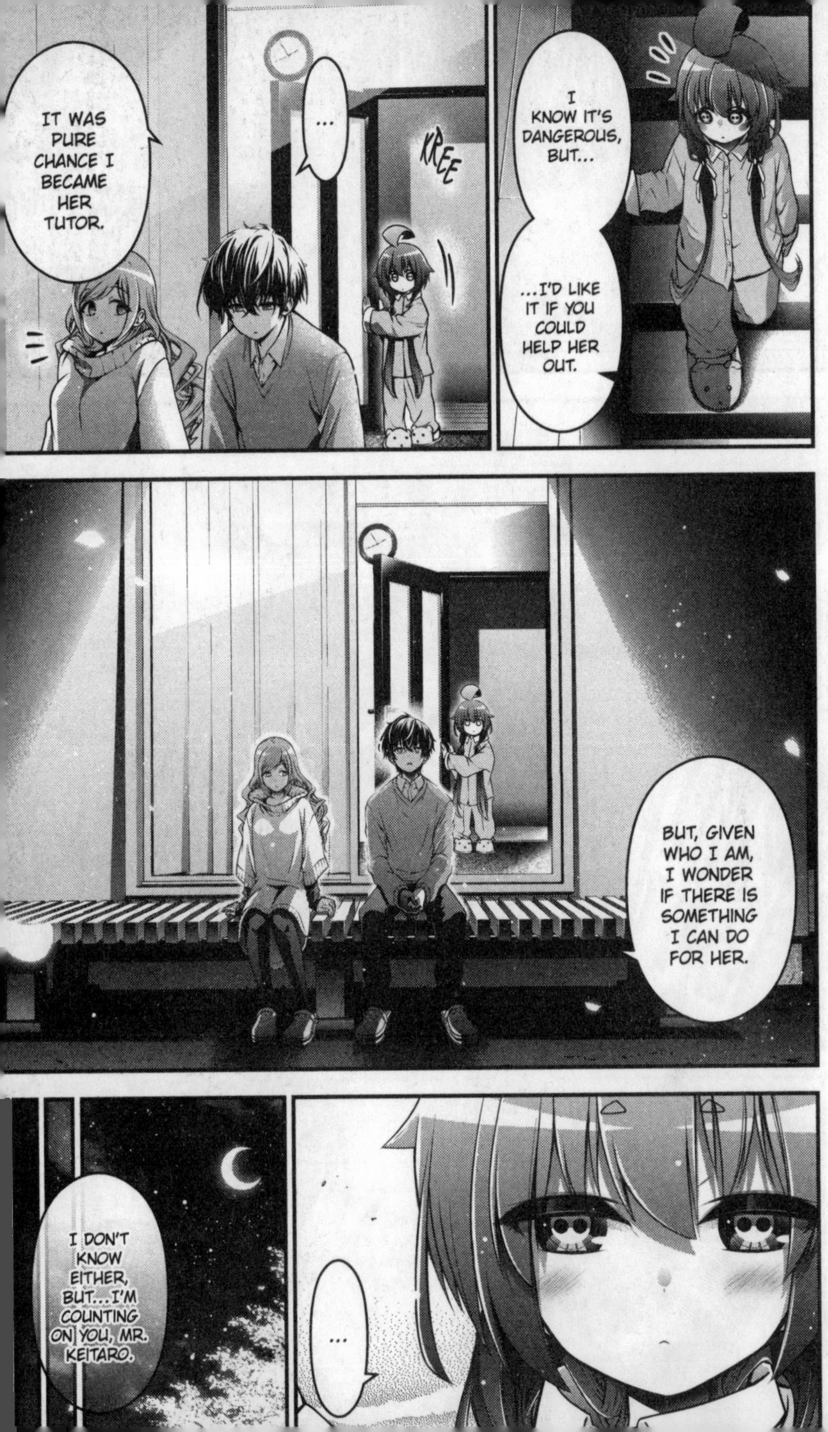
I KNOW IT'S DANGEROUS, BUT...
...I'D LIKE IT IF YOU COULD HELP HER OUT.
...
KREE
IT WAS PURE CHANCE I BECAME HER TUTOR.
BUT, GIVEN WHO I AM, I WONDER IF THERE IS SOMETHING I CAN DO FOR HER.
...
I DON'T KNOW EITHER, BUT... I'M COUNTING ON YOU, MR. KEITARO.

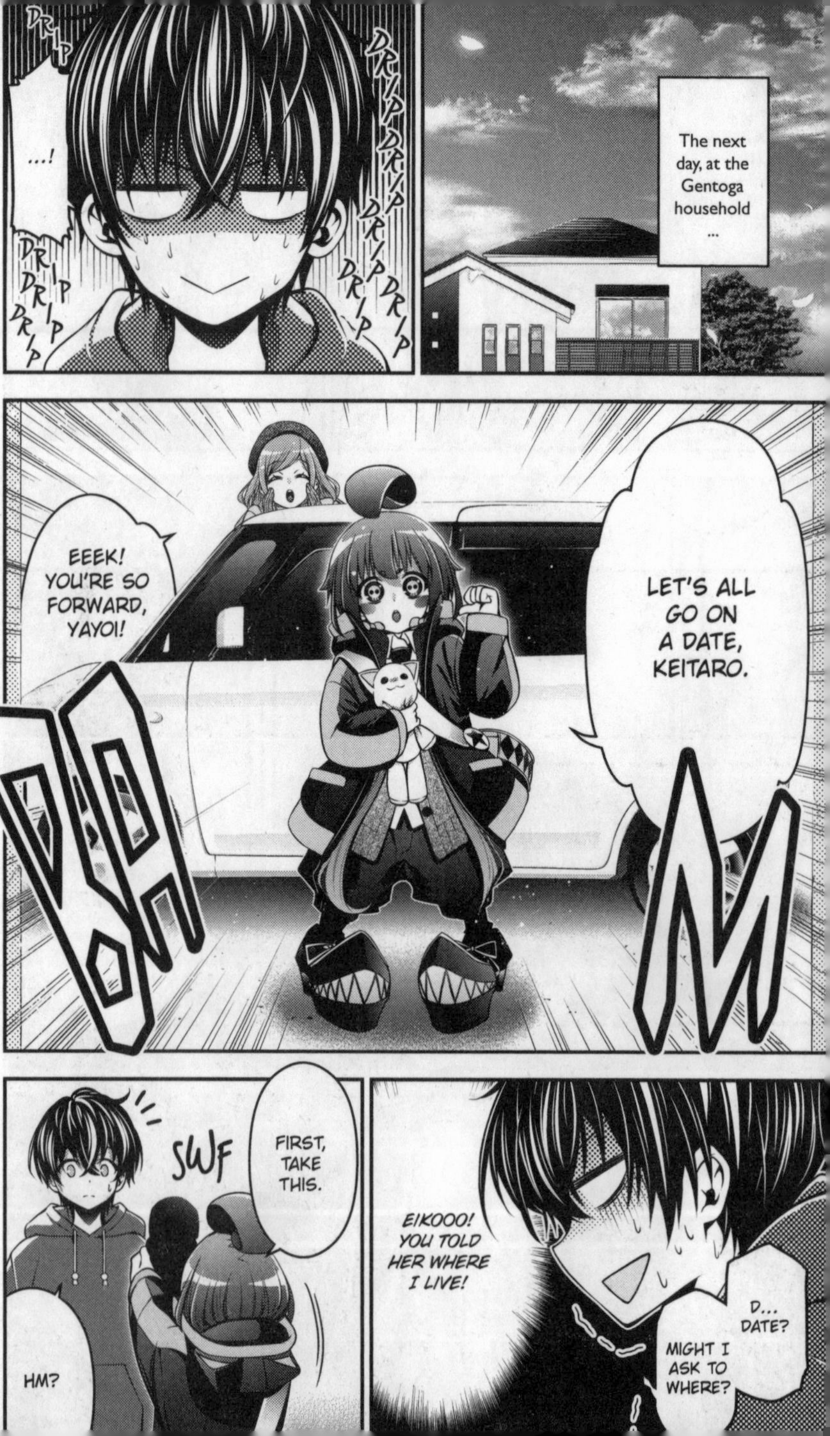
The next day, at the Gentoga household ...
DRIP DRIP DRIP DRIP DRIP DRIP
...!
DRIP DRIP DRIP
LET'S ALL GO ON A DATE, KEITARO.
EEEK! YOU'RE SO FORWARD, YAYOI!
D... DATE?
MIGHT I ASK TO WHERE?
EIKOOO! YOU TOLD HER WHERE I LIVE!
FIRST, TAKE THIS.
SWF
HM?

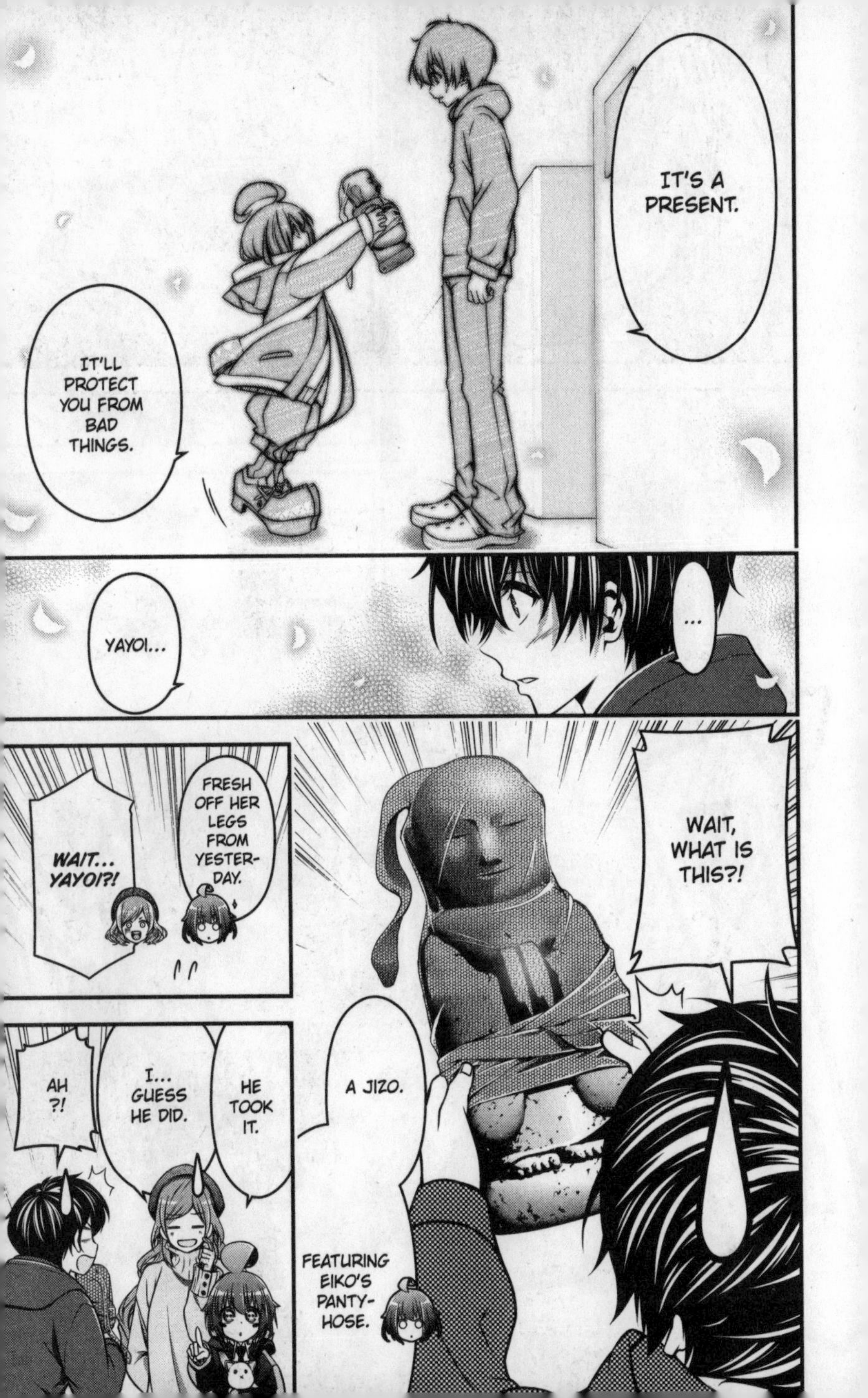
IT'S A PRESENT.
IT'LL PROTECT YOU FROM BAD THINGS.
...
YAYOI...
WAIT, WHAT IS THIS?!
A JIZO.
FEATURING EIKO'S PANTY-HOSE.
FRESH OFF HER LEGS FROM YESTER-DAY.
WAIT... YAYOI?!
HE TOOK IT.
I... GUESS HE DID.
AH ?!

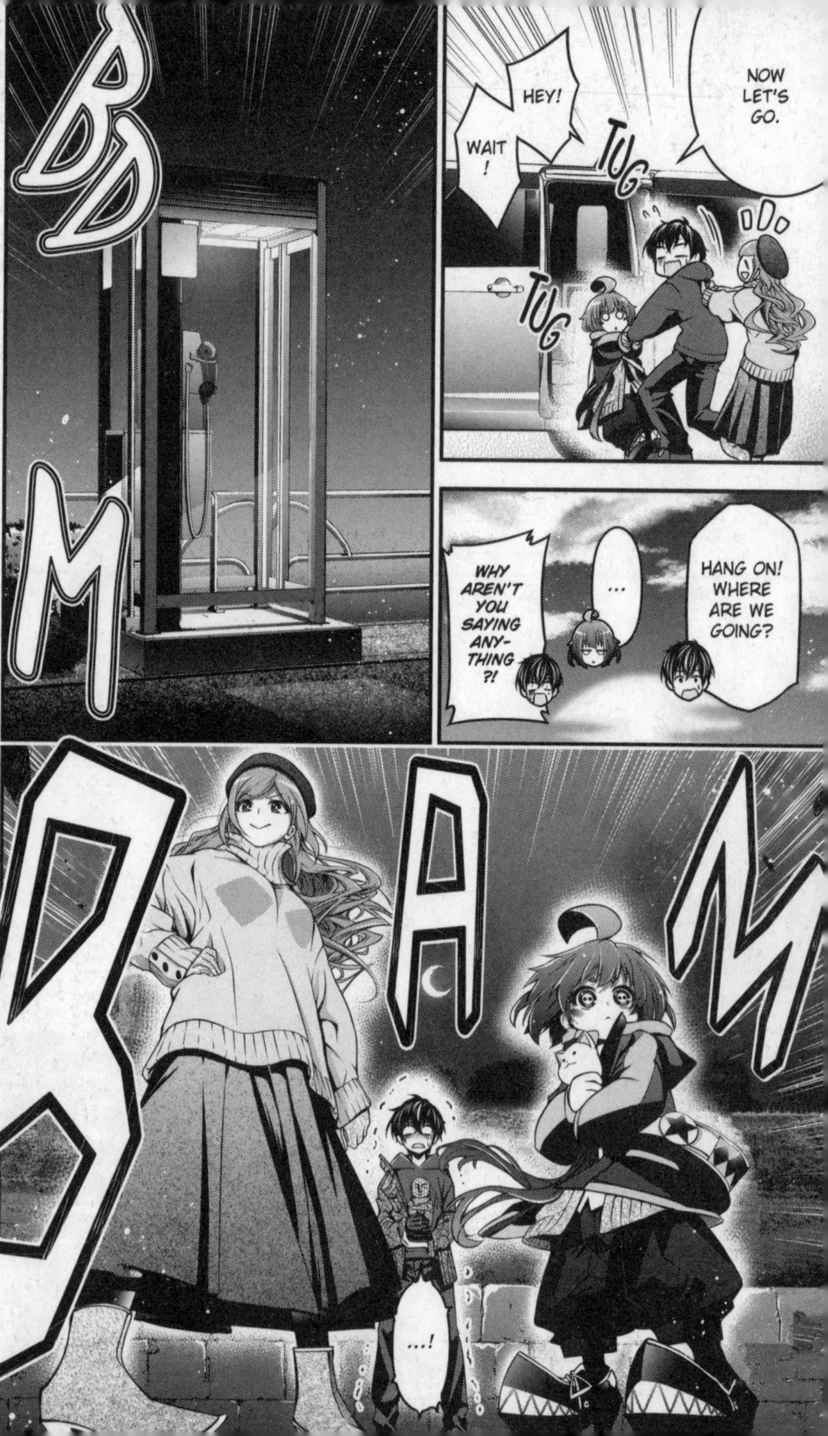
NOW LET'S GO.
TUG
HEY!
WAIT!
TUG
HANG ON! WHERE ARE WE GOING?
...
WHY AREN'T YOU SAYING ANYTHING?!
BDDM
BAM
...!

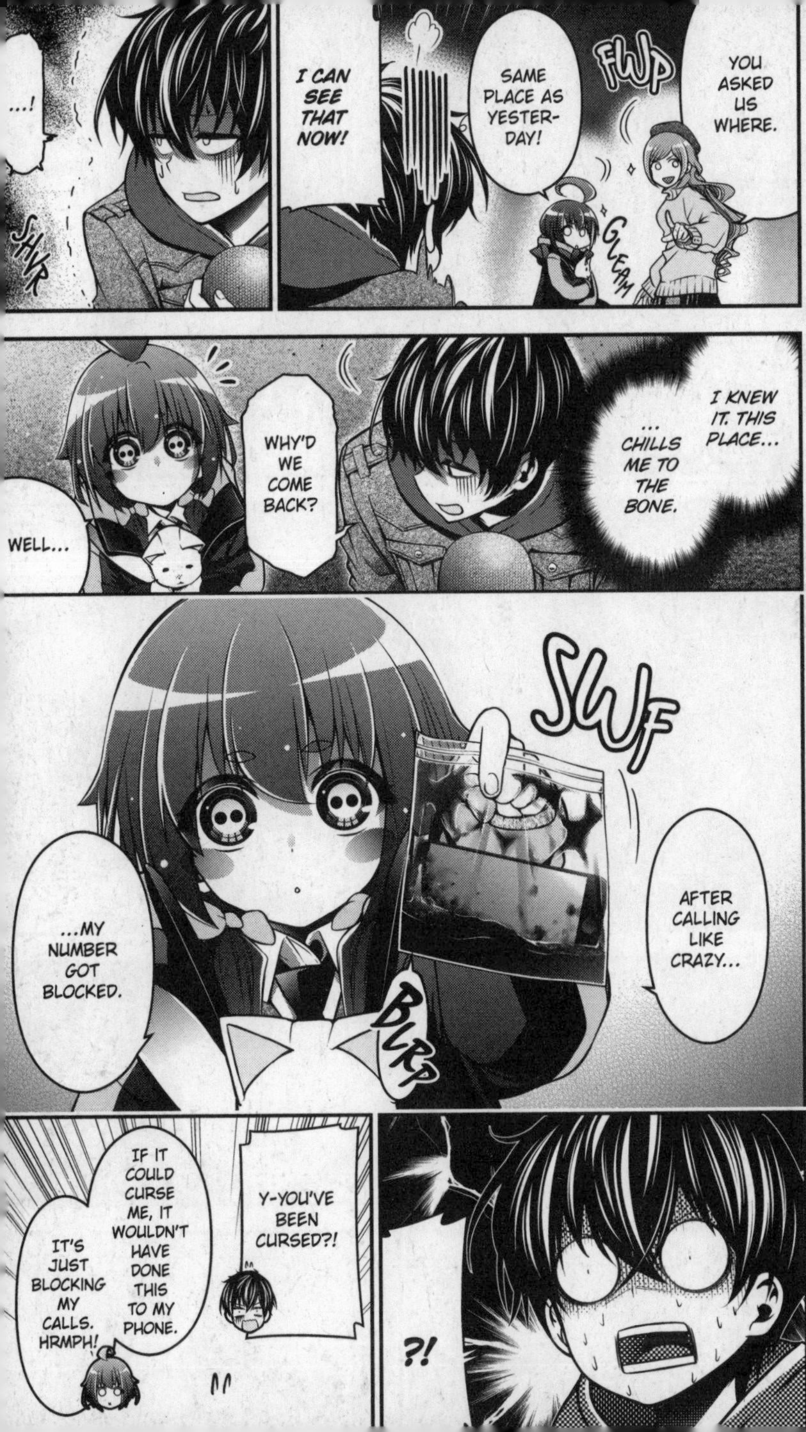
YOU ASKED US WHERE.
FWP
SAME PLACE AS YESTER-DAY!
GLEAM
I CAN SEE THAT NOW!
...!
SHVR
I KNEW IT. THIS PLACE...
...CHILLS ME TO THE BONE.
WHY'D WE COME BACK?
WELL...
SWF
AFTER CALLING LIKE CRAZY...
...MY NUMBER GOT BLOCKED.
BLRP
?!
Y-YOU'VE BEEN CURSED?!
IF IT COULD CURSE ME, IT WOULDN'T HAVE DONE THIS TO MY PHONE.
IT'S JUST BLOCKING MY CALLS. HRMPH!

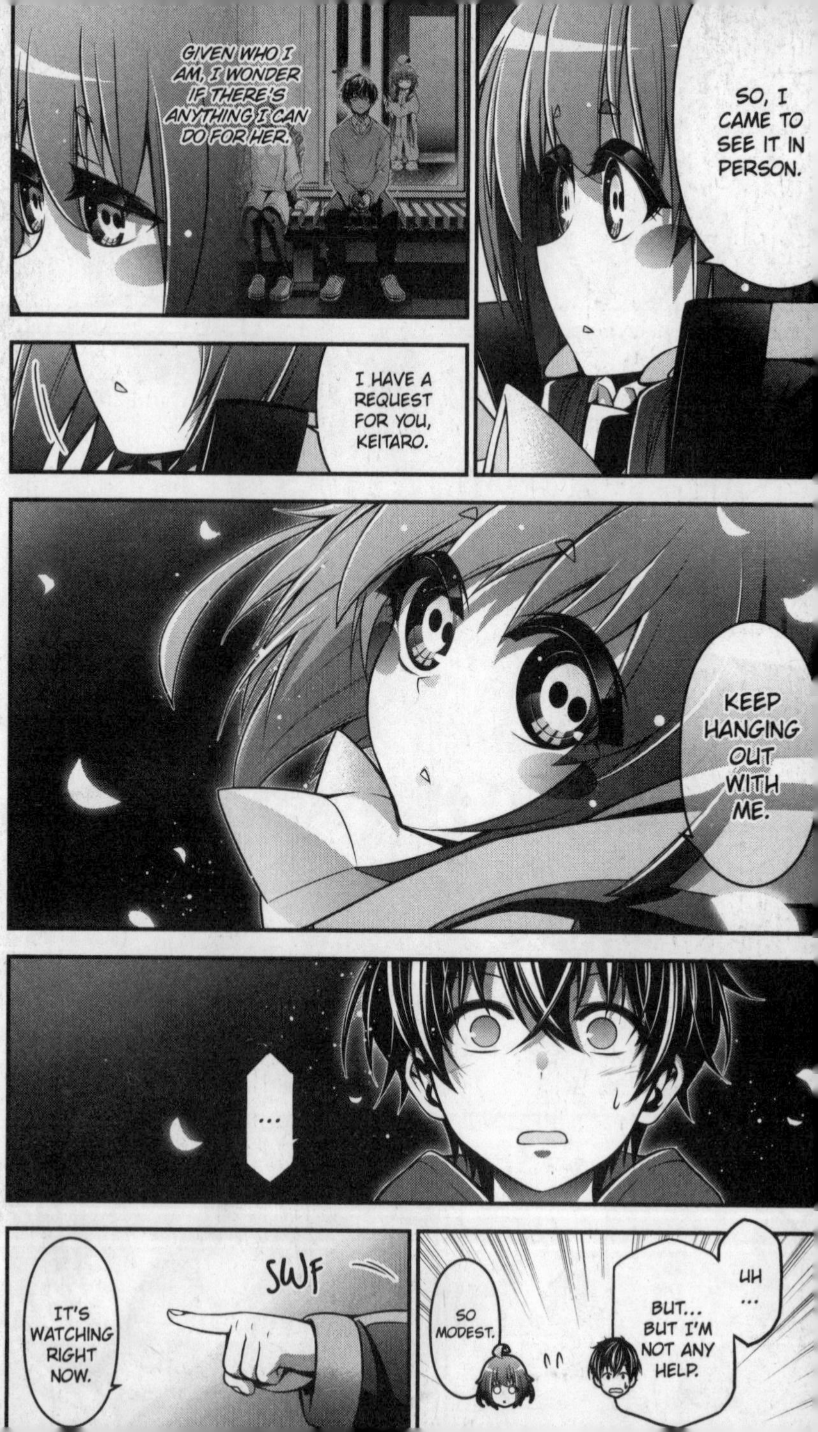
SO, I CAME TO SEE IT IN PERSON.
GIVEN WHO I AM, I WONDER IF THERE'S ANYTHING I CAN DO FOR HER.
I HAVE A REQUEST FOR YOU, KEITARO.
KEEP HANGING OUT WITH ME.
...
UH ...
BUT... BUT I'M NOT ANY HELP.
SO MODEST.
SWF
IT'S WATCHING RIGHT NOW.

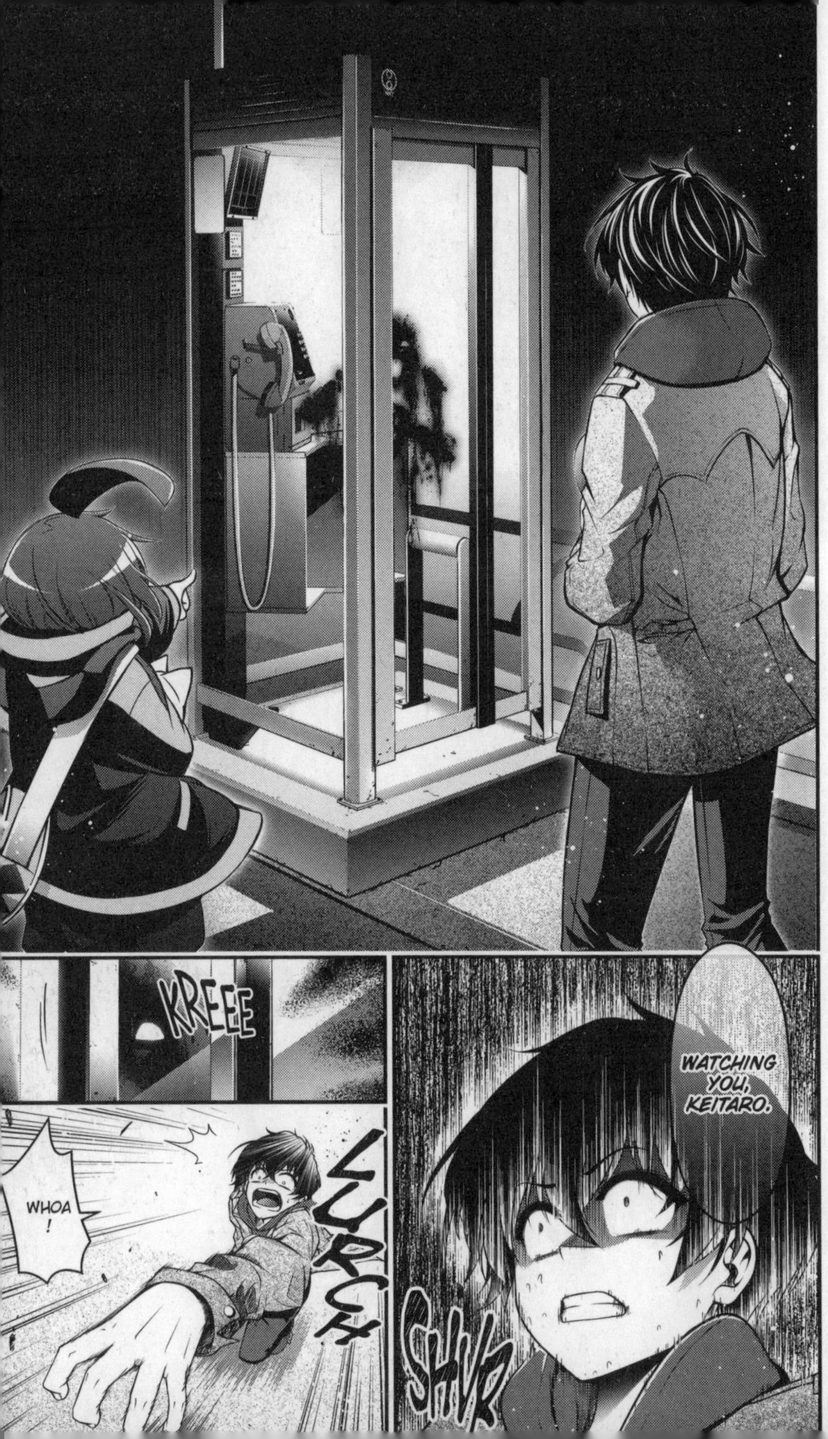
WATCHING YOU, KEITARO.
SHVK
KREEE
WHOA!
LURCH

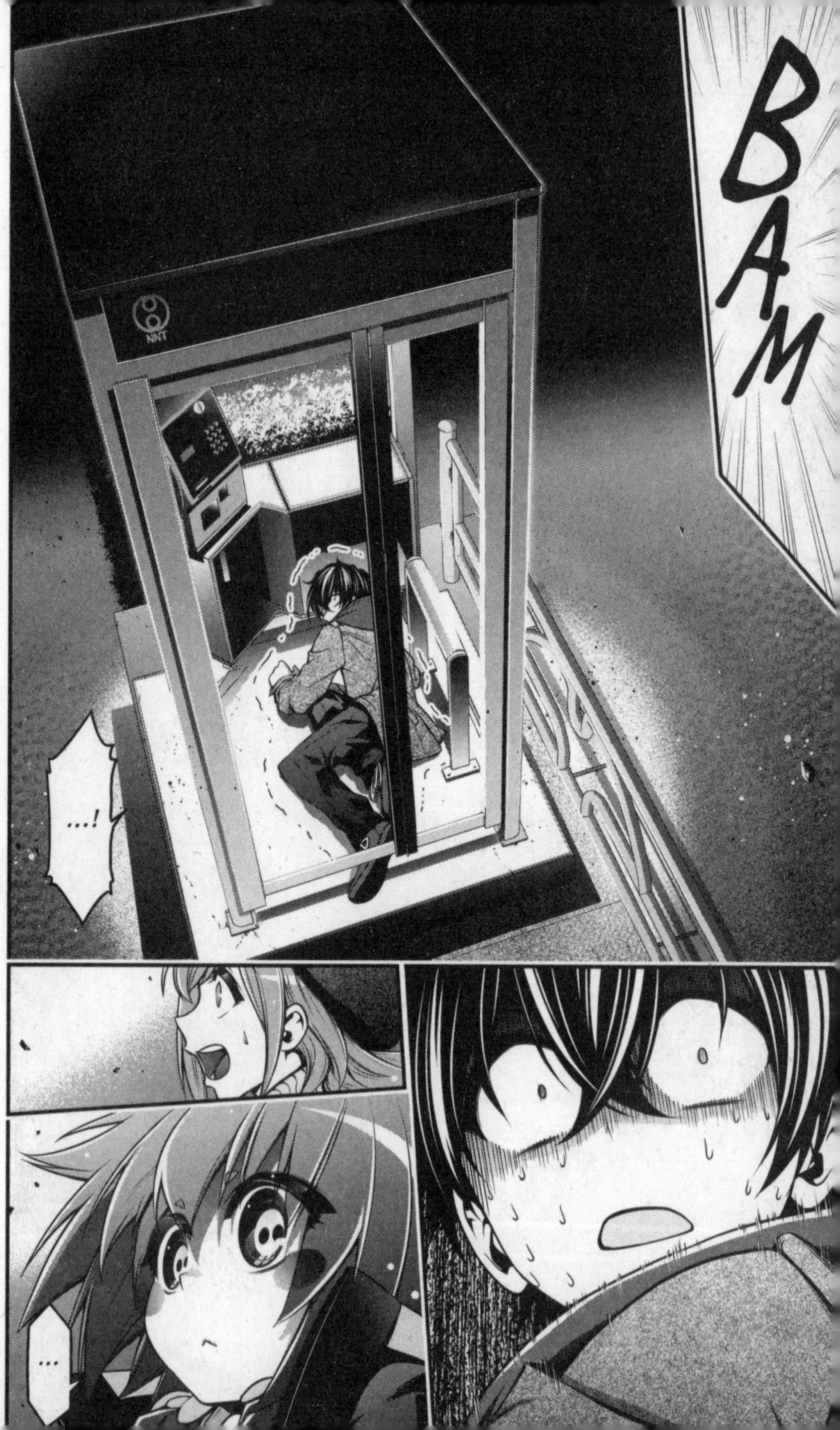
BAM
...!
...

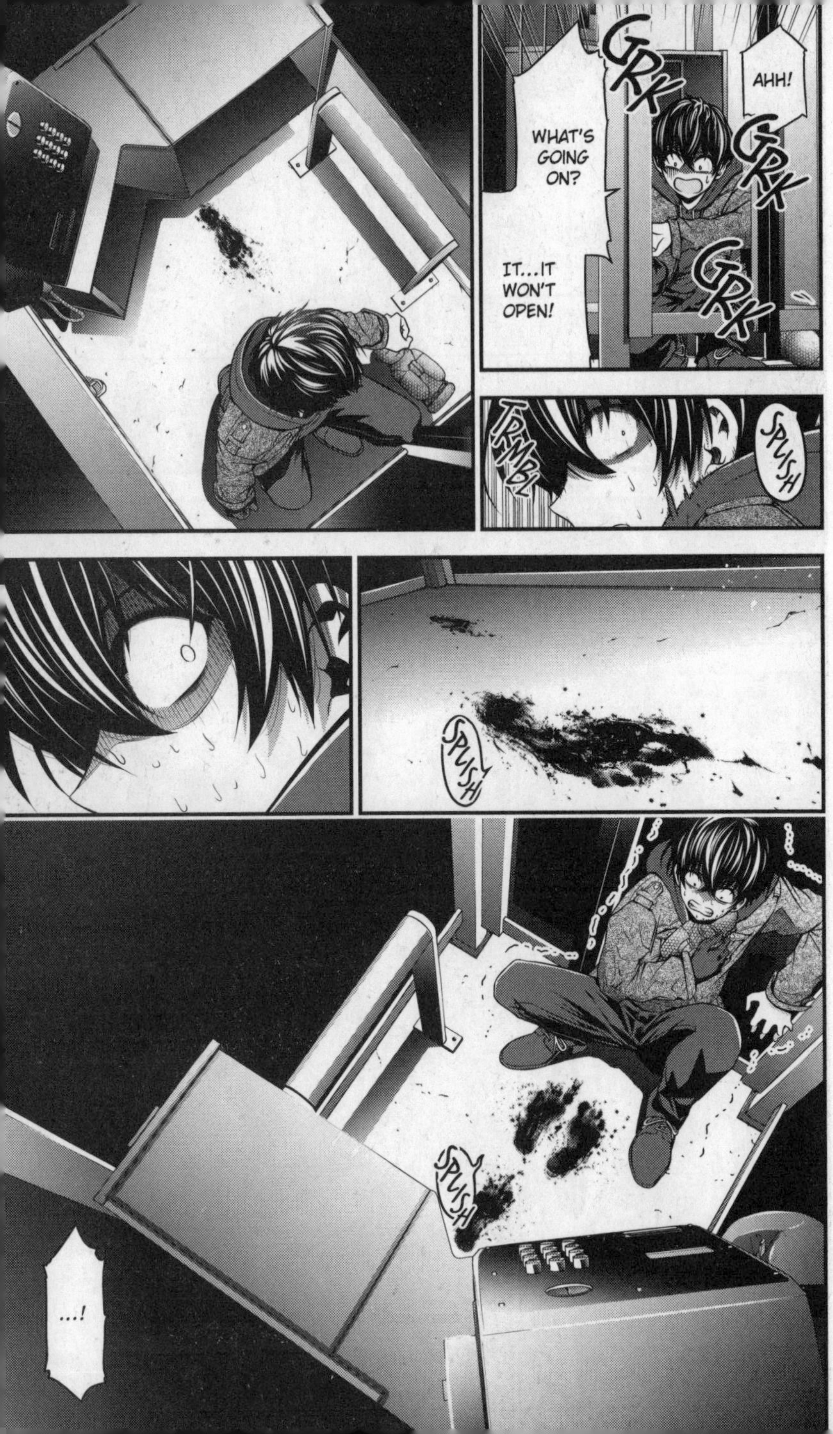
AHH!
GRK
GRK
GRK
WHAT'S GOING ON?
IT...IT WON'T OPEN!
SPLISH
TRMBL
SPLISH
SPLISH
...!

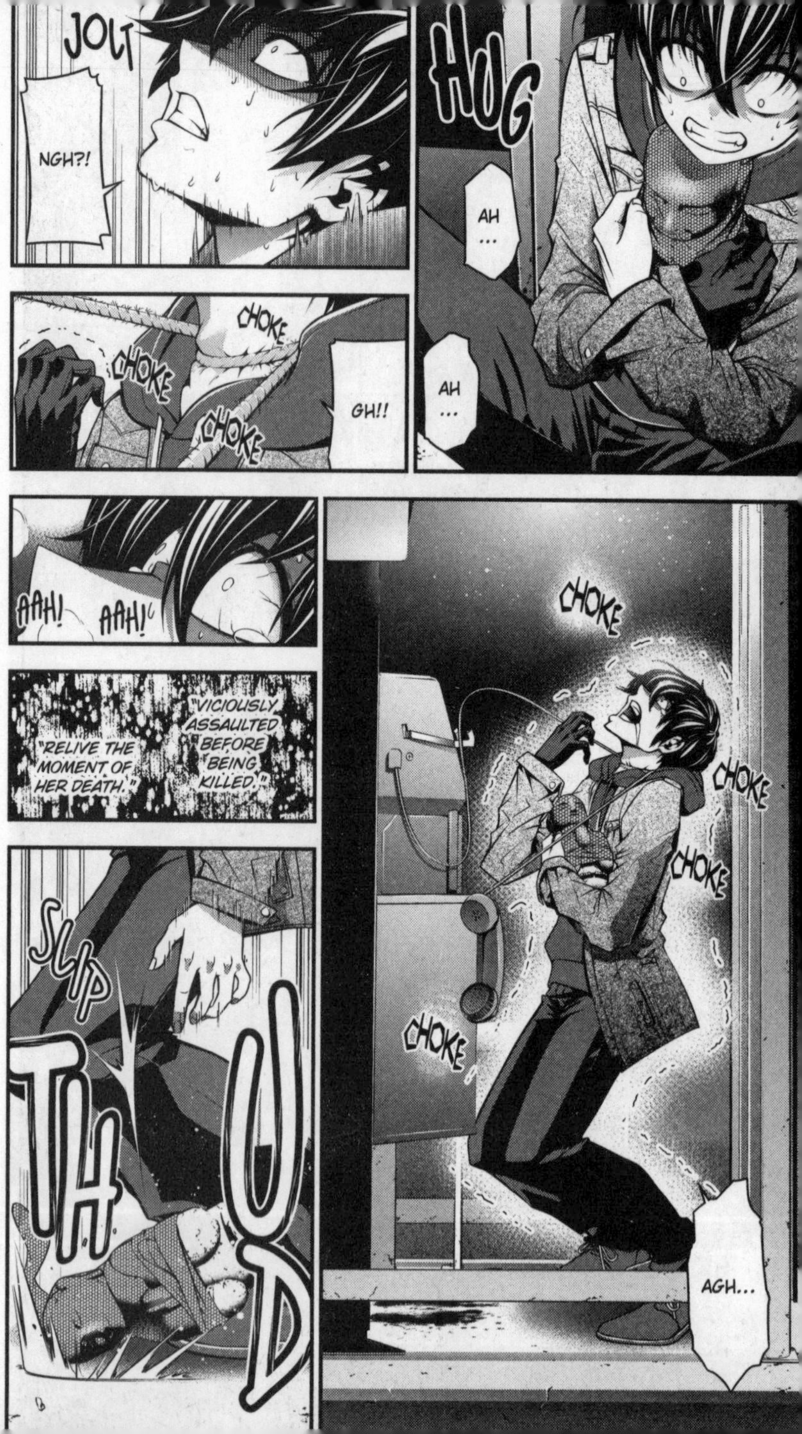
HUG
AH...
AH...
JOLT
NGH?!
CHOKE
GH!!
CHOKE
CHOKE
CHOKE
CHOKE
CHOKE
CHOKE
AGH...
AAH!
AAH!
"VICIOUSLY ASSAULTED BEFORE BEING KILLED."
"RELIVE THE MOMENT OF HER DEATH."
SLIP
THUD

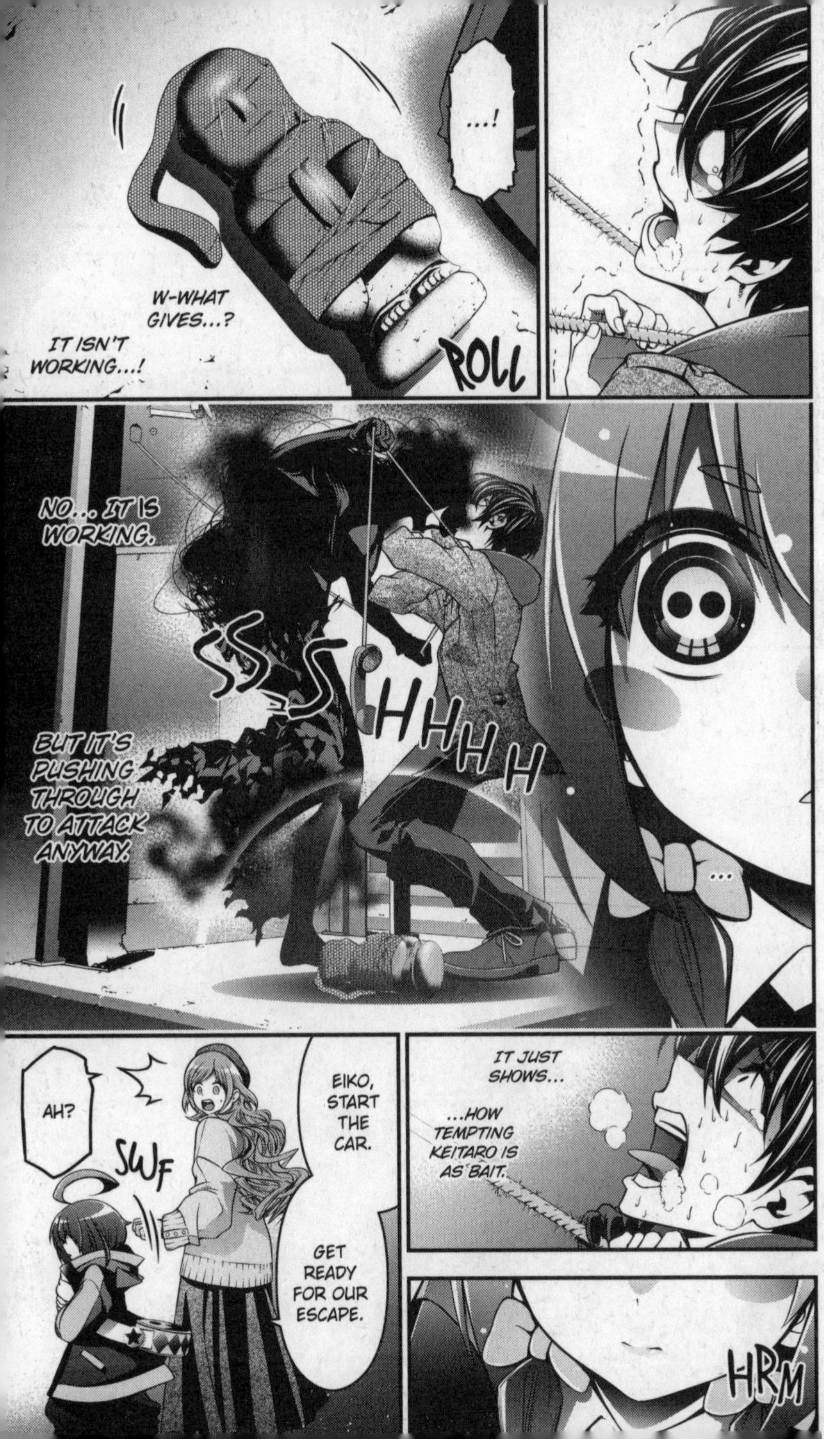

...!
W-WHAT GIVES...?
IT ISN'T WORKING...!
ROLL
...
SSSHHHHH
NO... IT IS WORKING.
BUT IT'S PUSHING THROUGH TO ATTACK ANYWAY.
IT JUST SHOWS...
...HOW TEMPTING KEITARO IS AS BAIT.
HRM
EIKO, START THE CAR.
GET READY FOR OUR ESCAPE.
AH?
SWF

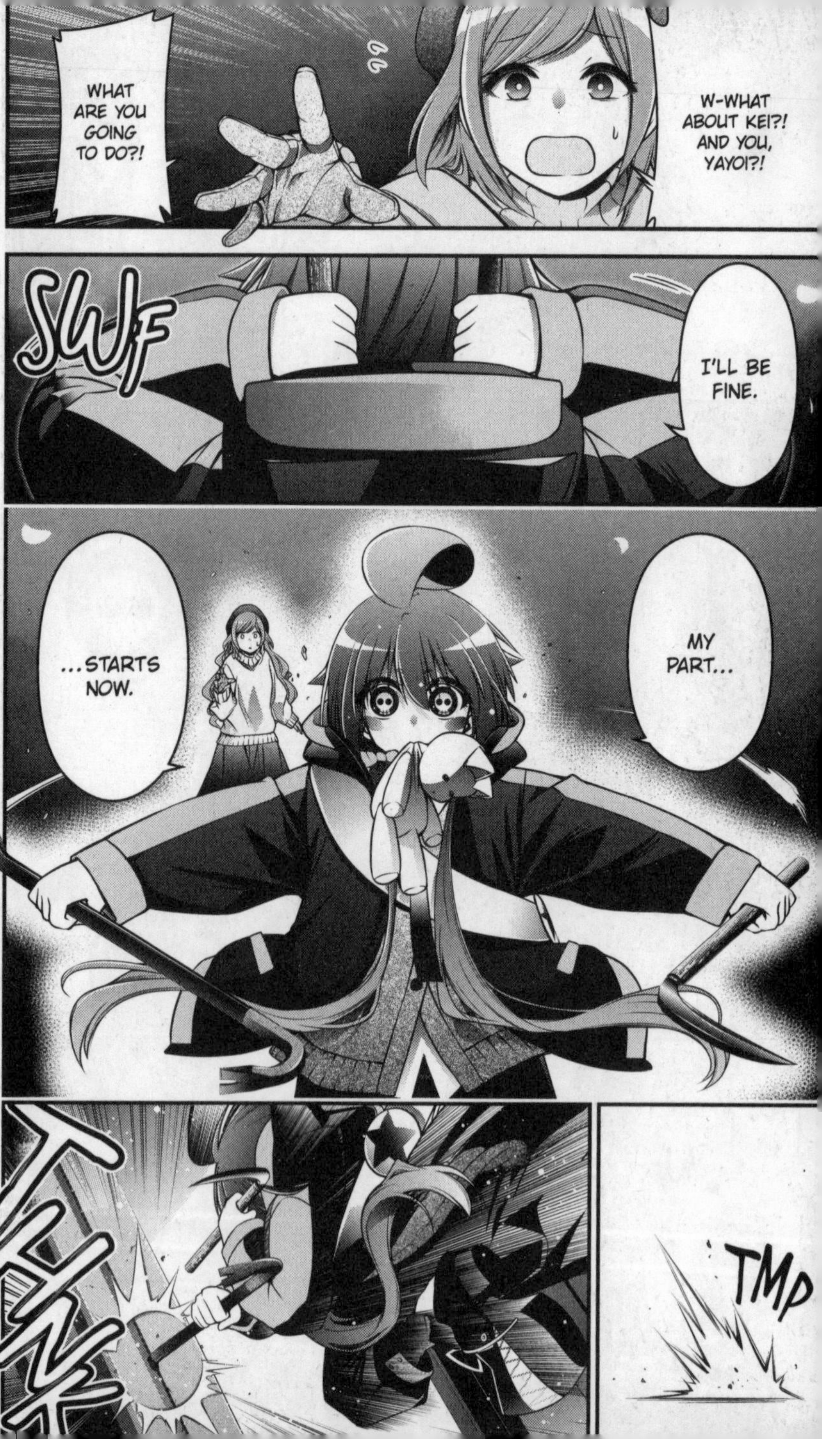
W-WHAT ABOUT KEI?! AND YOU, YAYOI?!
WHAT ARE YOU GOING TO DO?!
I'LL BE FINE.
SWF
MY PART...
...STARTS NOW.
TMP
TINK

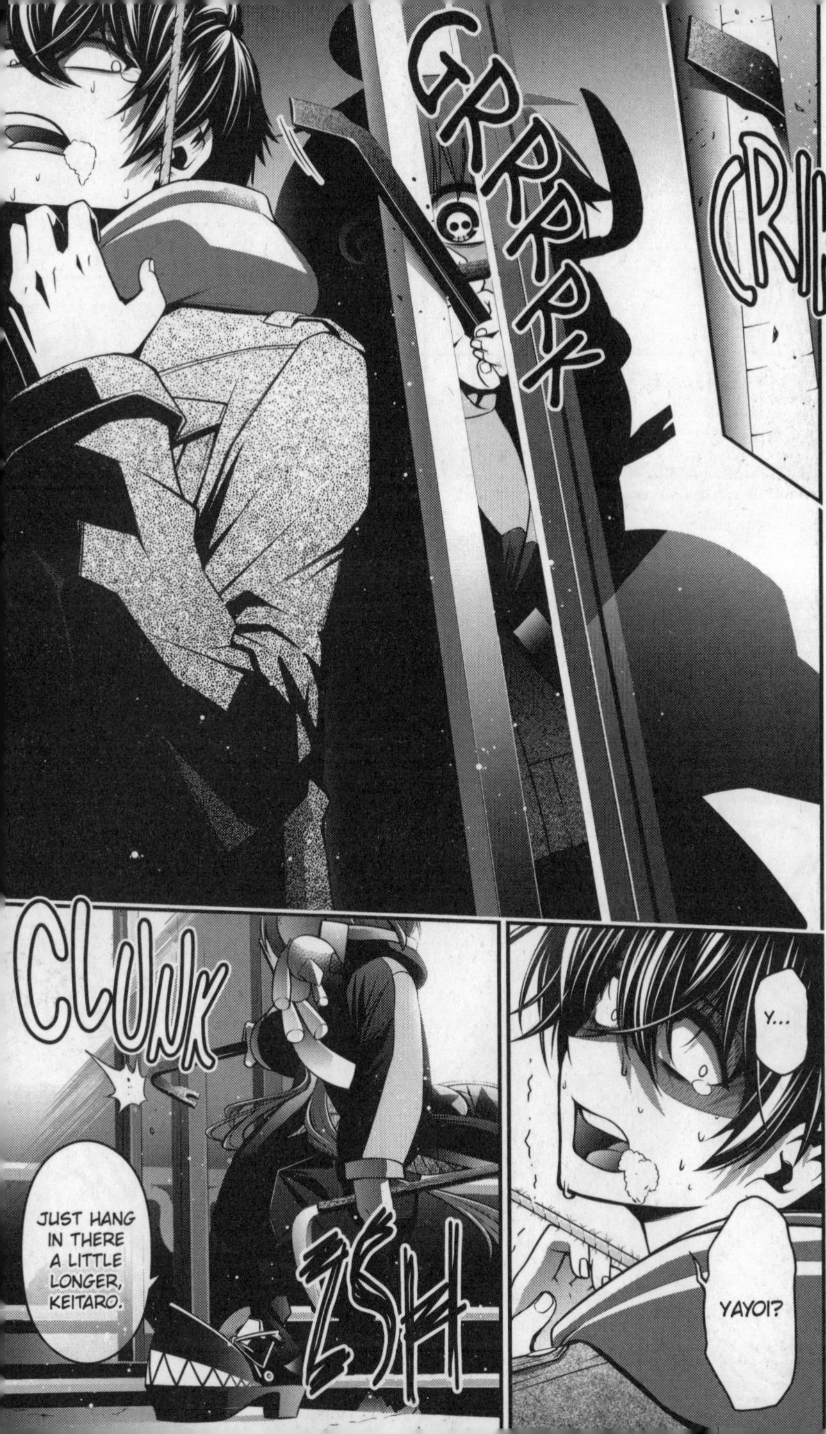
CRIK
GRRRRK
Y...
YAYOI?
CLUNK
JUST HANG IN THERE A LITTLE LONGER, KEITARO.
ZSH

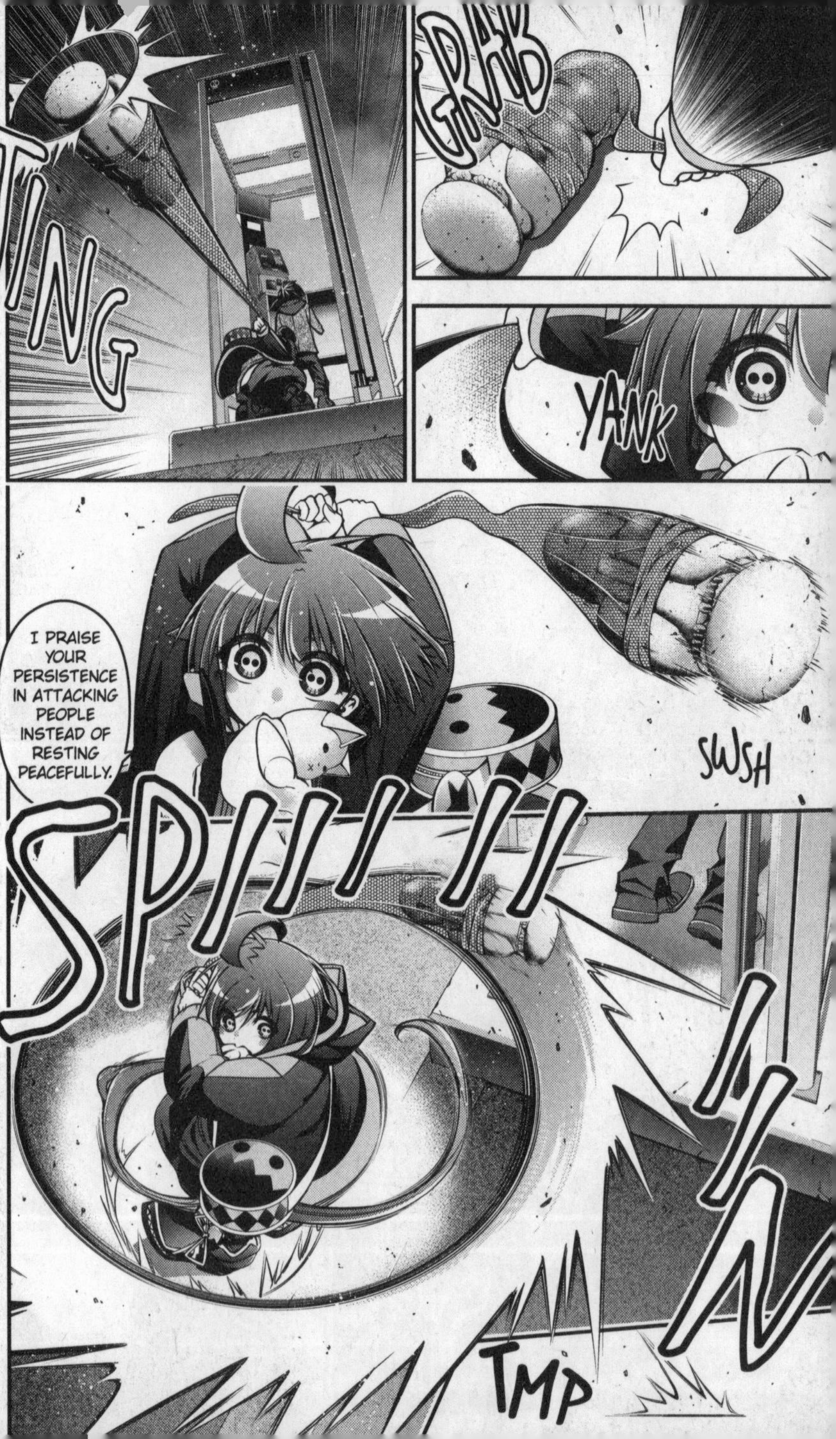
GRAB
YANK
TING
SWSH
I PRAISE YOUR PERSISTENCE IN ATTACKING PEOPLE INSTEAD OF RESTING PEACEFULLY.
SPIIIIIN
TMP

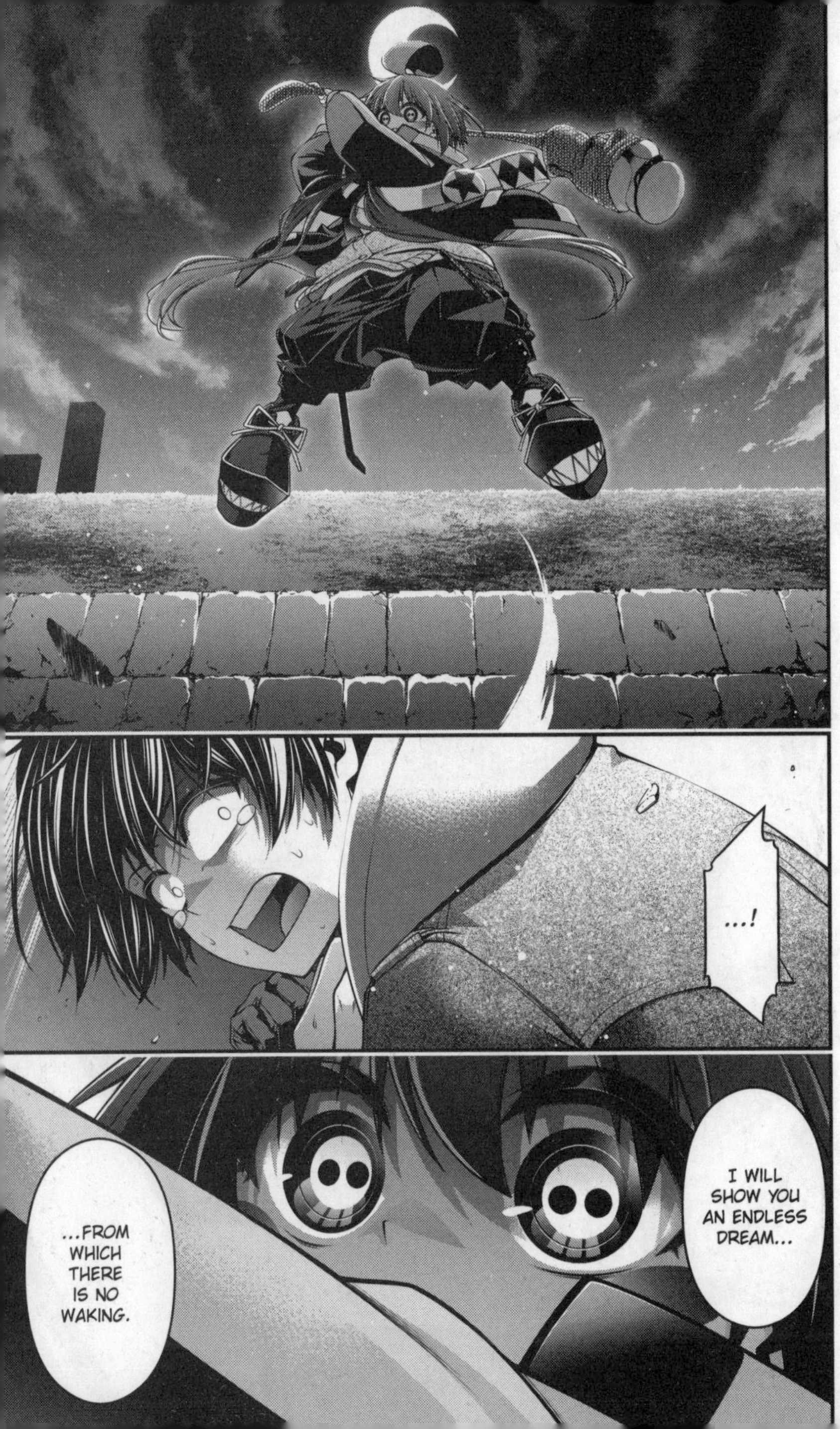
...!
I WILL SHOW YOU AN ENDLESS DREAM...
...FROM WHICH THERE IS NO WAKING.

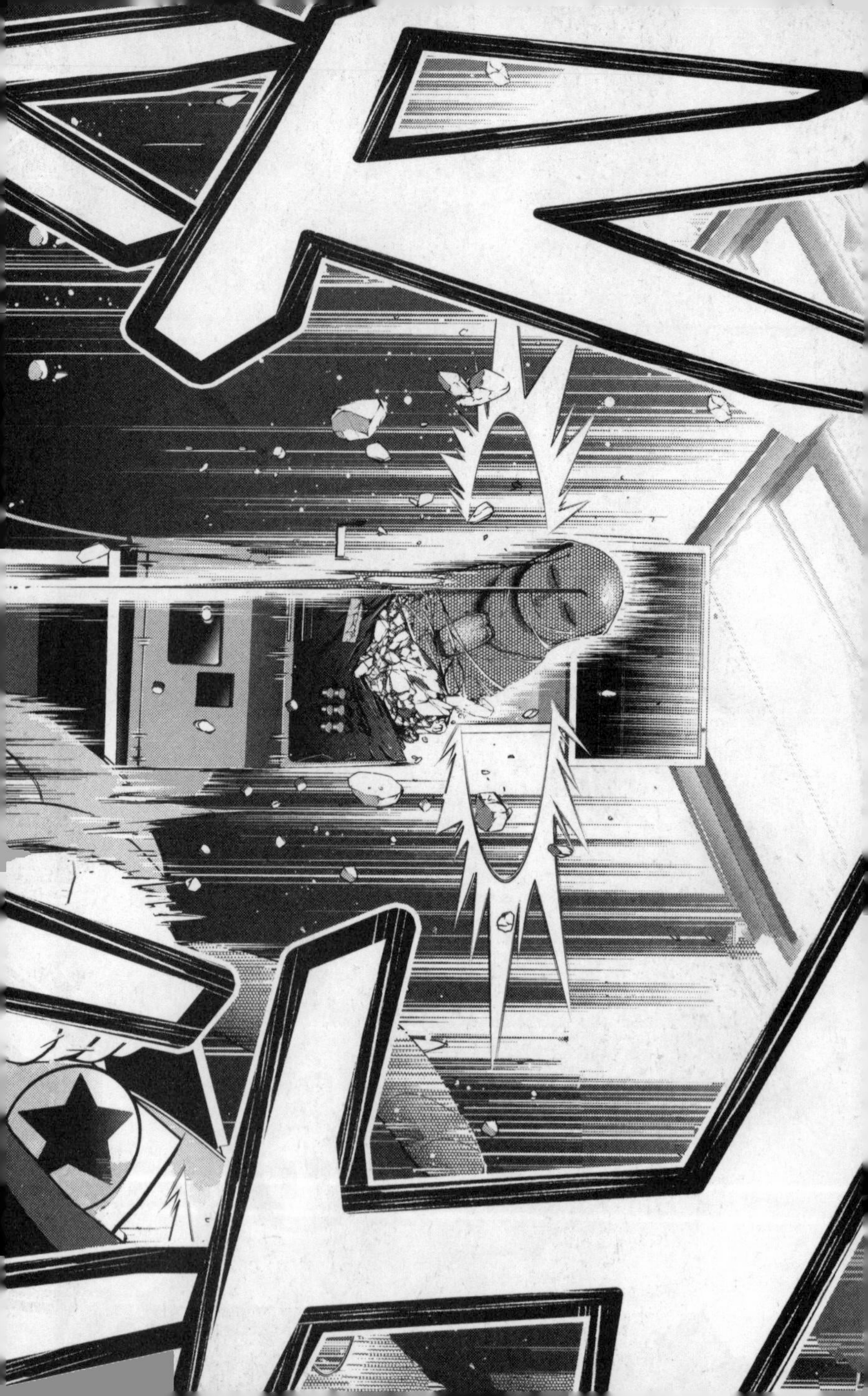

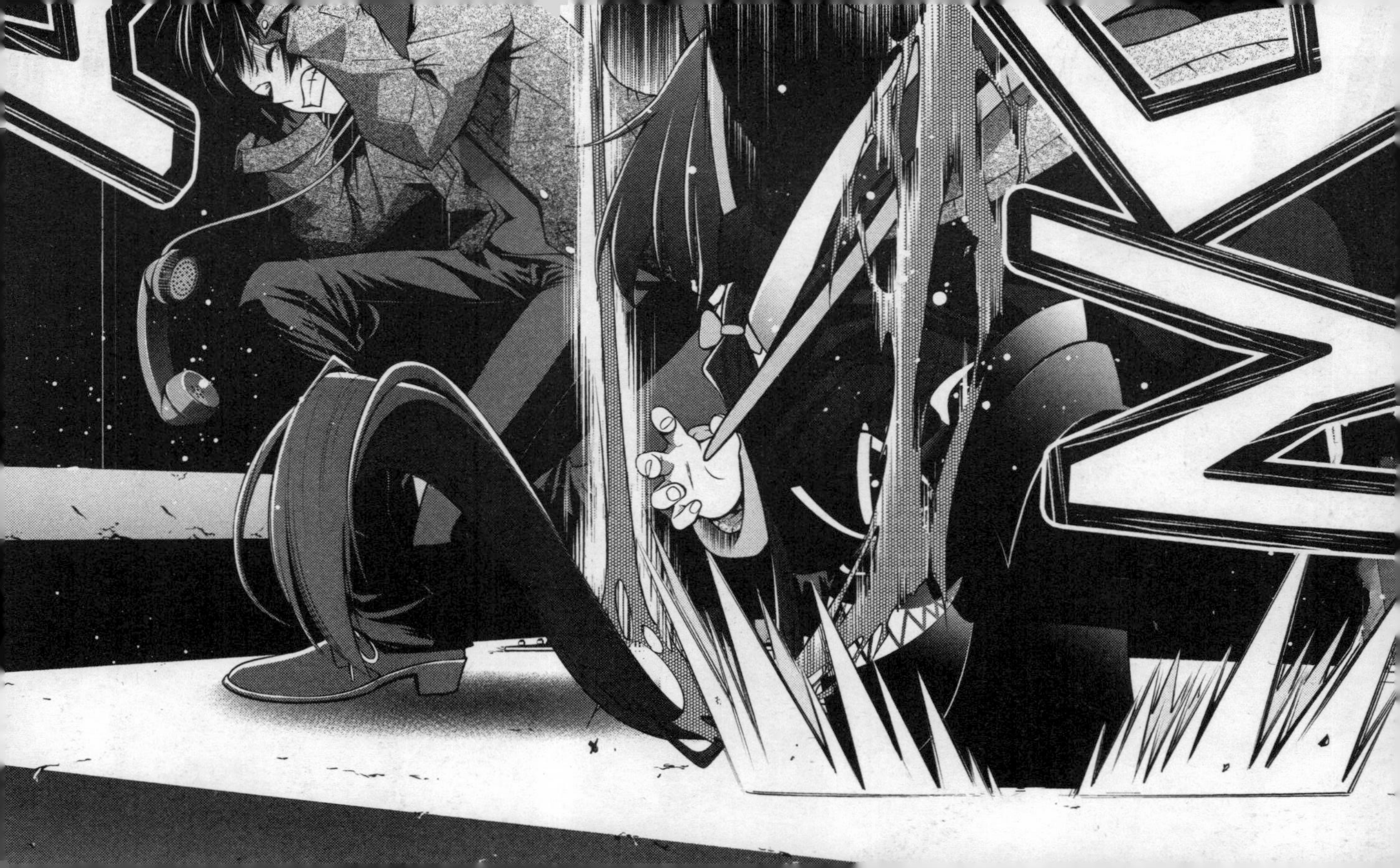

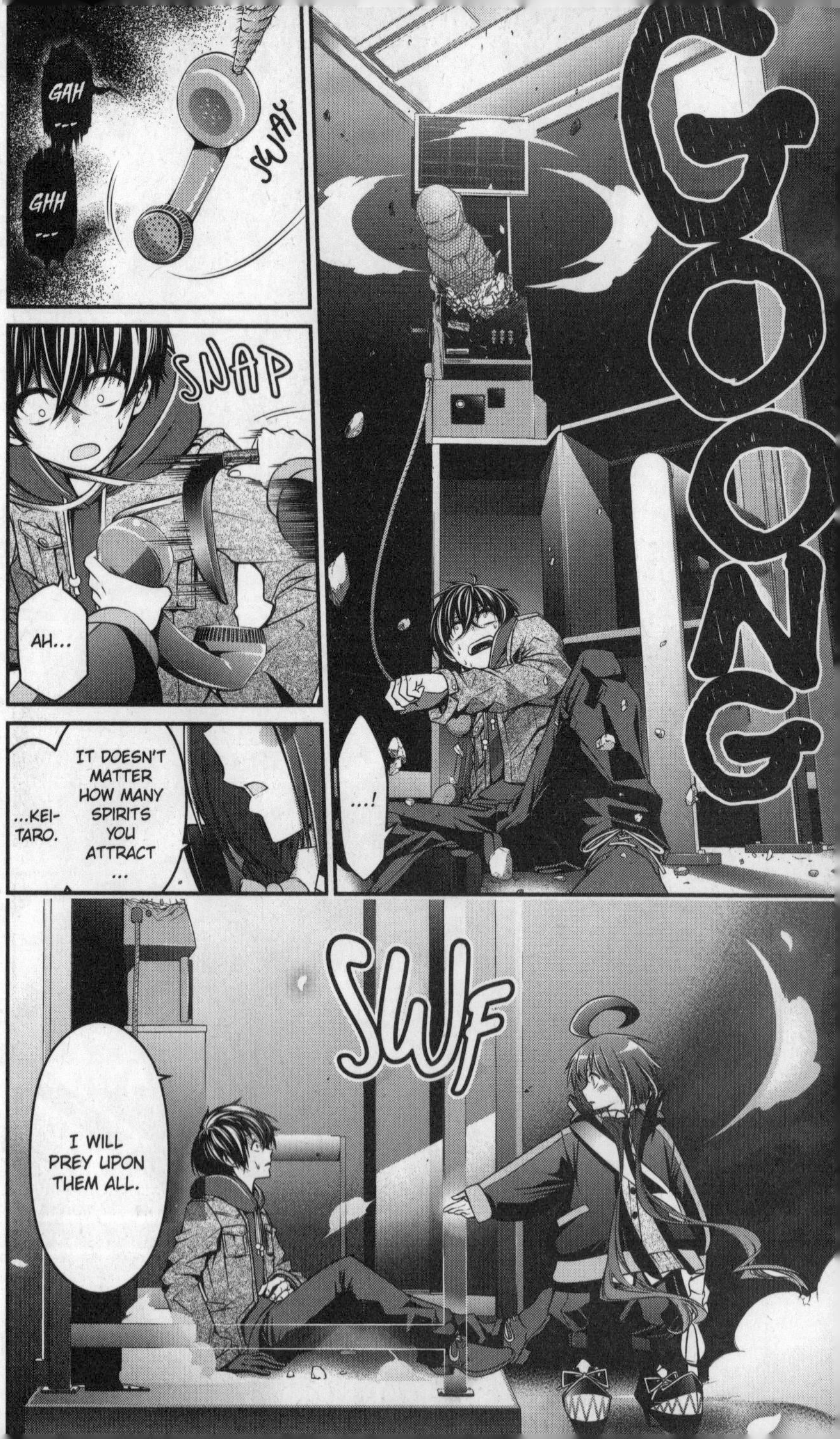
GOONG
...!
GAH...
GHH...
SWAY
SNAP
AH...
IT DOESN'T MATTER HOW MANY SPIRITS YOU ATTRACT...
...KEI-TARO.
SWF
I WILL PREY UPON THEM ALL.

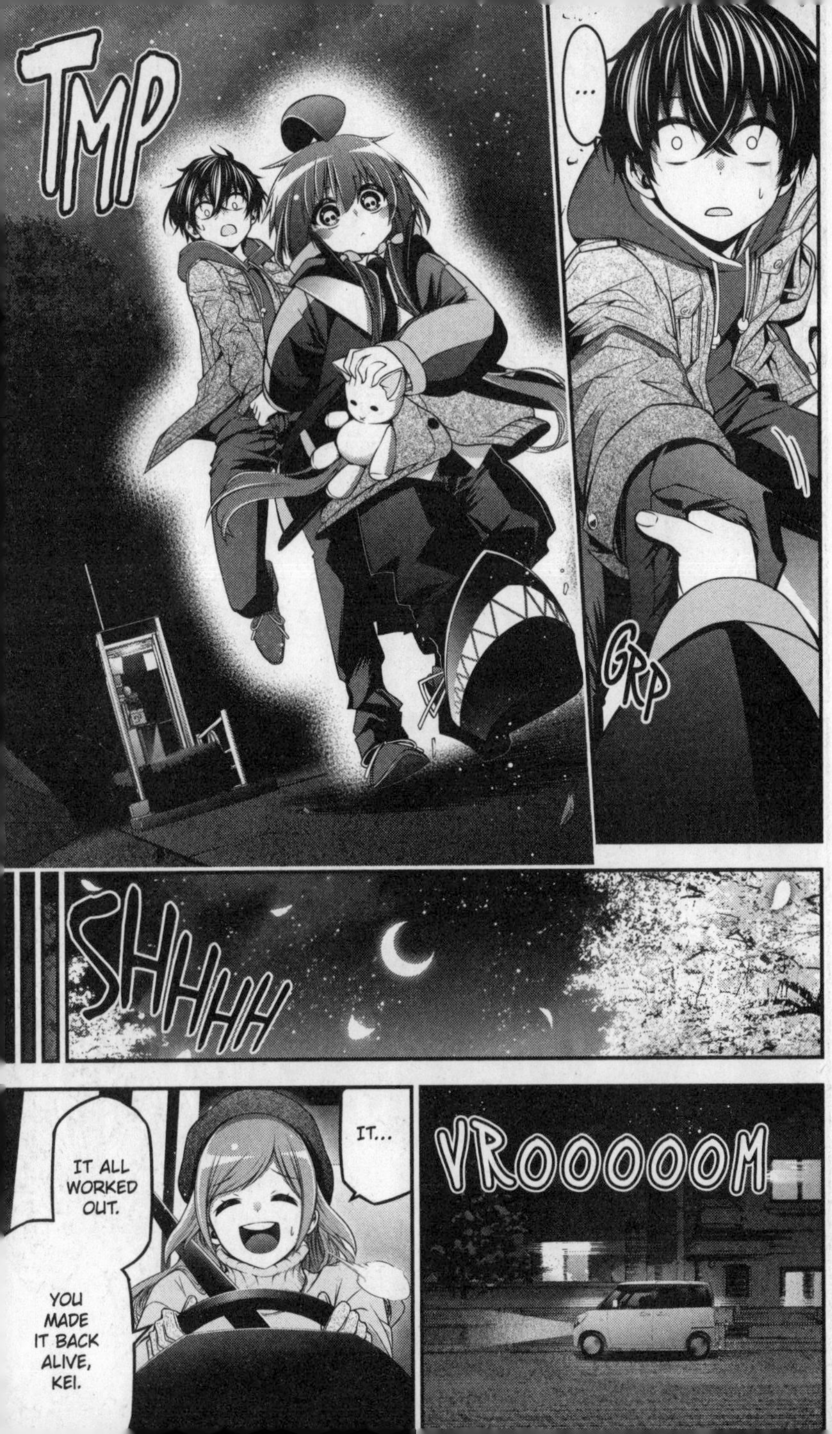
...
GRP
TMP
SHHHH
VROOOOOM
IT...
IT ALL WORKED OUT.
YOU MADE IT BACK ALIVE, KEI.

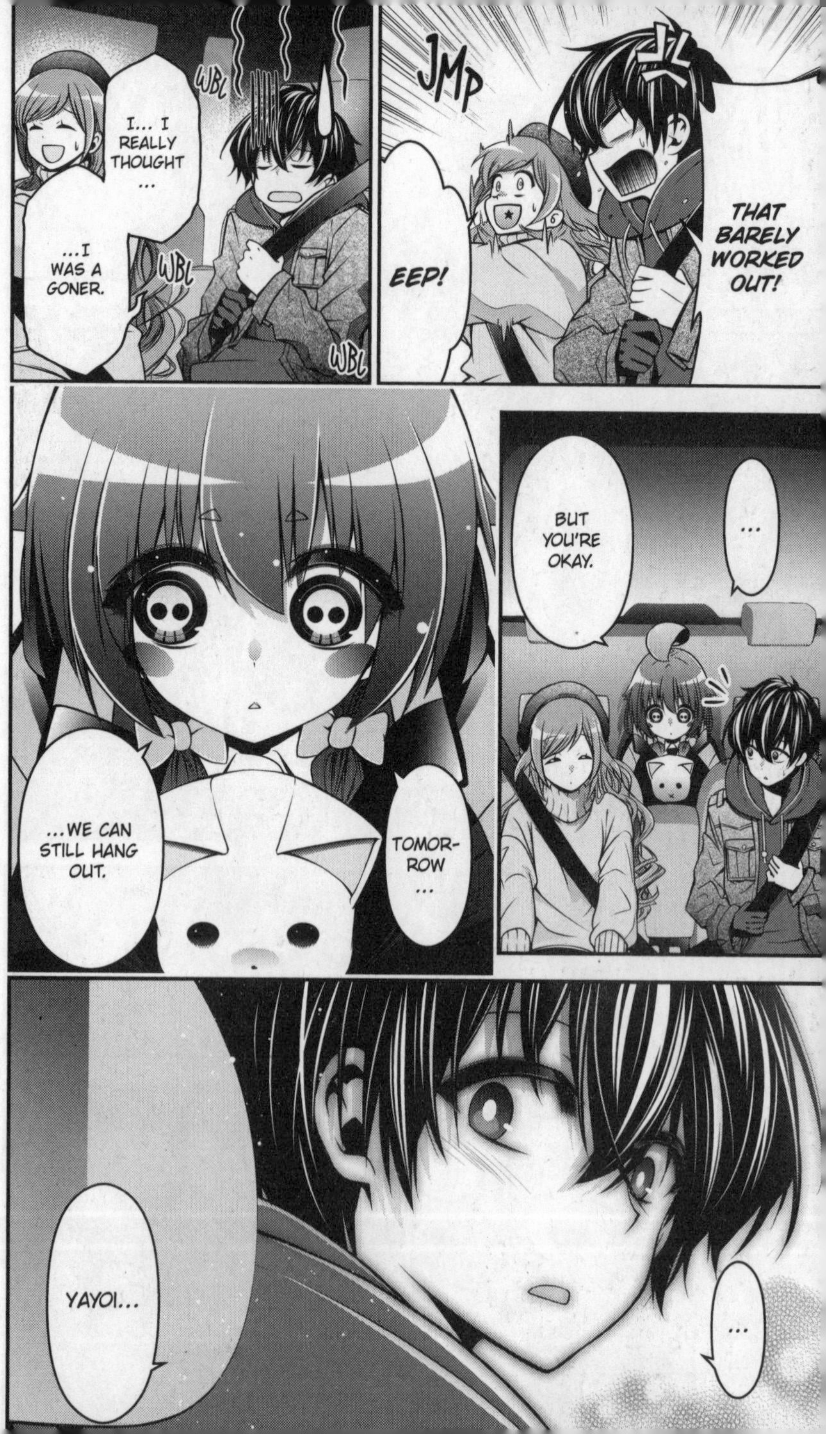
JMP
THAT BARELY WORKED OUT!
EEP!
WBL
I... I REALLY THOUGHT...
...I WAS A GONER.
WBL
WBL
...
BUT YOU'RE OKAY.
TOMORROW...
...WE CAN STILL HANG OUT.
...
YAYOI...

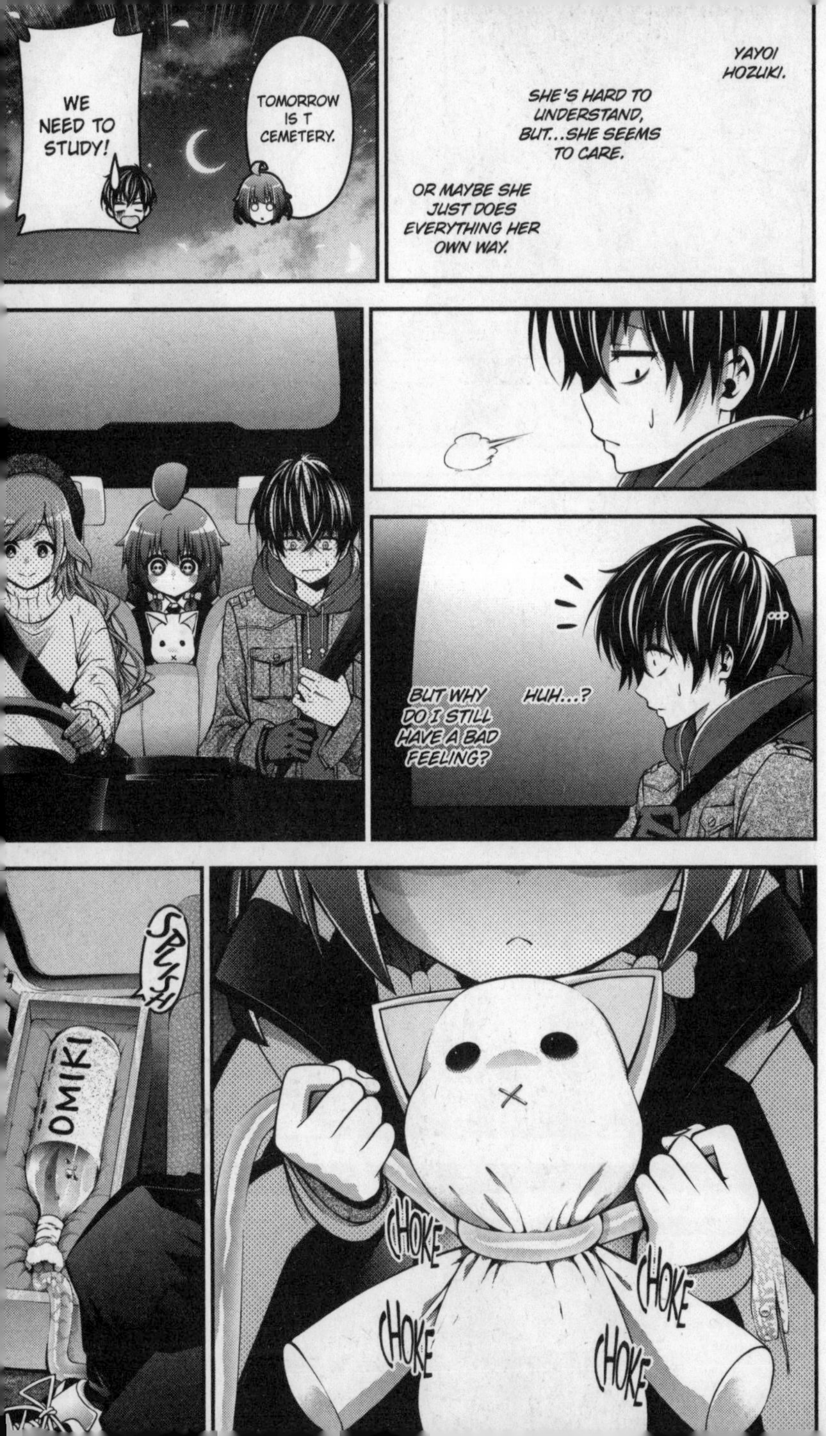
YAYOI HOZUKI.
SHE'S HARD TO UNDERSTAND, BUT...SHE SEEMS TO CARE.
OR MAYBE SHE JUST DOES EVERYTHING HER OWN WAY.
TOMORROW IS T CEMETERY.
WE NEED TO STUDY!
HUH...?
BUT WHY DO I STILL HAVE A BAD FEELING?
CHOKE
CHOKE
CHOKE
CHOKE
SPLISH
OMIKI

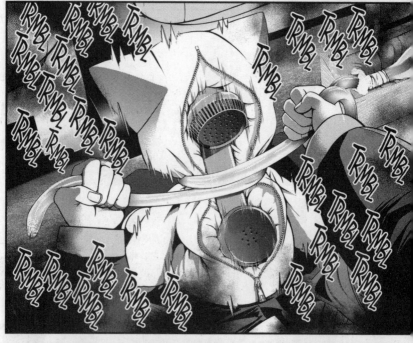

TRMBL TRMBL

...at the Hozuki home...

The next day...

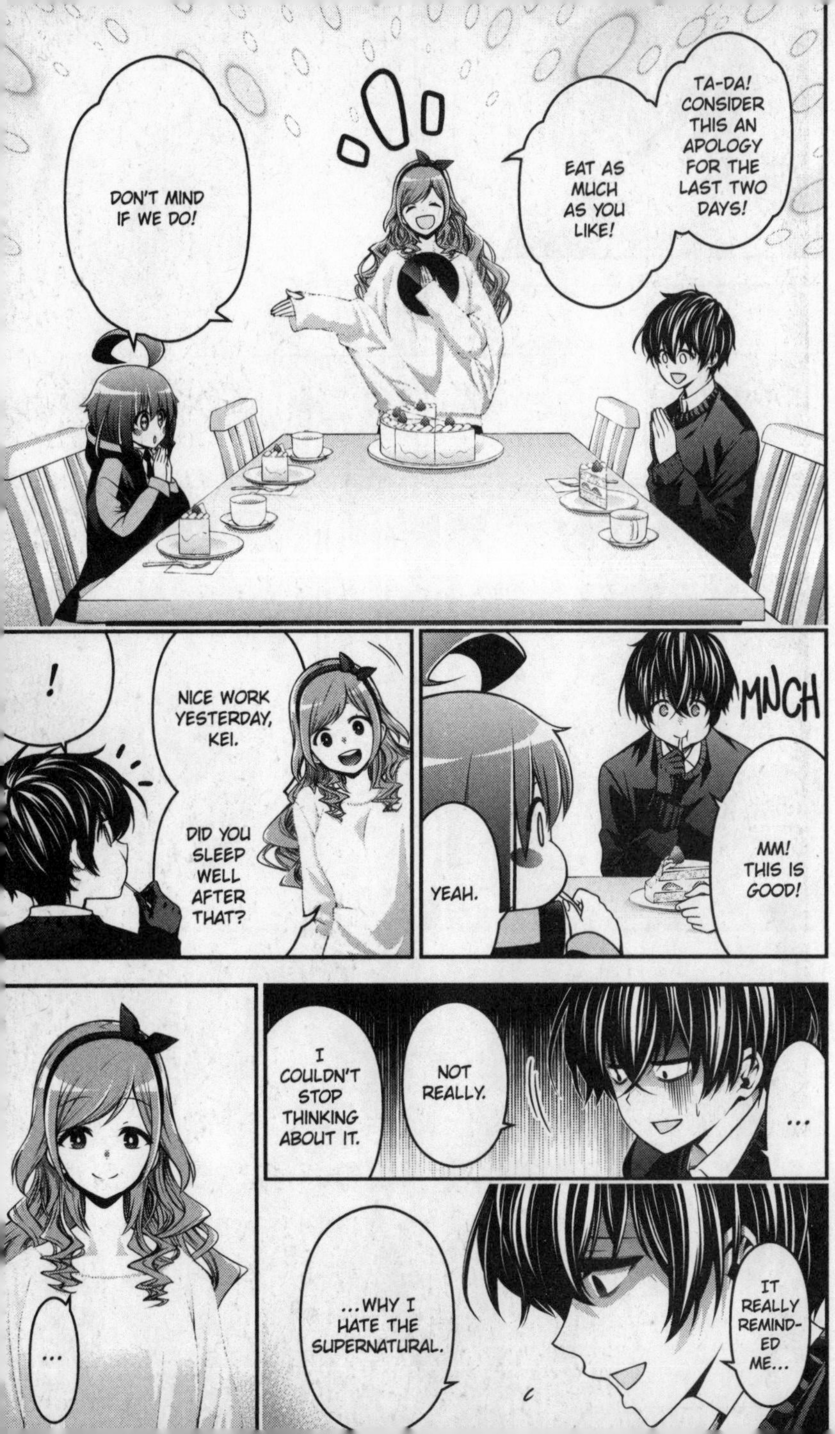
TA-DA! CONSIDER THIS AN APOLOGY FOR THE LAST TWO DAYS!
EAT AS MUCH AS YOU LIKE!
DON'T MIND IF WE DO!
MNCH
MM! THIS IS GOOD!
YEAH.
NICE WORK YESTERDAY, KEI.
DID YOU SLEEP WELL AFTER THAT?
!
...
NOT REALLY.
I COULDN'T STOP THINKING ABOUT IT.
IT REALLY REMIND-ED ME...
...WHY I HATE THE SUPERNATURAL.
...

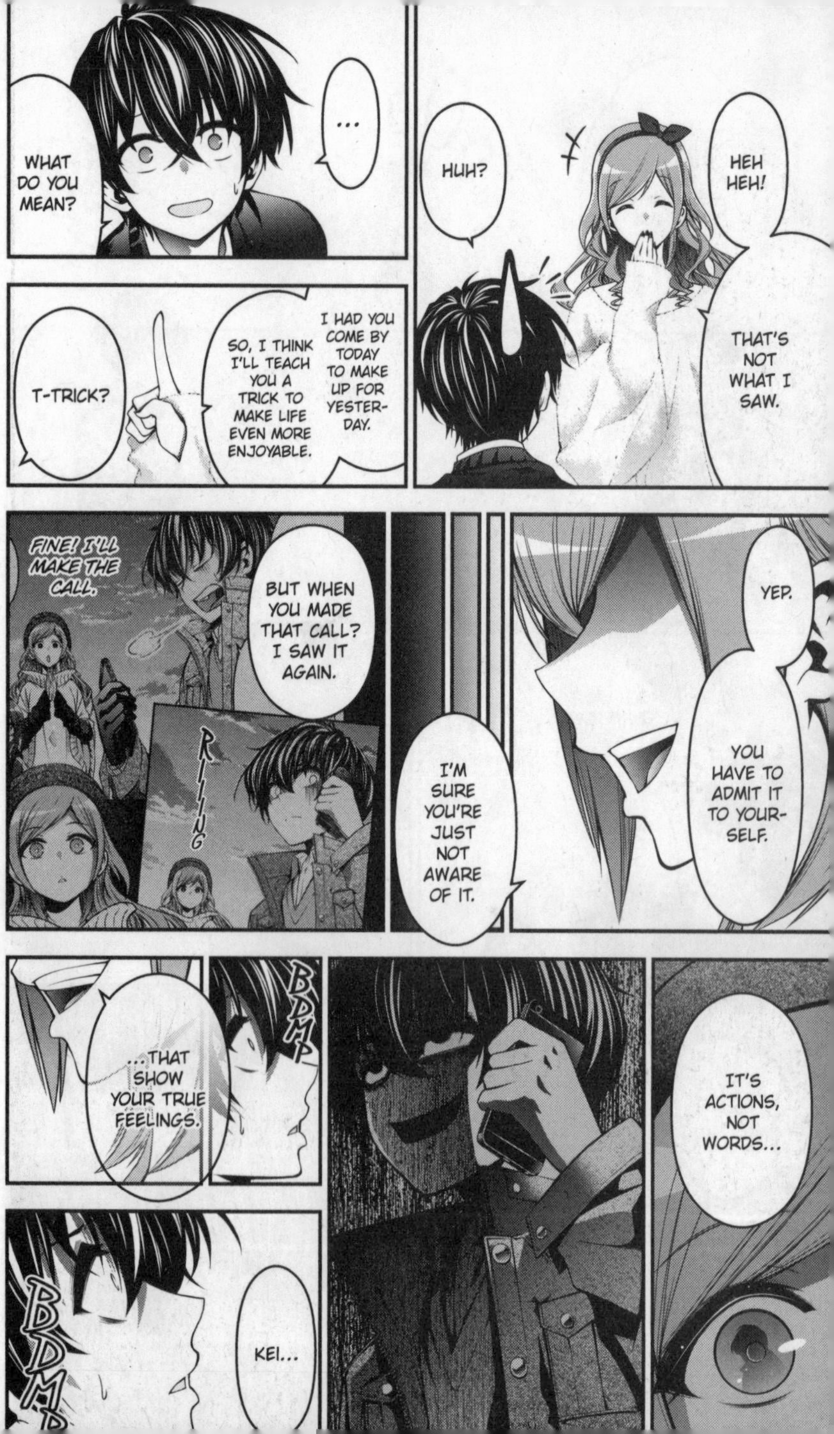
HEH HEH!
HUH?
THAT'S NOT WHAT I SAW.
...
WHAT DO YOU MEAN?
I HAD YOU COME BY TODAY TO MAKE UP FOR YESTER-DAY.
SO, I THINK I'LL TEACH YOU A TRICK TO MAKE LIFE EVEN MORE ENJOYABLE.
T-TRICK?
YEP.
YOU HAVE TO ADMIT IT TO YOUR-SELF.
I'M SURE YOU'RE JUST NOT AWARE OF IT.
BUT WHEN YOU MADE THAT CALL? I SAW IT AGAIN.
FINE! I'LL MAKE THE CALL.
RIIING
IT'S ACTIONS, NOT WORDS...
BDMP
...THAT SHOW YOUR TRUE FEELINGS.
BDMP
KEI...

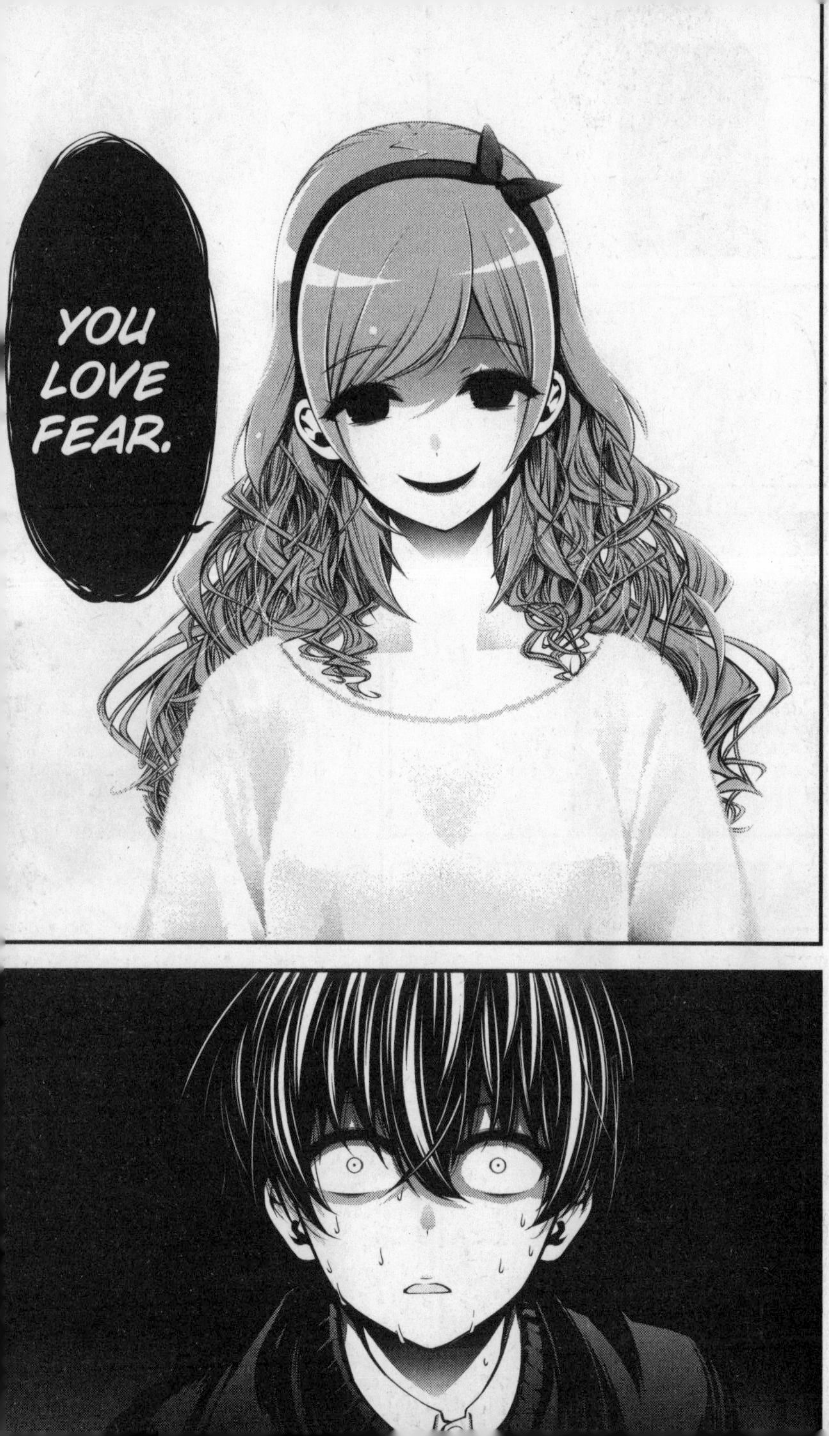
YOU LOVE FEAR.

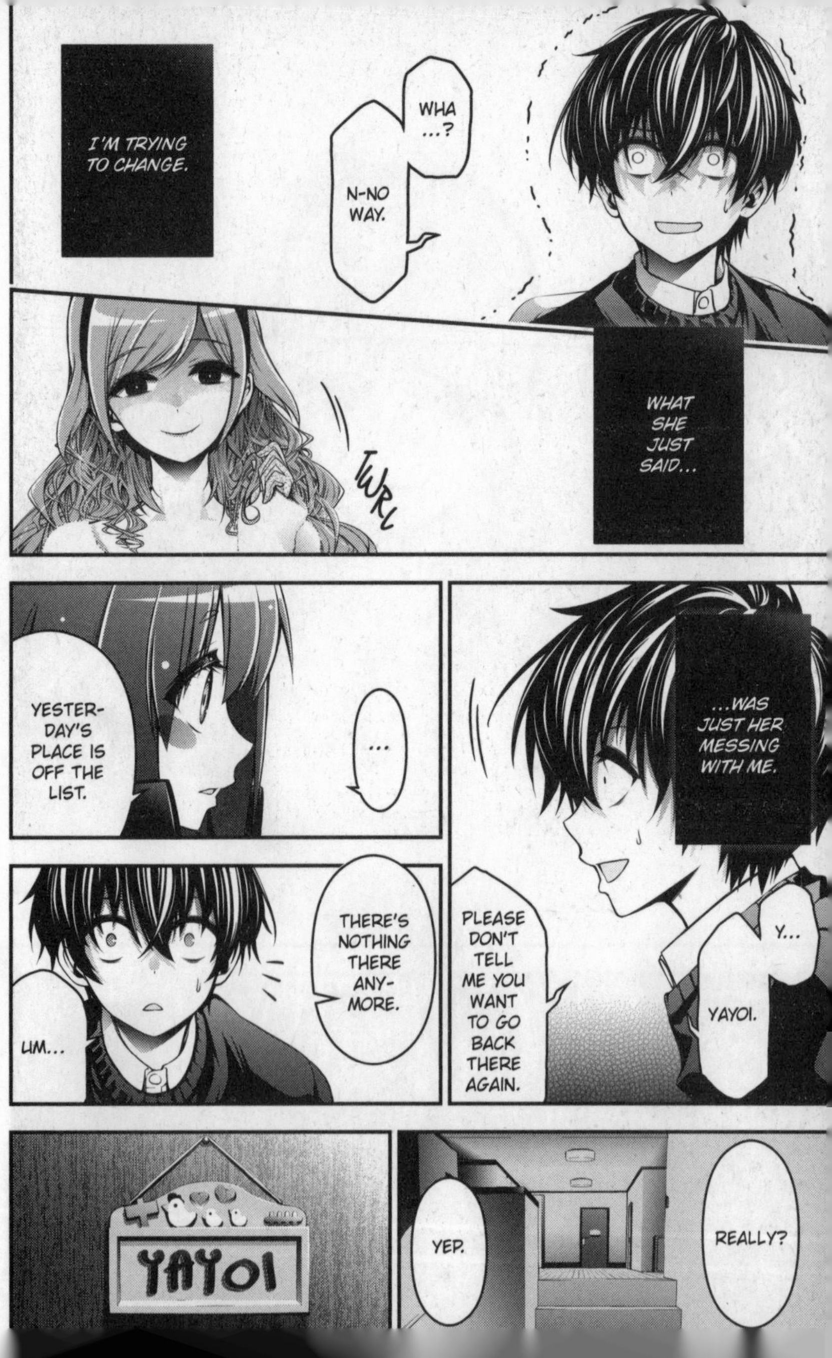
WHA ...?
N-NO WAY.
I'M TRYING TO CHANGE.
WHAT SHE JUST SAID...
TWRL
...WAS JUST HER MESSING WITH ME.
Y...
YAYOI.
PLEASE DON'T TELL ME YOU WANT TO GO BACK THERE AGAIN.
...
YESTER-DAY'S PLACE IS OFF THE LIST.
THERE'S NOTHING THERE ANY-MORE.
UM...
REALLY?
YEP.
YAYOI

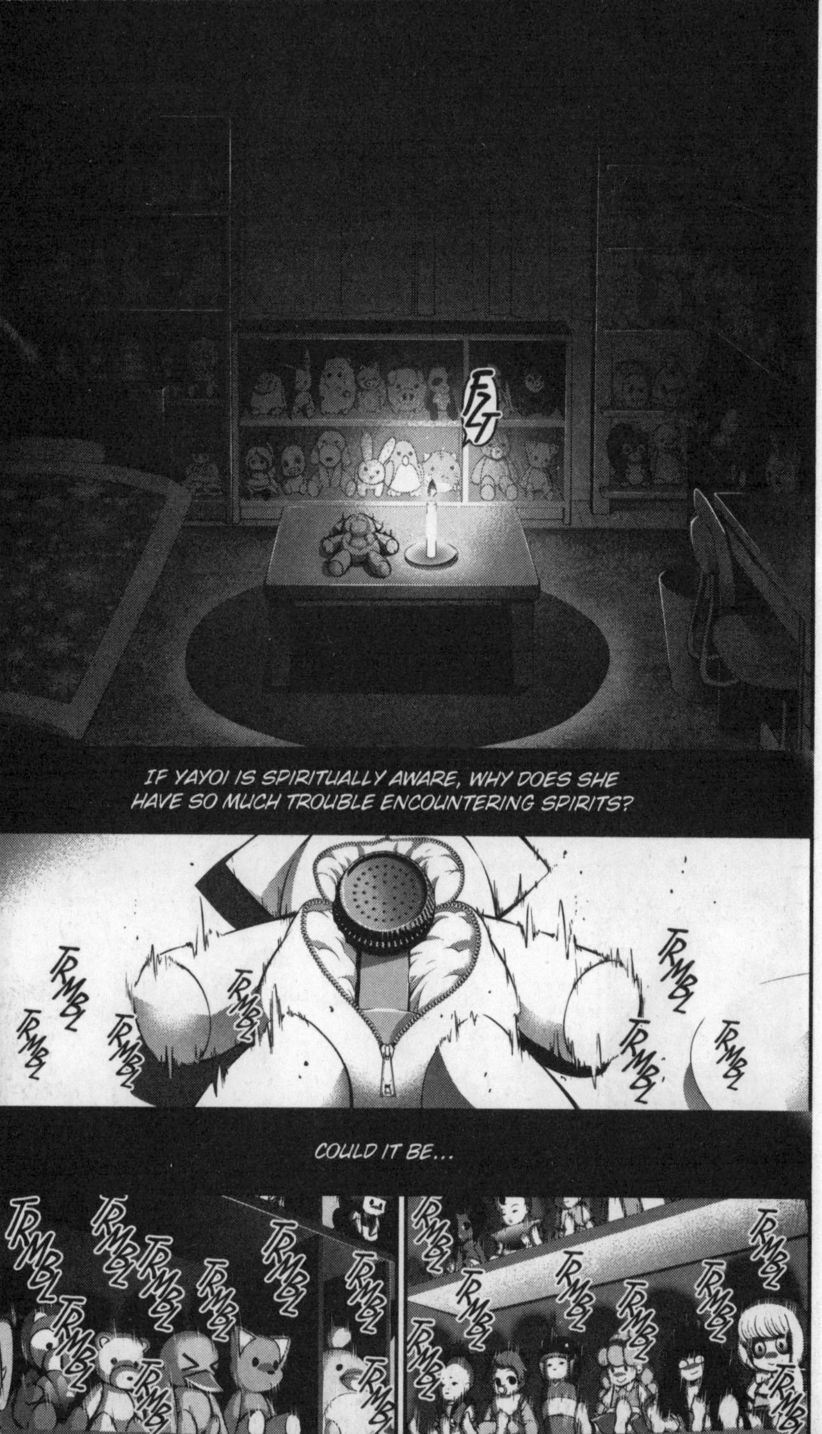
FZT
IF YAYOI IS SPIRITUALLY AWARE, WHY DOES SHE HAVE SO MUCH TROUBLE ENCOUNTERING SPIRITS?
TRMBL
TRMBL
TRMBL
TRMBL
TRMBL
TRMBL
TRMBL
COULD IT BE...
TRMBL
TRMBL
TRMBL
TRMBL
TRMBL
TRMBL
TRMBL
TRMBL
TRMBL
TRMBL
TRMBL
TRMBL
TRMBL
TRMBL
TRMBL
TRMBL
TRMBL

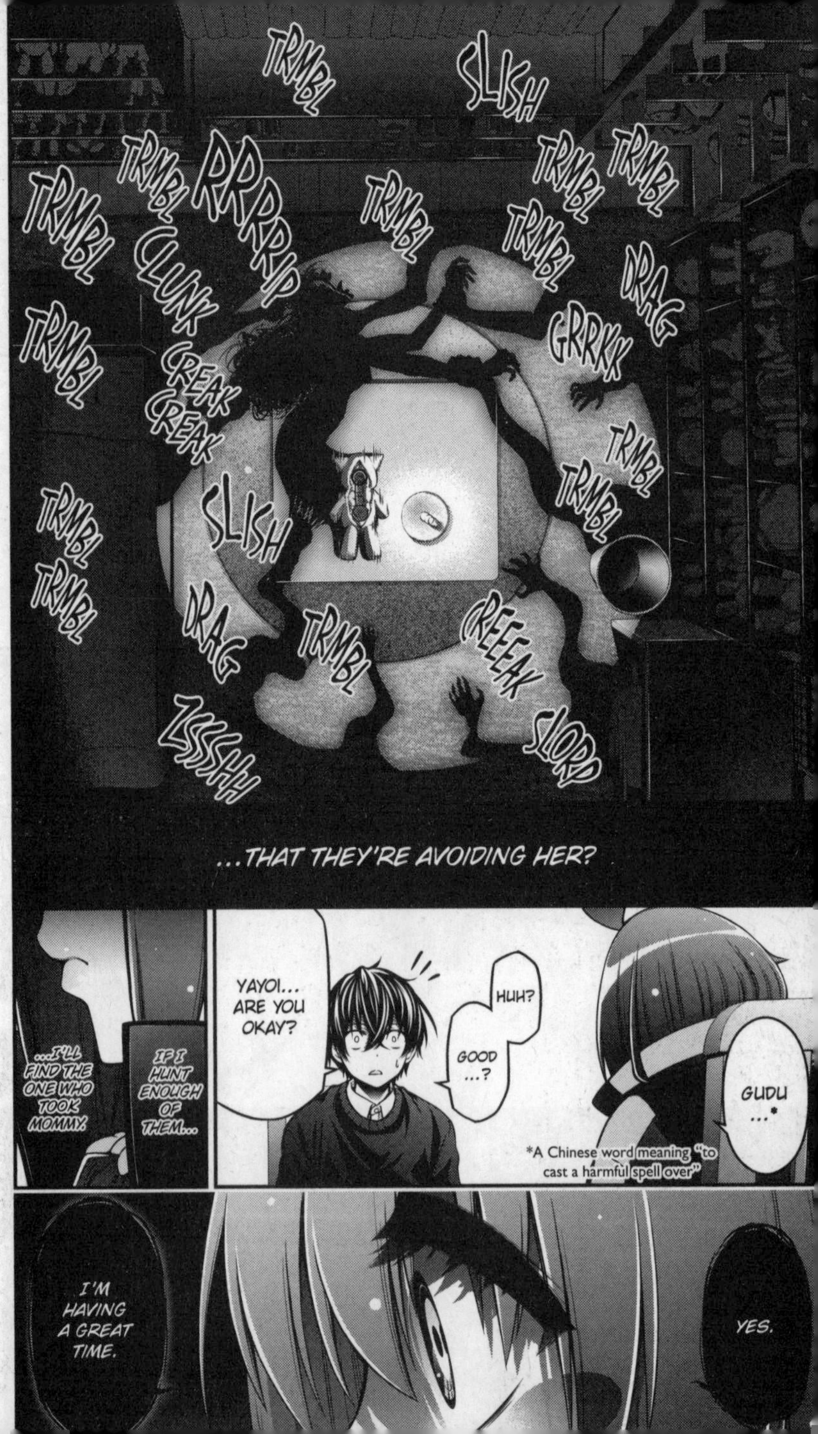
SLISH
TRMBL
TRMBL
TRMBL
TRMBL
TRMBL
RRRRRIP
TRMBL
TRMBL
DRAG
GRRKK
CLUNK
TRMBL
CREAK
CREAK
TRMBL
TRMBL
SLISH
TRMBL
TRMBL
CREEEAK
DRAG
TRMBL
SLORP
ZSSSHH
...THAT THEY'RE AVOIDING HER?
GUDU...*
HUH?
YAYOI... ARE YOU OKAY?
GOOD...?
*A Chinese word meaning "to cast a harmful spell over"
IF I HUNT ENOUGH OF THEM...
...I'LL FIND THE ONE WHO TOOK MOMMY.
YES.
I'M HAVING A GREAT TIME.

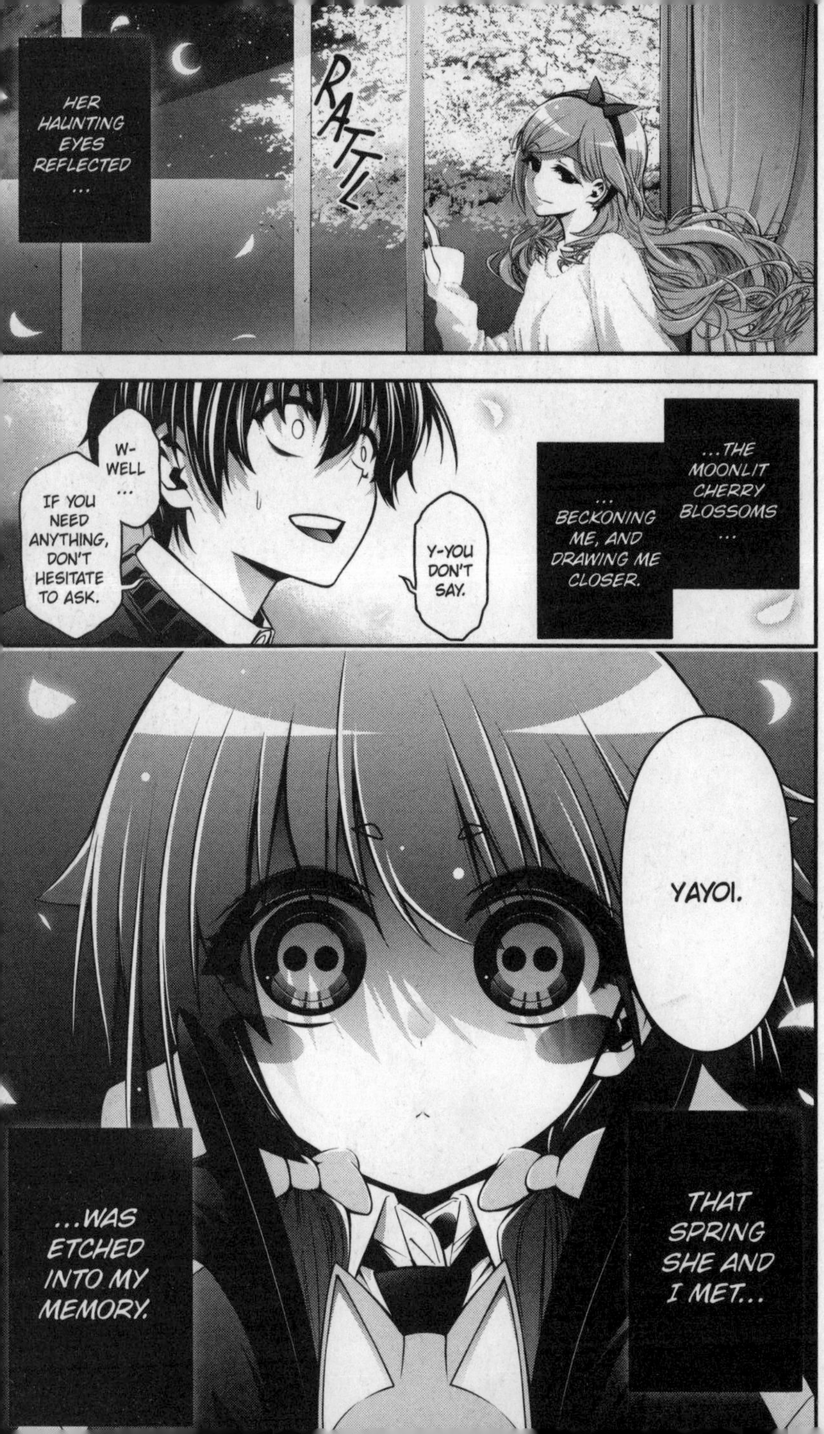
RATTL
HER HAUNTING EYES REFLECTED…
…THE MOONLIT CHERRY BLOSSOMS…
…BECKONING ME, AND DRAWING ME CLOSER.
Y-YOU DON'T SAY.
W-WELL… IF YOU NEED ANYTHING, DON'T HESITATE TO ASK.
YAYOI.
THAT SPRING SHE AND I MET…
…WAS ETCHED INTO MY MEMORY.

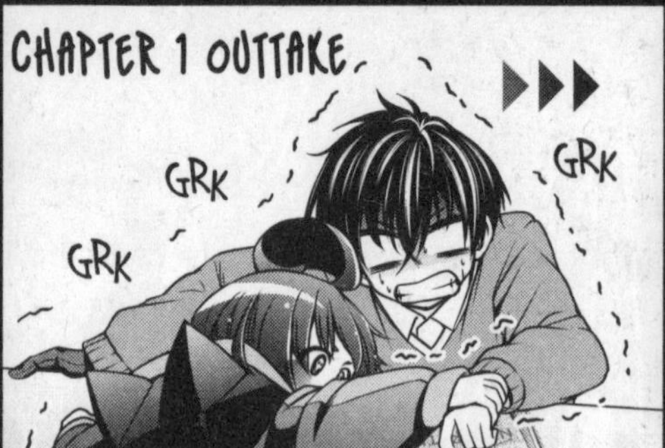
CHAPTER 1 OUTTAKE
GRK
GRK
GRK

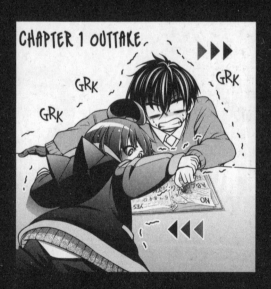

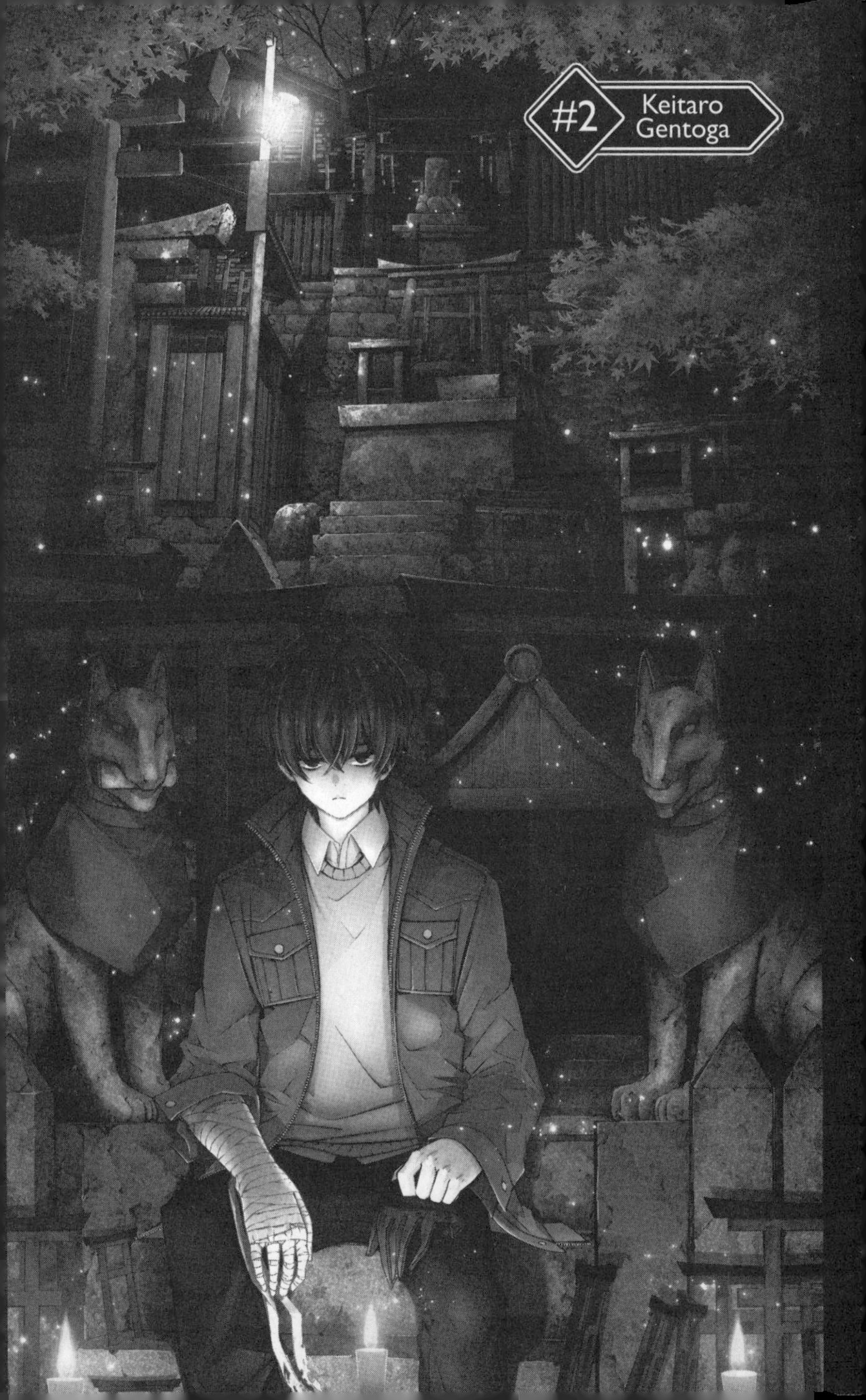
#2
Keitaro Gentoga

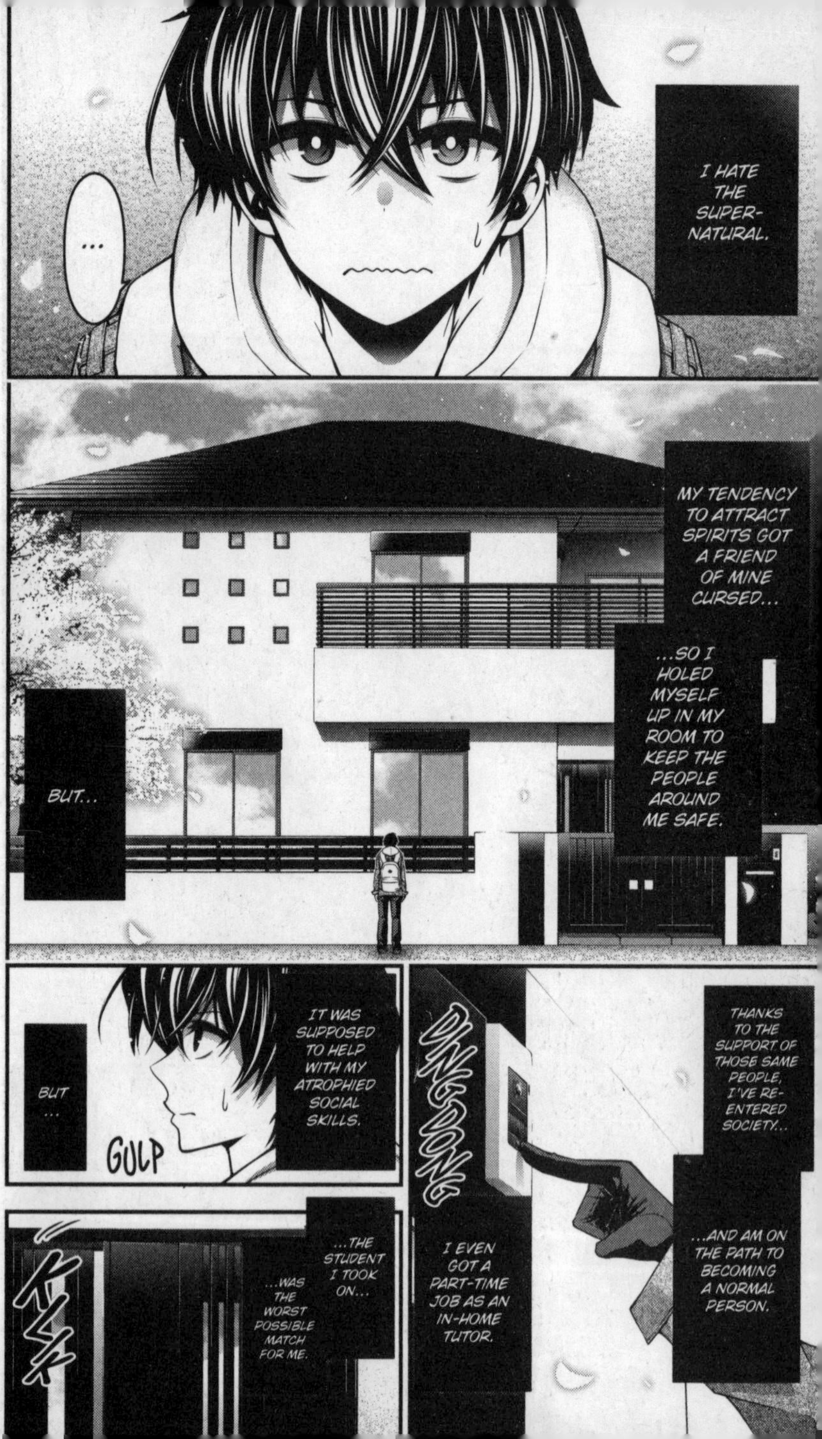
I HATE THE SUPER-NATURAL.
...
MY TENDENCY TO ATTRACT SPIRITS GOT A FRIEND OF MINE CURSED...
...SO I HOLED MYSELF UP IN MY ROOM TO KEEP THE PEOPLE AROUND ME SAFE.
BUT...
THANKS TO THE SUPPORT OF THOSE SAME PEOPLE, I'VE RE-ENTERED SOCIETY...
...AND AM ON THE PATH TO BECOMING A NORMAL PERSON.
DING DONG
I EVEN GOT A PART-TIME JOB AS AN IN-HOME TUTOR.
IT WAS SUPPOSED TO HELP WITH MY ATROPHIED SOCIAL SKILLS.
BUT ...
GULP
...THE STUDENT I TOOK ON...
...WAS THE WORST POSSIBLE MATCH FOR ME.
KLIK

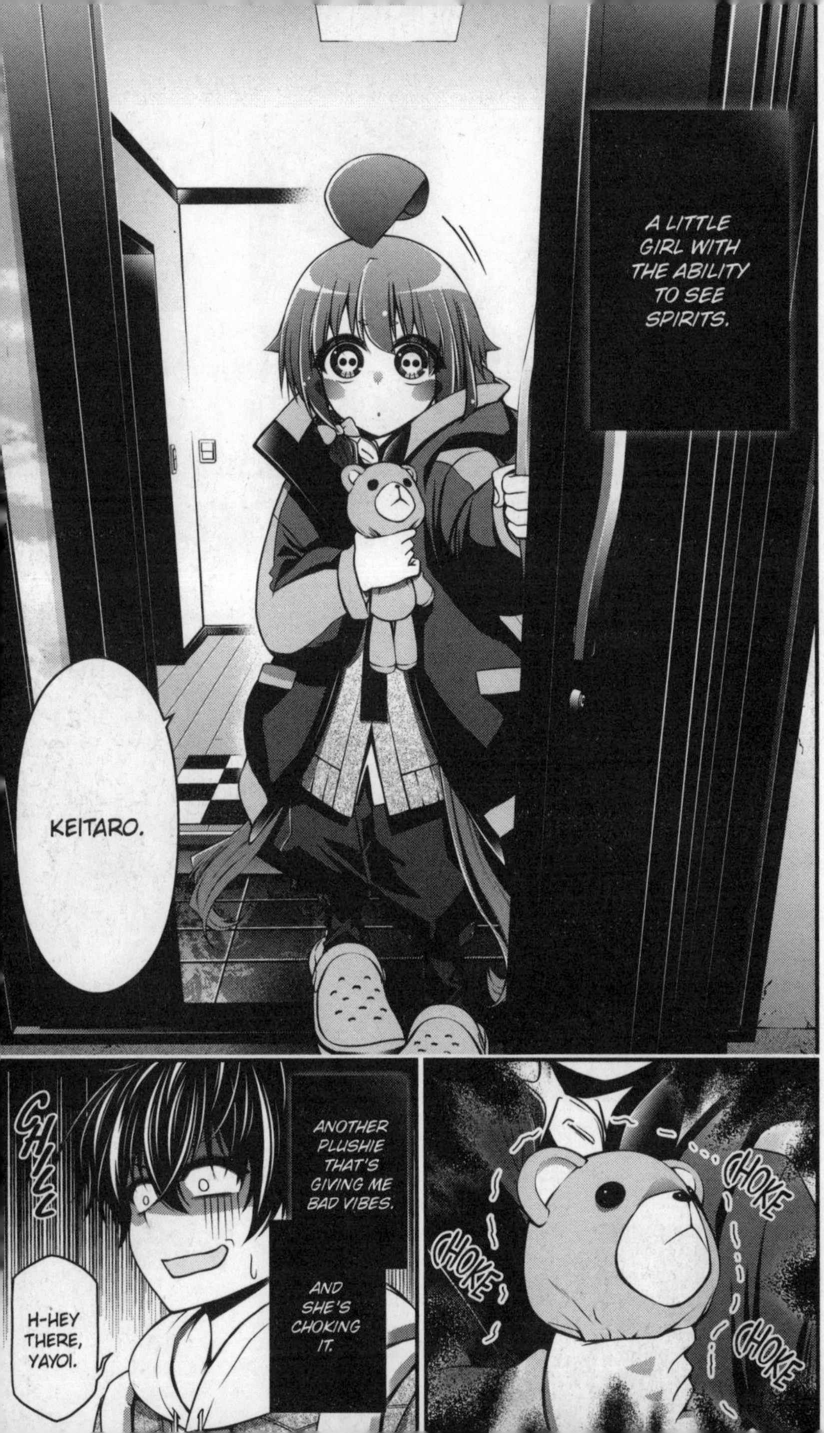
A LITTLE GIRL WITH THE ABILITY TO SEE SPIRITS.
KEITARO.
CHOKE
CHOKE
CHOKE
ANOTHER PLUSHIE THAT'S GIVING ME BAD VIBES.
CHILL
AND SHE'S CHOKING IT.
H-HEY THERE, YAYOI.

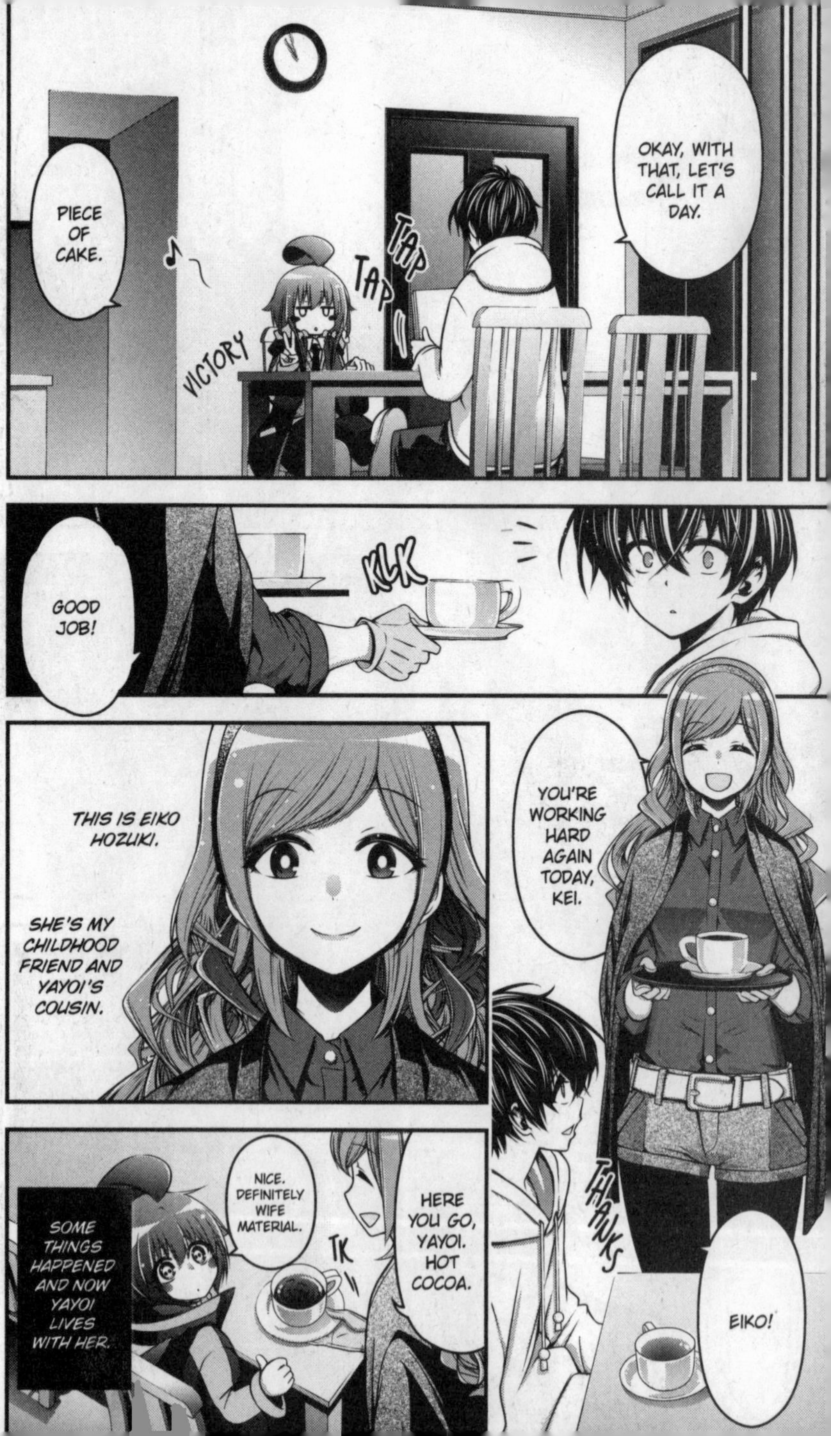
OKAY, WITH THAT, LET'S CALL IT A DAY.
TAP TAP
PIECE OF CAKE.
VICTORY
KLK
GOOD JOB!
YOU'RE WORKING HARD AGAIN TODAY, KEI.
THANKS
EIKO!
THIS IS EIKO HOZUKI.
SHE'S MY CHILDHOOD FRIEND AND YAYOI'S COUSIN.
HERE YOU GO, YAYOI. HOT COCOA.
TK
NICE. DEFINITELY WIFE MATERIAL.
SOME THINGS HAPPENED AND NOW YAYOI LIVES WITH HER.

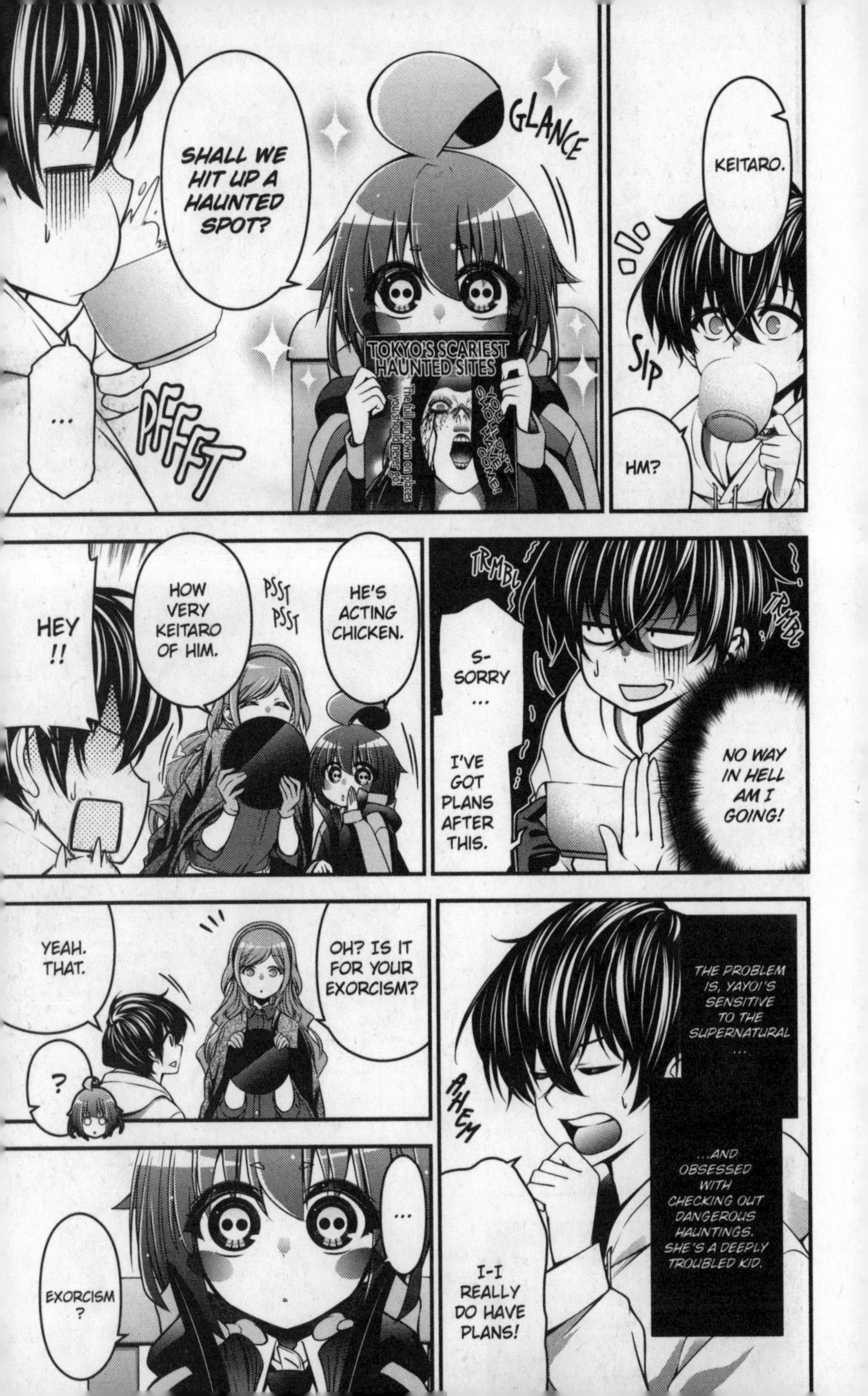
KEITARO.
SIP
HM?
GLANCE
TOKYO'S SCARIEST HAUNTED SITES
YOU SHOULDN'T HAVE COME!
The full rundown on places you should never go!
SHALL WE HIT UP A HAUNTED SPOT?
PFFFT
...
TRMBL
TRMBL
NO WAY IN HELL AM I GOING!
S-SORRY...
I'VE GOT PLANS AFTER THIS.
HE'S ACTING CHICKEN.
PSST PSST
HOW VERY KEITARO OF HIM.
HEY!!
THE PROBLEM IS, YAYOI'S SENSITIVE TO THE SUPERNATURAL...
...AND OBSESSED WITH CHECKING OUT DANGEROUS HAUNTINGS. SHE'S A DEEPLY TROUBLED KID.
AHEM
I-I REALLY DO HAVE PLANS!
OH? IS IT FOR YOUR EXORCISM?
YEAH. THAT.
?
...
EXORCISM?

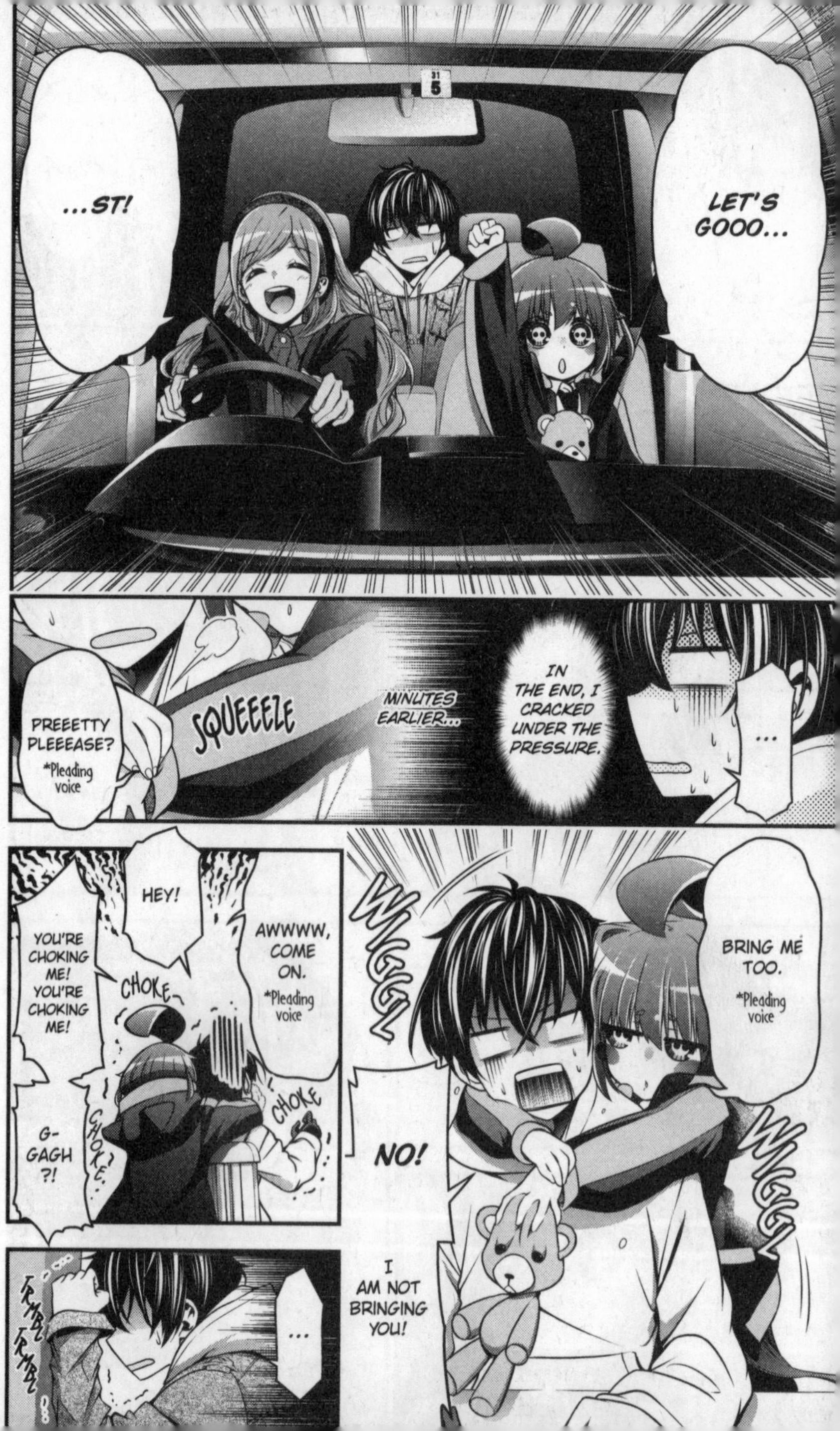
LET'S GOOO...
...ST!
...
IN THE END, I CRACKED UNDER THE PRESSURE.
MINUTES EARLIER...
SQUEEEZE
PREEETTY PLEEEASE?
*Pleading voice
BRING ME TOO.
*Pleading voice
WIGGL
WIGGL
NO!
I AM NOT BRINGING YOU!
AWWWW, COME ON.
*Pleading voice
HEY!
YOU'RE CHOKING ME! YOU'RE CHOKING ME!
CHOKE
CHOKE
CHOKE...
G-GAGH?!
...
TRMBL
TRMBL

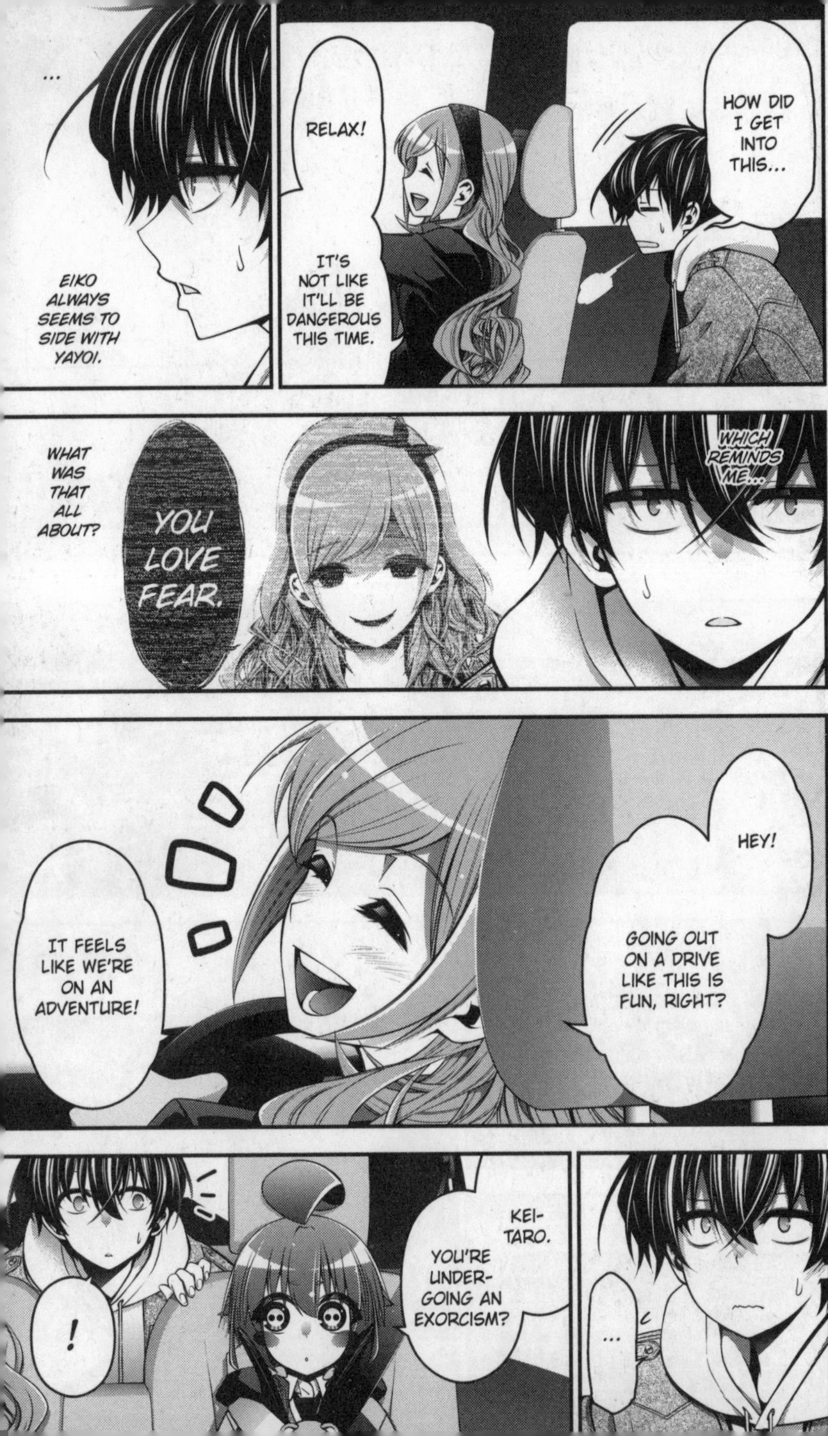
HOW DID I GET INTO THIS...
RELAX!
IT'S NOT LIKE IT'LL BE DANGEROUS THIS TIME.
...
EIKO ALWAYS SEEMS TO SIDE WITH YAYOI.
WHICH REMINDS ME...
YOU LOVE FEAR.
WHAT WAS THAT ALL ABOUT?
HEY!
GOING OUT ON A DRIVE LIKE THIS IS FUN, RIGHT?
IT FEELS LIKE WE'RE ON AN ADVENTURE!
...
KEI-TARO.
YOU'RE UNDER-GOING AN EXORCISM?
!

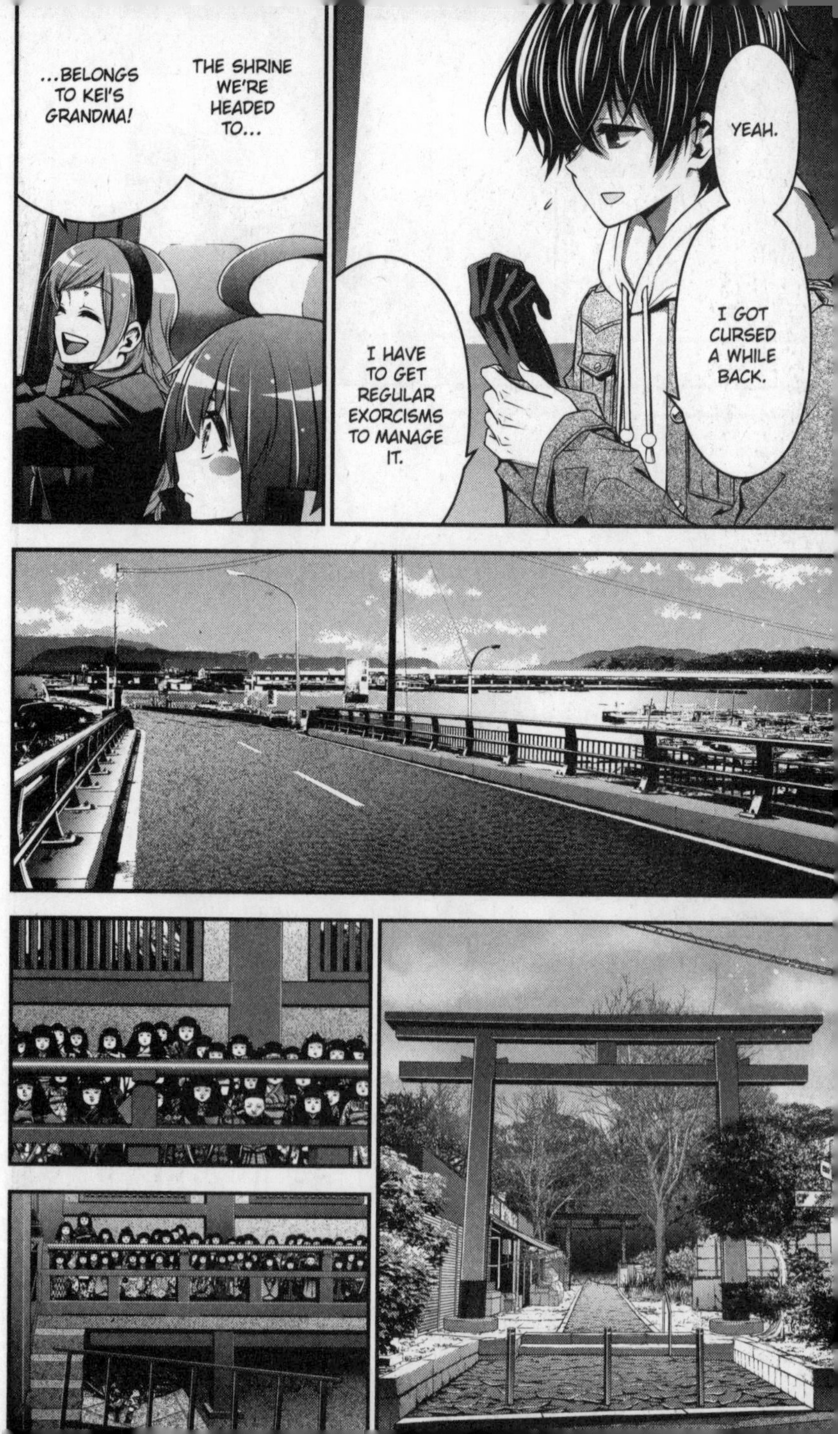
YEAH.
I GOT CURSED A WHILE BACK.
I HAVE TO GET REGULAR EXORCISMS TO MANAGE IT.
THE SHRINE WE'RE HEADED TO...
...BELONGS TO KEI'S GRANDMA!

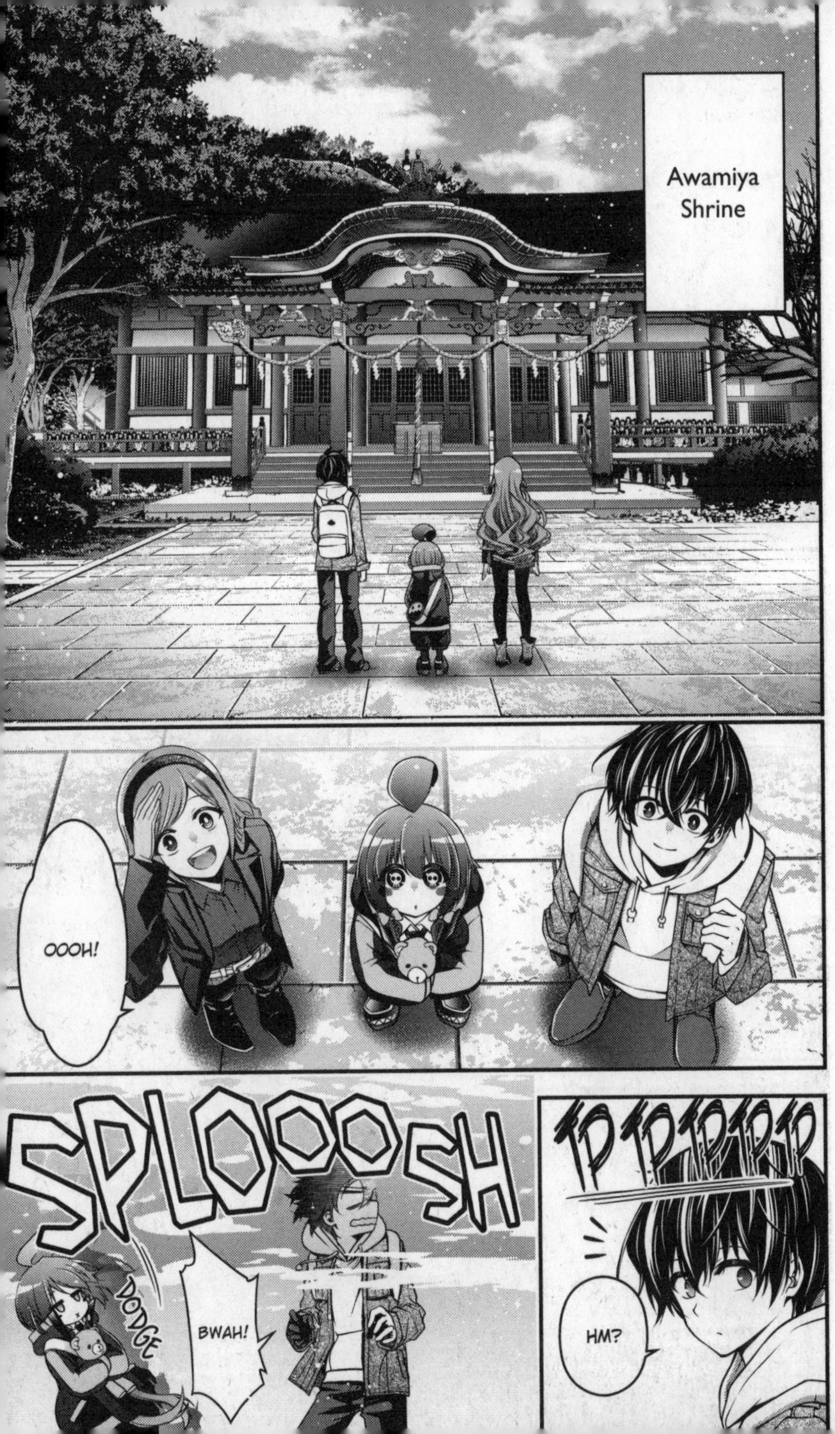
Awamiya Shrine
OOOH!
TP TP TP TP TP
HM?
SPLOOOSH
BWAH!
DODGE

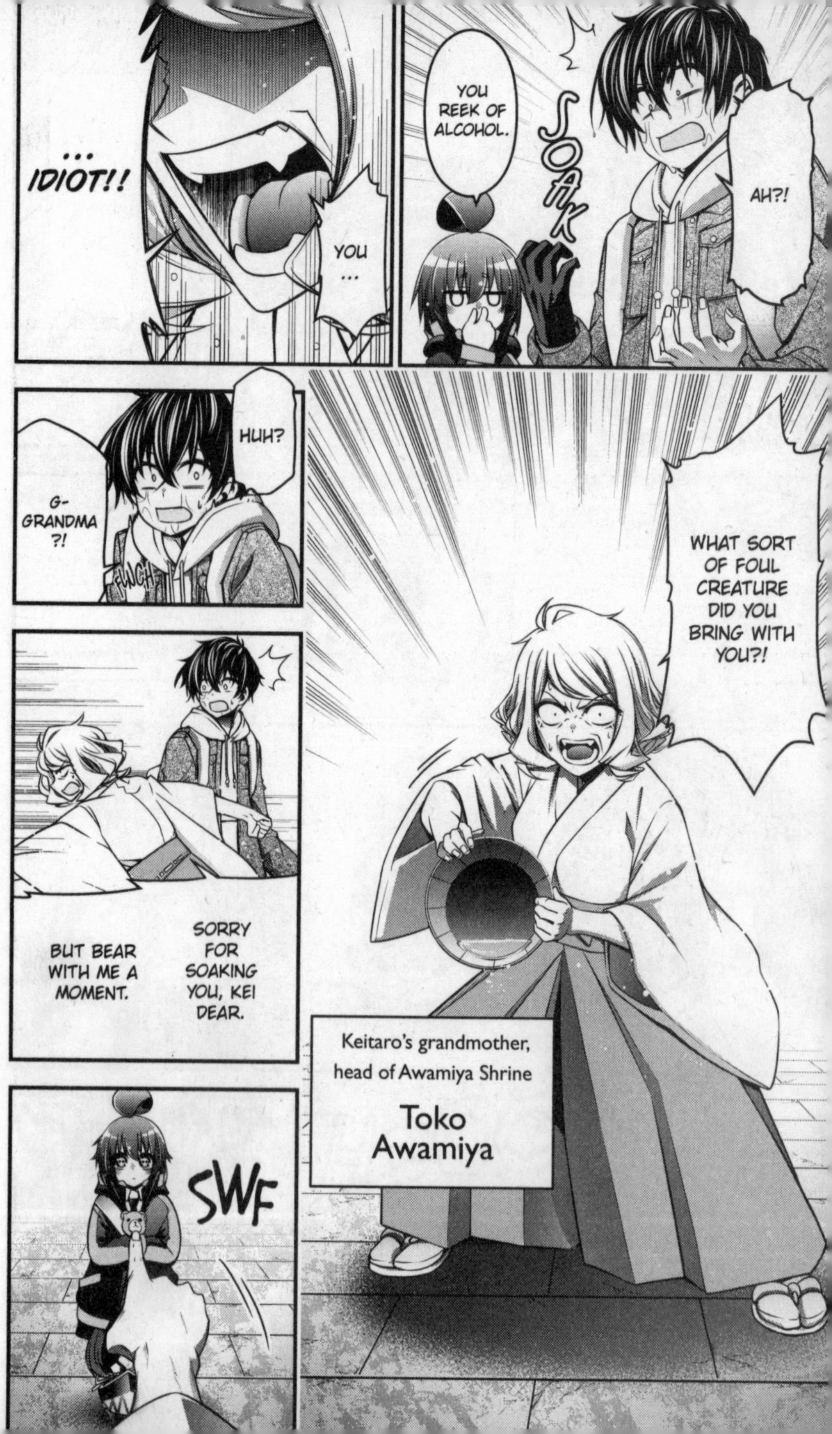
AH?!
SOAK
YOU REEK OF ALCOHOL.
YOU ...
... IDIOT!!
WHAT SORT OF FOUL CREATURE DID YOU BRING WITH YOU?!
Keitaro's grandmother, head of Awamiya Shrine
Toko Awamiya
HUH?
G-GRANDMA?!
FLINCH
SORRY FOR SOAKING YOU, KEI DEAR.
BUT BEAR WITH ME A MOMENT.
SWF

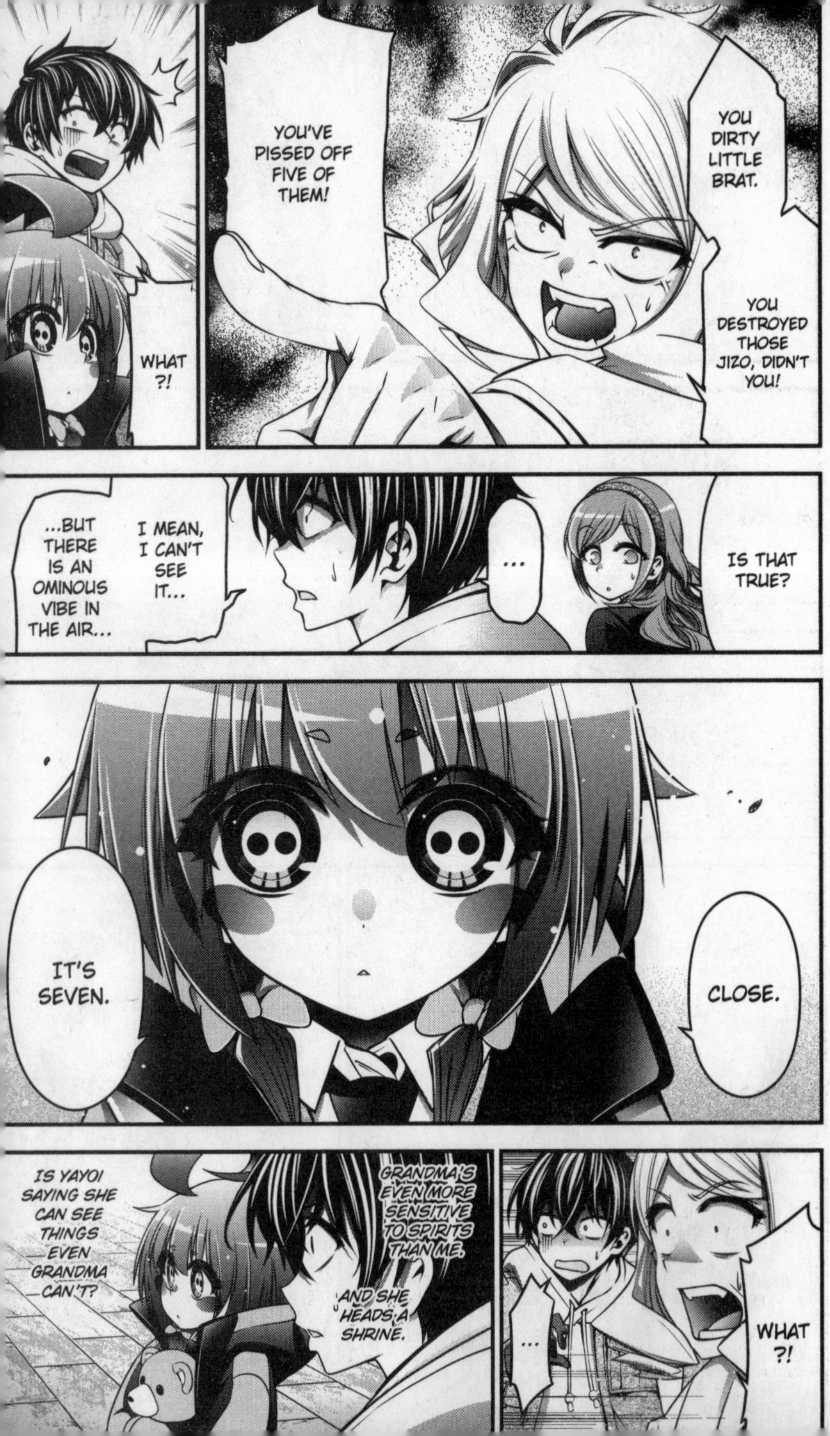
YOU DIRTY LITTLE BRAT.
YOU DESTROYED THOSE JIZO, DIDN'T YOU!
YOU'VE PISSED OFF FIVE OF THEM!
WHAT ?!
IS THAT TRUE?
...
I MEAN, I CAN'T SEE IT...
...BUT THERE IS AN OMINOUS VIBE IN THE AIR...
CLOSE.
IT'S SEVEN.
WHAT ?!
...
GRANDMA'S EVEN MORE SENSITIVE TO SPIRITS THAN ME.
AND SHE HEADS A SHRINE.
IS YAYOI SAYING SHE CAN SEE THINGS EVEN GRANDMA CAN'T?

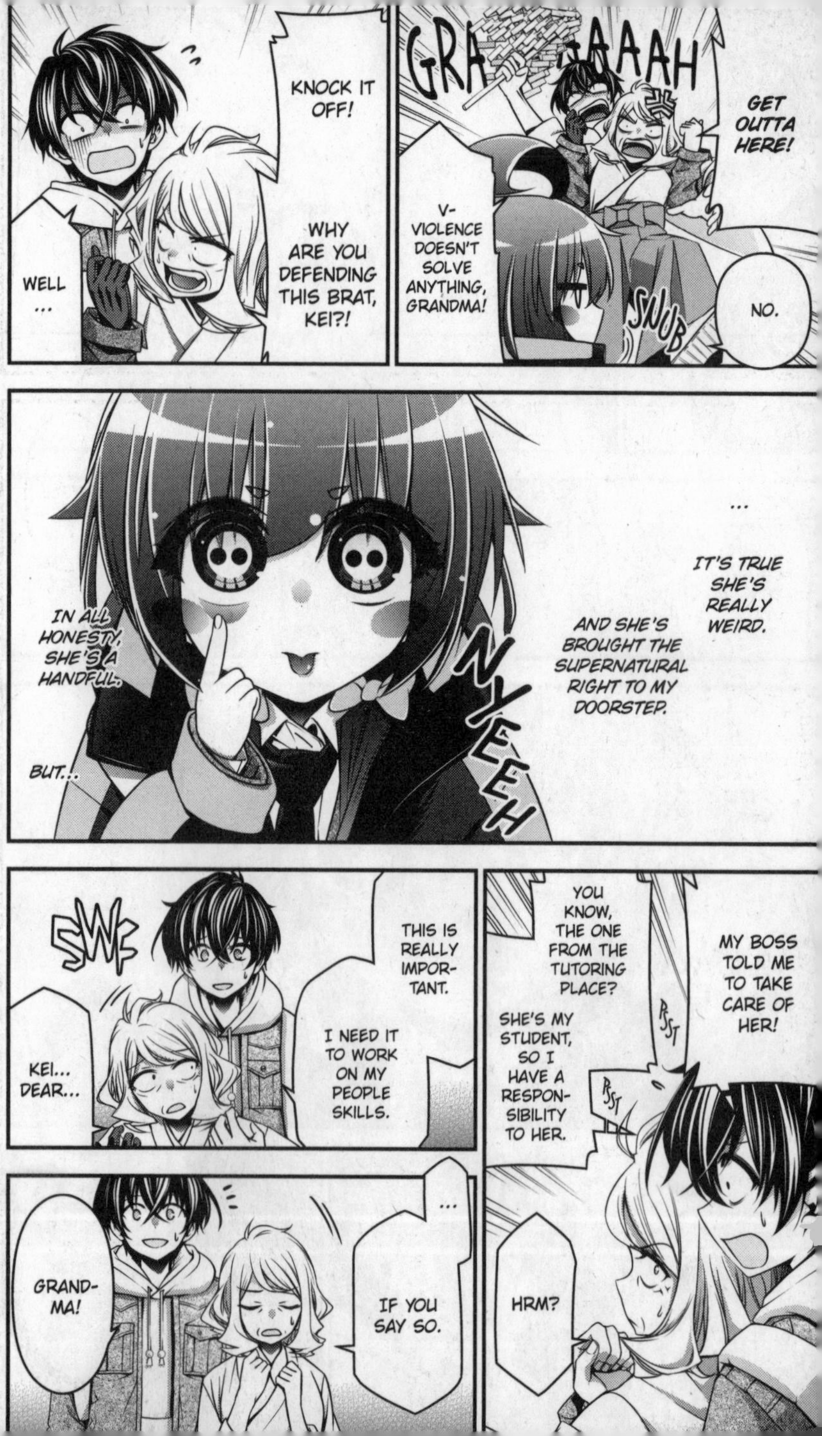
KNOCK IT OFF!
WHY ARE YOU DEFENDING THIS BRAT, KEI?!
WELL ...
GRA AAAH
GET OUTTA HERE!
V-VIOLENCE DOESN'T SOLVE ANYTHING, GRANDMA!
SNUB
NO.
...
IT'S TRUE SHE'S REALLY WEIRD.
AND SHE'S BROUGHT THE SUPERNATURAL RIGHT TO MY DOORSTEP.
NYEEH
IN ALL HONESTY, SHE'S A HANDFUL.
BUT...
MY BOSS TOLD ME TO TAKE CARE OF HER!
YOU KNOW, THE ONE FROM THE TUTORING PLACE?
PSST
SHE'S MY STUDENT, SO I HAVE A RESPONSIBILITY TO HER.
PSST
HRM?
SWF
THIS IS REALLY IMPORTANT.
I NEED IT TO WORK ON MY PEOPLE SKILLS.
KEI... DEAR...
...
IF YOU SAY SO.
GRAND-MA!

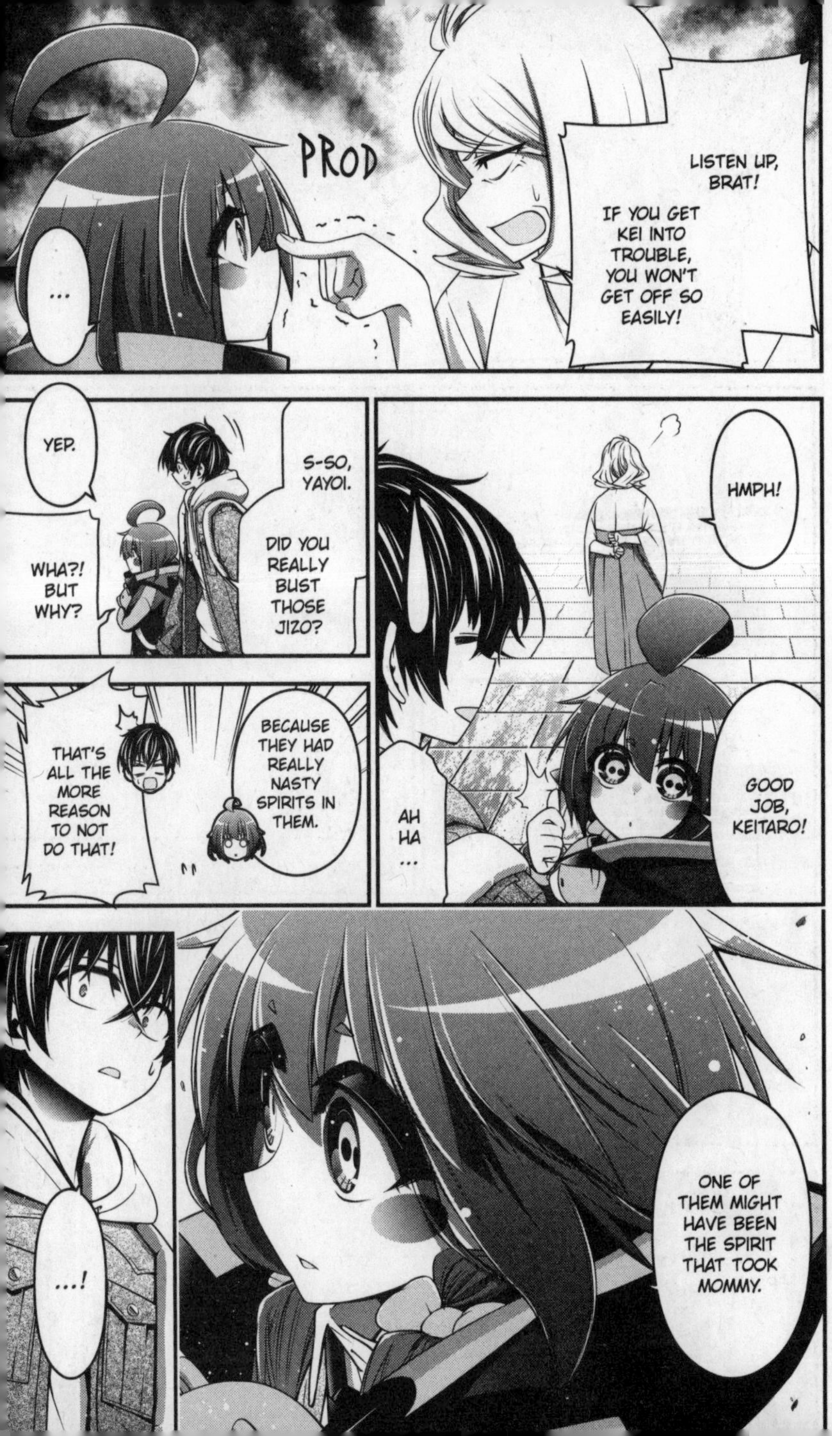
LISTEN UP, BRAT!
IF YOU GET KEI INTO TROUBLE, YOU WON'T GET OFF SO EASILY!
PROD
...
HMPH!
GOOD JOB, KEITARO!
AH HA ...
S-SO, YAYOI.
DID YOU REALLY BUST THOSE JIZO?
YEP.
WHA?! BUT WHY?
BECAUSE THEY HAD REALLY NASTY SPIRITS IN THEM.
THAT'S ALL THE MORE REASON TO NOT DO THAT!
ONE OF THEM MIGHT HAVE BEEN THE SPIRIT THAT TOOK MOMMY.
...!

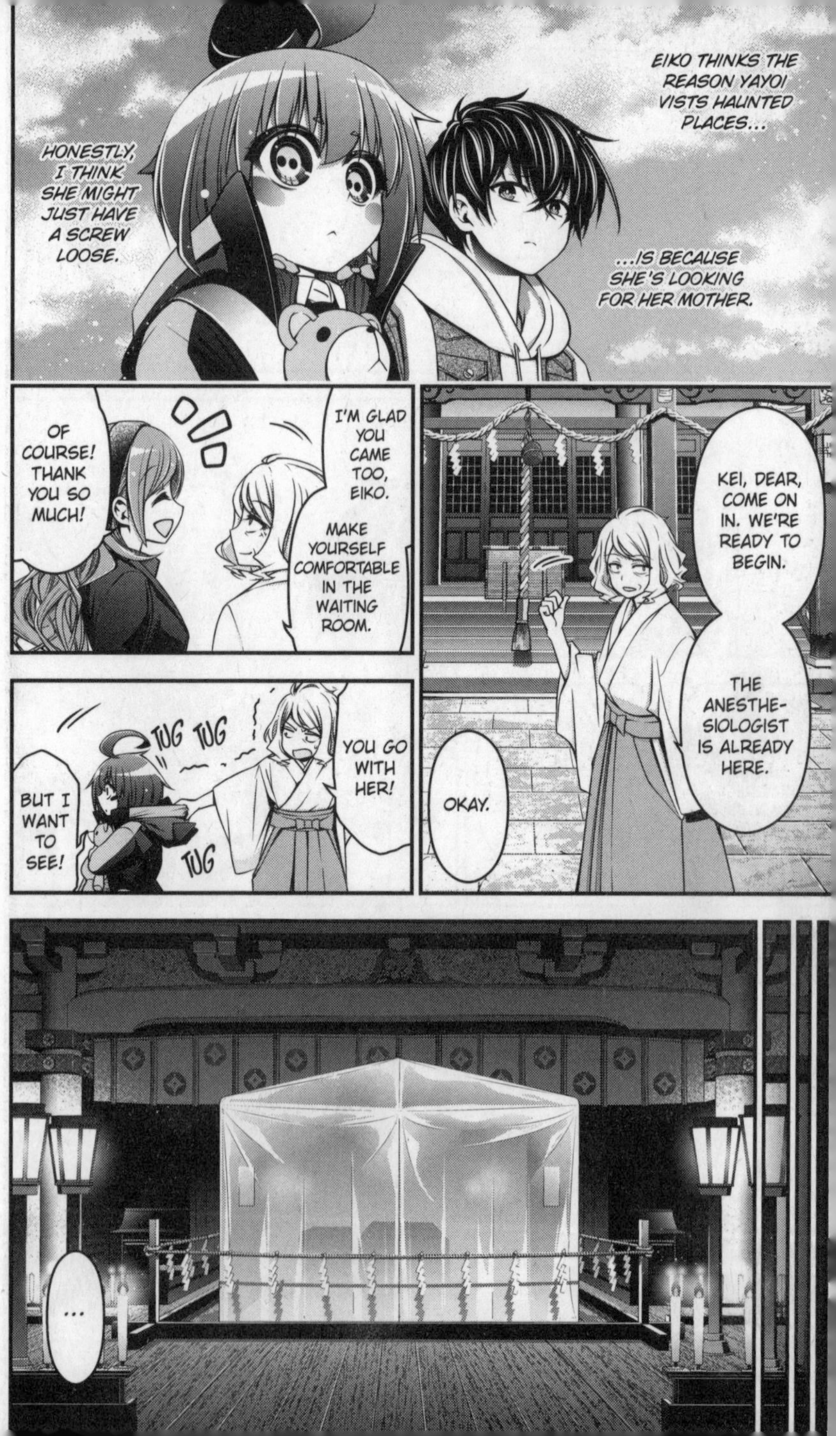
EIKO THINKS THE REASON YAYOI VISTS HAUNTED PLACES...
...IS BECAUSE SHE'S LOOKING FOR HER MOTHER.
HONESTLY, I THINK SHE MIGHT JUST HAVE A SCREW LOOSE.
KEI, DEAR, COME ON IN. WE'RE READY TO BEGIN.
THE ANESTHE-SIOLOGIST IS ALREADY HERE.
OKAY.
I'M GLAD YOU CAME TOO, EIKO.
MAKE YOURSELF COMFORTABLE IN THE WAITING ROOM.
OF COURSE! THANK YOU SO MUCH!
YOU GO WITH HER!
TUG TUG
BUT I WANT TO SEE!
TUG
...

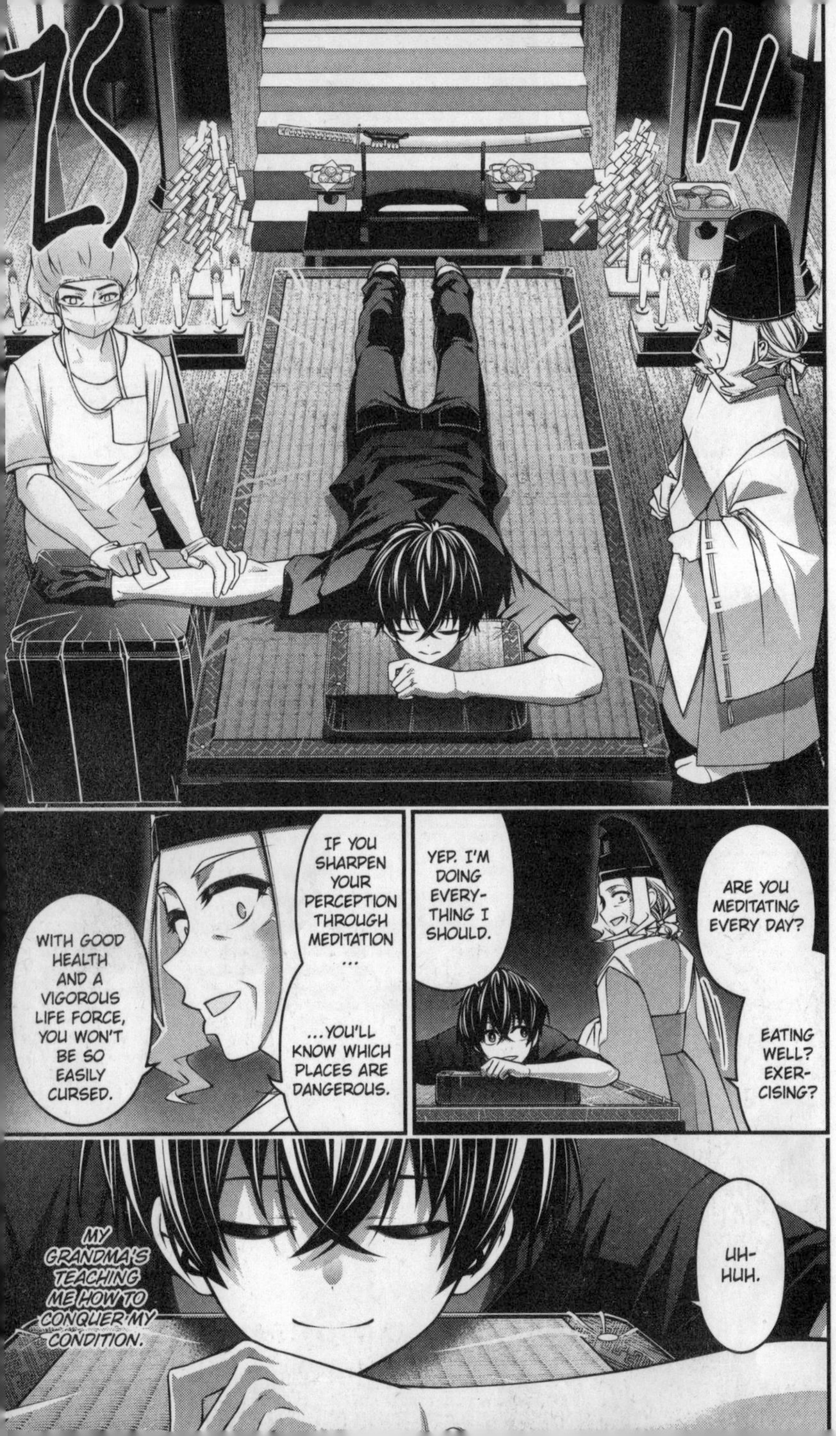
H
ZS
ARE YOU MEDITATING EVERY DAY?
EATING WELL? EXER-CISING?
YEP. I'M DOING EVERY-THING I SHOULD.
IF YOU SHARPEN YOUR PERCEPTION THROUGH MEDITATION ...
...YOU'LL KNOW WHICH PLACES ARE DANGEROUS.
WITH GOOD HEALTH AND A VIGOROUS LIFE FORCE, YOU WON'T BE SO EASILY CURSED.
UH-HUH.
MY GRANDMA'S TEACHING ME HOW TO CONQUER MY CONDITION.

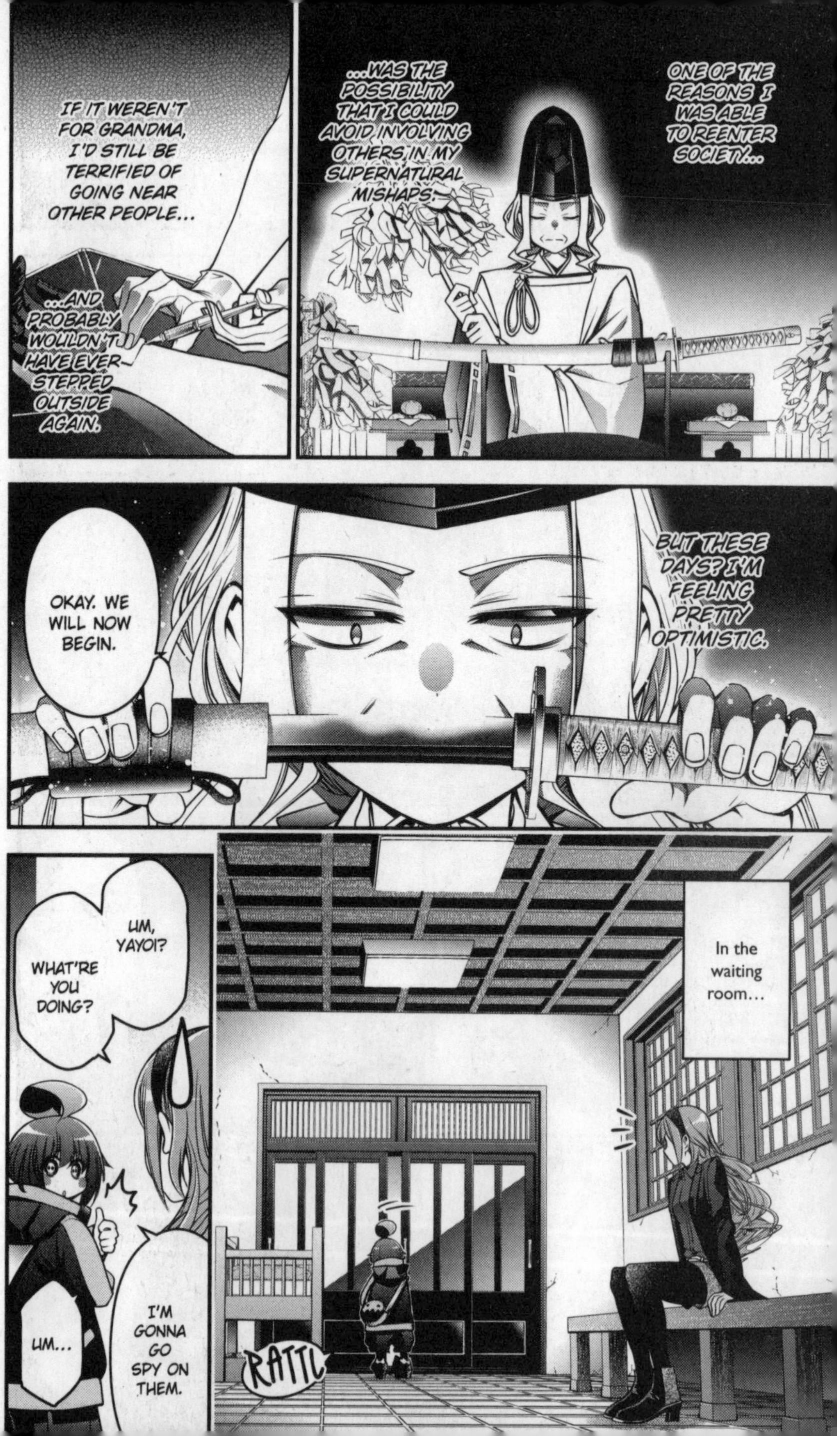
ONE OF THE REASONS I WAS ABLE TO REENTER SOCIETY...
...WAS THE POSSIBILITY THAT I COULD AVOID INVOLVING OTHERS IN MY SUPERNATURAL MISHAPS.
IF IT WEREN'T FOR GRANDMA, I'D STILL BE TERRIFIED OF GOING NEAR OTHER PEOPLE...
...AND PROBABLY WOULDN'T HAVE EVER STEPPED OUTSIDE AGAIN.
BUT THESE DAYS? I'M FEELING PRETTY OPTIMISTIC.
OKAY. WE WILL NOW BEGIN.
In the waiting room...
RATTL
UM, YAYOI?
WHAT'RE YOU DOING?
I'M GONNA GO SPY ON THEM.
UM...

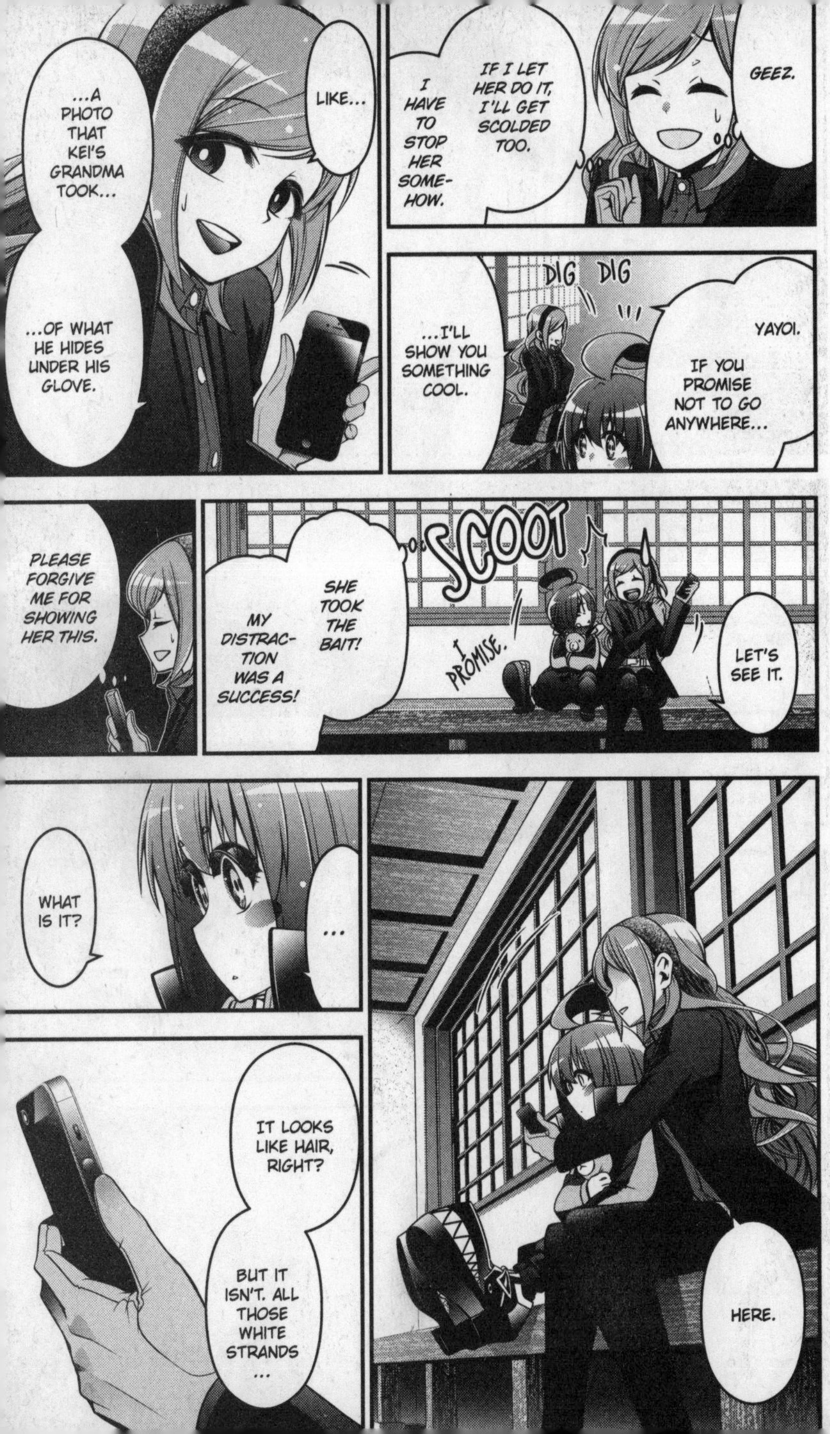
GEEZ.
IF I LET HER DO IT, I'LL GET SCOLDED TOO.
I HAVE TO STOP HER SOMEHOW.
DIG DIG
YAYOI.
IF YOU PROMISE NOT TO GO ANYWHERE...
...I'LL SHOW YOU SOMETHING COOL.
LIKE...
...A PHOTO THAT KEI'S GRANDMA TOOK...
...OF WHAT HE HIDES UNDER HIS GLOVE.
LET'S SEE IT.
SCOOT
I PROMISE.
SHE TOOK THE BAIT!
MY DISTRACTION WAS A SUCCESS!
PLEASE FORGIVE ME FOR SHOWING HER THIS.
HERE.
...
WHAT IS IT?
IT LOOKS LIKE HAIR, RIGHT?
BUT IT ISN'T. ALL THOSE WHITE STRANDS ...

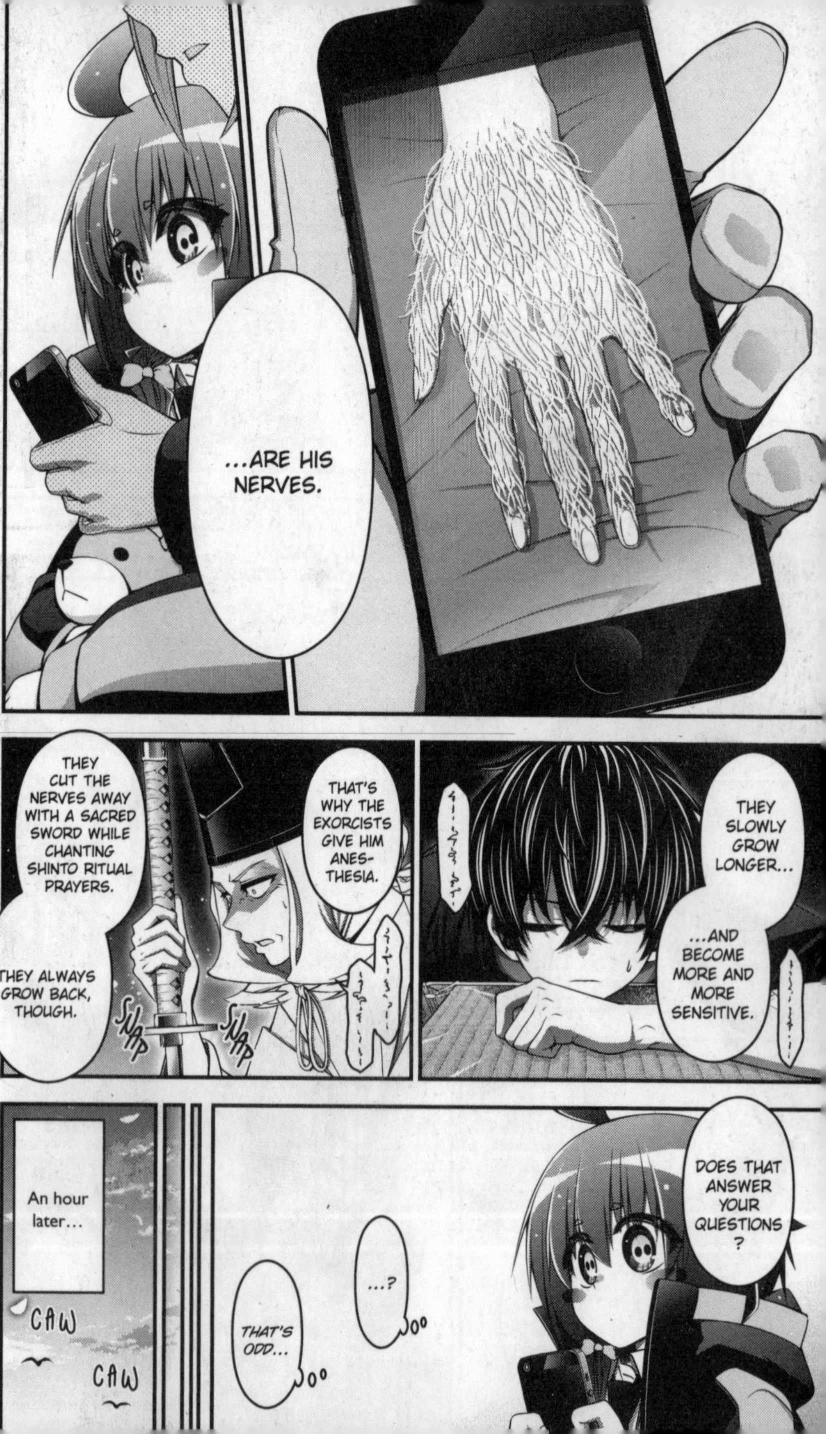
...ARE HIS NERVES.
THEY SLOWLY GROW LONGER...
...AND BECOME MORE AND MORE SENSITIVE.
THAT'S WHY THE EXORCISTS GIVE HIM ANES-THESIA.
THEY CUT THE NERVES AWAY WITH A SACRED SWORD WHILE CHANTING SHINTO RITUAL PRAYERS.
THEY ALWAYS GROW BACK, THOUGH.
SNAP
SNAP
DOES THAT ANSWER YOUR QUESTIONS?
...?
THAT'S ODD...
An hour later...
CAW
CAW

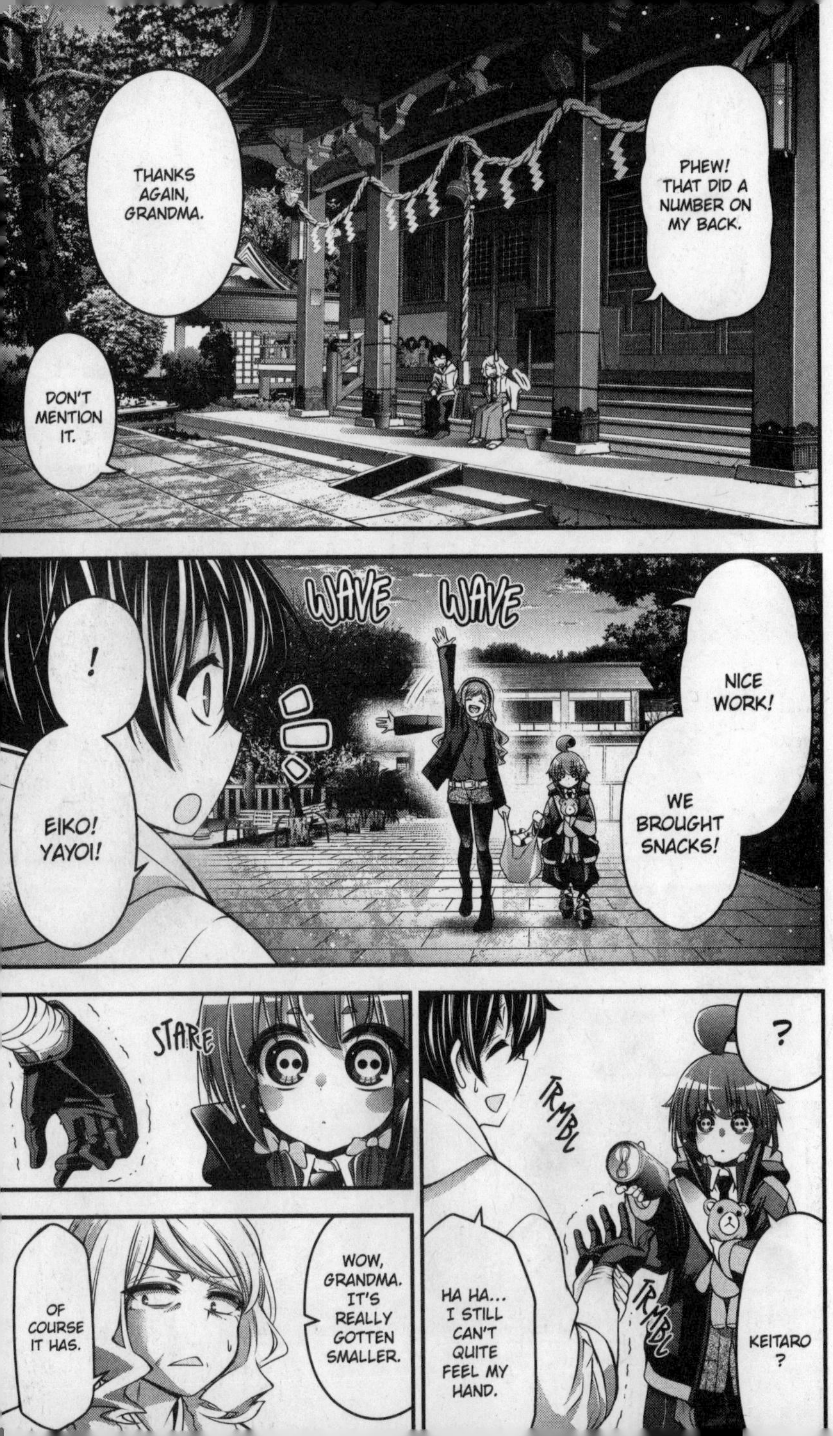
PHEW! THAT DID A NUMBER ON MY BACK.
THANKS AGAIN, GRANDMA.
DON'T MENTION IT.
NICE WORK!
WE BROUGHT SNACKS!
WAVE WAVE
!
EIKO! YAYOI!
?
TRMBL
KEITARO?
HA HA... I STILL CAN'T QUITE FEEL MY HAND.
TRMBL
STARE
WOW, GRANDMA. IT'S REALLY GOTTEN SMALLER.
OF COURSE IT HAS.

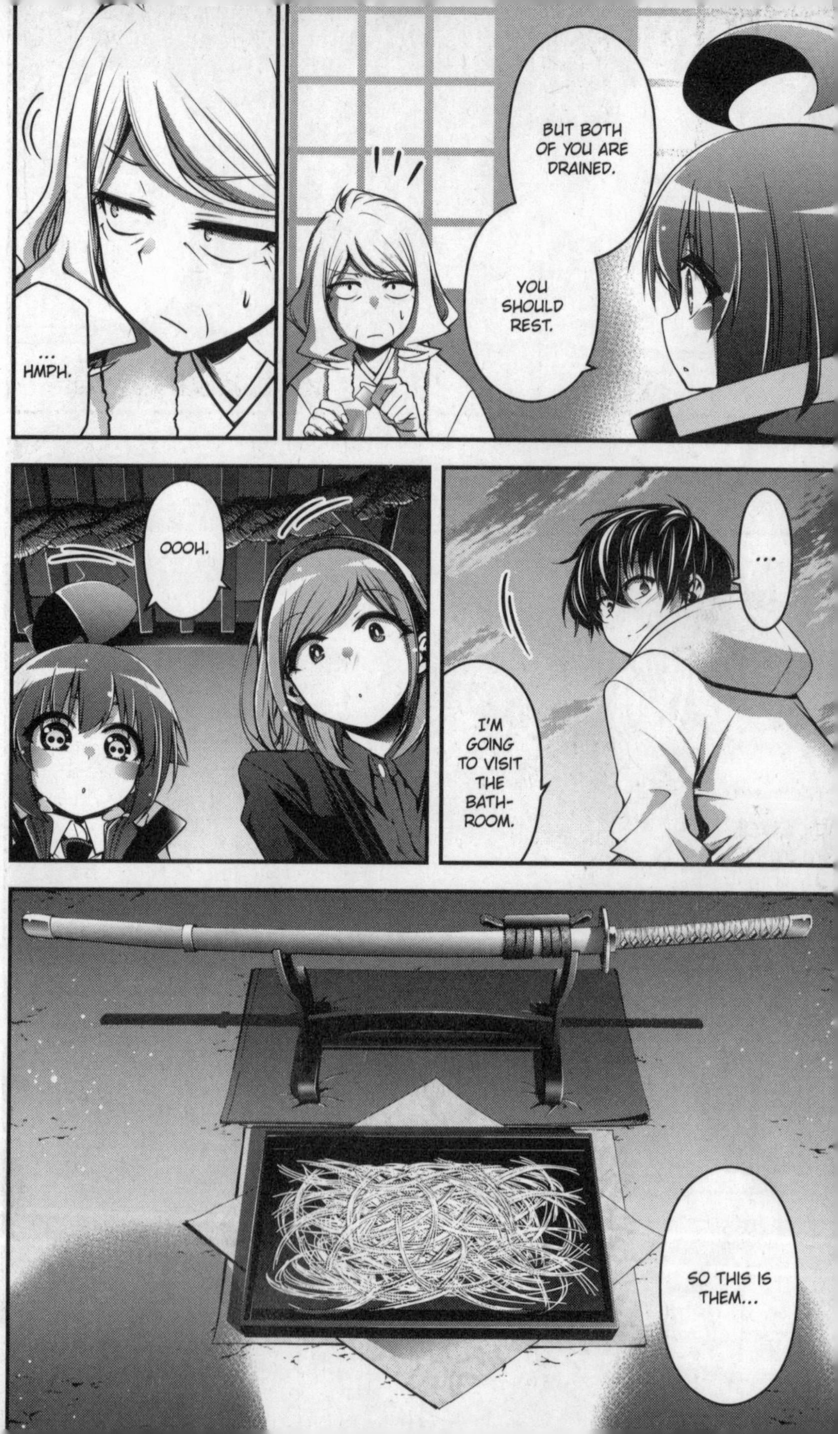
BUT BOTH OF YOU ARE DRAINED.
YOU SHOULD REST.
... HMPH.
...
I'M GOING TO VISIT THE BATH-ROOM.
OOOH.
SO THIS IS THEM...

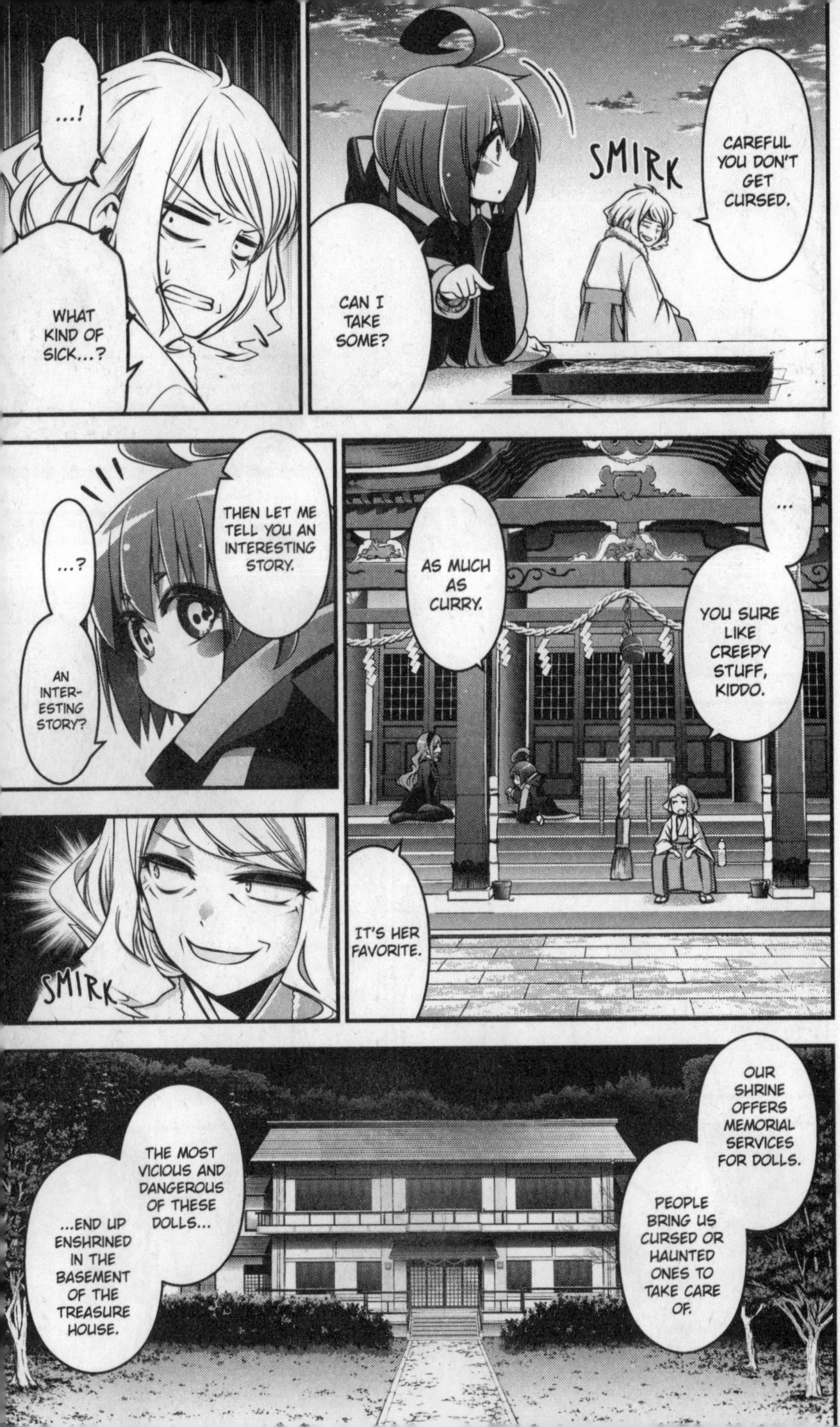
CAREFUL YOU DON'T GET CURSED.
SMIRK
CAN I TAKE SOME?
...!
WHAT KIND OF SICK...?
...
YOU SURE LIKE CREEPY STUFF, KIDDO.
AS MUCH AS CURRY.
IT'S HER FAVORITE.
THEN LET ME TELL YOU AN INTERESTING STORY.
...?
AN INTER-ESTING STORY?
SMIRK
OUR SHRINE OFFERS MEMORIAL SERVICES FOR DOLLS.
PEOPLE BRING US CURSED OR HAUNTED ONES TO TAKE CARE OF.
THE MOST VICIOUS AND DANGEROUS OF THESE DOLLS...
...END UP ENSHRINED IN THE BASEMENT OF THE TREASURE HOUSE.

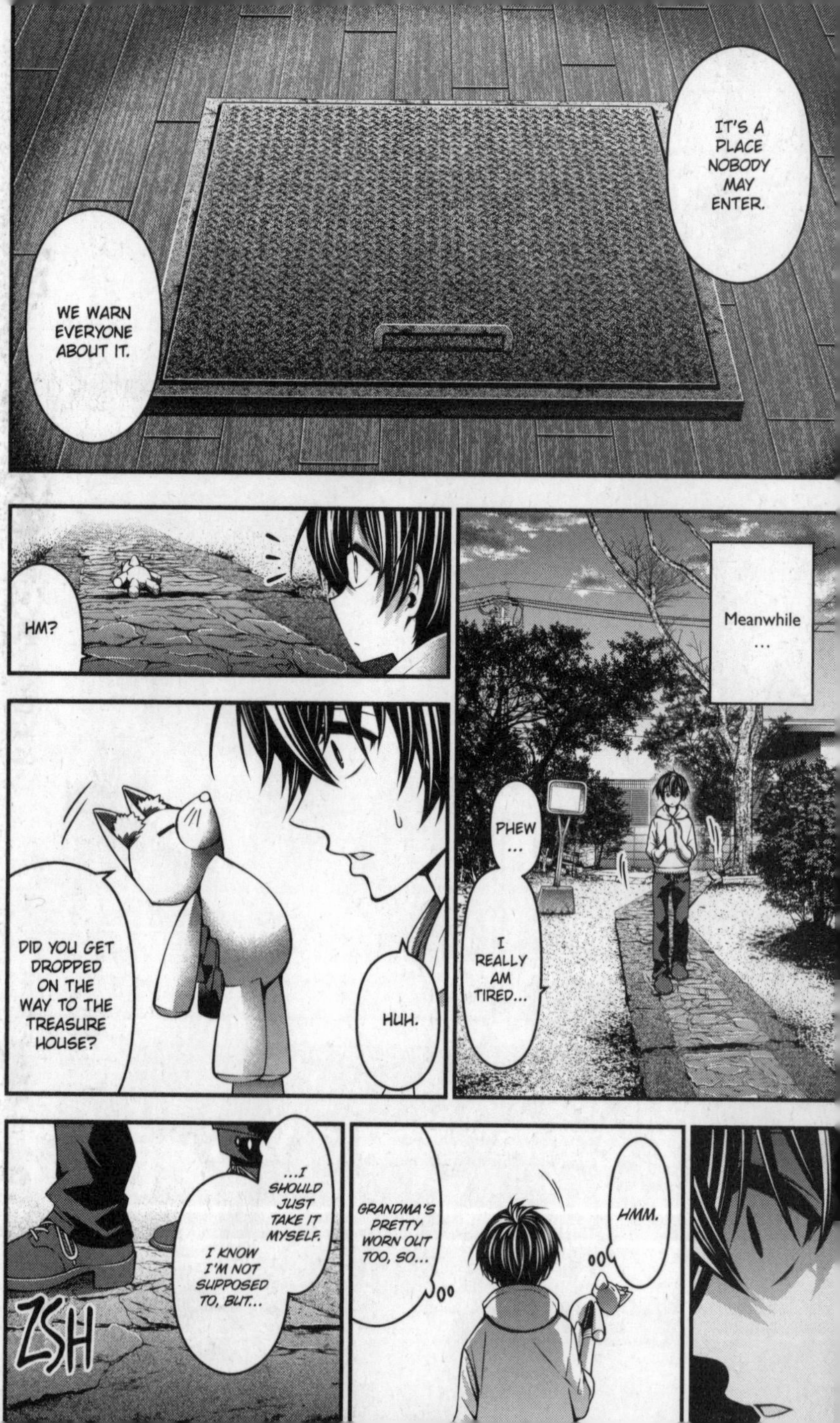
IT'S A PLACE NOBODY MAY ENTER.
WE WARN EVERYONE ABOUT IT.
Meanwhile...
PHEW...
I REALLY AM TIRED...
HM?
HUH.
DID YOU GET DROPPED ON THE WAY TO THE TREASURE HOUSE?
HMM.
GRANDMA'S PRETTY WORN OUT TOO, SO...
...I SHOULD JUST TAKE IT MYSELF.
I KNOW I'M NOT SUPPOSED TO, BUT...
ZSH

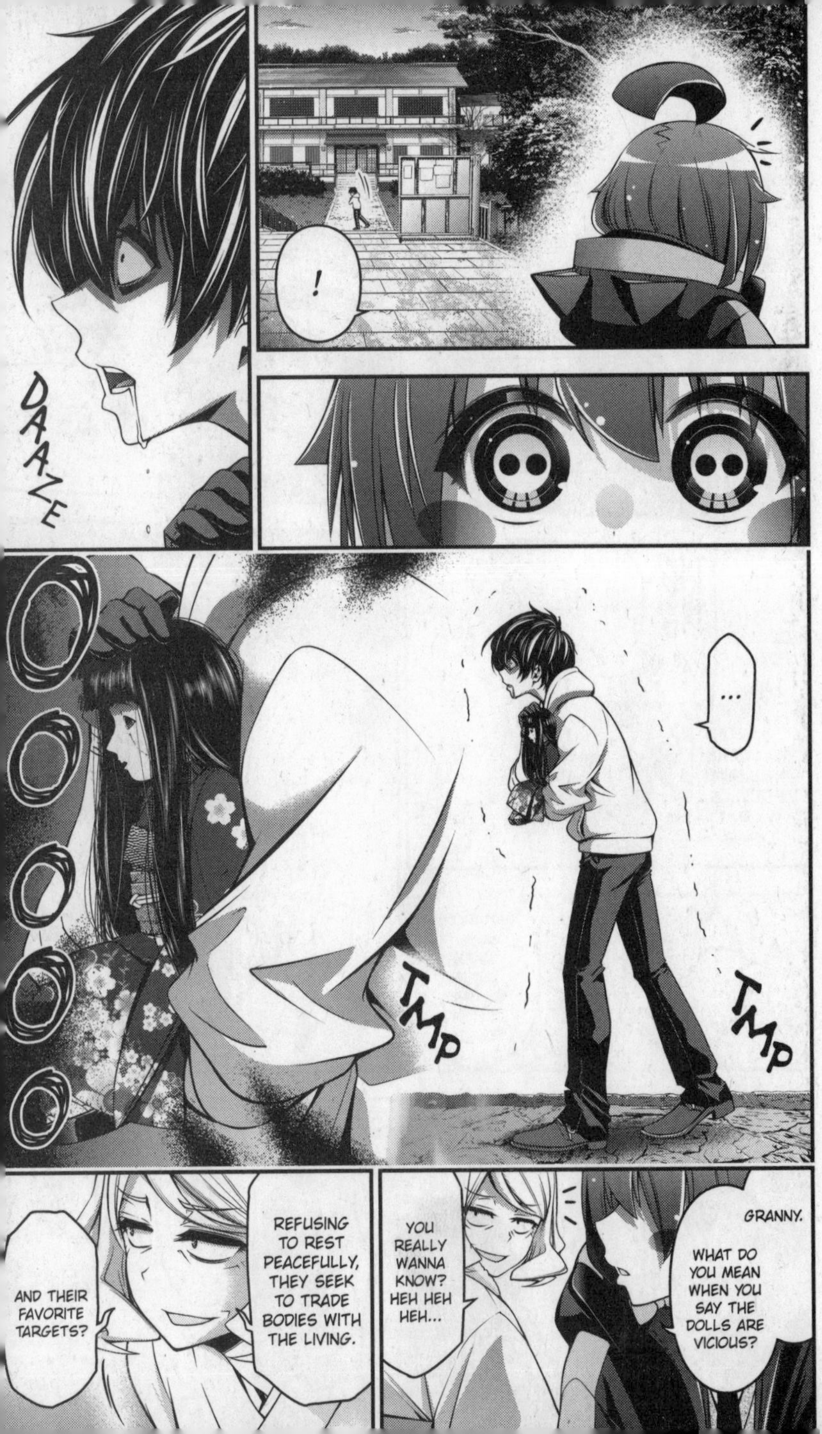
!
DAAAZE
...
TMP
TMP
GRANNY.
WHAT DO YOU MEAN WHEN YOU SAY THE DOLLS ARE VICIOUS?
YOU REALLY WANNA KNOW? HEH HEH HEH...
REFUSING TO REST PEACEFULLY, THEY SEEK TO TRADE BODIES WITH THE LIVING.
AND THEIR FAVORITE TARGETS?

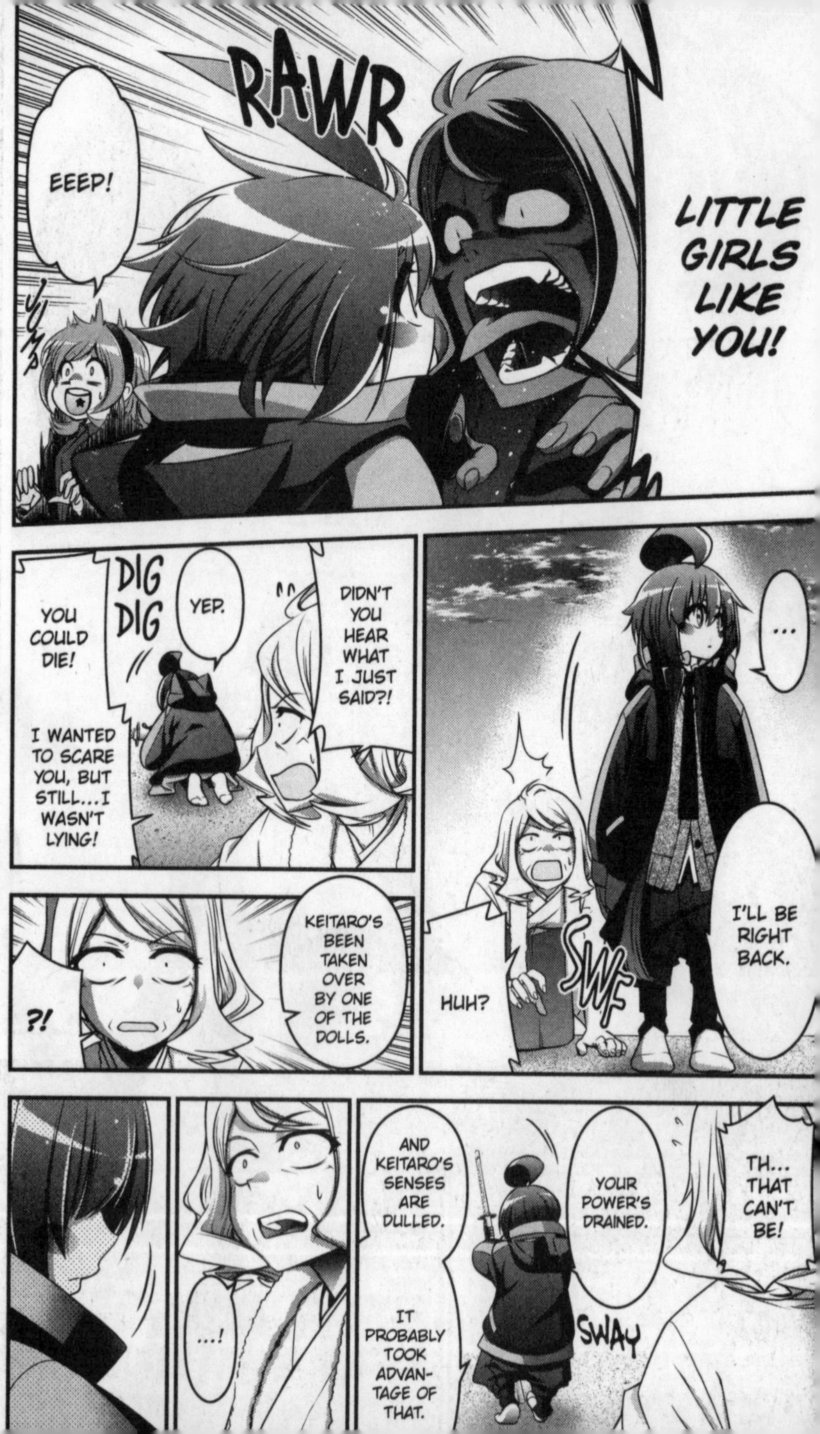
LITTLE GIRLS LIKE YOU!
RAWR
EEEP!
JUMP
...
I'LL BE RIGHT BACK.
HUH?
SWF
DIDN'T YOU HEAR WHAT I JUST SAID?!
YEP.
DIG DIG
YOU COULD DIE!
I WANTED TO SCARE YOU, BUT STILL...I WASN'T LYING!
KEITARO'S BEEN TAKEN OVER BY ONE OF THE DOLLS.
?!
TH... THAT CAN'T BE!
YOUR POWER'S DRAINED.
AND KEITARO'S SENSES ARE DULLED.
IT PROBABLY TOOK ADVAN-TAGE OF THAT.
SWAY
...!

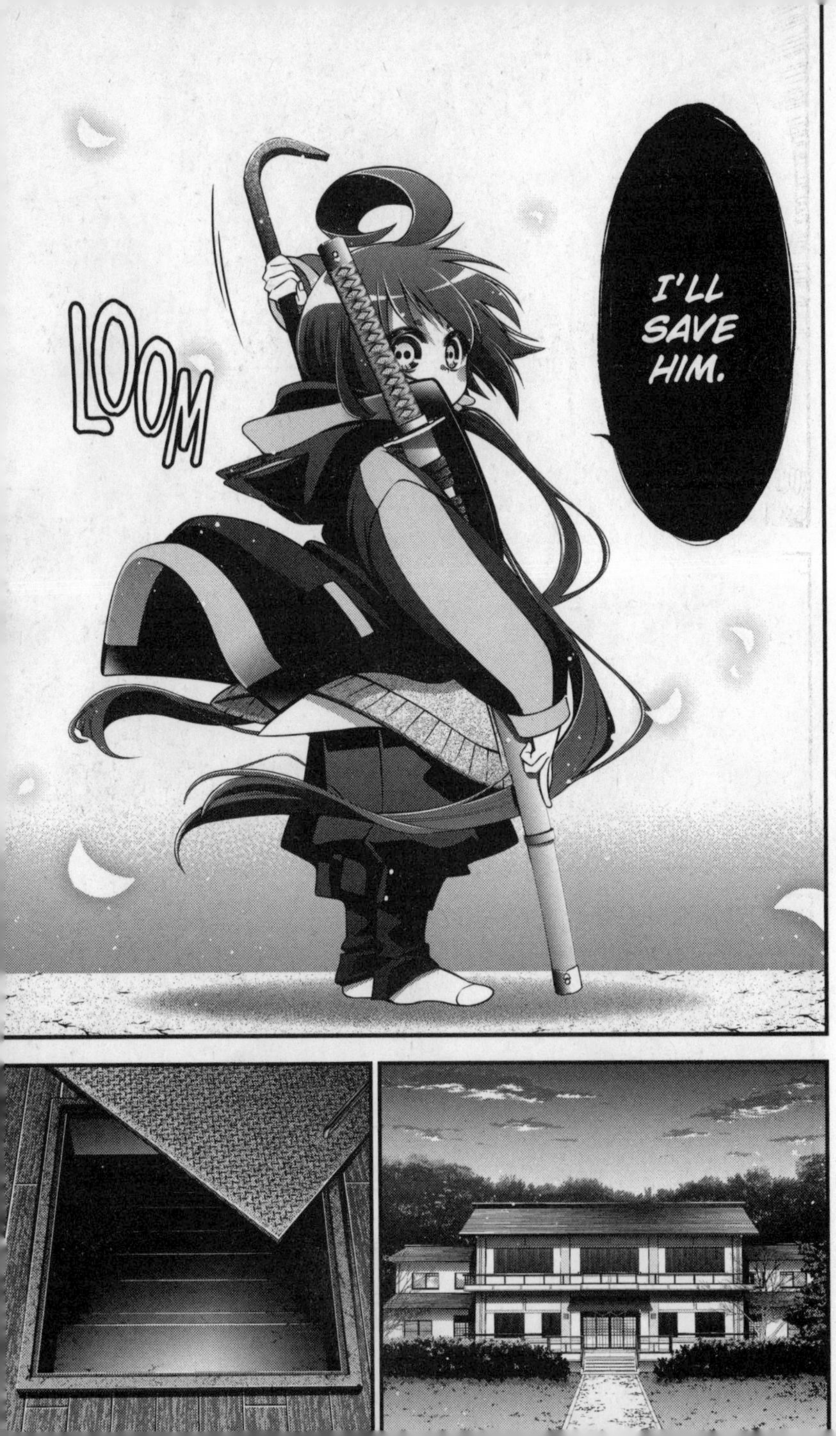
I'LL SAVE HIM.
LOOM

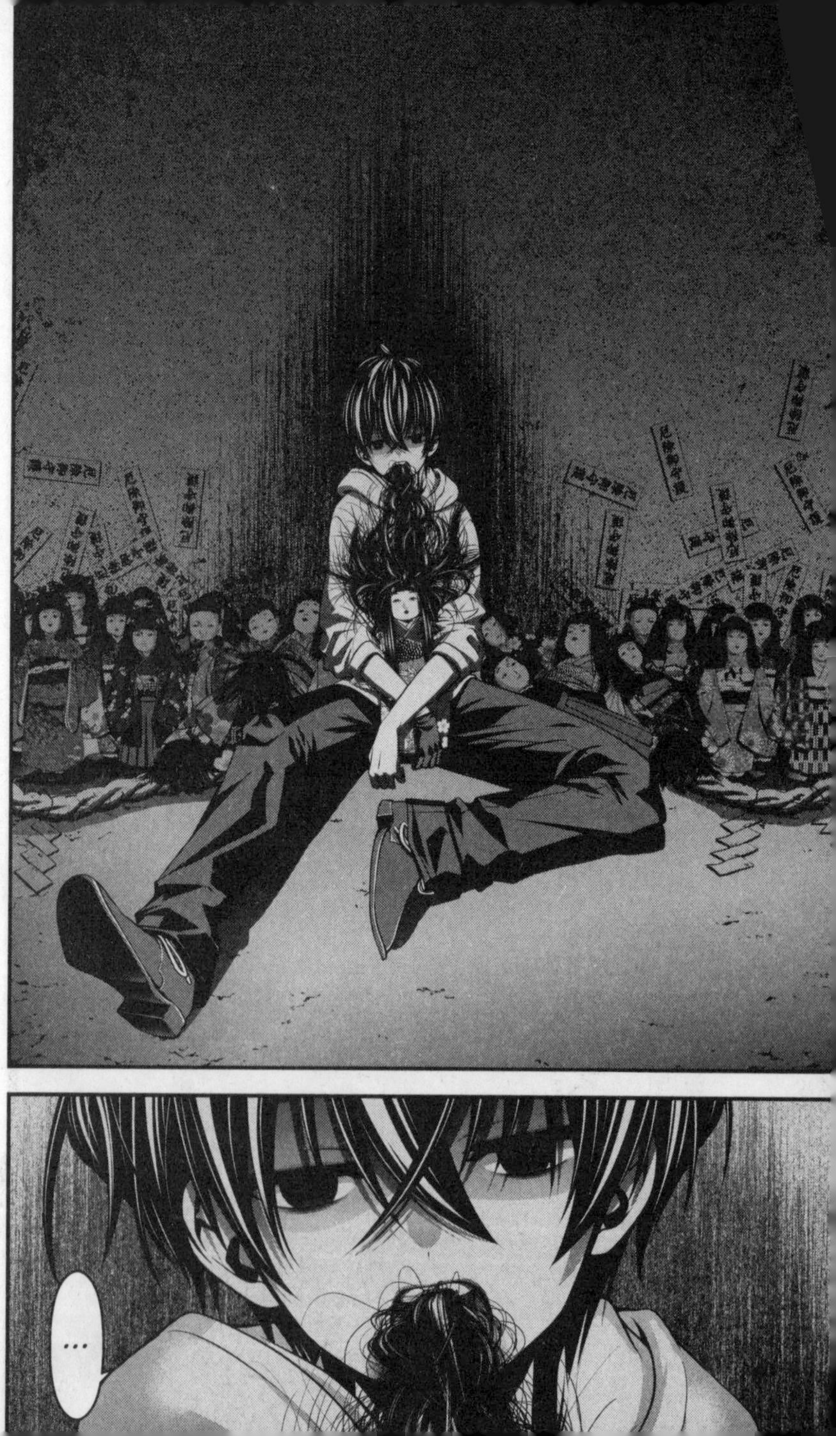
...

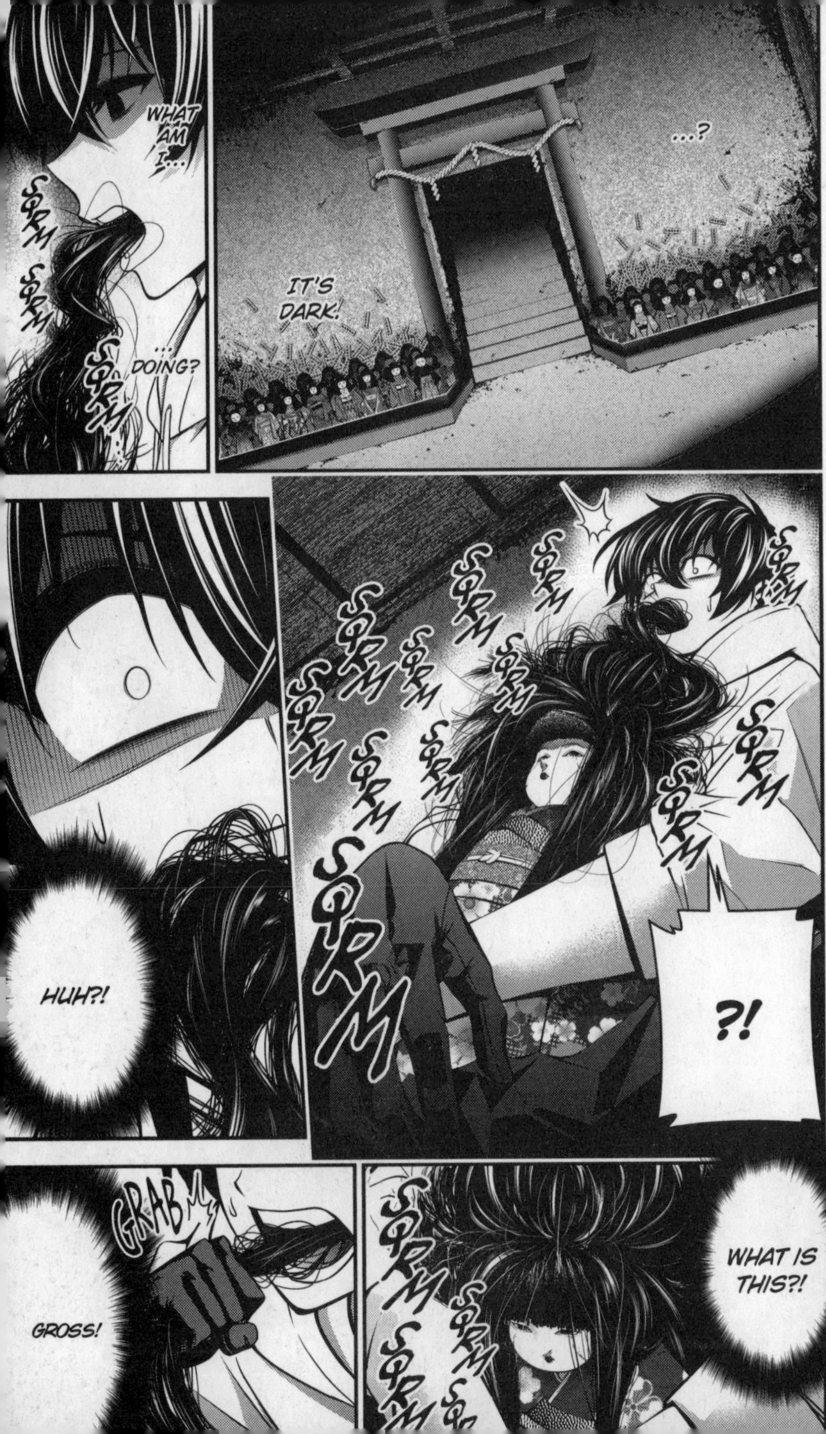
...?
IT'S DARK.
WHAT AM I...
...DOING?
SQRM SQRM SQRM
SQRM
SQRM
SQRM SQRM SQRM SQRM SQRM SQRM SQRM SQRM SQRM SQRM
?!
HUH?!
WHAT IS THIS?!
SQRM SQRM SQRM
GRAB
GROSS!

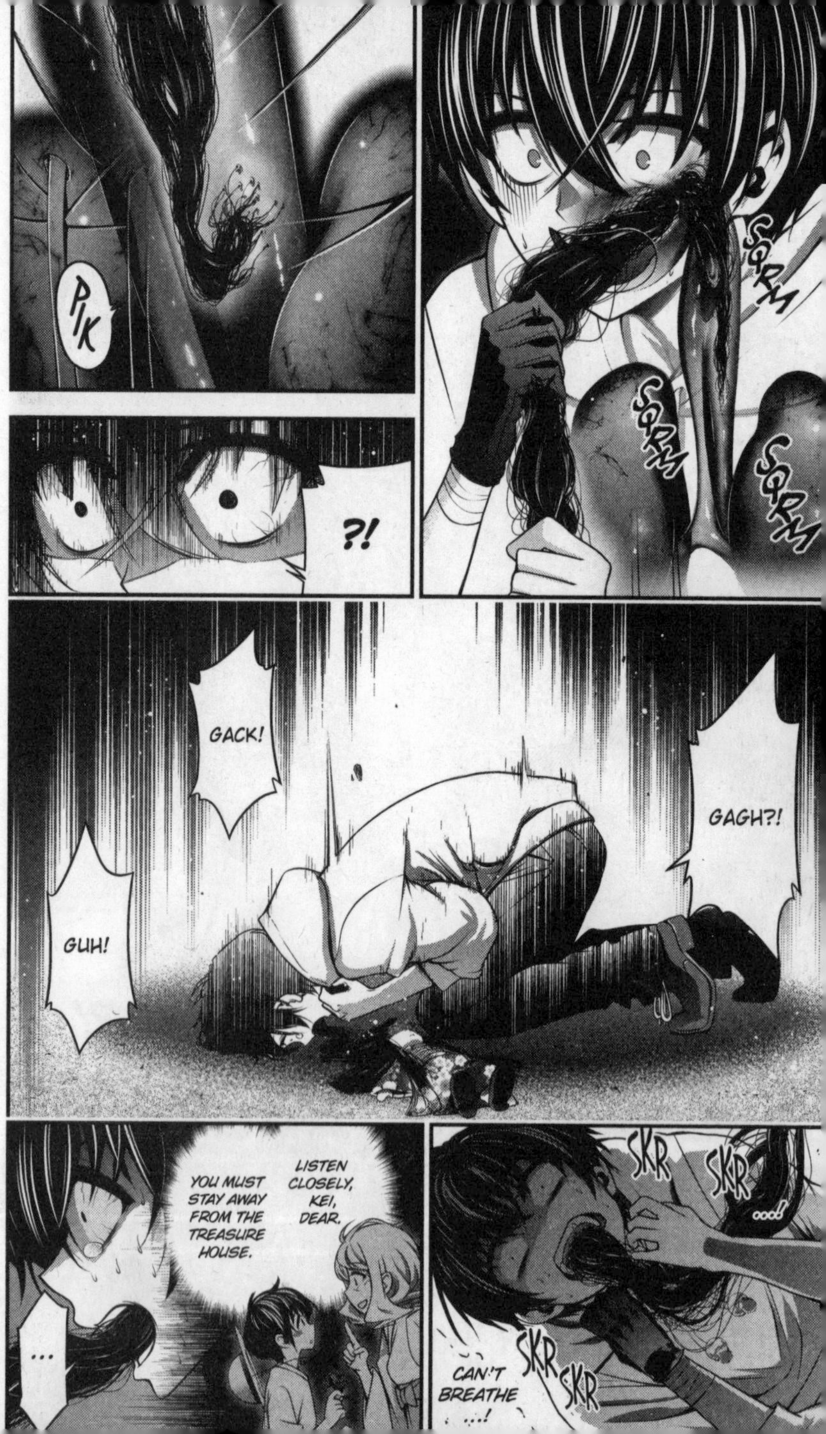
SQRM
SQRM
SQRM
PIK
?!
GAGH?!
GACK!
GUH!
SKR
SKR
...!
SKR
SKR
CAN'T BREATHE ...!
LISTEN CLOSELY, KEI, DEAR.
YOU MUST STAY AWAY FROM THE TREASURE HOUSE.
...

W...

...WHY...

WHY DID I
IGNORE HER
WARNING?   ...!

I'M
USUALLY SO
CAREFUL...

KLAK

...

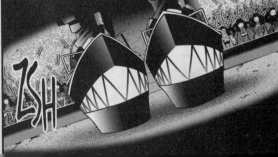

ZSH

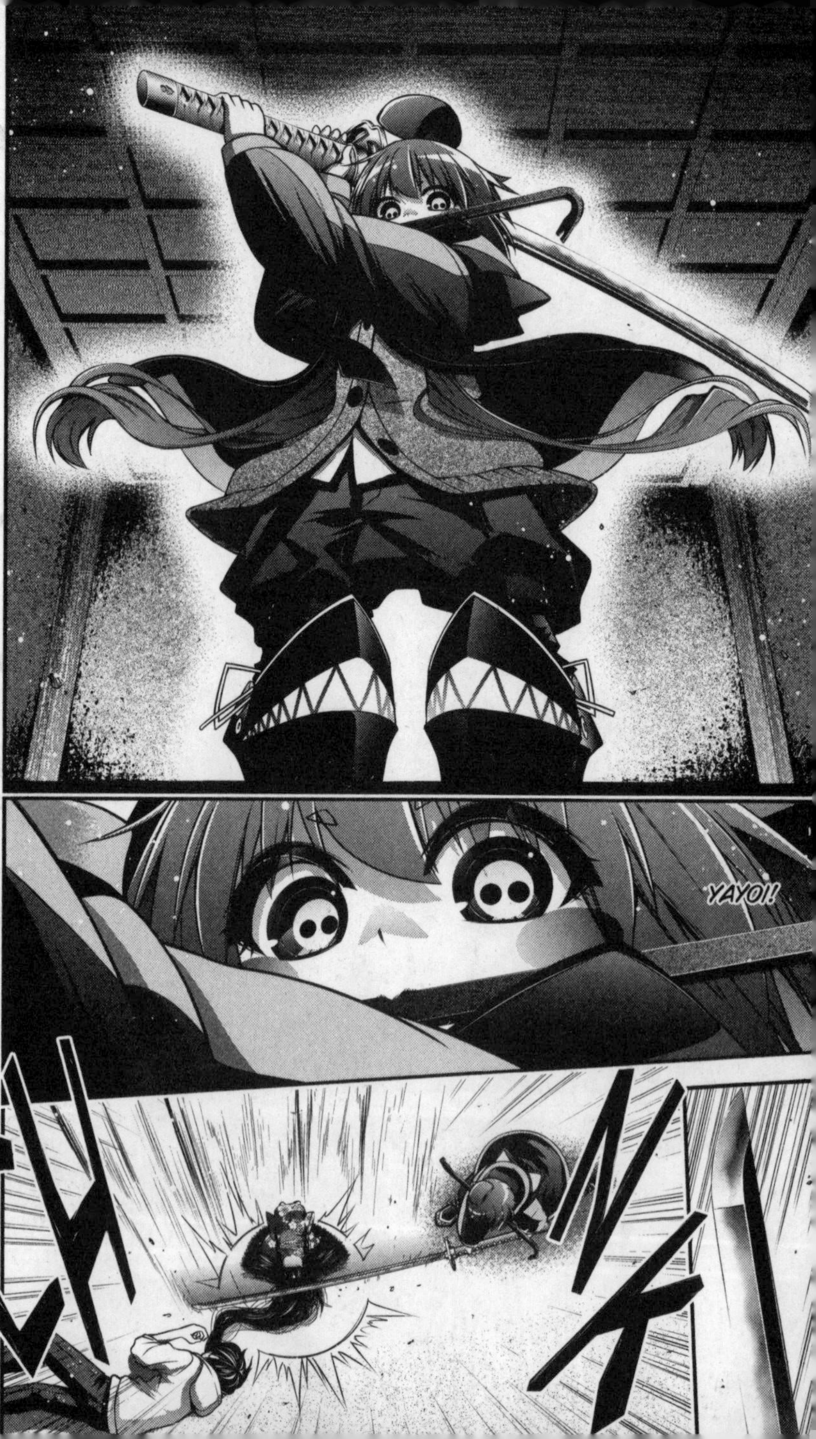
YAYOI!
CLINK

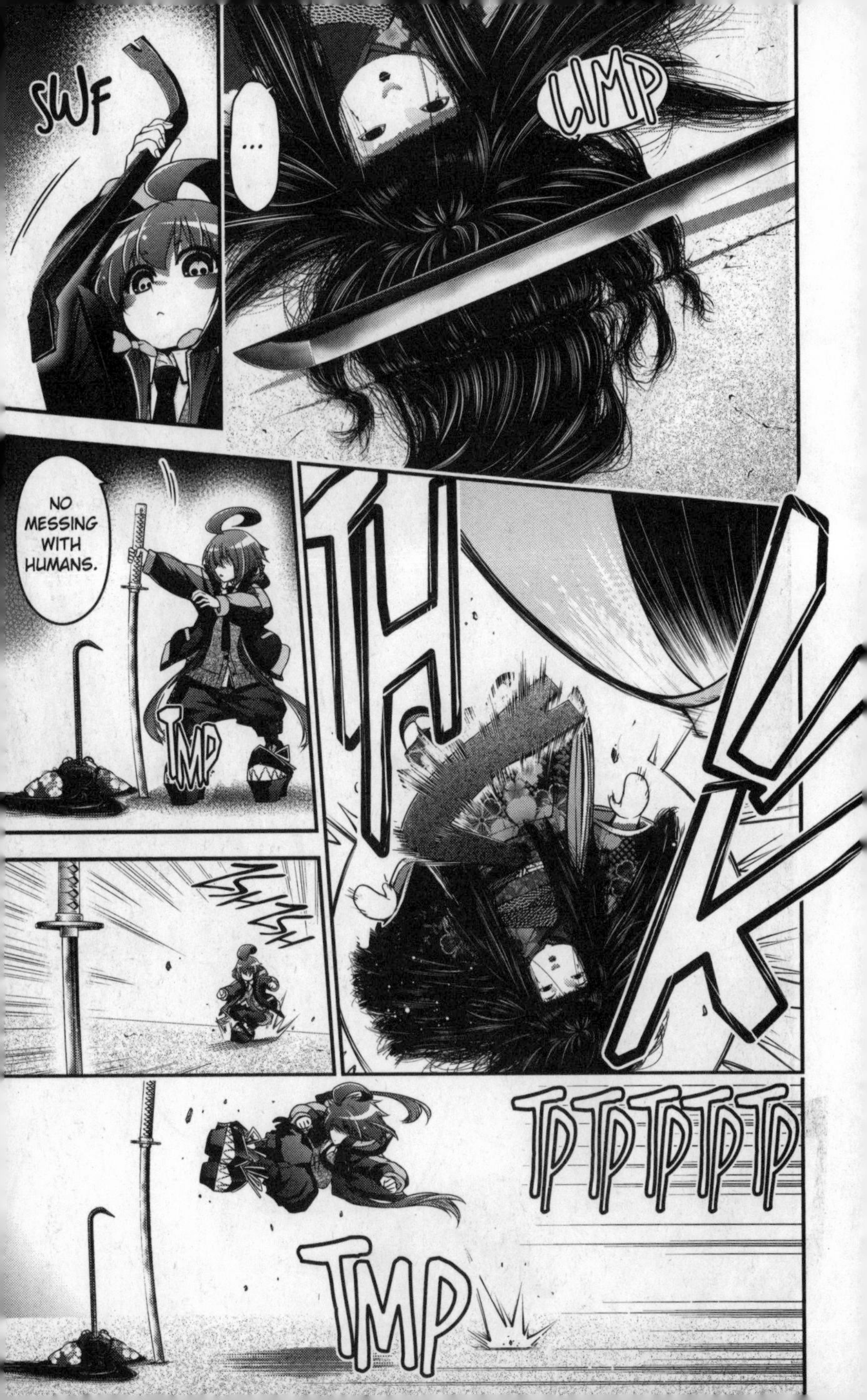
LIMP
...
SWF
THWK
NO MESSING WITH HUMANS.
TMP
TPTPTPTPTP
TMP

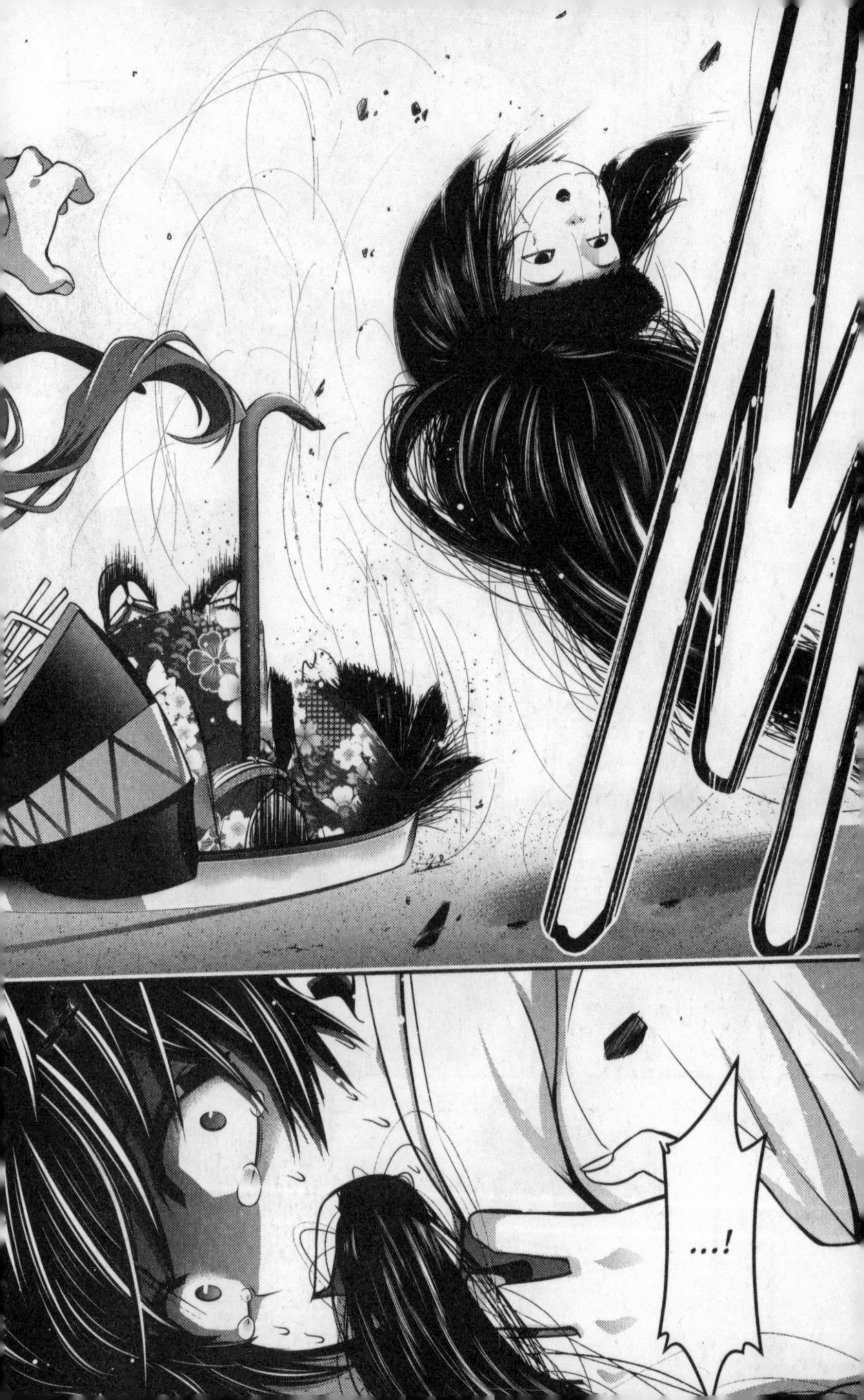
...!

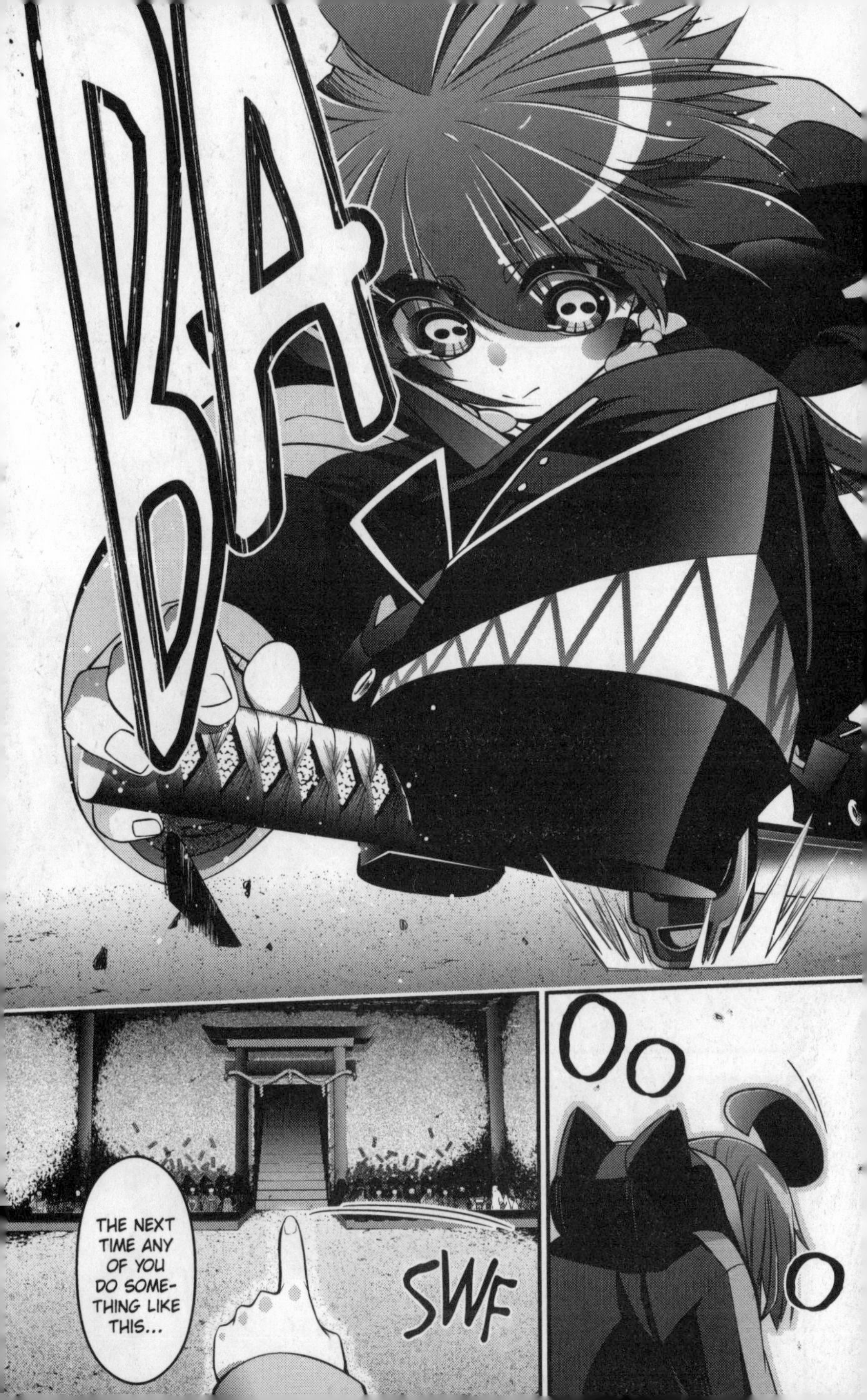
THE NEXT TIME ANY OF YOU DO SOME-THING LIKE THIS...
SWF

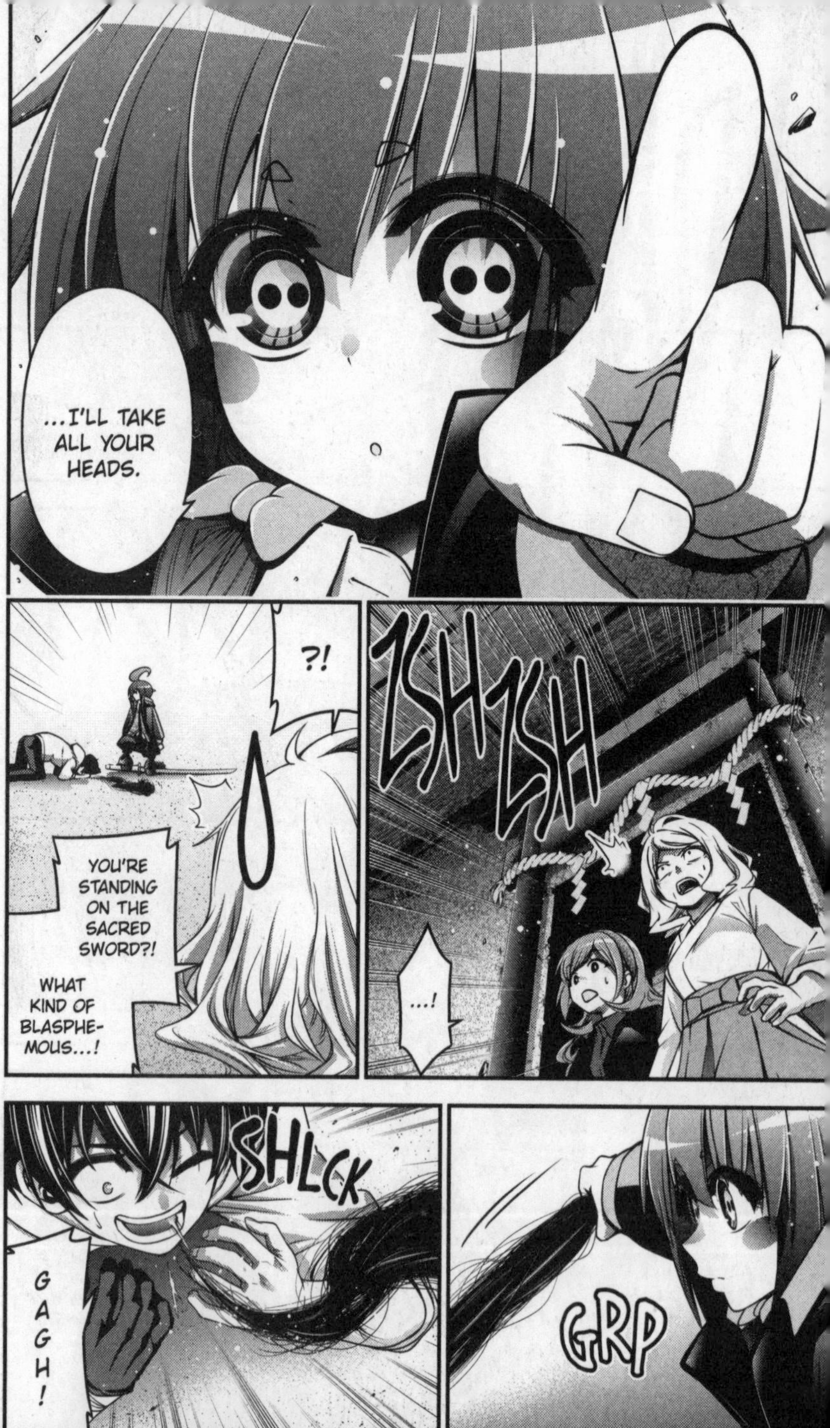
...I'LL TAKE ALL YOUR HEADS.
ZSH ZSH
...!
?!
YOU'RE STANDING ON THE SACRED SWORD?!
WHAT KIND OF BLASPHE-MOUS...!
GRP
SHLCK
GAGH!

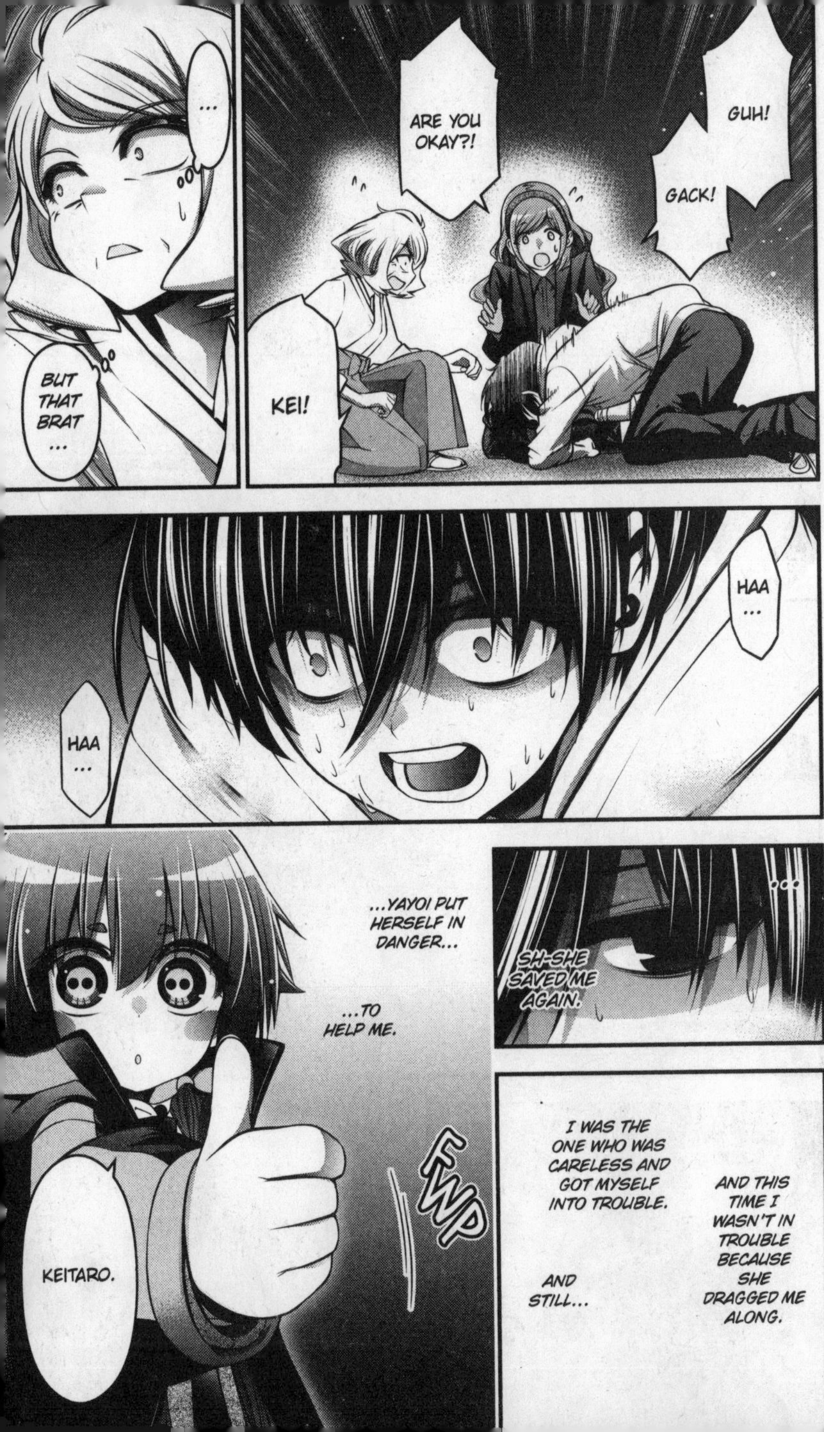
GUH!
GACK!
ARE YOU OKAY?!
KEI!
...
BUT THAT BRAT ...
HAA ...
HAA ...
...
SH-SHE SAVED ME AGAIN.
I WAS THE ONE WHO WAS CARELESS AND GOT MYSELF INTO TROUBLE.
AND THIS TIME I WASN'T IN TROUBLE BECAUSE SHE DRAGGED ME ALONG.
AND STILL...
...YAYOI PUT HERSELF IN DANGER...
...TO HELP ME.
FWP
KEITARO.

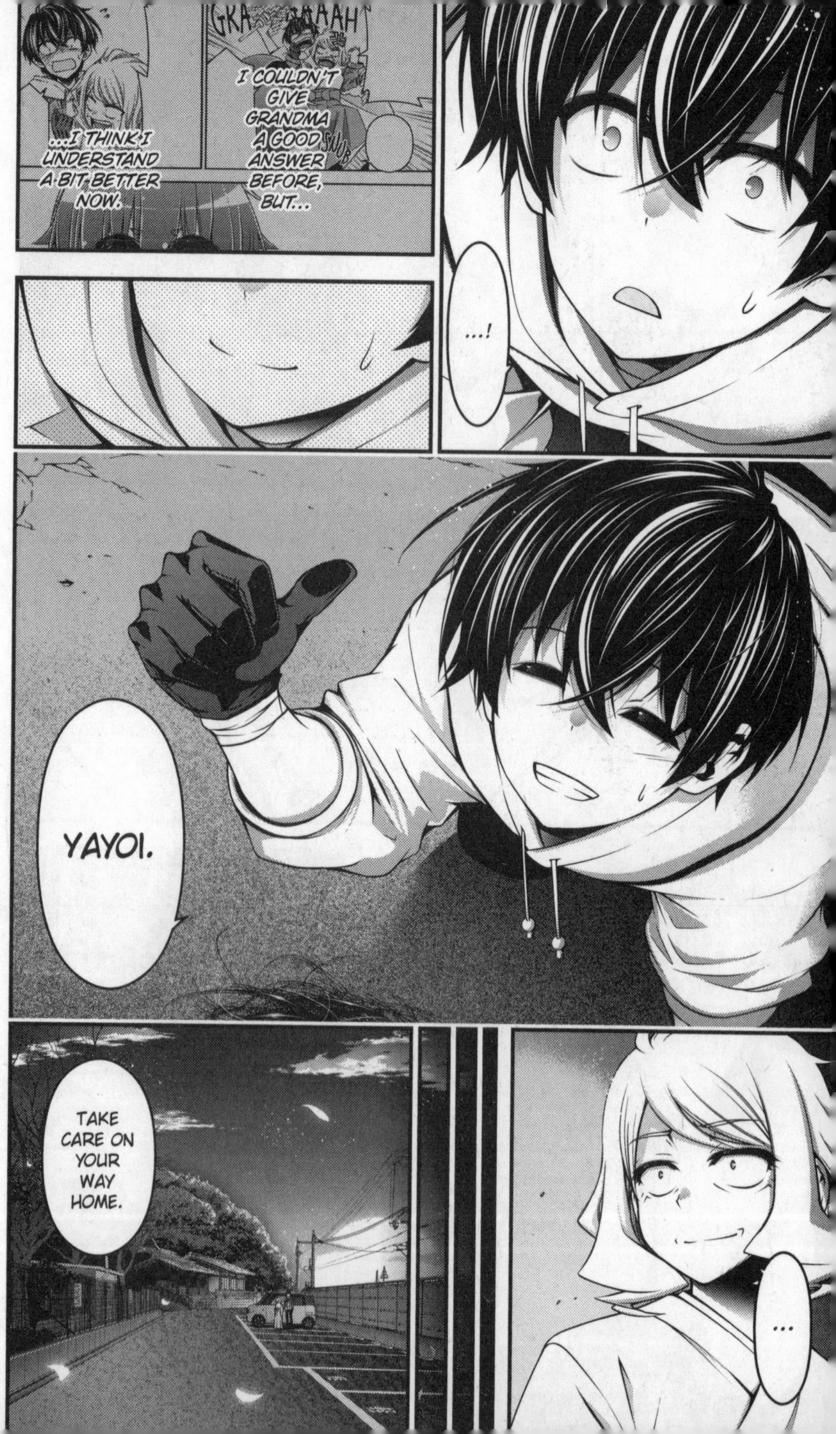
...!
I COULDN'T GIVE GRANDMA A GOOD ANSWER BEFORE, BUT...
...I THINK I UNDERSTAND A BIT BETTER NOW.
YAYOI.
...
TAKE CARE ON YOUR WAY HOME.

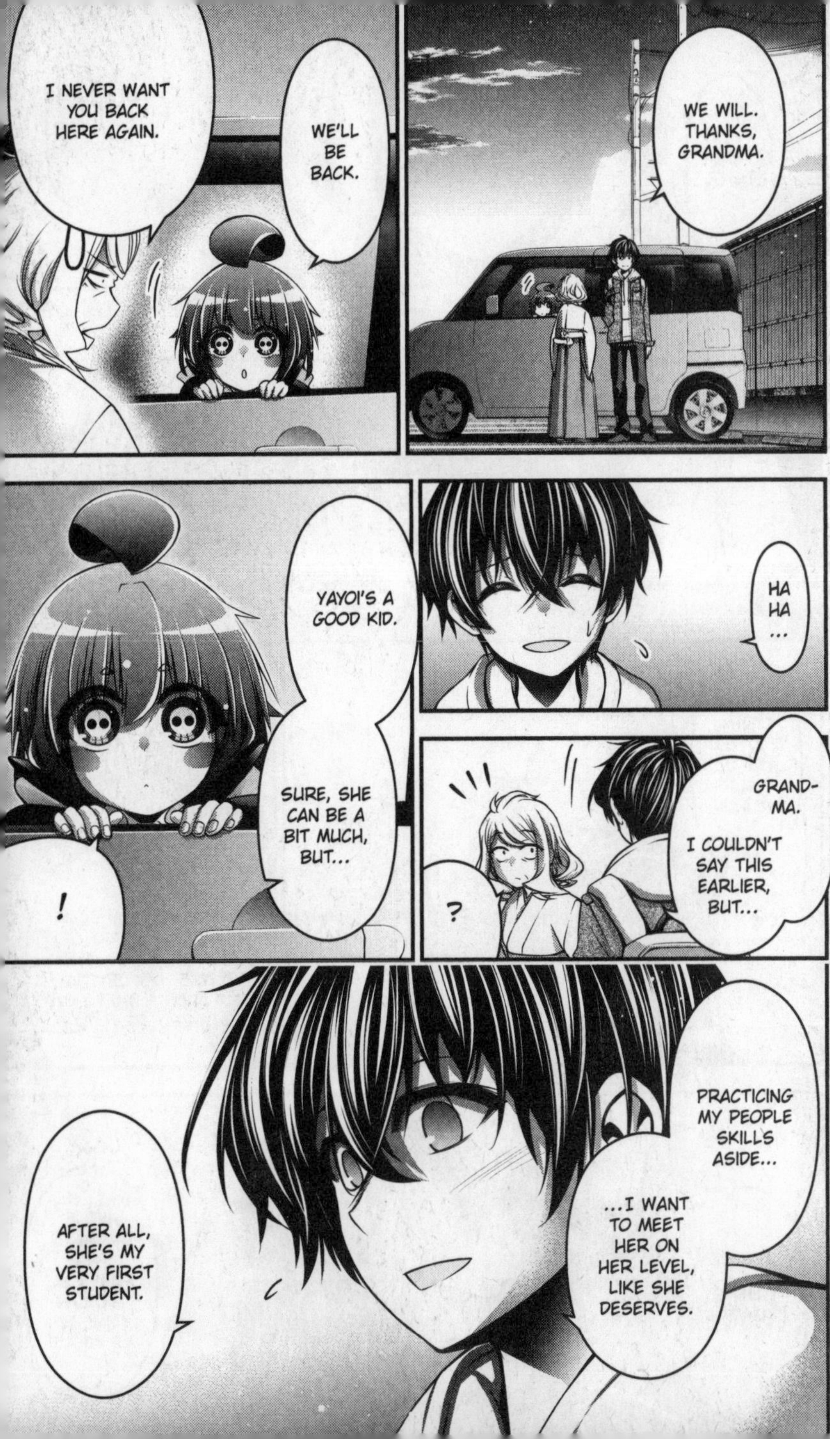
WE WILL. THANKS, GRANDMA.
WE'LL BE BACK.
I NEVER WANT YOU BACK HERE AGAIN.
HA HA...
GRAND-MA.
I COULDN'T SAY THIS EARLIER, BUT...
?
YAYOI'S A GOOD KID.
SURE, SHE CAN BE A BIT MUCH, BUT...
!
PRACTICING MY PEOPLE SKILLS ASIDE...
...I WANT TO MEET HER ON HER LEVEL, LIKE SHE DESERVES.
AFTER ALL, SHE'S MY VERY FIRST STUDENT.

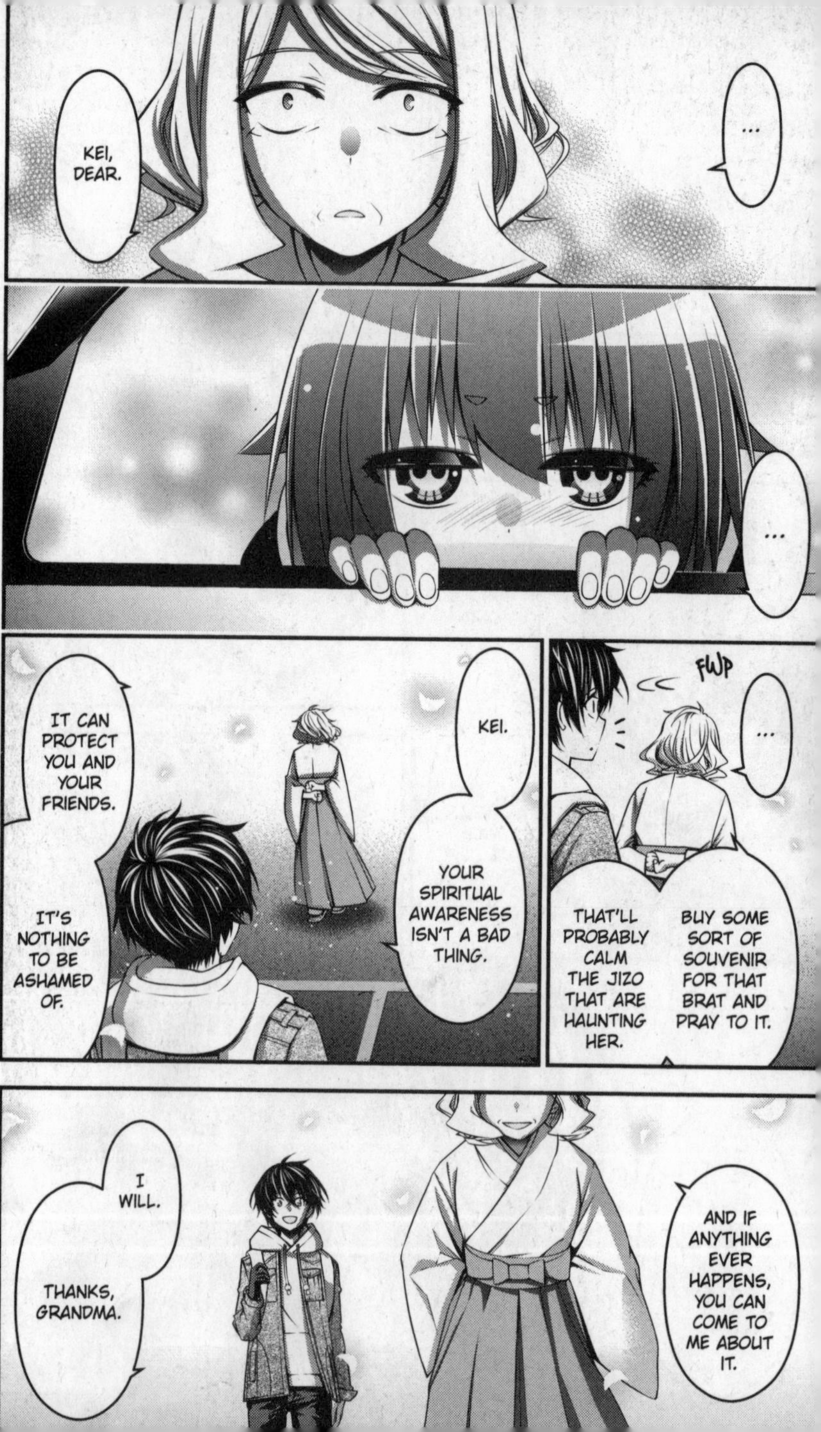
...
KEI, DEAR.
...
FWP
...
BUY SOME SORT OF SOUVENIR FOR THAT BRAT AND PRAY TO IT.
THAT'LL PROBABLY CALM THE JIZO THAT ARE HAUNTING HER.
KEI.
YOUR SPIRITUAL AWARENESS ISN'T A BAD THING.
IT CAN PROTECT YOU AND YOUR FRIENDS.
IT'S NOTHING TO BE ASHAMED OF.
AND IF ANYTHING EVER HAPPENS, YOU CAN COME TO ME ABOUT IT.
I WILL.
THANKS, GRANDMA.

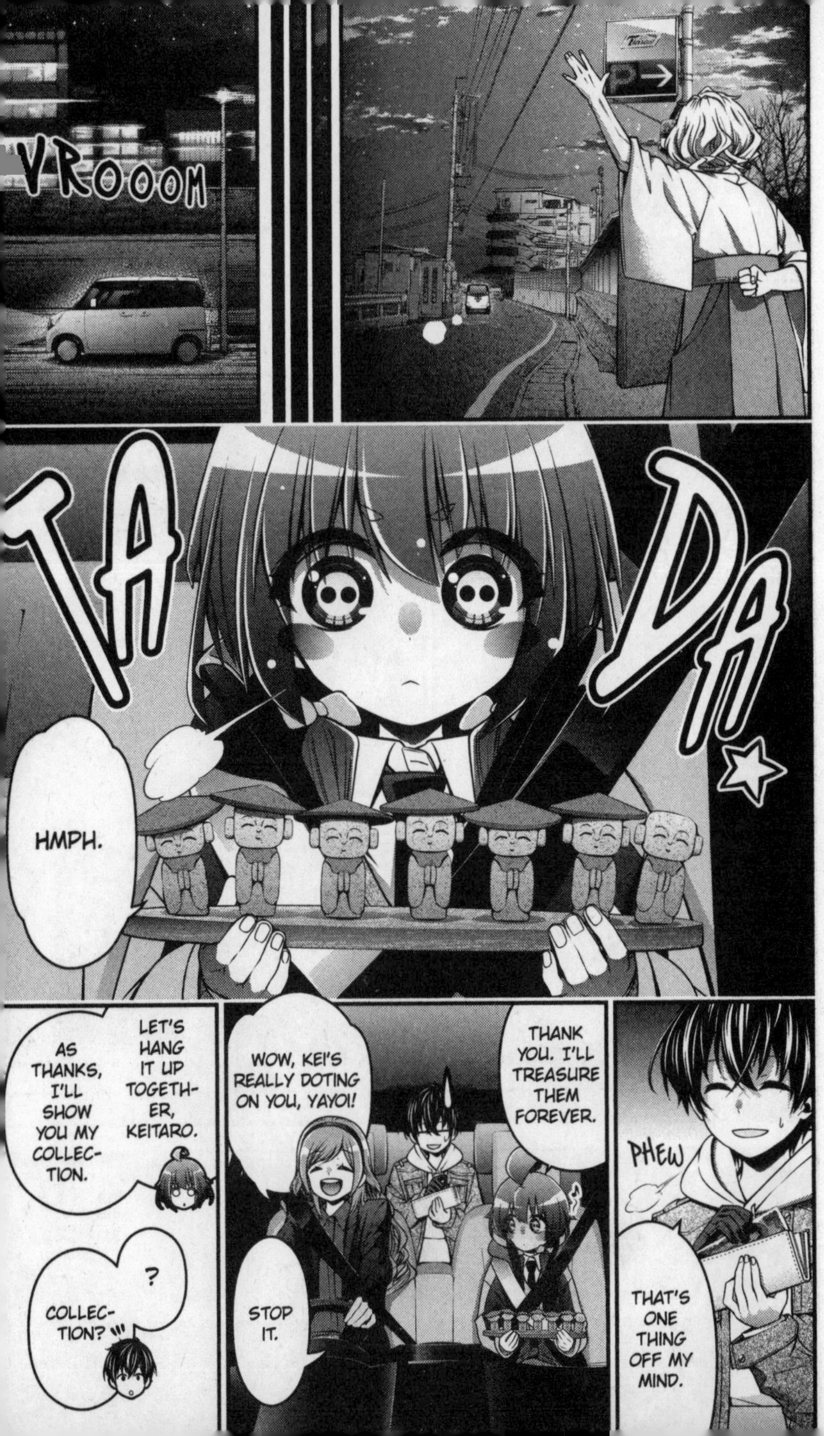
VROOOM
TA DA
HMPH.
PHEW
THAT'S ONE THING OFF MY MIND.
THANK YOU. I'LL TREASURE THEM FOREVER.
WOW, KEI'S REALLY DOTING ON YOU, YAYOI!
STOP IT.
LET'S HANG IT UP TOGETH-ER, KEITARO.
AS THANKS, I'LL SHOW YOU MY COLLEC-TION.
?
COLLEC-TION?

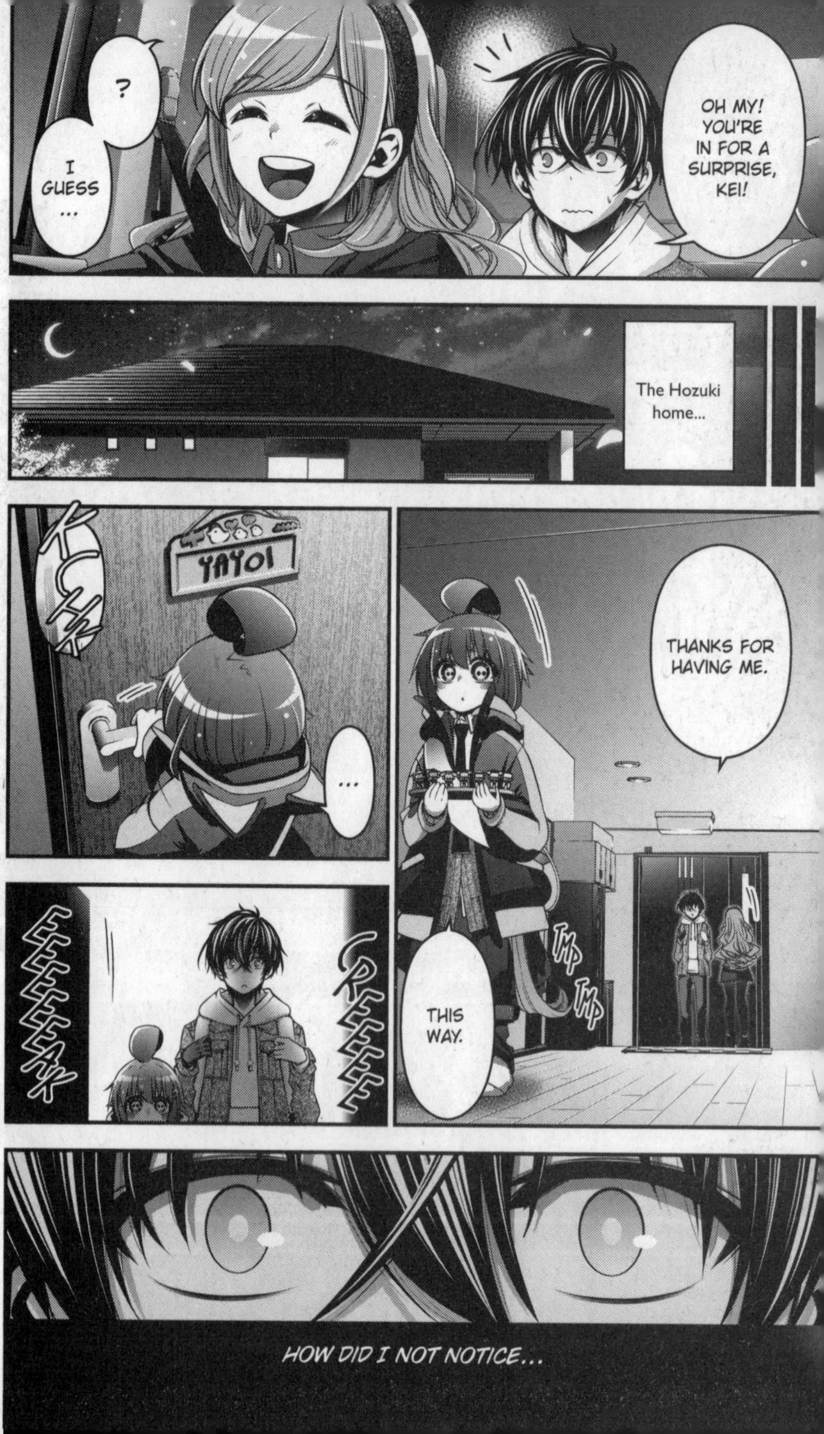
OH MY! YOU'RE IN FOR A SURPRISE, KEI!
?
I GUESS ...
The Hozuki home...
THANKS FOR HAVING ME.
TMP TMP
THIS WAY.
KCHK
...
CREEEEE
EEEEEEAK
HOW DID I NOT NOTICE...

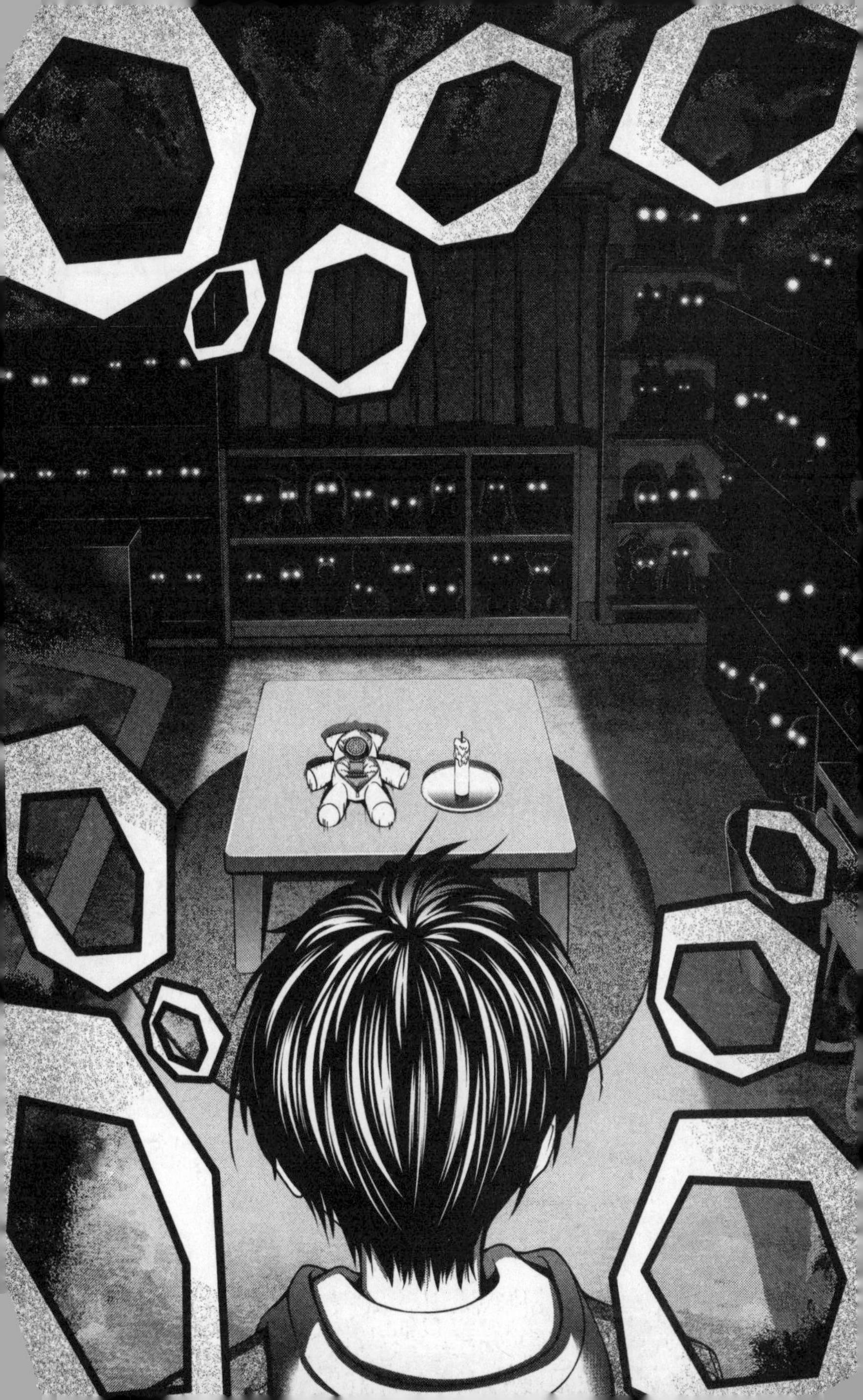

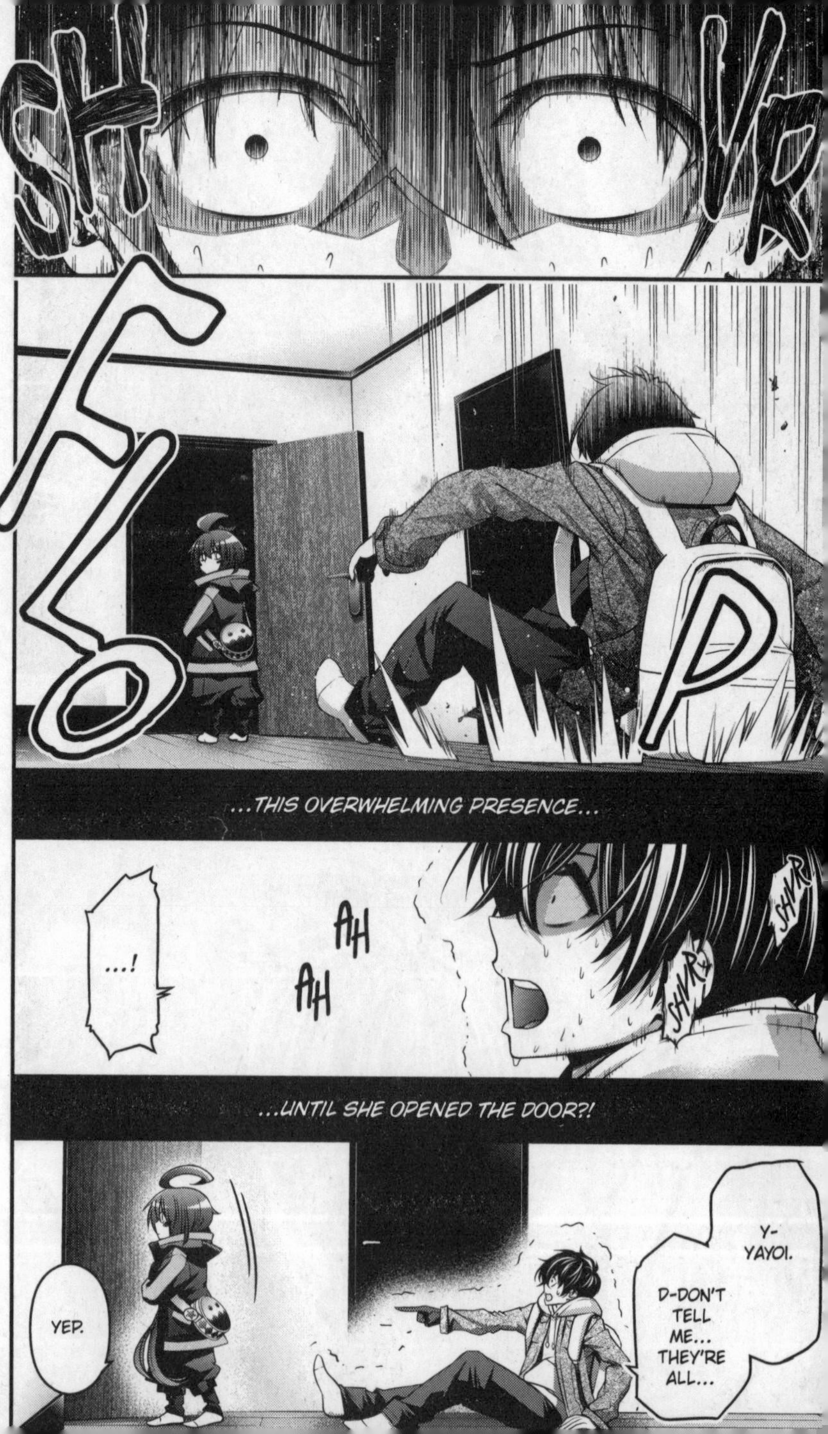
SHVR
FLOP
...THIS OVERWHELMING PRESENCE...
SHVR
SHVR
AH AH
...!
...UNTIL SHE OPENED THE DOOR?!
Y-YAYOI.
D-DON'T TELL ME... THEY'RE ALL...
YEP.

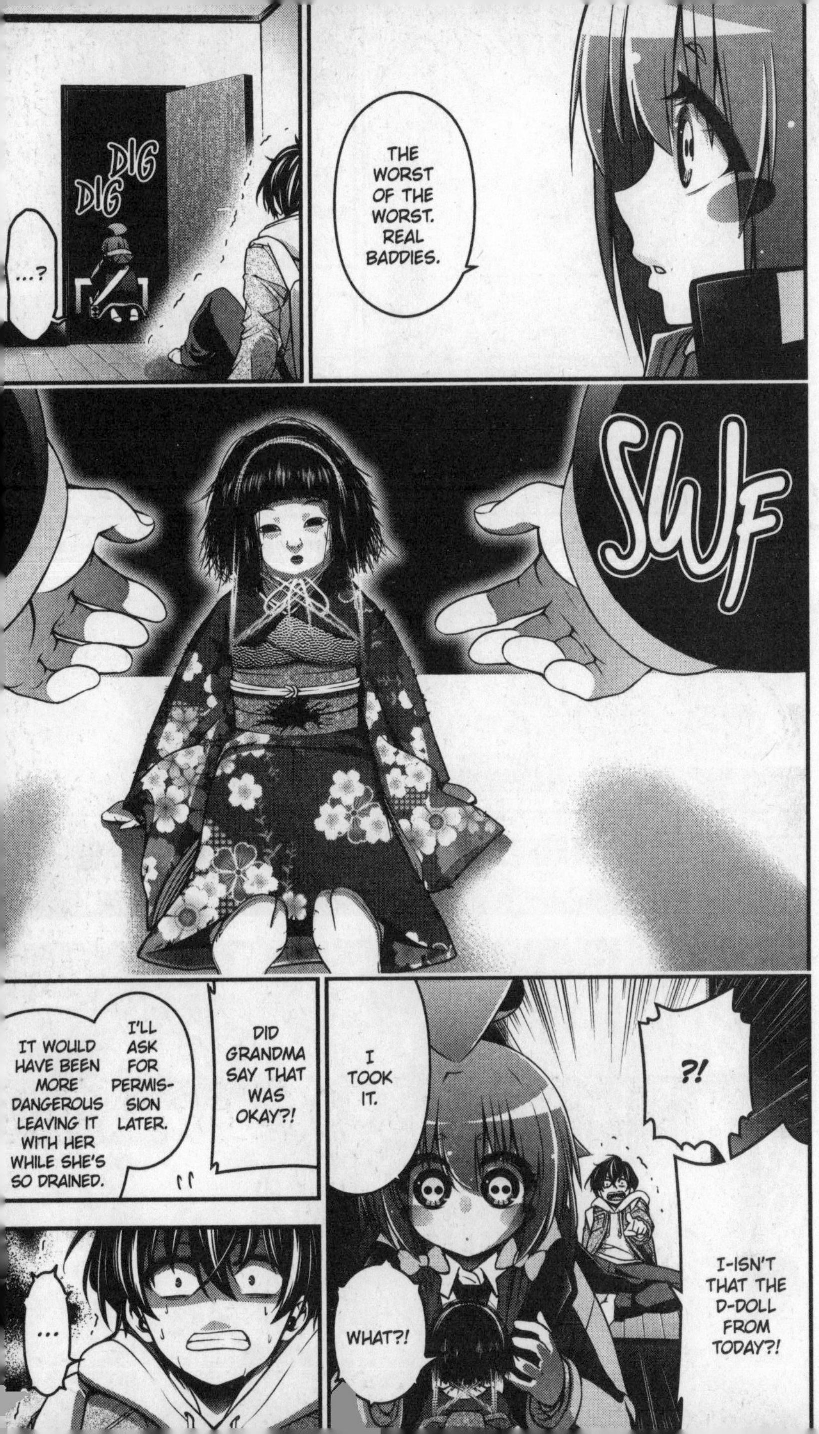
THE WORST OF THE WORST. REAL BADDIES.
DIG DIG
...?
SWF
?!
I-ISN'T THAT THE D-DOLL FROM TODAY?!
I TOOK IT.
WHAT?!
DID GRANDMA SAY THAT WAS OKAY?!
I'LL ASK FOR PERMIS-SION LATER.
IT WOULD HAVE BEEN MORE DANGEROUS LEAVING IT WITH HER WHILE SHE'S SO DRAINED.
...

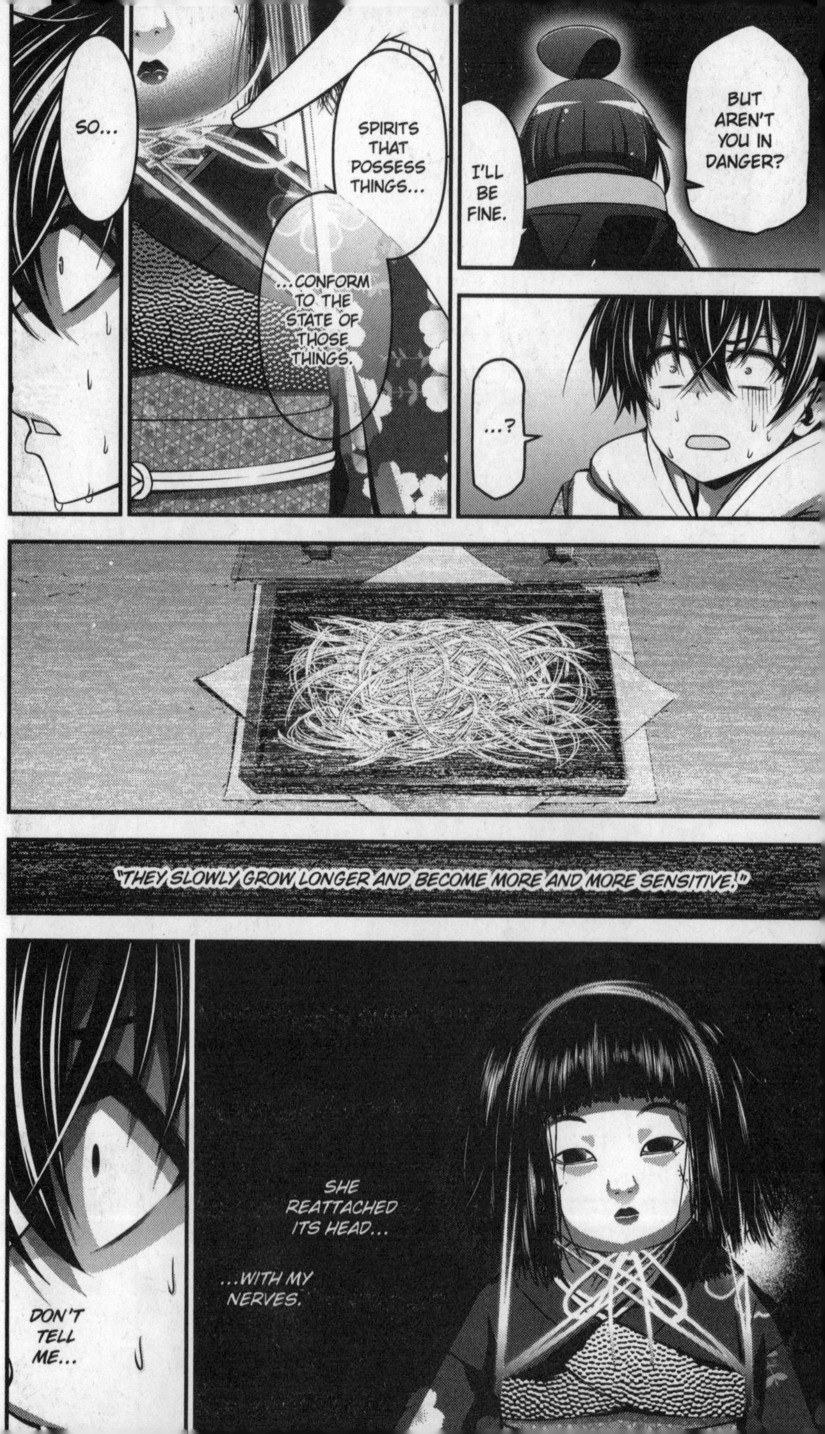
BUT AREN'T YOU IN DANGER?
I'LL BE FINE.
...?
SPIRITS THAT POSSESS THINGS...
...CONFORM TO THE STATE OF THOSE THINGS.
SO...
"THEY SLOWLY GROW LONGER AND BECOME MORE AND MORE SENSITIVE."
SHE REATTACHED ITS HEAD...
...WITH MY NERVES.
DON'T TELL ME...

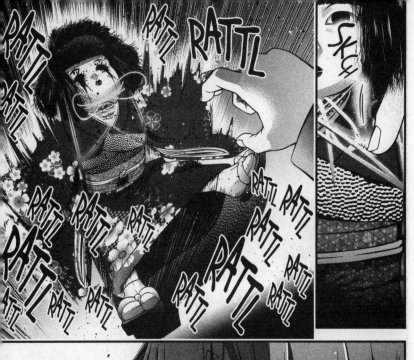

RATTL RATTL RATTL RATTL RATTL

SKCH

RATTI RATTI RATTI RATTI RATTI RATTI RATTI RATTI RATTI RATTI RATTI

SEE? IT'S SYNCHRONIZED.

I'M ALREADY REGRETTING...

...SAYING THAT I SHOULD MEET THIS GIRL ON HER LEVEL.

ZSSH

...!

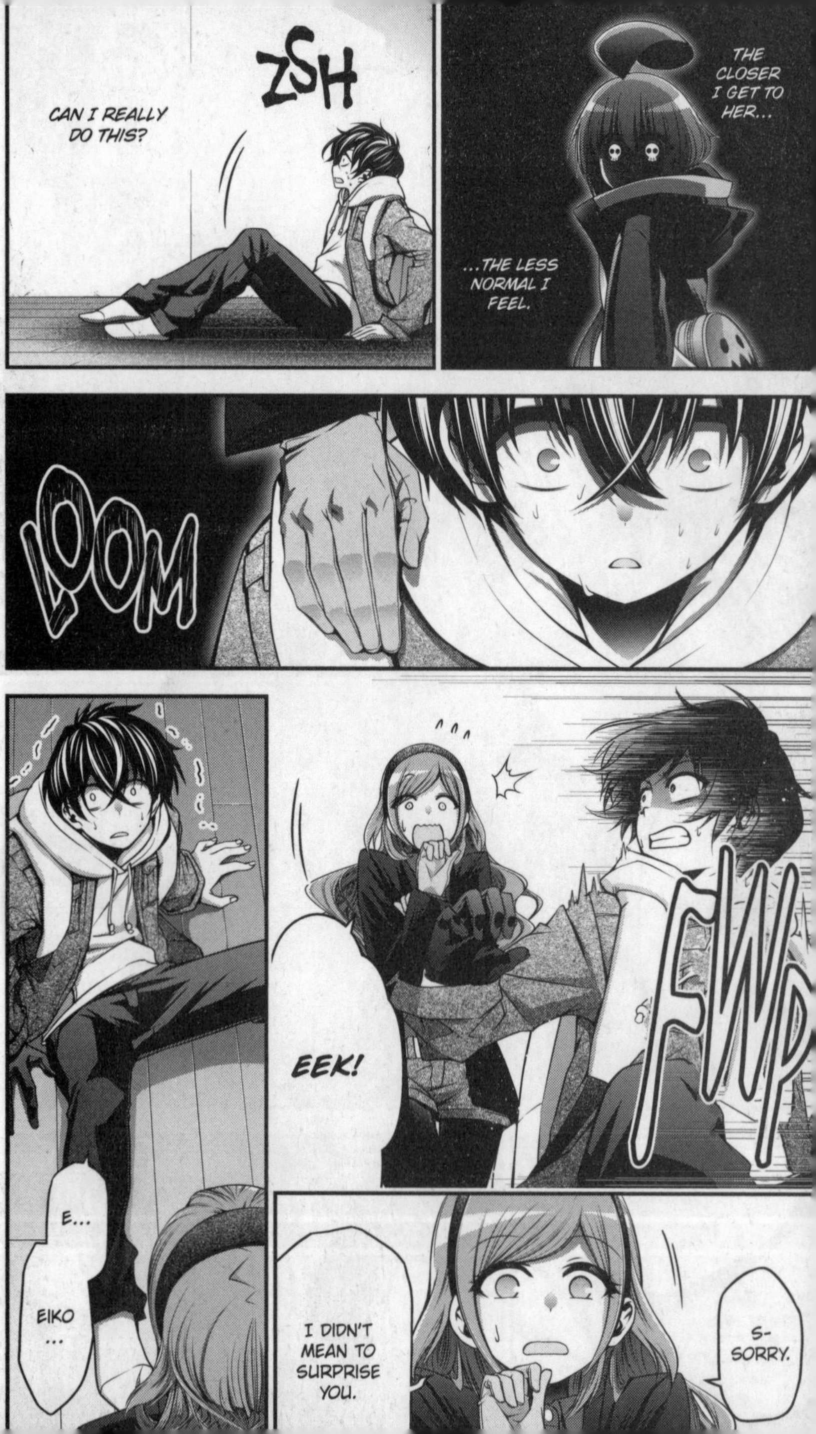

THE CLOSER I GET TO HER...
...THE LESS NORMAL I FEEL.
ZSH
CAN I REALLY DO THIS?
LOOM
FWP
EEK!
S-SORRY.
I DIDN'T MEAN TO SURPRISE YOU.
E...
EIKO...

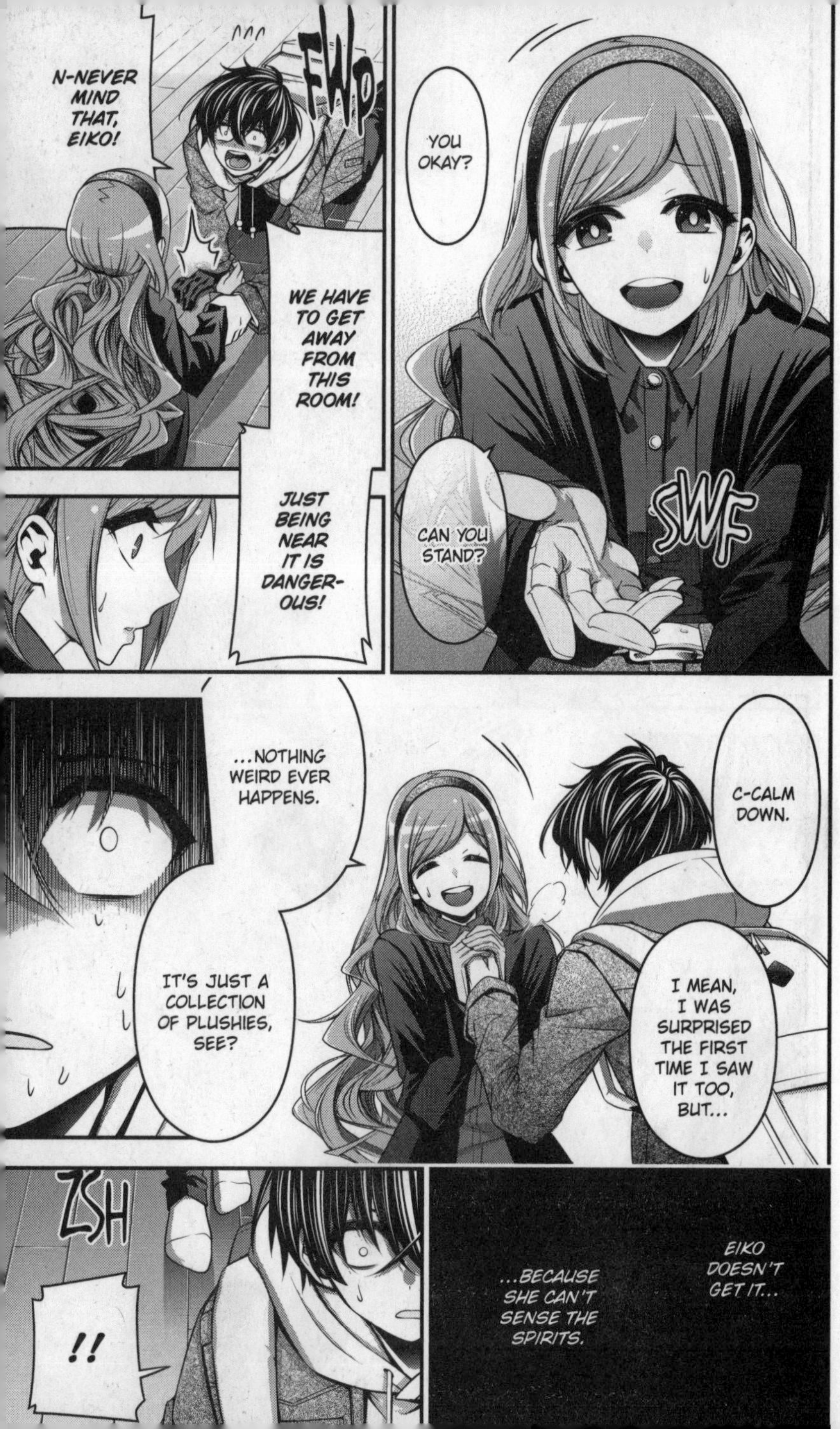
YOU OKAY?
SWF
CAN YOU STAND?
FWP
N-NEVER MIND THAT, EIKO!
WE HAVE TO GET AWAY FROM THIS ROOM!
JUST BEING NEAR IT IS DANGER-OUS!
C-CALM DOWN.
I MEAN, I WAS SURPRISED THE FIRST TIME I SAW IT TOO, BUT...
...NOTHING WEIRD EVER HAPPENS.
IT'S JUST A COLLECTION OF PLUSHIES, SEE?
EIKO DOESN'T GET IT...
...BECAUSE SHE CAN'T SENSE THE SPIRITS.
ZSH
!!

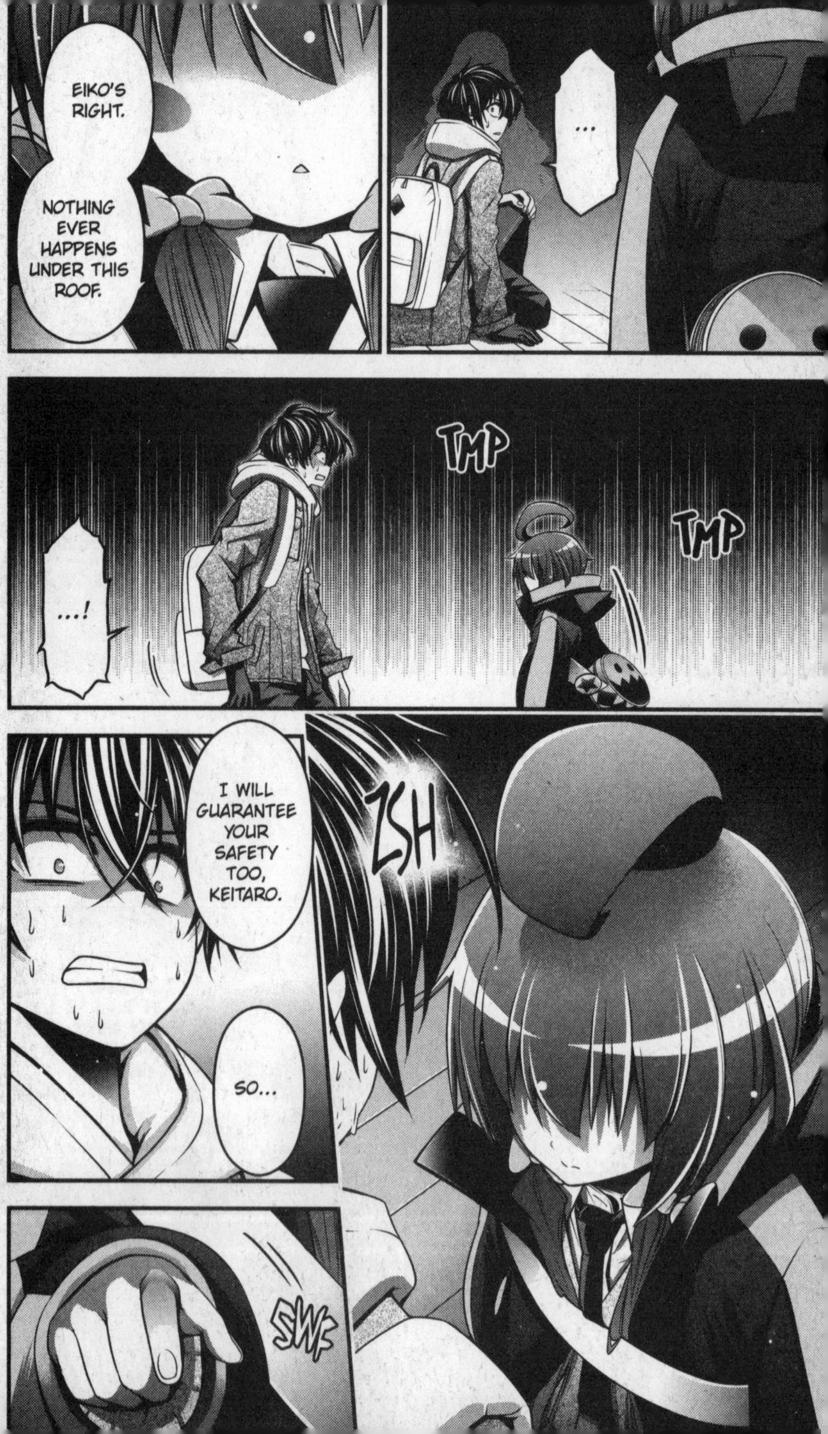
...
EIKO'S RIGHT.
NOTHING EVER HAPPENS UNDER THIS ROOF.
TMP
TMP
...!
ZSH
I WILL GUARANTEE YOUR SAFETY TOO, KEITARO.
SO...
SWF

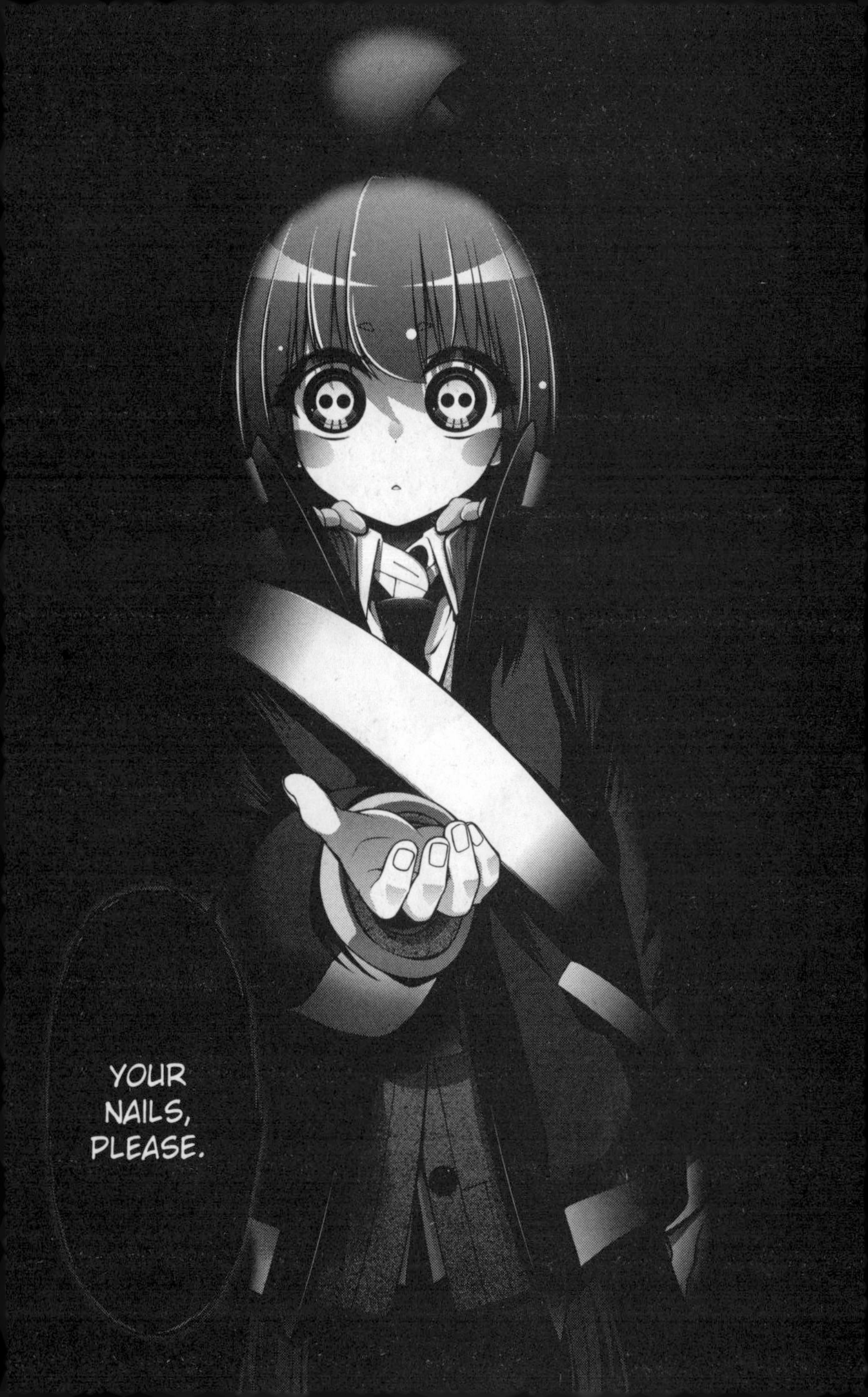
YOUR NAILS, PLEASE.

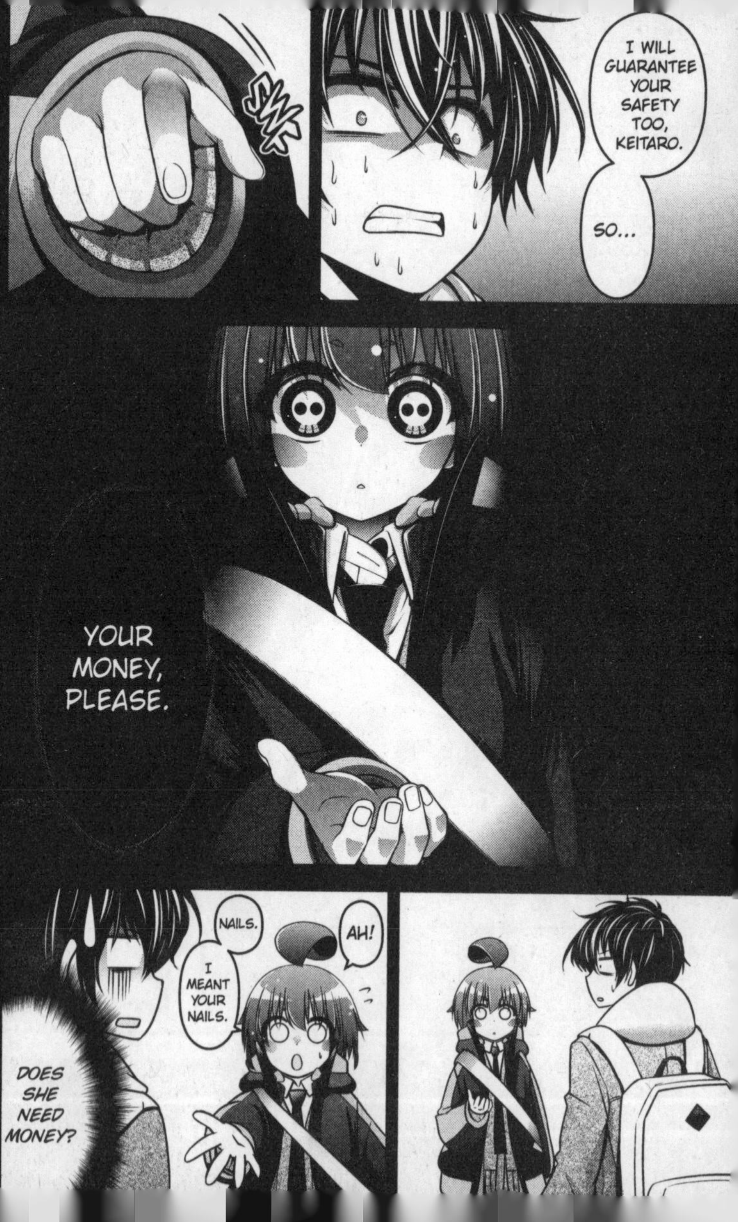
I WILL GUARANTEE YOUR SAFETY TOO, KEITARO.
SO...
SWK
YOUR MONEY, PLEASE.
AH!
NAILS.
I MEANT YOUR NAILS.
DOES SHE NEED MONEY?

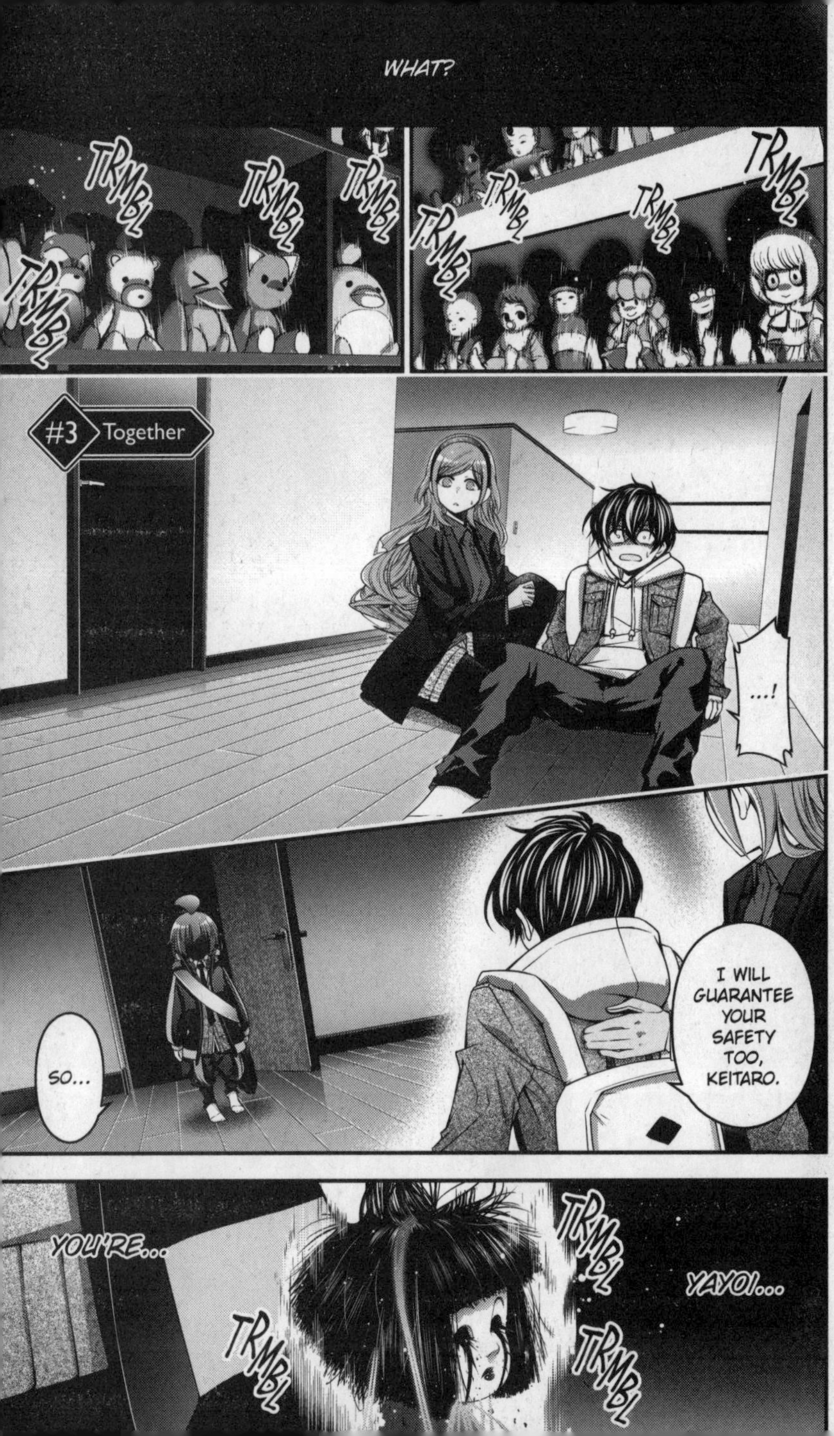
WHAT?
TRMBL
TRMBL
TRMBL
TRMBL
TRMBL
TRMBL
TRMBL
TRMBL
#3 Together
...!
I WILL GUARANTEE YOUR SAFETY TOO, KEITARO.
SO...
TRMBL
YOU'RE...
YAYOI...
TRMBL
TRMBL

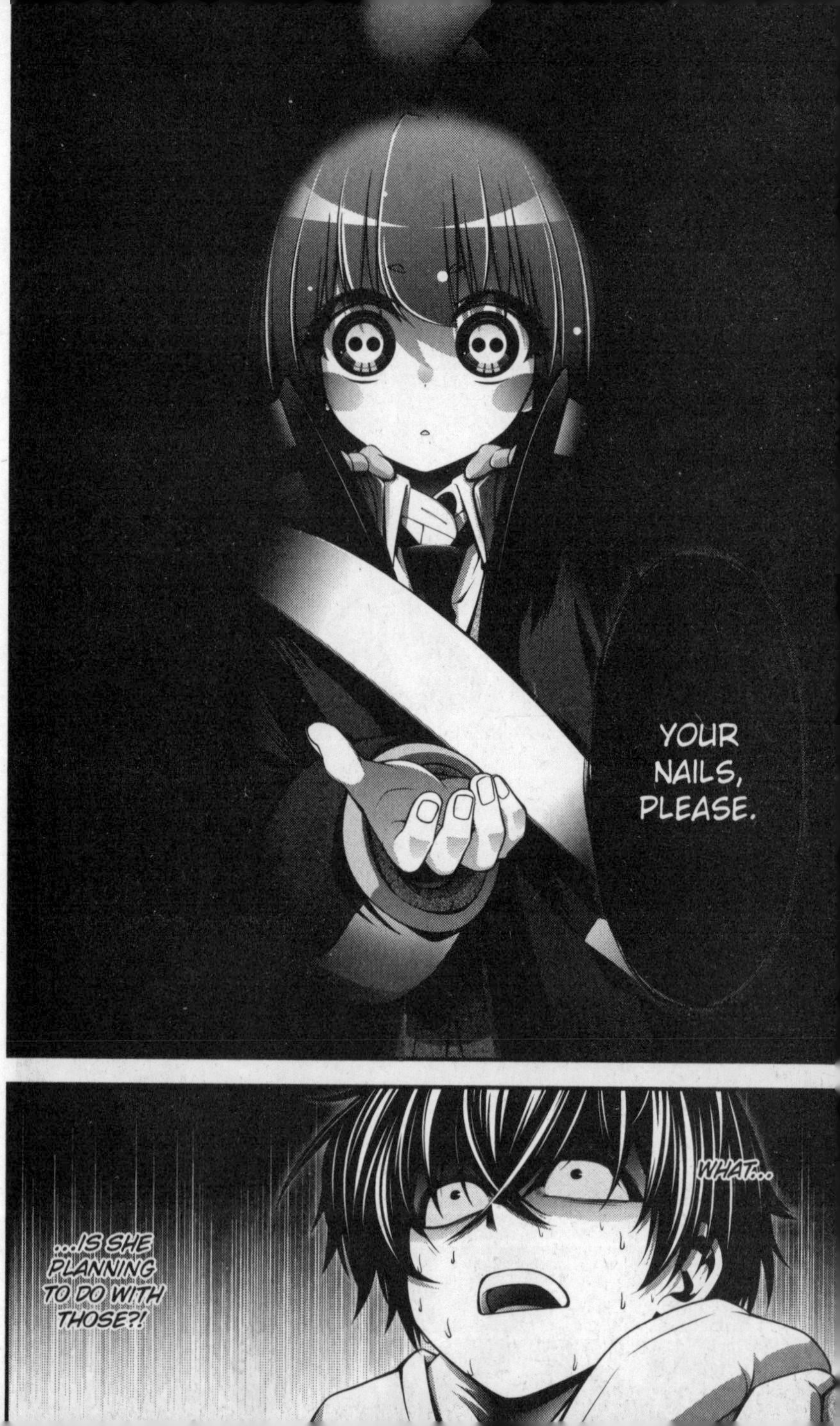
YOUR NAILS, PLEASE.
WHAT...
...IS SHE PLANNING TO DO WITH THOSE?!

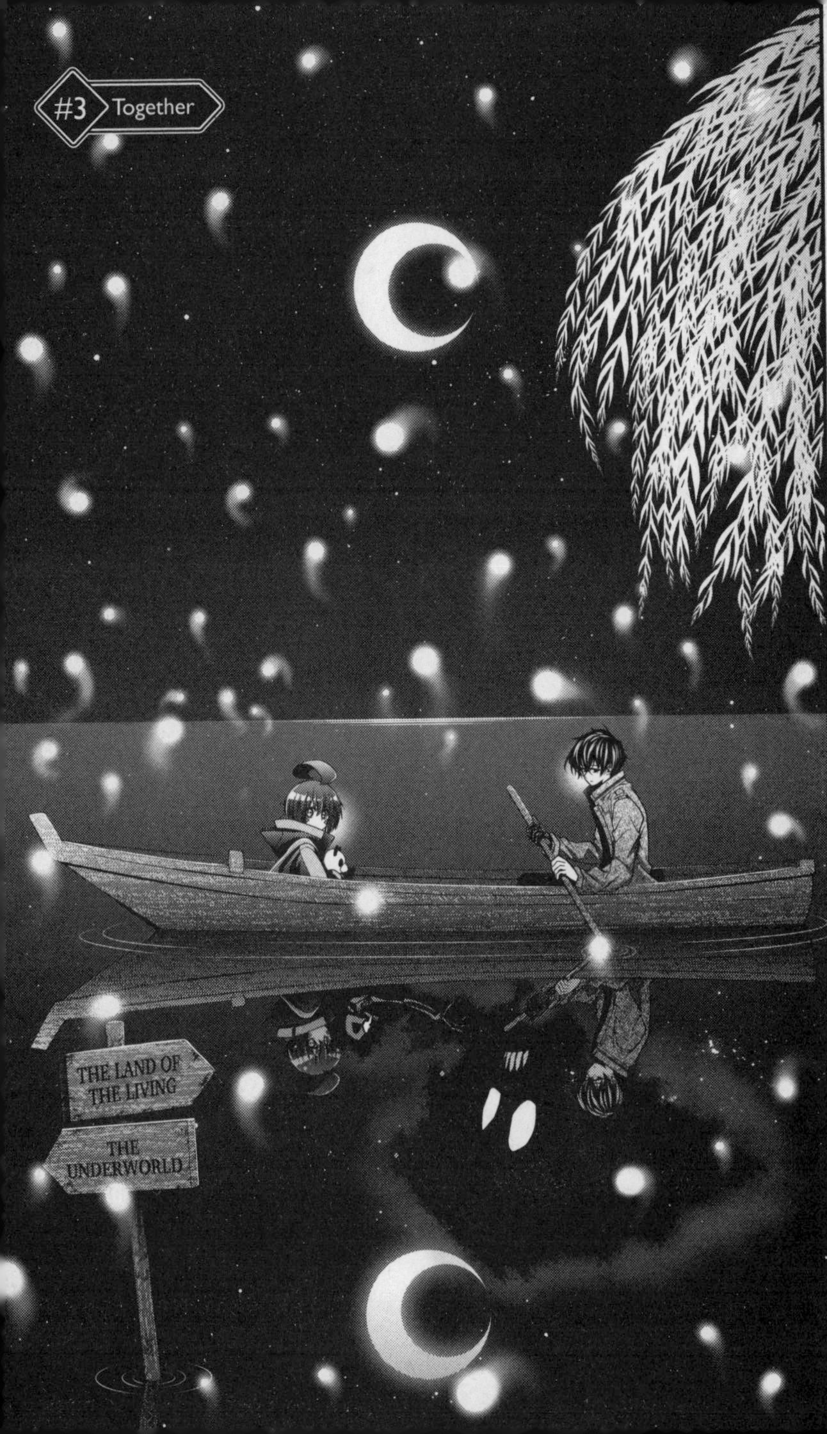
#3 Together
THE LAND OF THE LIVING
THE UNDERWORLD

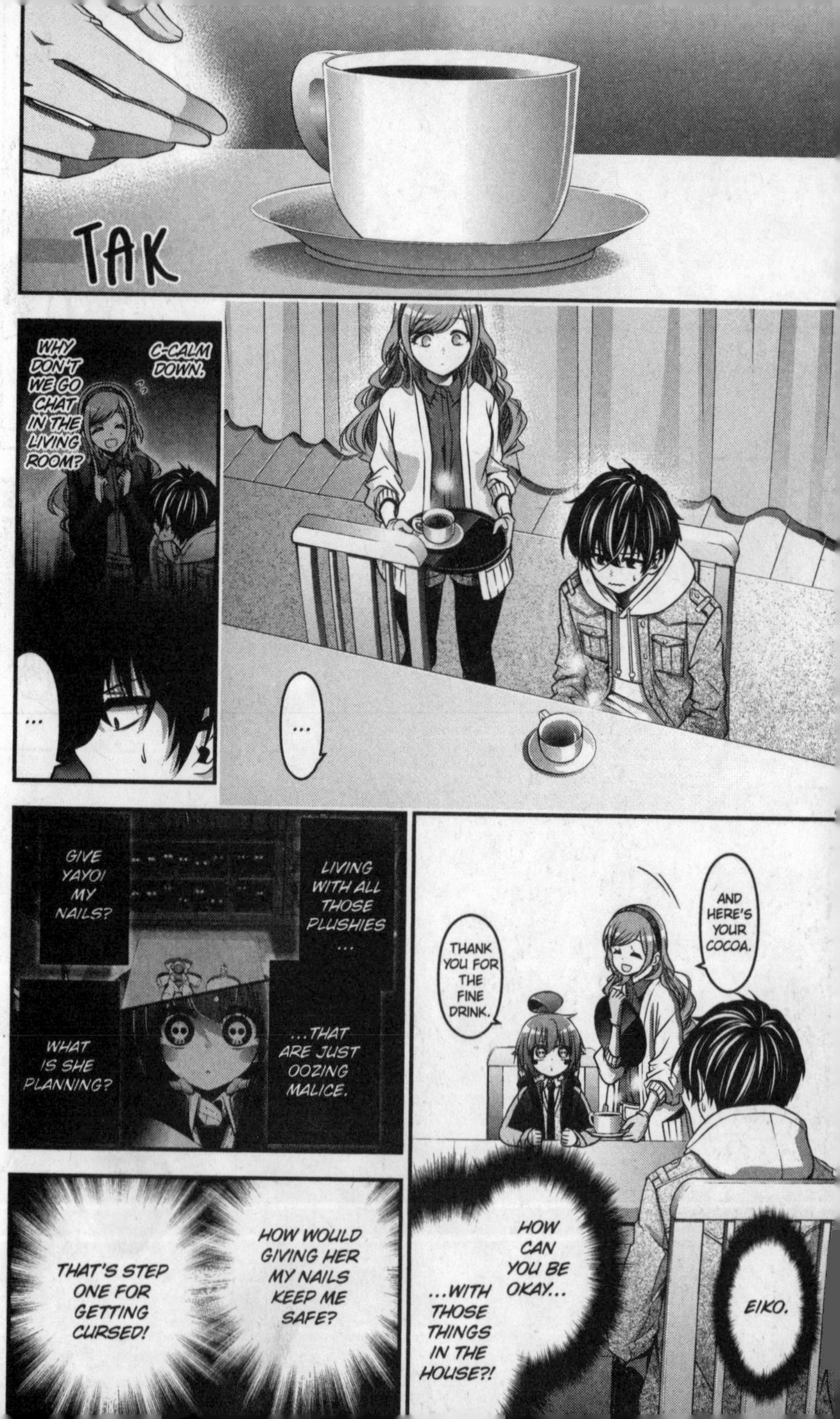
TAK
...
C-CALM DOWN.
WHY DON'T WE GO CHAT IN THE LIVING ROOM?
...
AND HERE'S YOUR COCOA.
THANK YOU FOR THE FINE DRINK.
EIKO.
HOW CAN YOU BE OKAY...
...WITH THOSE THINGS IN THE HOUSE?!
LIVING WITH ALL THOSE PLUSHIES...
...THAT ARE JUST OOZING MALICE.
GIVE YAYOI MY NAILS?
WHAT IS SHE PLANNING?
HOW WOULD GIVING HER MY NAILS KEEP ME SAFE?
THAT'S STEP ONE FOR GETTING CURSED!

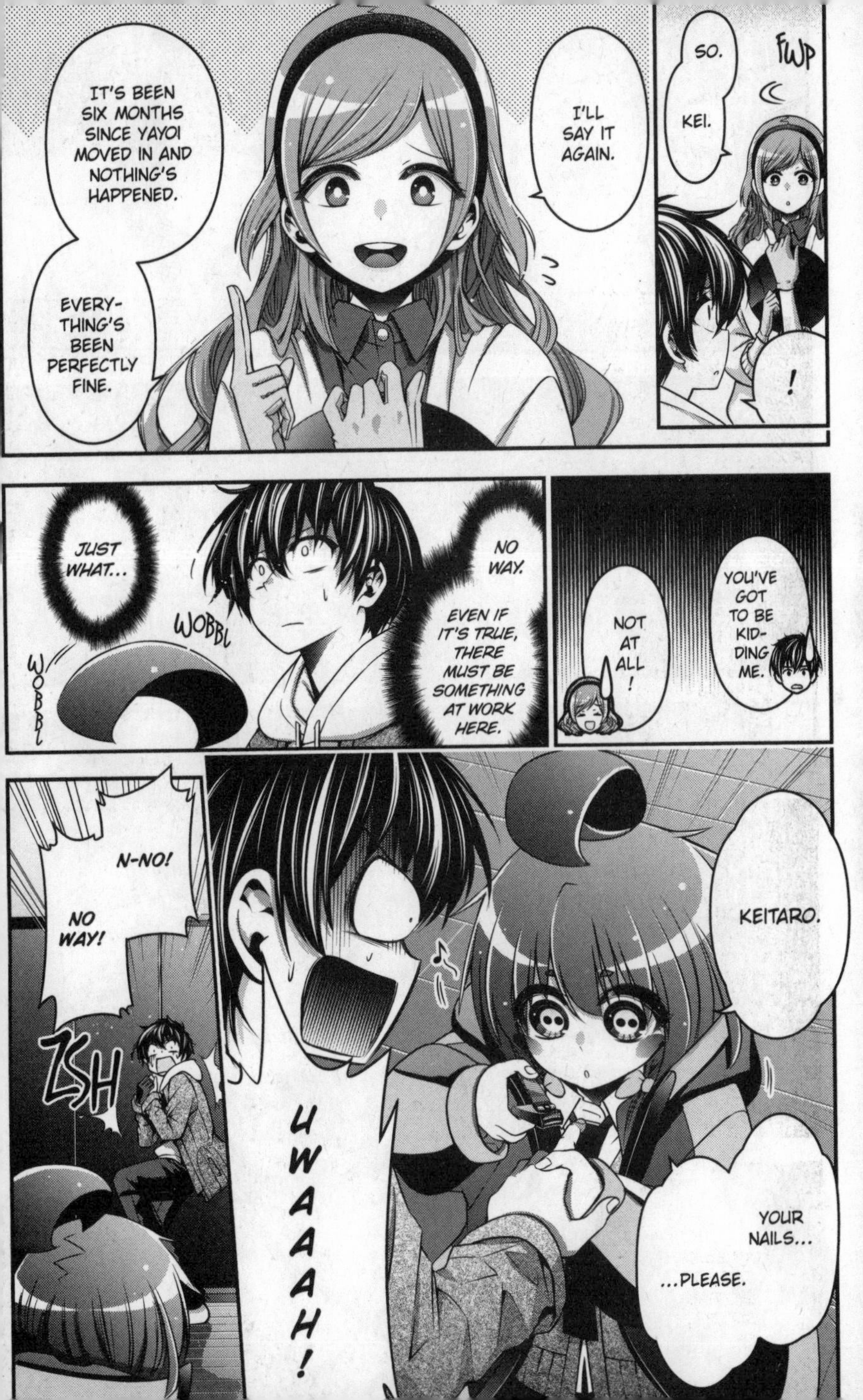
SO.
FWP
KEI.
!
I'LL SAY IT AGAIN.
IT'S BEEN SIX MONTHS SINCE YAYOI MOVED IN AND NOTHING'S HAPPENED.
EVERYTHING'S BEEN PERFECTLY FINE.
YOU'VE GOT TO BE KIDDING ME.
NOT AT ALL!
NO WAY.
EVEN IF IT'S TRUE, THERE MUST BE SOMETHING AT WORK HERE.
JUST WHAT...
WOBBL
WOBBL
KEITARO.
YOUR NAILS...
...PLEASE.
UWAAAAH!
N-NO!
NO WAY!
ZSH

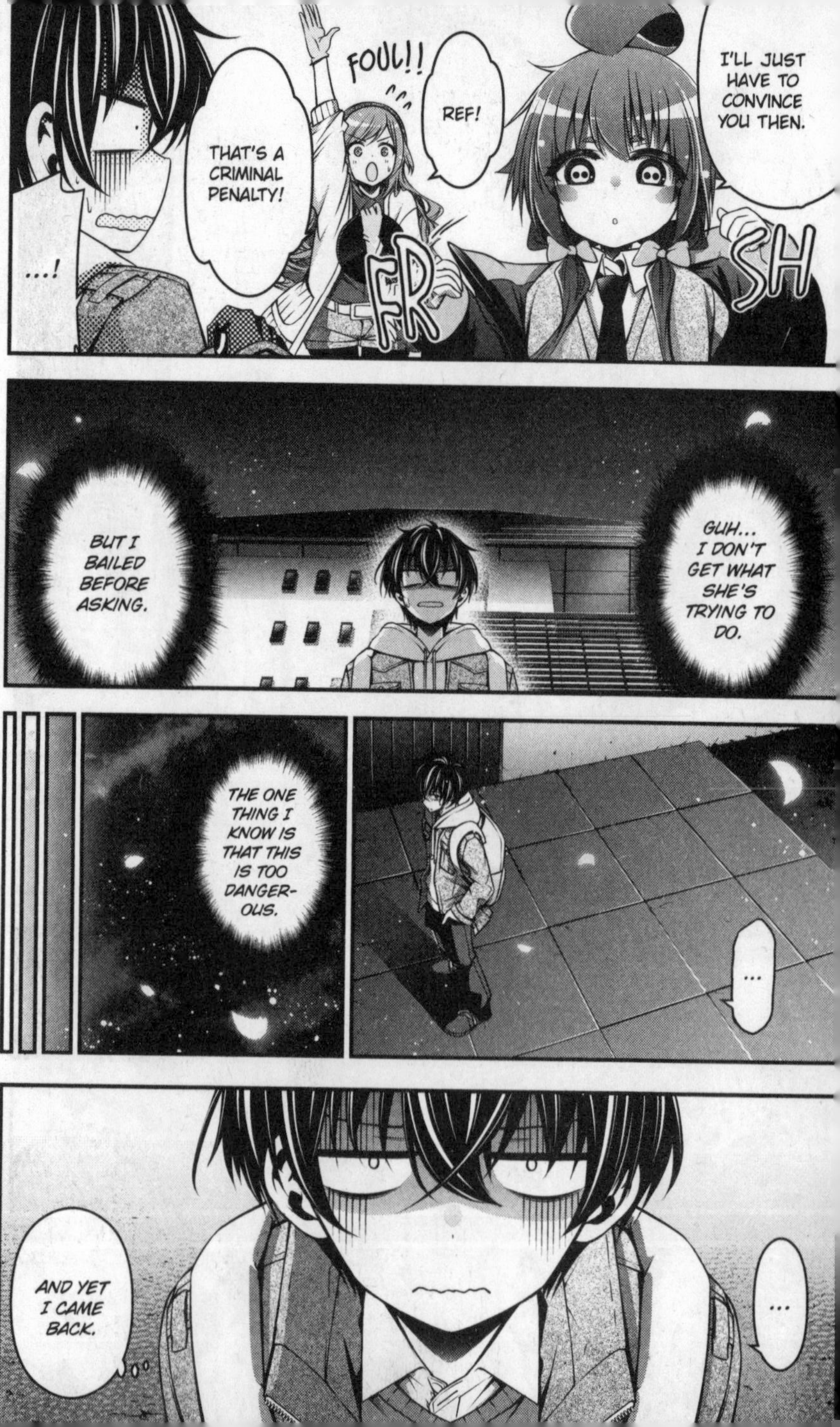
I'LL JUST HAVE TO CONVINCE YOU THEN.
FRSH
REF!
FOUL!!
THAT'S A CRIMINAL PENALTY!
...!
GUH... I DON'T GET WHAT SHE'S TRYING TO DO.
BUT I BAILED BEFORE ASKING.
...
THE ONE THING I KNOW IS THAT THIS IS TOO DANGER-OUS.
...
AND YET I CAME BACK.

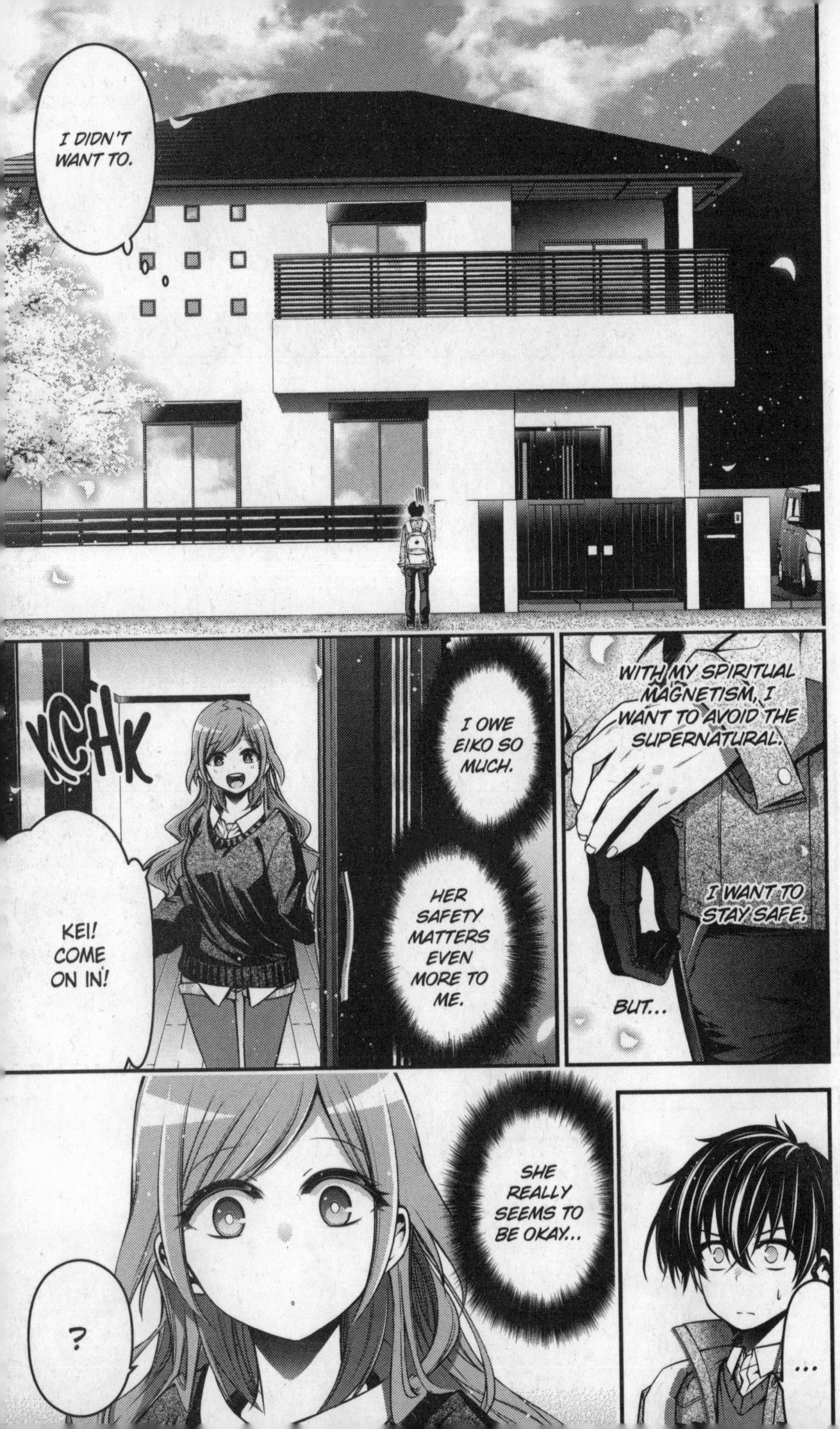
I DIDN'T WANT TO.
WITH MY SPIRITUAL MAGNETISM, I WANT TO AVOID THE SUPERNATURAL.
I WANT TO STAY SAFE.
BUT...
I OWE EIKO SO MUCH.
HER SAFETY MATTERS EVEN MORE TO ME.
KCHK
KEI! COME ON IN!
...
SHE REALLY SEEMS TO BE OKAY...
?

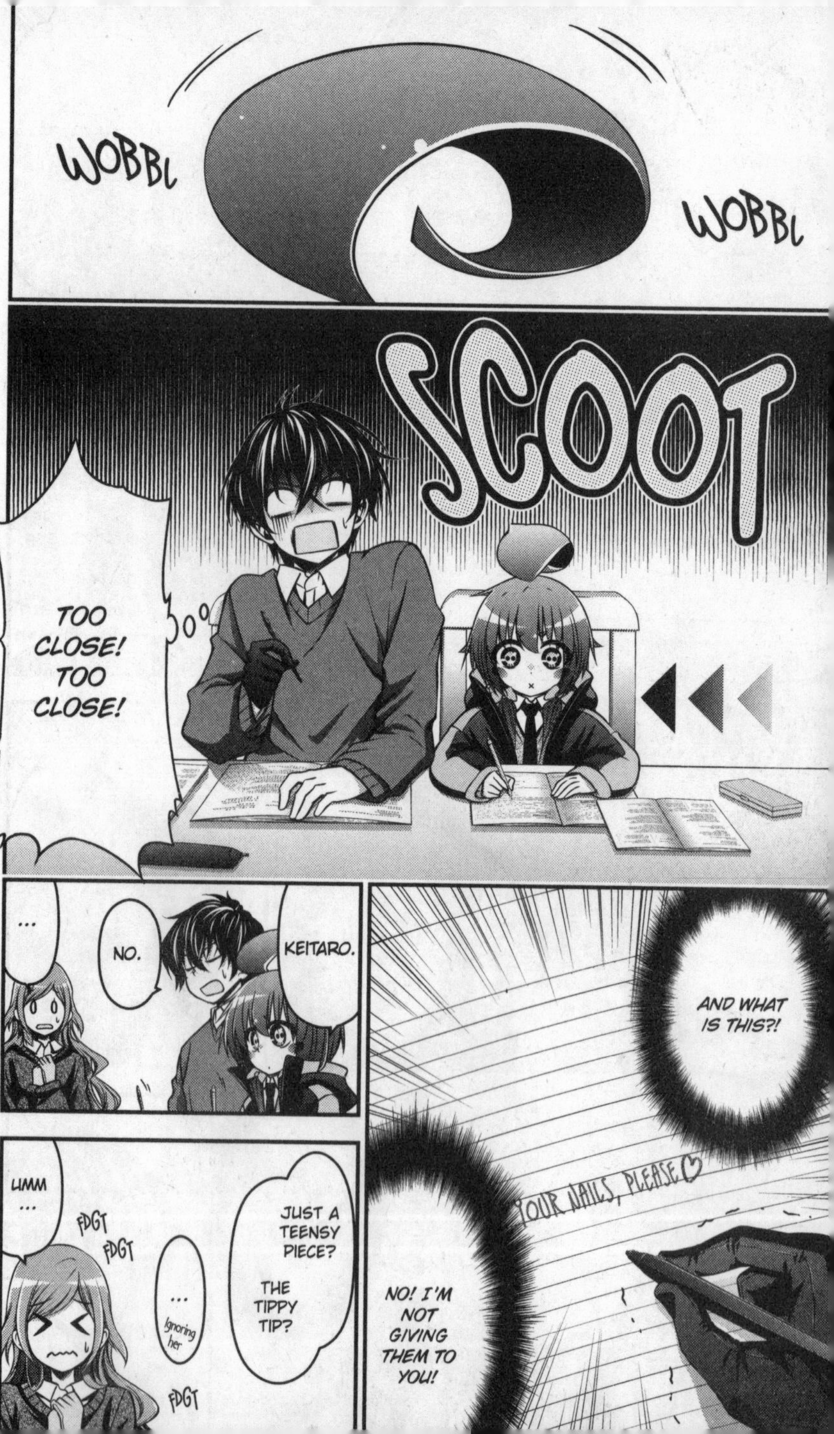
WOBBL
WOBBL
SCOOT
TOO CLOSE! TOO CLOSE!
AND WHAT IS THIS?!
YOUR NAILS, PLEASE
NO! I'M NOT GIVING THEM TO YOU!
KEITARO.
NO.
...
JUST A TEENSY PIECE?
THE TIPPY TIP?
...
Ignoring her
UMM ...
FDGT
FDGT
FDGT

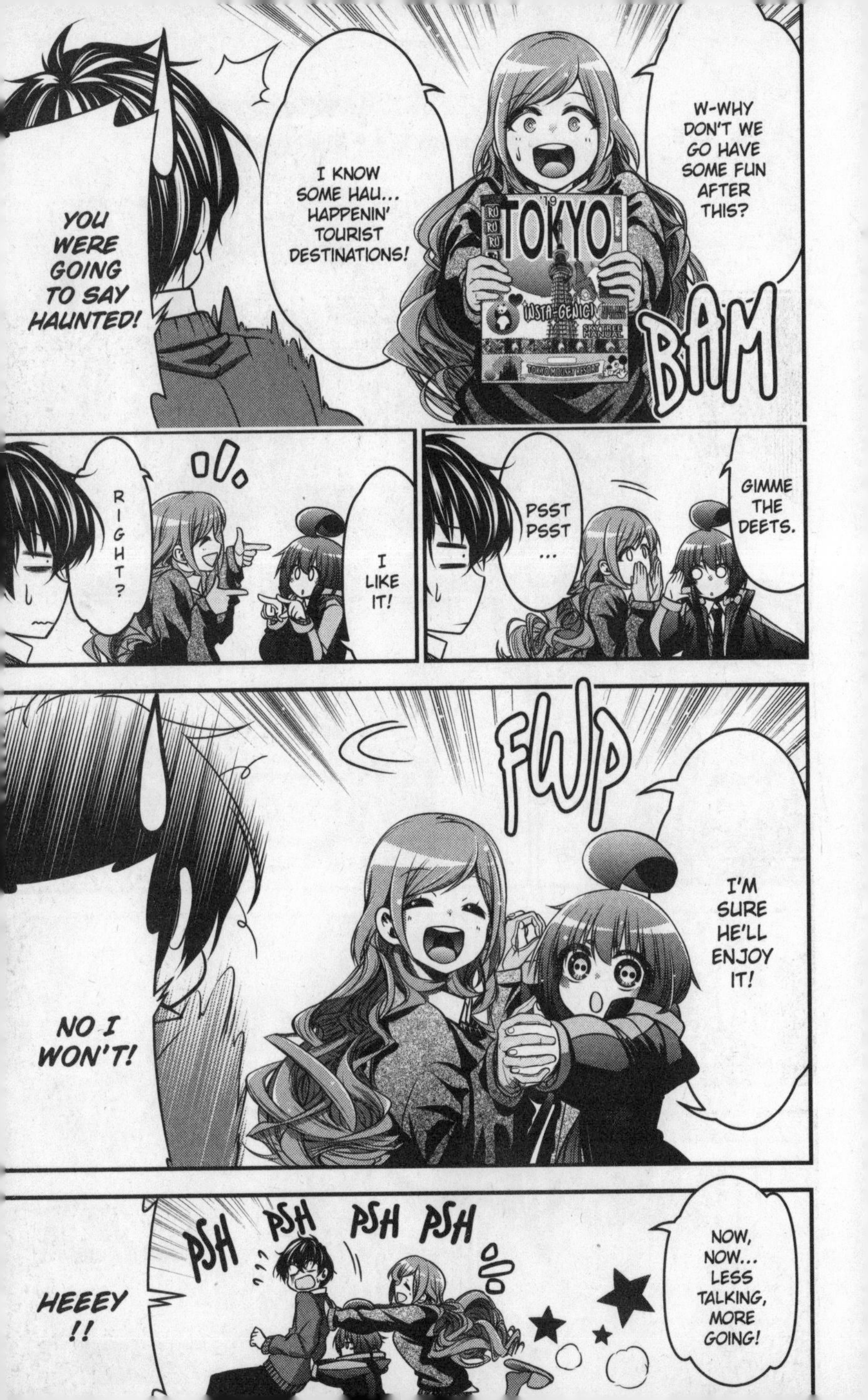
W-WHY DON'T WE GO HAVE SOME FUN AFTER THIS?
BAM
'19
TOKYO
INSTA-GENIC!
SKYTREE MANUAL
TOKYO MOUSEY RESORT
I KNOW SOME HAU... HAPPENIN' TOURIST DESTINATIONS!
YOU WERE GOING TO SAY HAUNTED!
GIMME THE DEETS.
PSST PSST ...
I LIKE IT!
RIGHT?
FWP
I'M SURE HE'LL ENJOY IT!
NO I WON'T!
NOW, NOW... LESS TALKING, MORE GOING!
PSH PSH PSH PSH
HEEEY!!

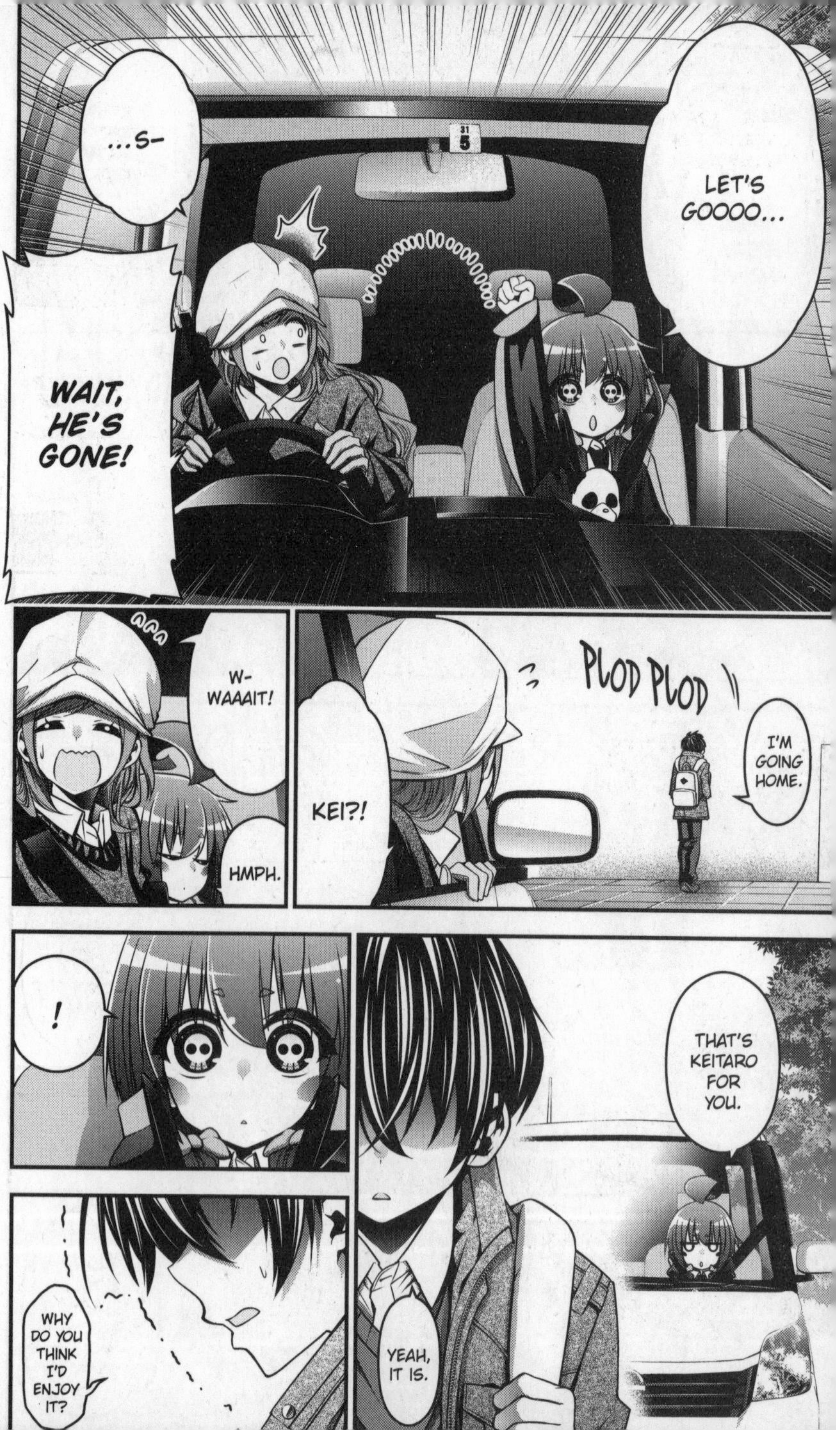
LET'S GOOOO...
...S-
WAIT, HE'S GONE!
PLOD PLOD
I'M GOING HOME.
KEI?!
W-WAAAIT!
HMPH.
THAT'S KEITARO FOR YOU.
YEAH, IT IS.
!
WHY DO YOU THINK I'D ENJOY IT?

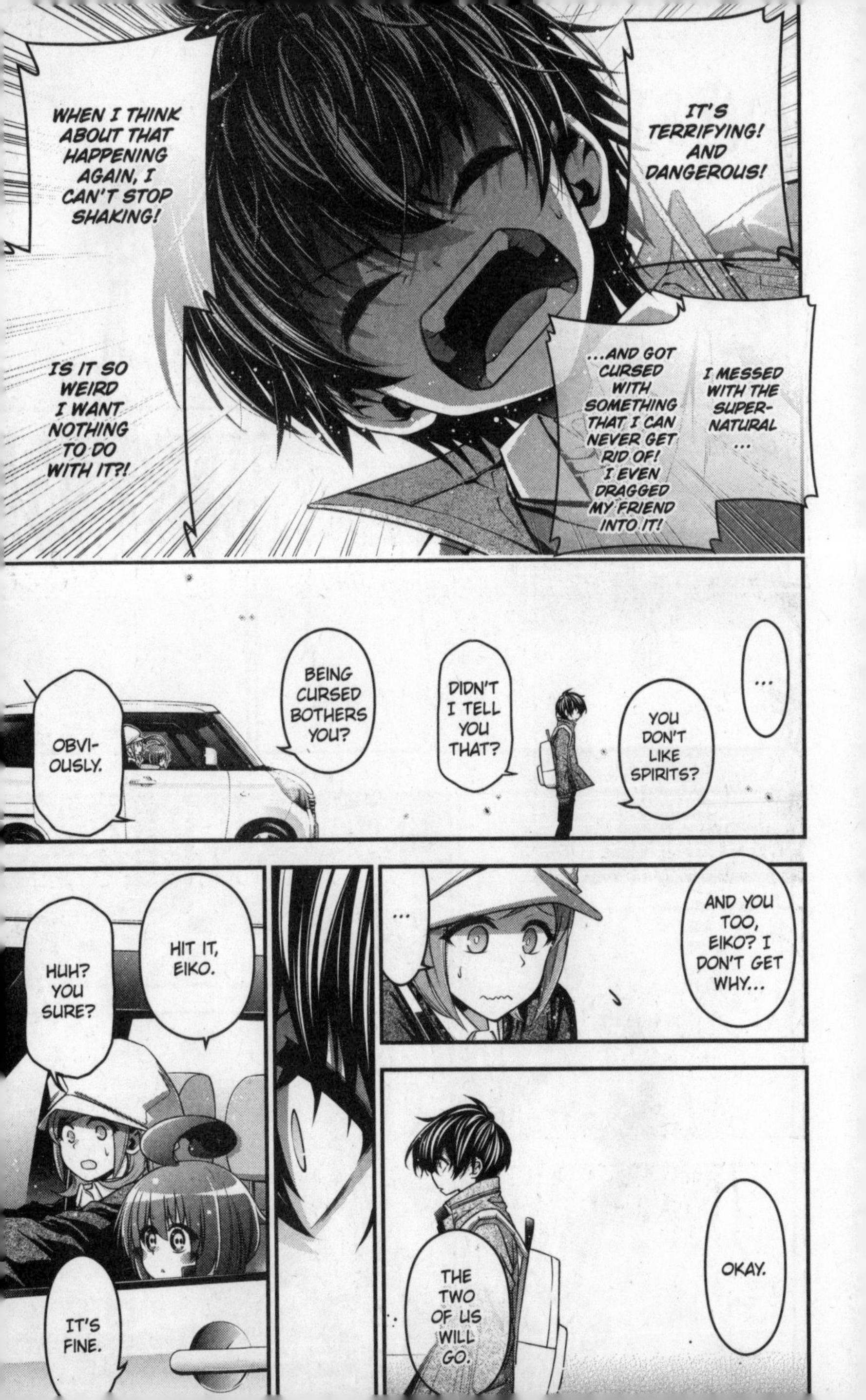
IT'S TERRIFYING! AND DANGEROUS!
WHEN I THINK ABOUT THAT HAPPENING AGAIN, I CAN'T STOP SHAKING!
I MESSED WITH THE SUPER-NATURAL ...
...AND GOT CURSED WITH SOMETHING THAT I CAN NEVER GET RID OF! I EVEN DRAGGED MY FRIEND INTO IT!
IS IT SO WEIRD I WANT NOTHING TO DO WITH IT?!
...
YOU DON'T LIKE SPIRITS?
DIDN'T I TELL YOU THAT?
BEING CURSED BOTHERS YOU?
OBVI-OUSLY.
AND YOU TOO, EIKO? I DON'T GET WHY...
...
OKAY.
THE TWO OF US WILL GO.
HIT IT, EIKO.
HUH? YOU SURE?
IT'S FINE.

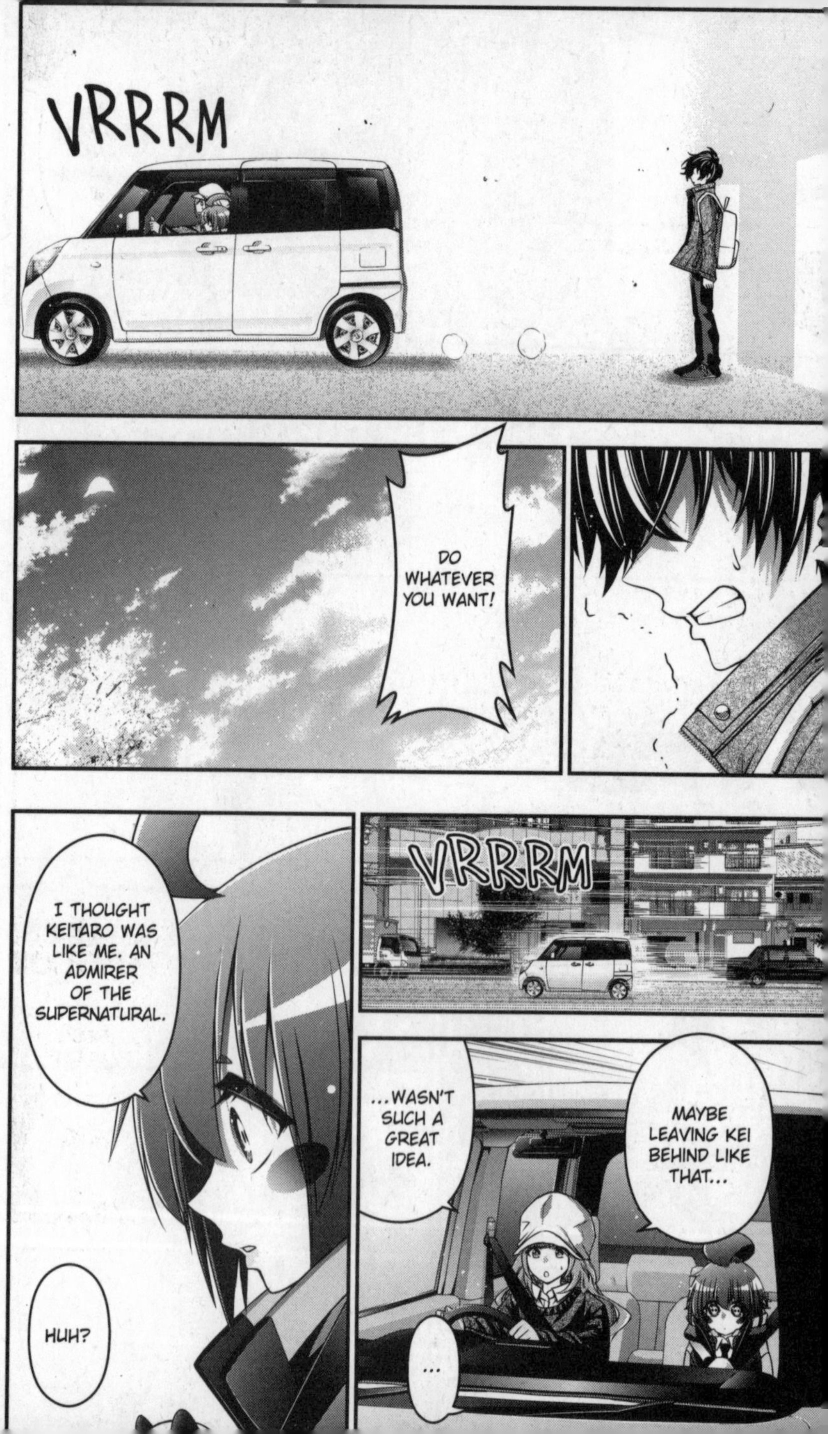
VRRRM
DO WHATEVER YOU WANT!
VRRRM
MAYBE LEAVING KEI BEHIND LIKE THAT...
...WASN'T SUCH A GREAT IDEA.
...
I THOUGHT KEITARO WAS LIKE ME. AN ADMIRER OF THE SUPERNATURAL.
HUH?

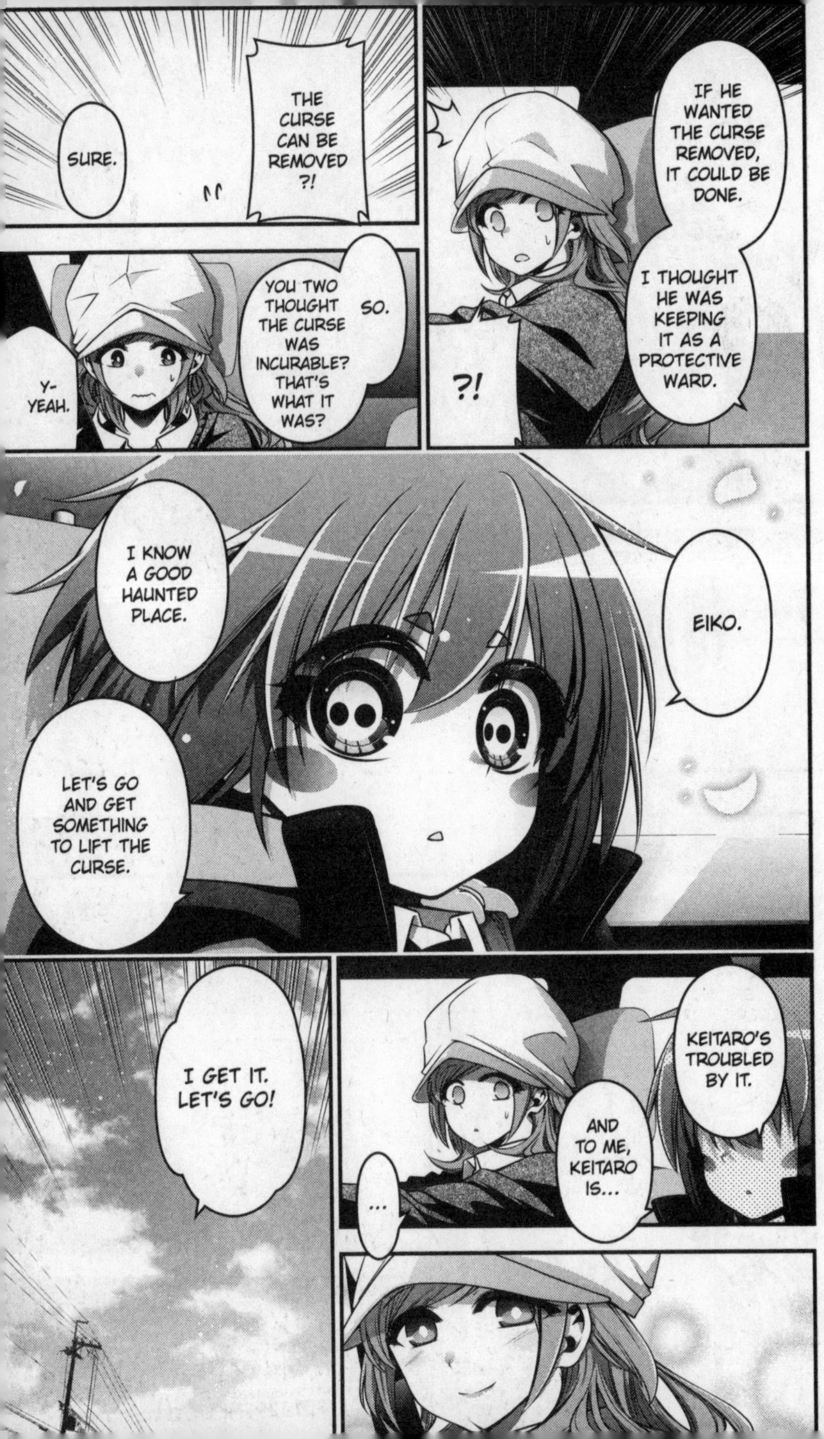
IF HE WANTED THE CURSE REMOVED, IT COULD BE DONE.
I THOUGHT HE WAS KEEPING IT AS A PROTECTIVE WARD.
?!
THE CURSE CAN BE REMOVED ?!
SURE.
SO.
YOU TWO THOUGHT THE CURSE WAS INCURABLE? THAT'S WHAT IT WAS?
Y- YEAH.
EIKO.
I KNOW A GOOD HAUNTED PLACE.
LET'S GO AND GET SOMETHING TO LIFT THE CURSE.
KEITARO'S TROUBLED BY IT.
AND TO ME, KEITARO IS...
...
I GET IT. LET'S GO!

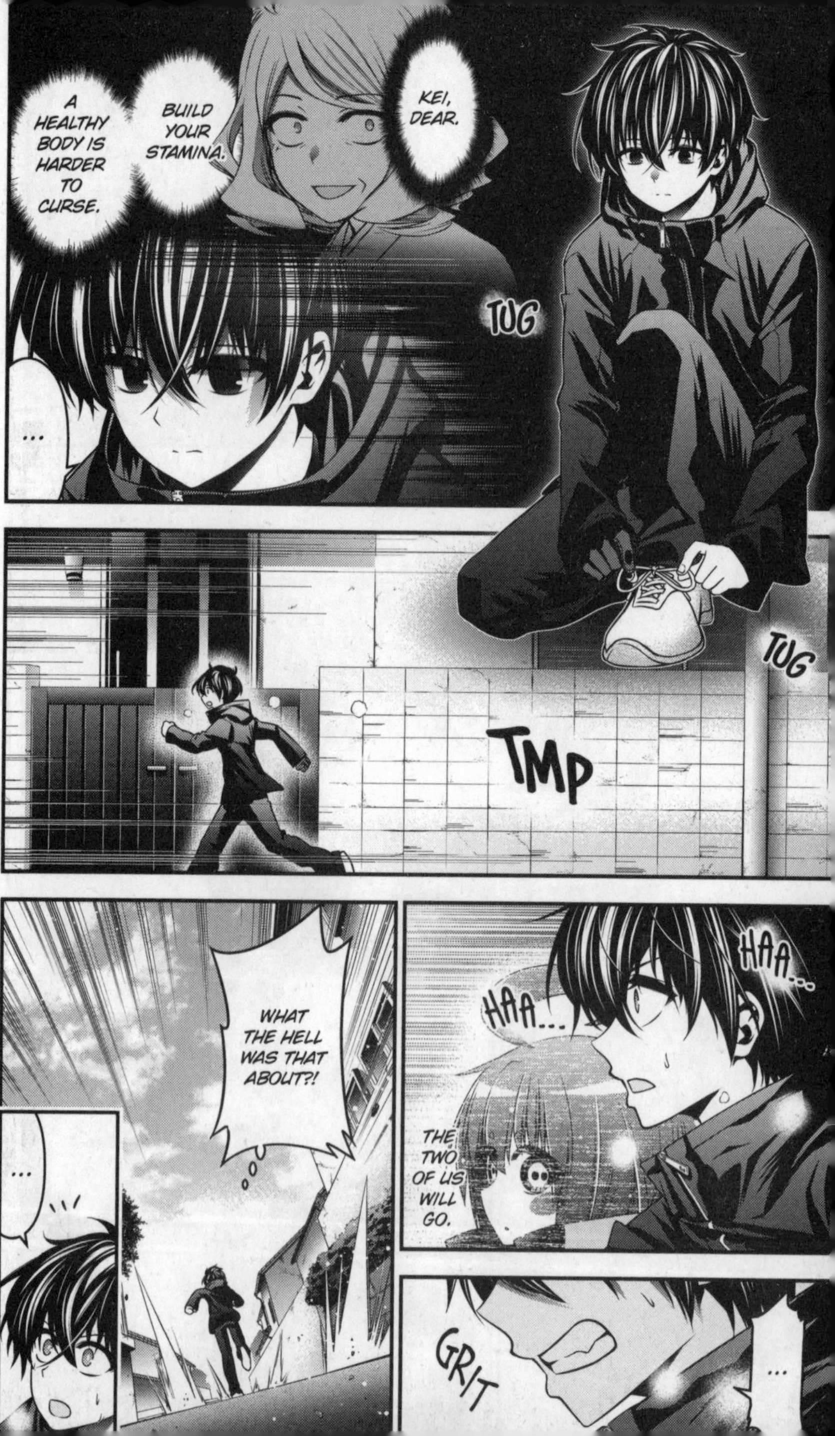
KEI, DEAR.
BUILD YOUR STAMINA.
A HEALTHY BODY IS HARDER TO CURSE.
TUG
...
TUG
TMP
HAA...
HAA...
THE TWO OF US WILL GO.
GRIT
...
WHAT THE HELL WAS THAT ABOUT?!
...

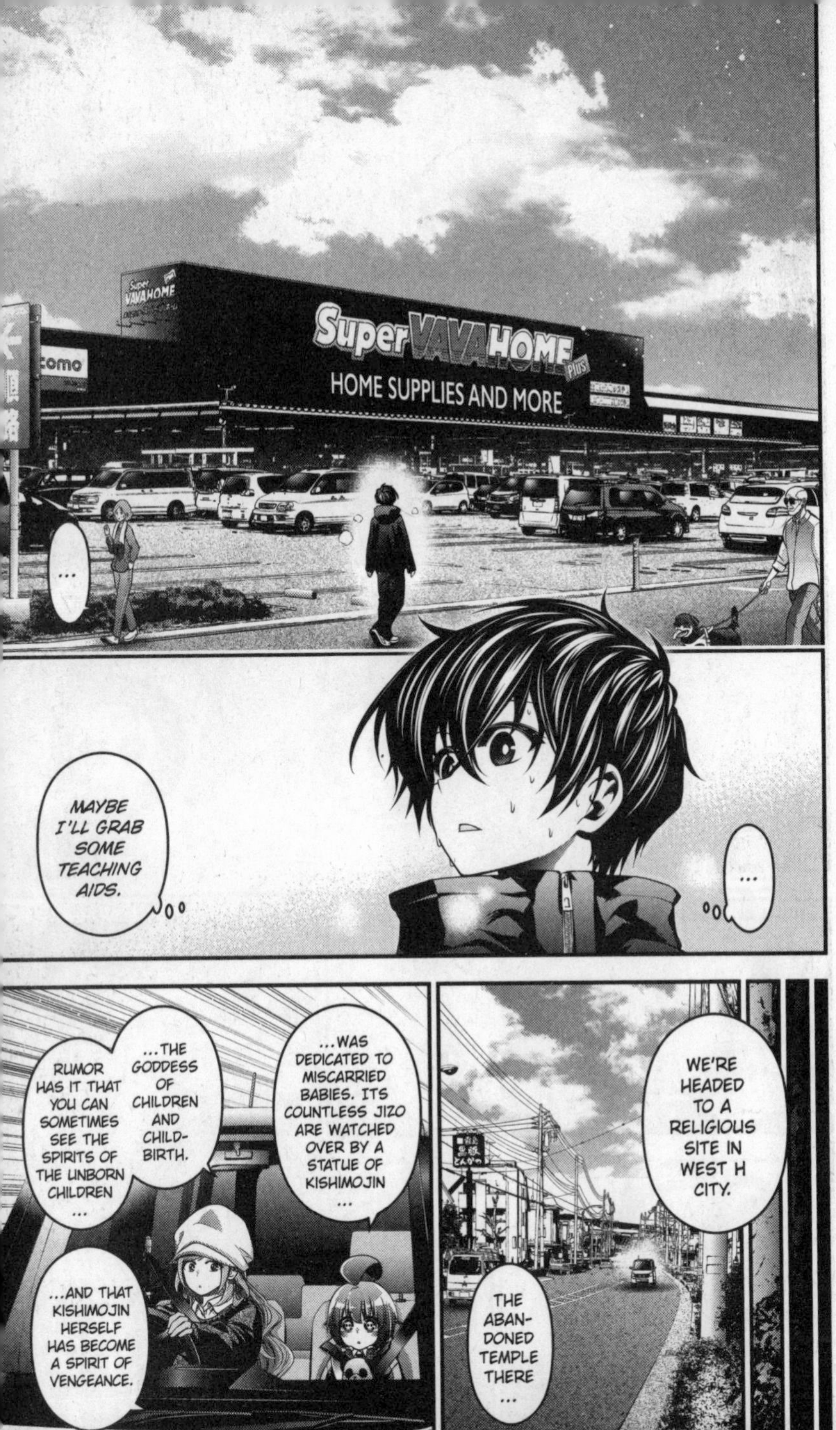
Super VAVAHOME Plus
HOME SUPPLIES AND MORE
...
...
MAYBE I'LL GRAB SOME TEACHING AIDS.
WE'RE HEADED TO A RELIGIOUS SITE IN WEST H CITY.
THE ABAN-DONED TEMPLE THERE ...
...WAS DEDICATED TO MISCARRIED BABIES. ITS COUNTLESS JIZO ARE WATCHED OVER BY A STATUE OF KISHIMOJIN ...
...THE GODDESS OF CHILDREN AND CHILD-BIRTH.
RUMOR HAS IT THAT YOU CAN SOMETIMES SEE THE SPIRITS OF THE UNBORN CHILDREN ...
...AND THAT KISHIMOJIN HERSELF HAS BECOME A SPIRIT OF VENGEANCE.

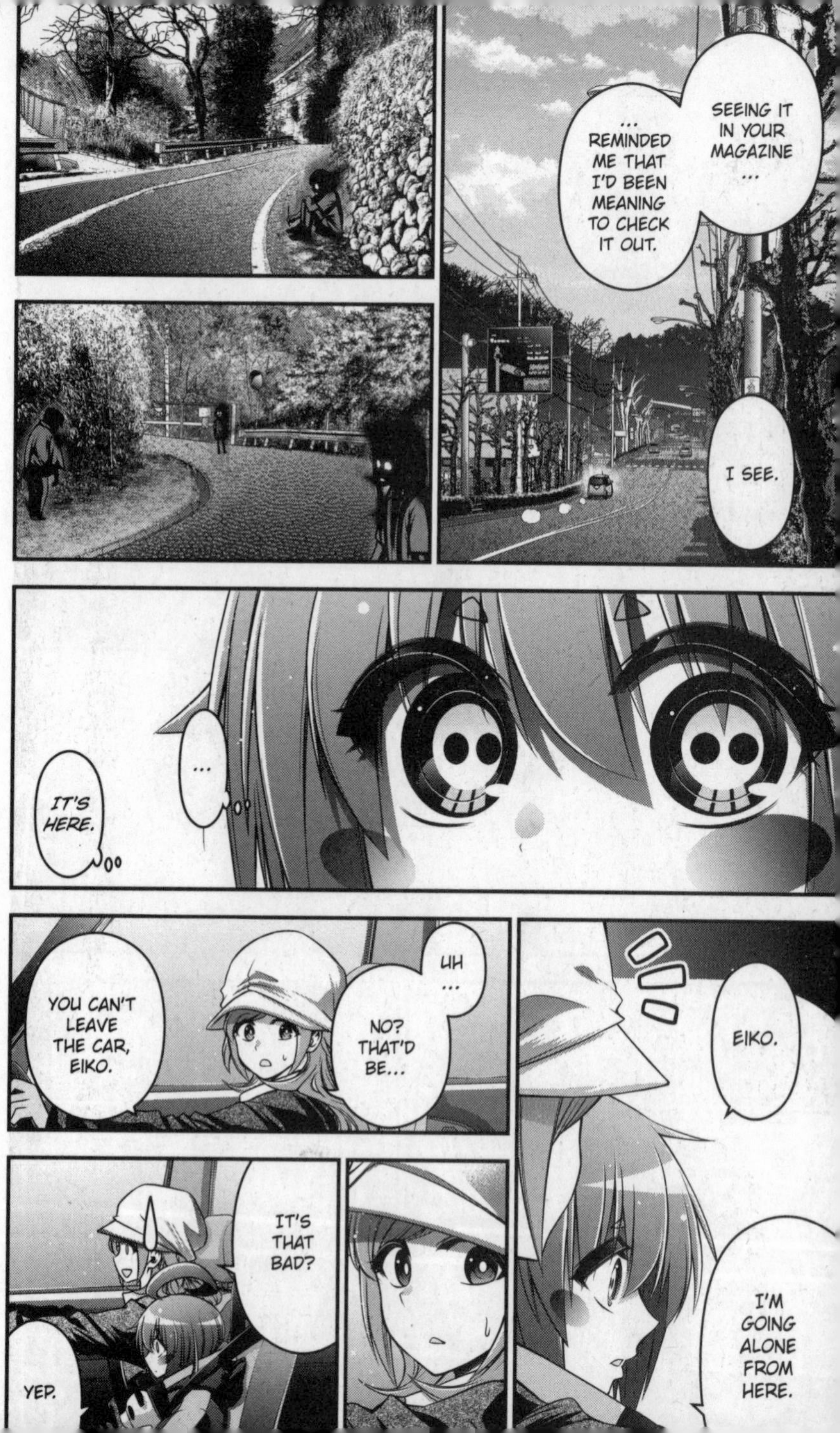
SEEING IT IN YOUR MAGAZINE ...
... REMINDED ME THAT I'D BEEN MEANING TO CHECK IT OUT.
I SEE.
...
IT'S HERE.
EIKO.
I'M GOING ALONE FROM HERE.
UH ...
NO? THAT'D BE...
YOU CAN'T LEAVE THE CAR, EIKO.
IT'S THAT BAD?
YEP.

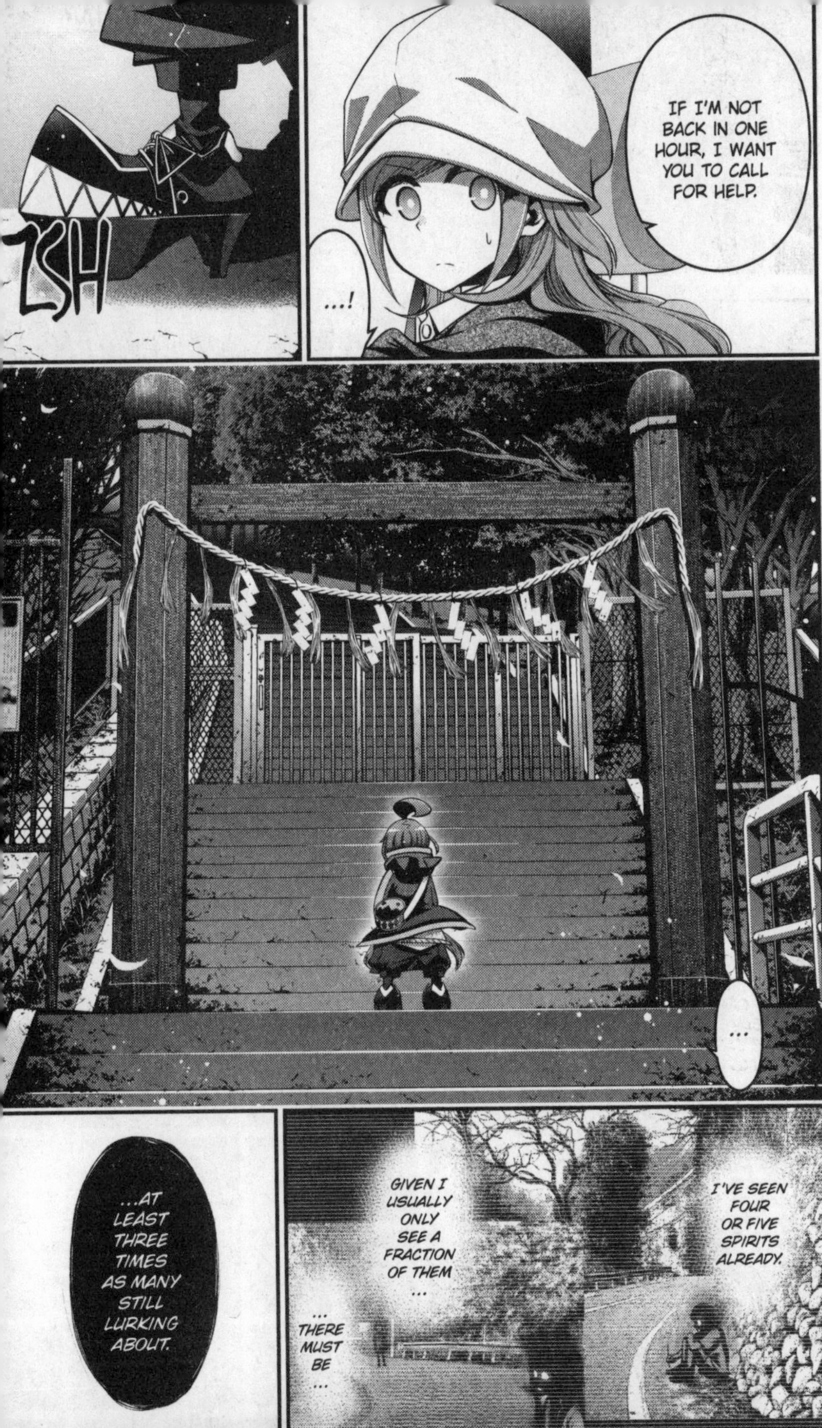
IF I'M NOT BACK IN ONE HOUR, I WANT YOU TO CALL FOR HELP.
...!
ZSH
...
I'VE SEEN FOUR OR FIVE SPIRITS ALREADY.
GIVEN I USUALLY ONLY SEE A FRACTION OF THEM ...
... THERE MUST BE ...
...AT LEAST THREE TIMES AS MANY STILL LURKING ABOUT.

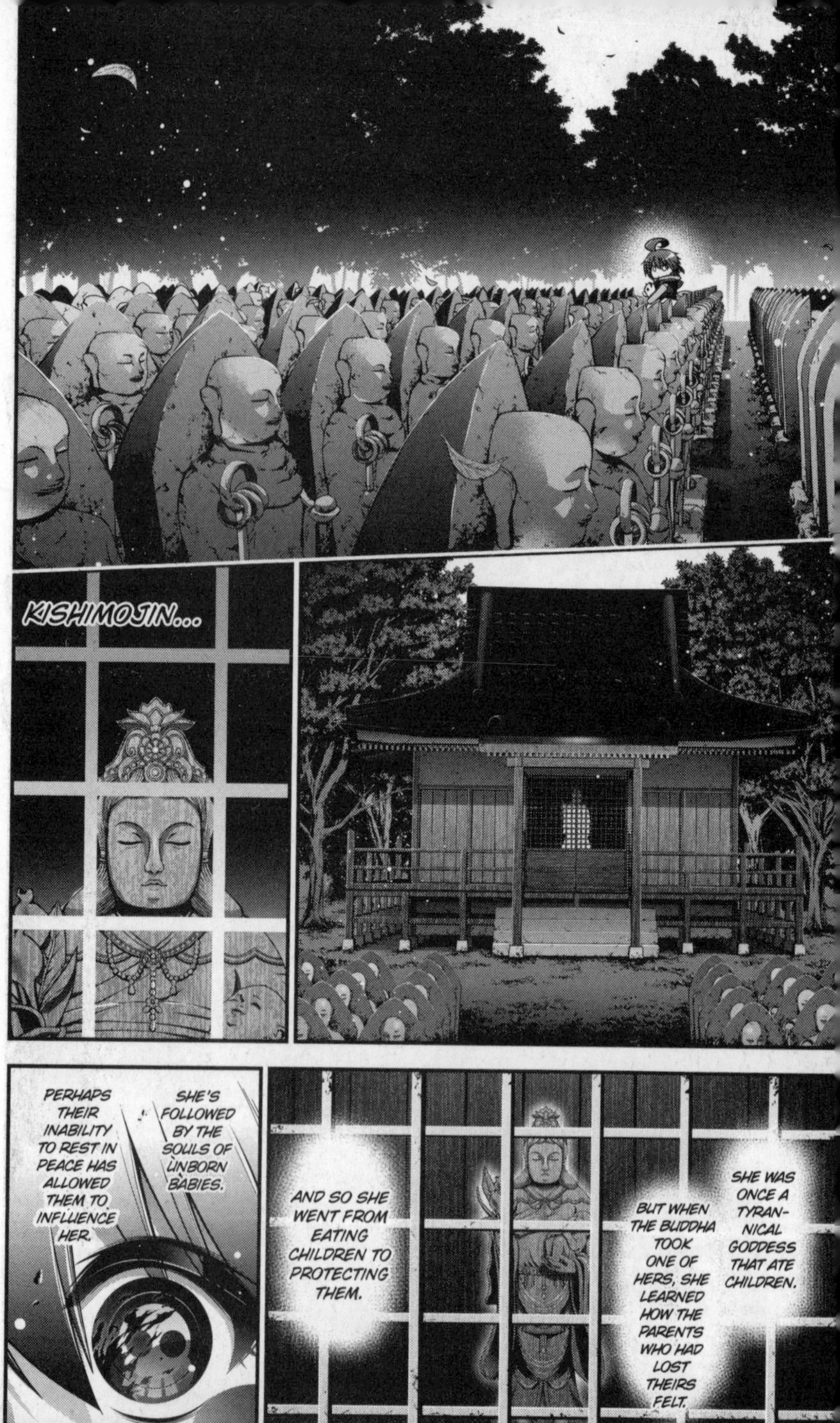
KISHIMOJIN...
SHE WAS ONCE A TYRANNICAL GODDESS THAT ATE CHILDREN.
BUT WHEN THE BUDDHA TOOK ONE OF HERS, SHE LEARNED HOW THE PARENTS WHO HAD LOST THEIRS FELT.
AND SO SHE WENT FROM EATING CHILDREN TO PROTECTING THEM.
SHE'S FOLLOWED BY THE SOULS OF UNBORN BABIES.
PERHAPS THEIR INABILITY TO REST IN PEACE HAS ALLOWED THEM TO INFLUENCE HER.

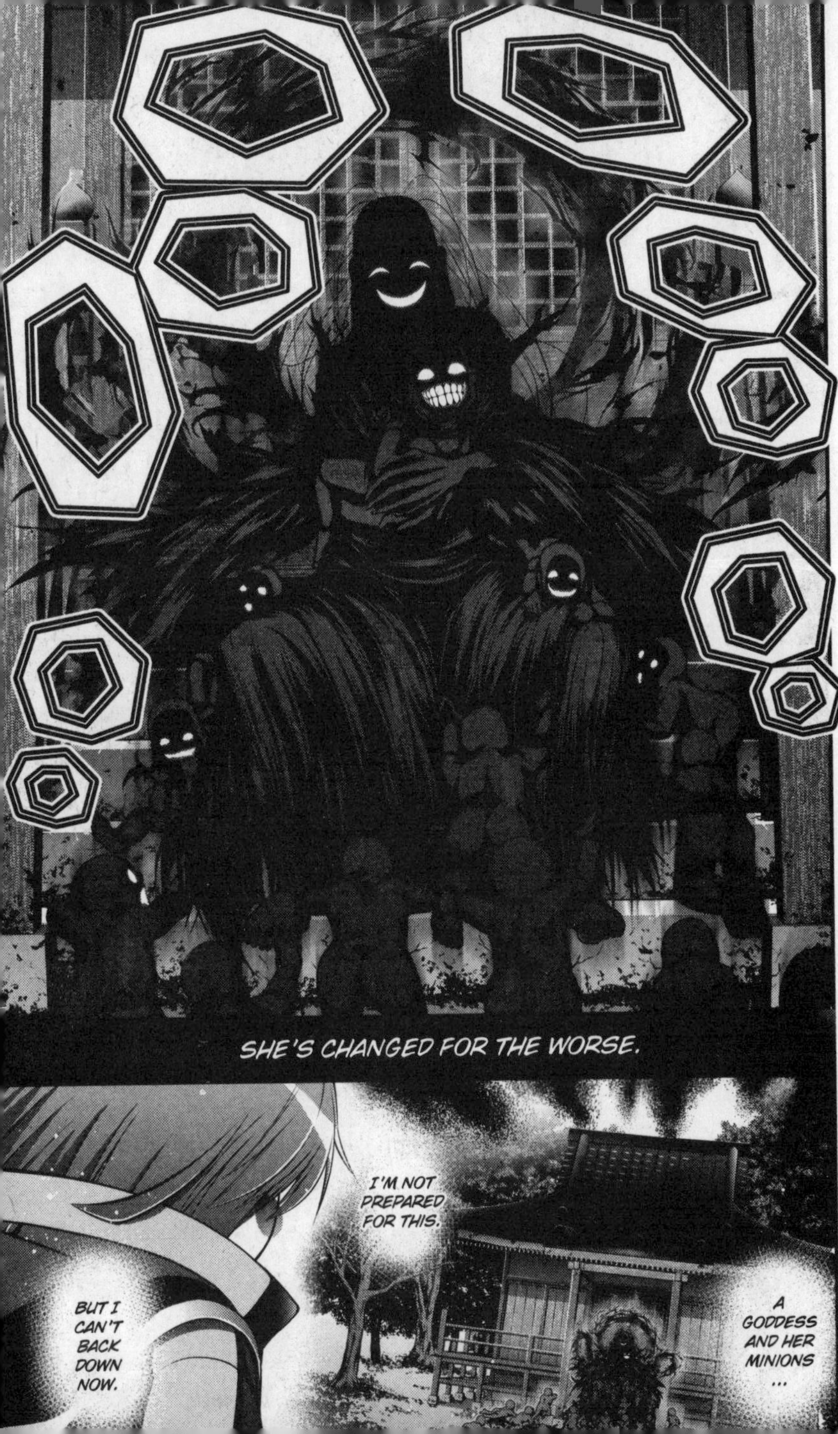
SHE'S CHANGED FOR THE WORSE.
A GODDESS AND HER MINIONS ...
I'M NOT PREPARED FOR THIS.
BUT I CAN'T BACK DOWN NOW.

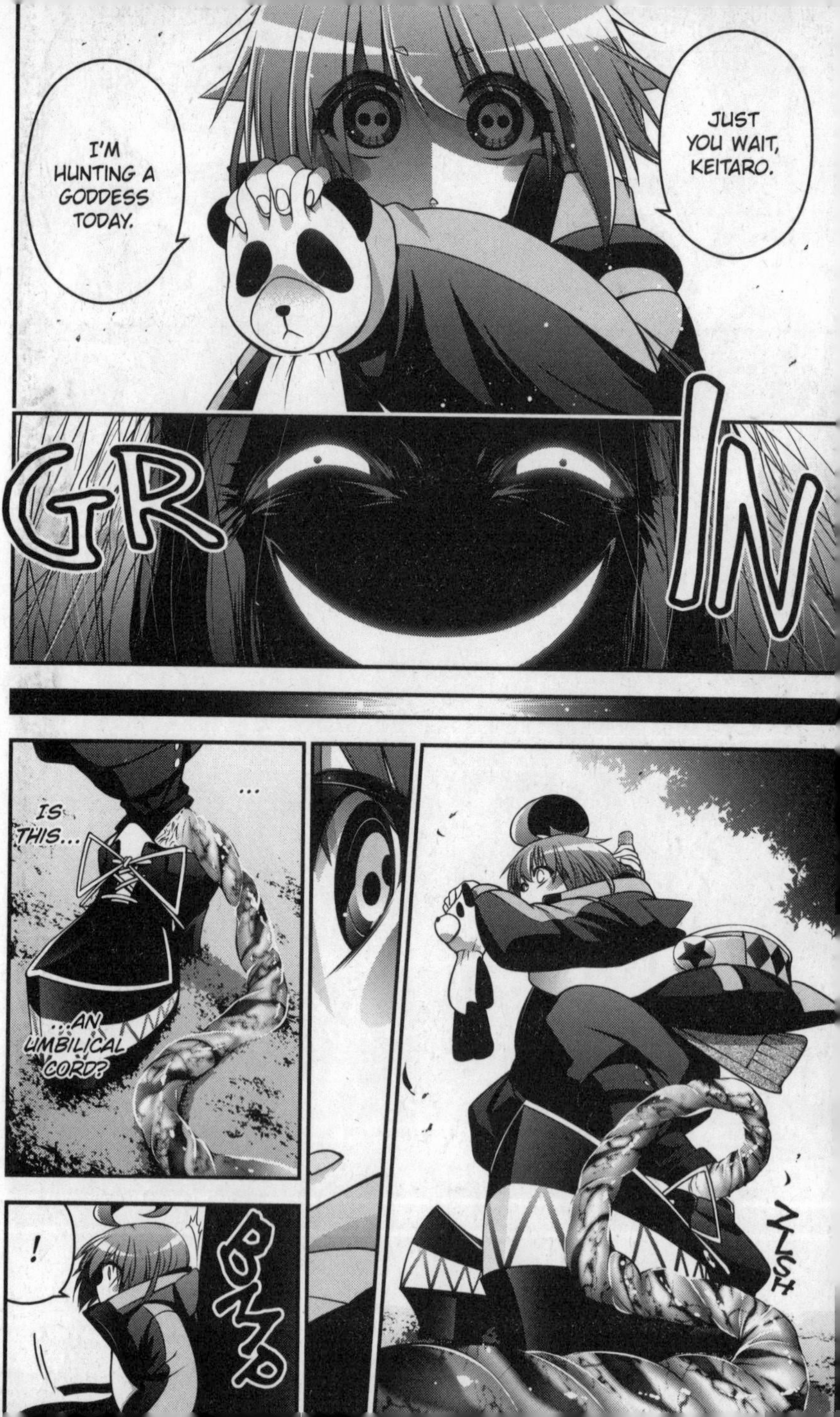
JUST YOU WAIT, KEITARO.
I'M HUNTING A GODDESS TODAY.
GRIN
ZLSH
...
IS THIS...
...AN UMBILICAL CORD?
!
BOMP

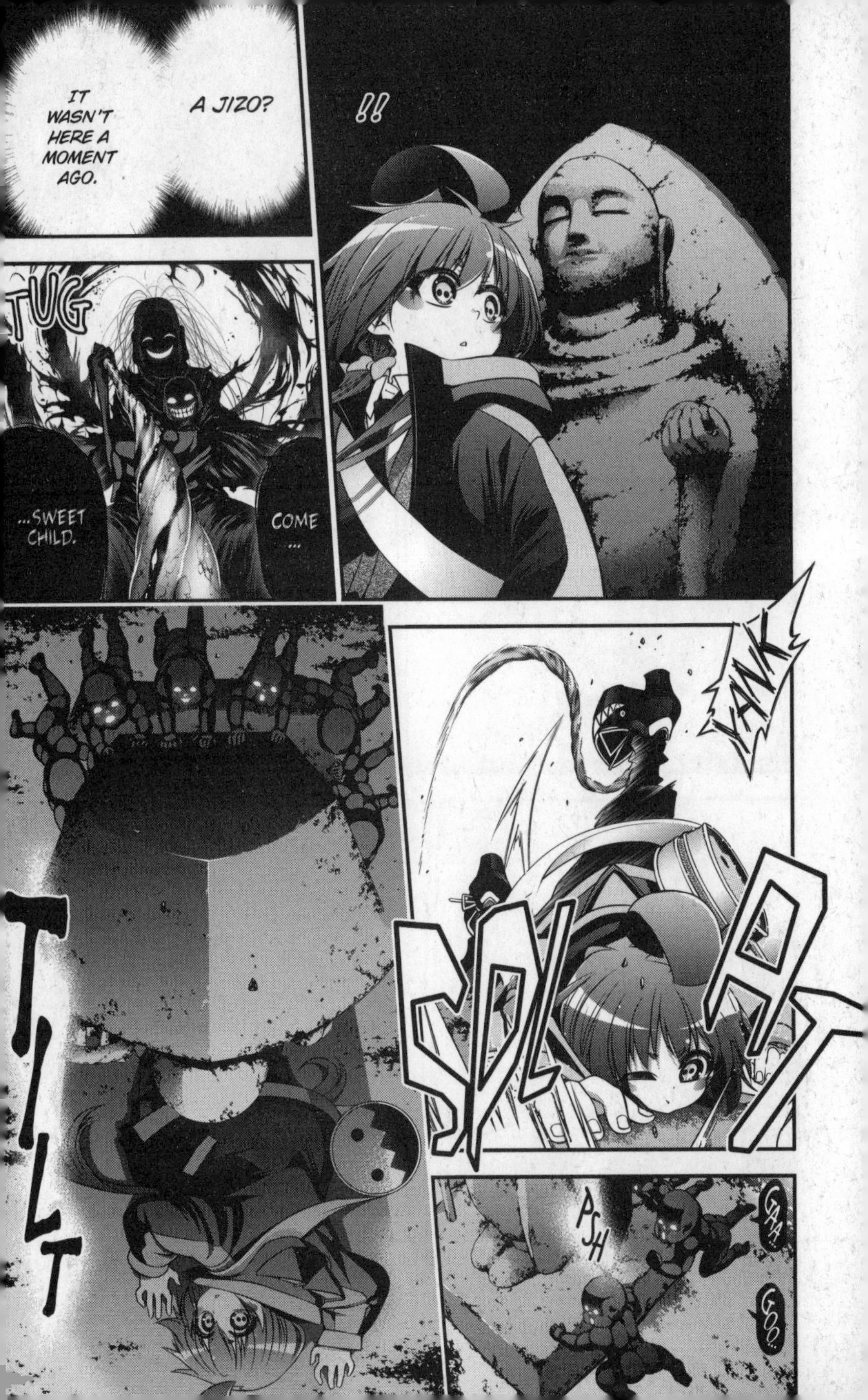
!!
A JIZO?
IT WASN'T HERE A MOMENT AGO.
TUG
COME ...
...SWEET CHILD.
YANK
SPLAT
PSH
GAA...
GOO...
TILT

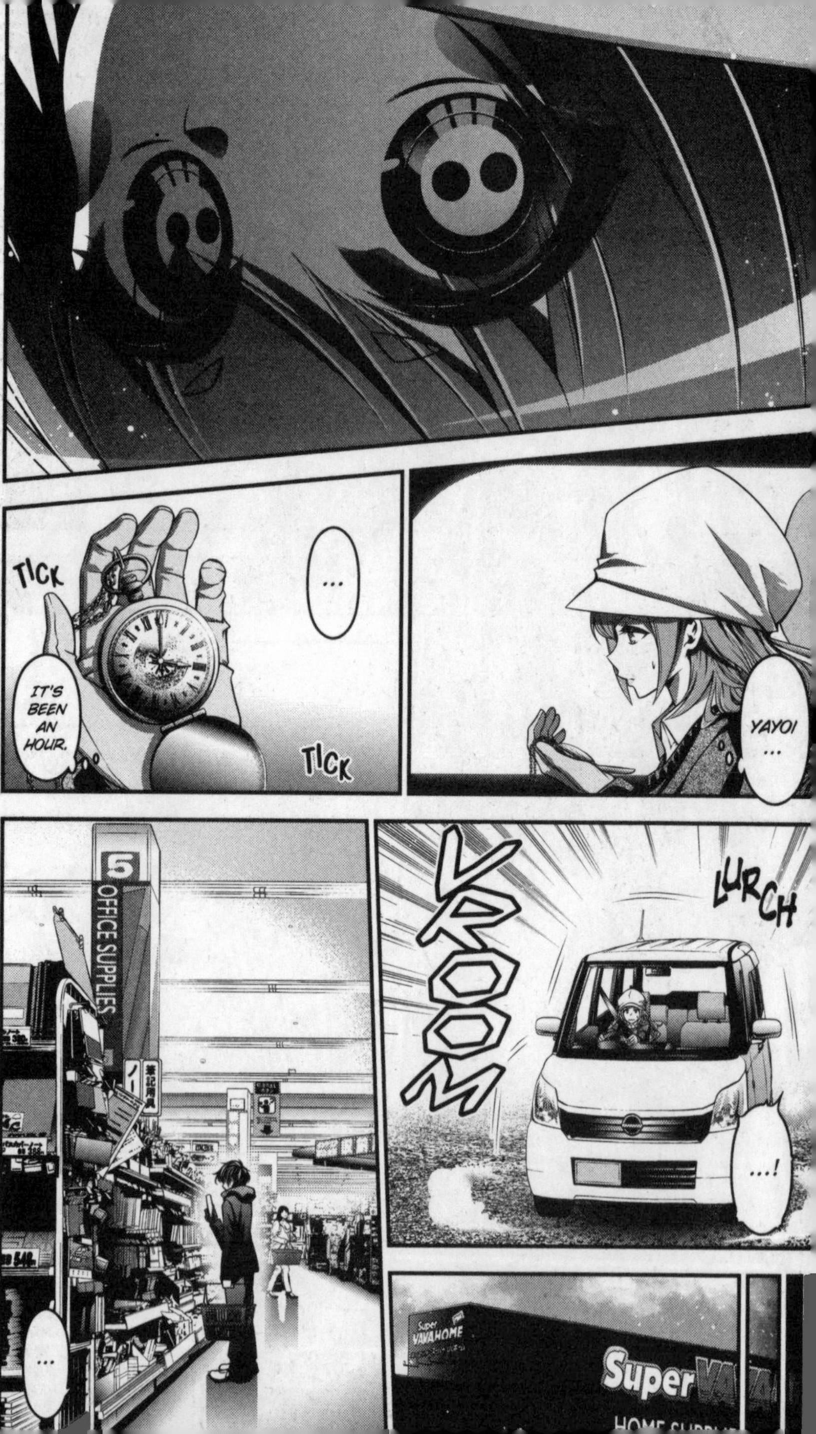
YAYOI ...
...
TICK
IT'S BEEN AN HOUR.
TICK
LURCH
VROOM
...!
5
OFFICE SUPPLIES
...
Super VAVAHOME

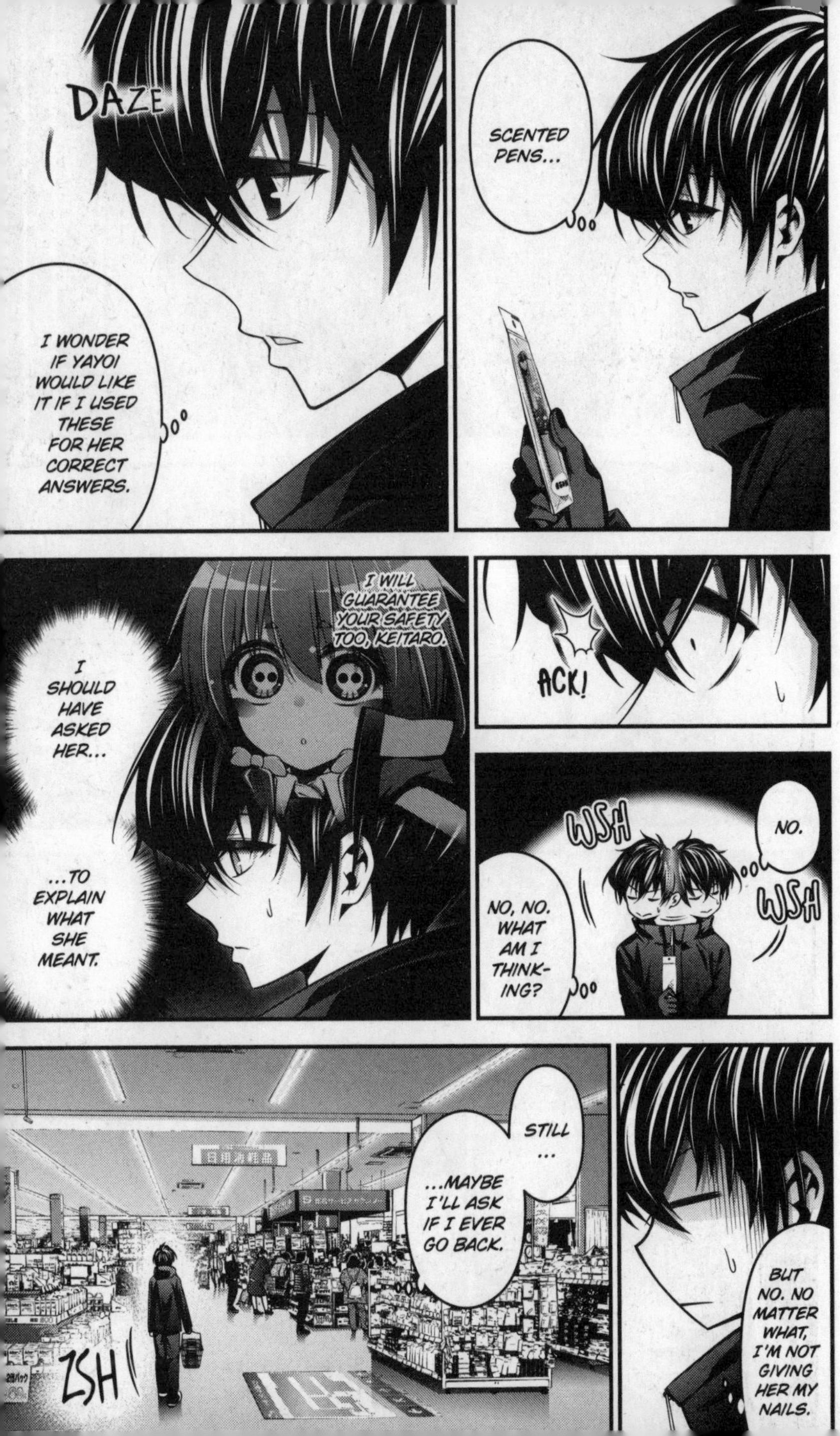
SCENTED PENS...
DAZE
I WONDER IF YAYOI WOULD LIKE IT IF I USED THESE FOR HER CORRECT ANSWERS.
ACK!
NO.
WSH
WSH
NO, NO. WHAT AM I THINKING?
I WILL GUARANTEE YOUR SAFETY TOO, KEITARO.
I SHOULD HAVE ASKED HER...
...TO EXPLAIN WHAT SHE MEANT.
BUT NO. NO MATTER WHAT, I'M NOT GIVING HER MY NAILS.
STILL...
...MAYBE I'LL ASK IF I EVER GO BACK.
ZSH

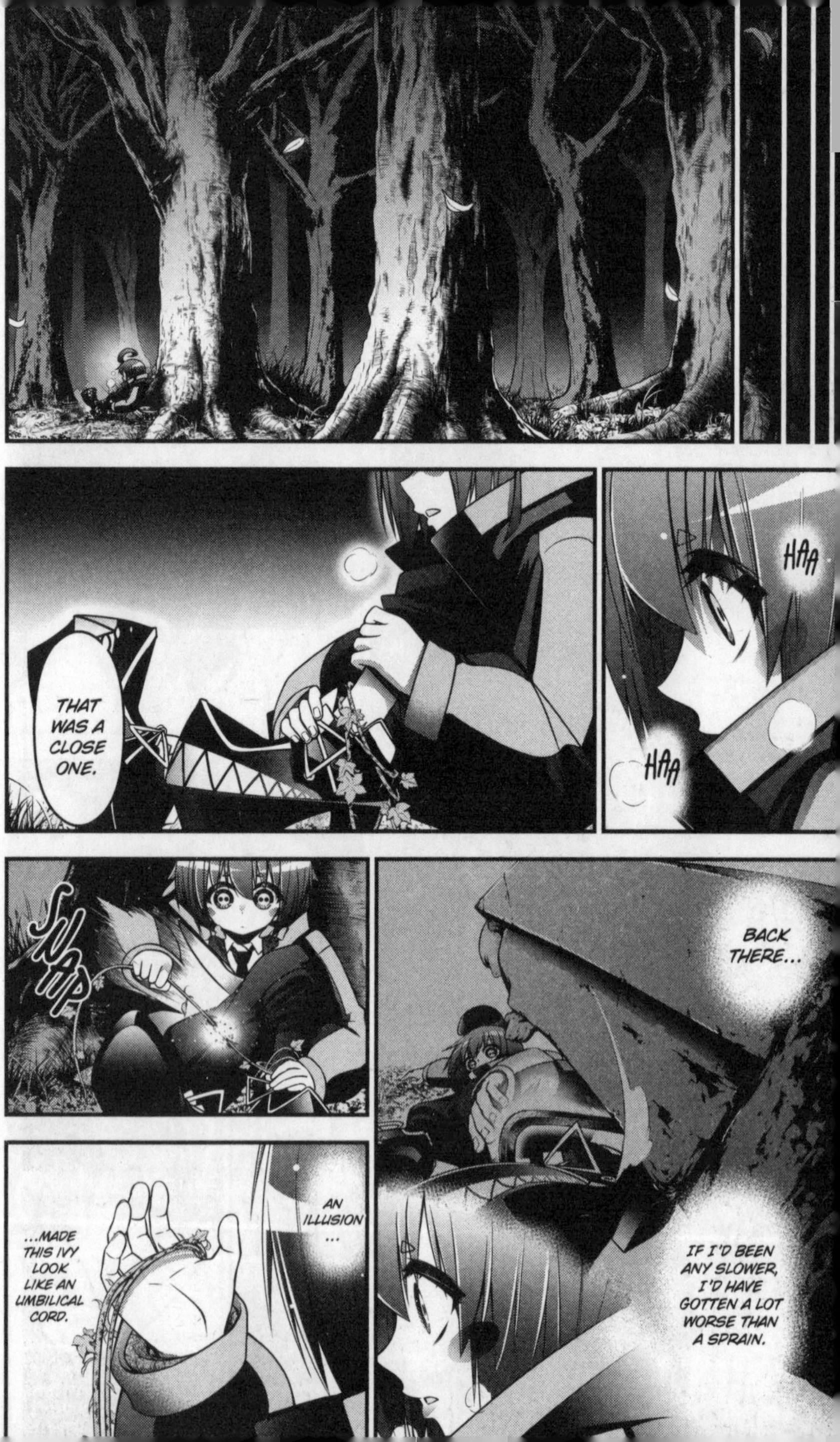
HAA
HAA
THAT WAS A CLOSE ONE.
BACK THERE...
IF I'D BEEN ANY SLOWER, I'D HAVE GOTTEN A LOT WORSE THAN A SPRAIN.
SNAP
AN ILLUSION...
...MADE THIS IVY LOOK LIKE AN UMBILICAL CORD.

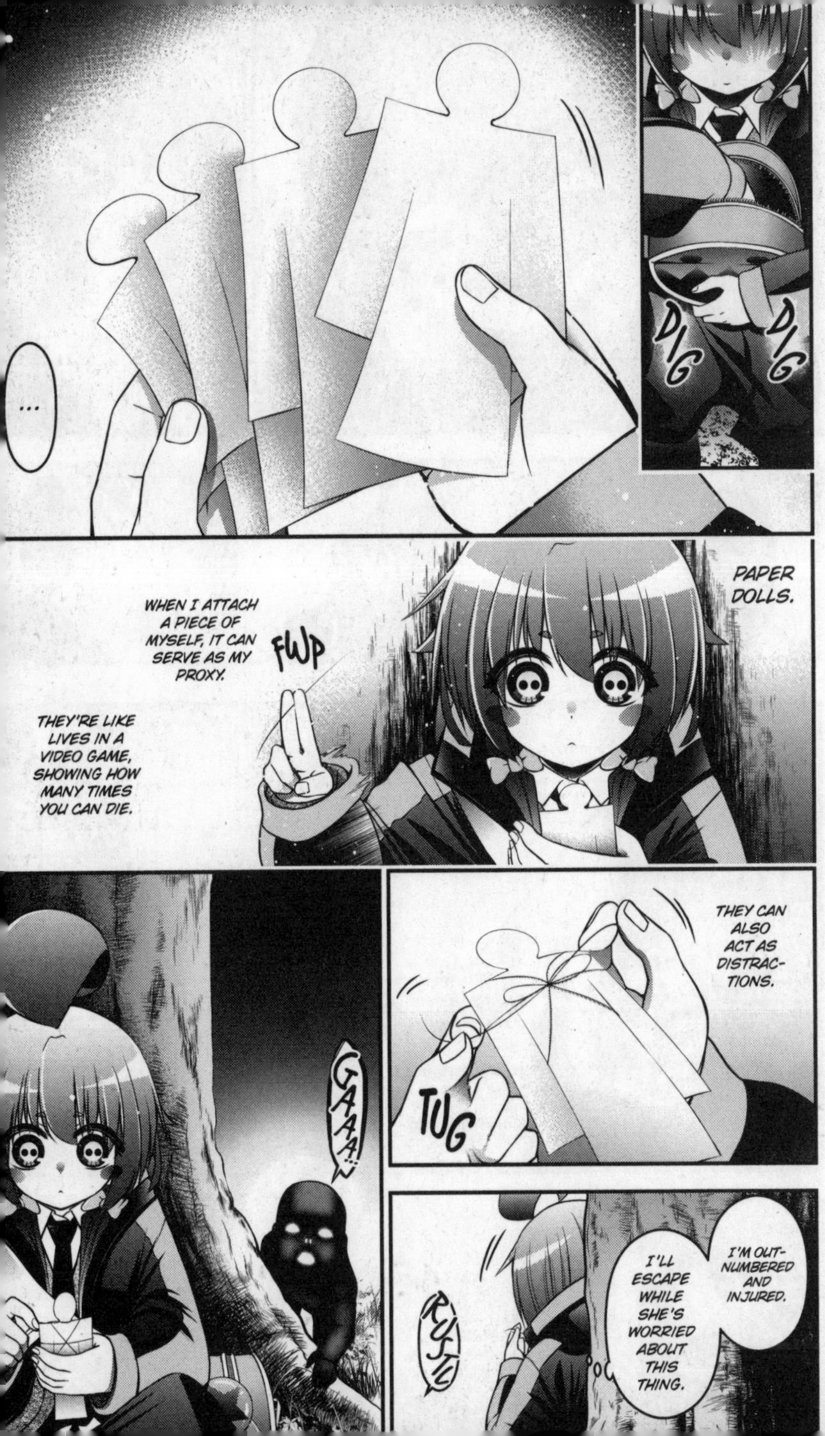
DIG
DIG
...
PAPER DOLLS.
WHEN I ATTACH A PIECE OF MYSELF, IT CAN SERVE AS MY PROXY.
FWP
THEY'RE LIKE LIVES IN A VIDEO GAME, SHOWING HOW MANY TIMES YOU CAN DIE.
THEY CAN ALSO ACT AS DISTRAC-TIONS.
TUG
I'M OUT-NUMBERED AND INJURED.
I'LL ESCAPE WHILE SHE'S WORRIED ABOUT THIS THING.
RUSTL
GAAA..!!

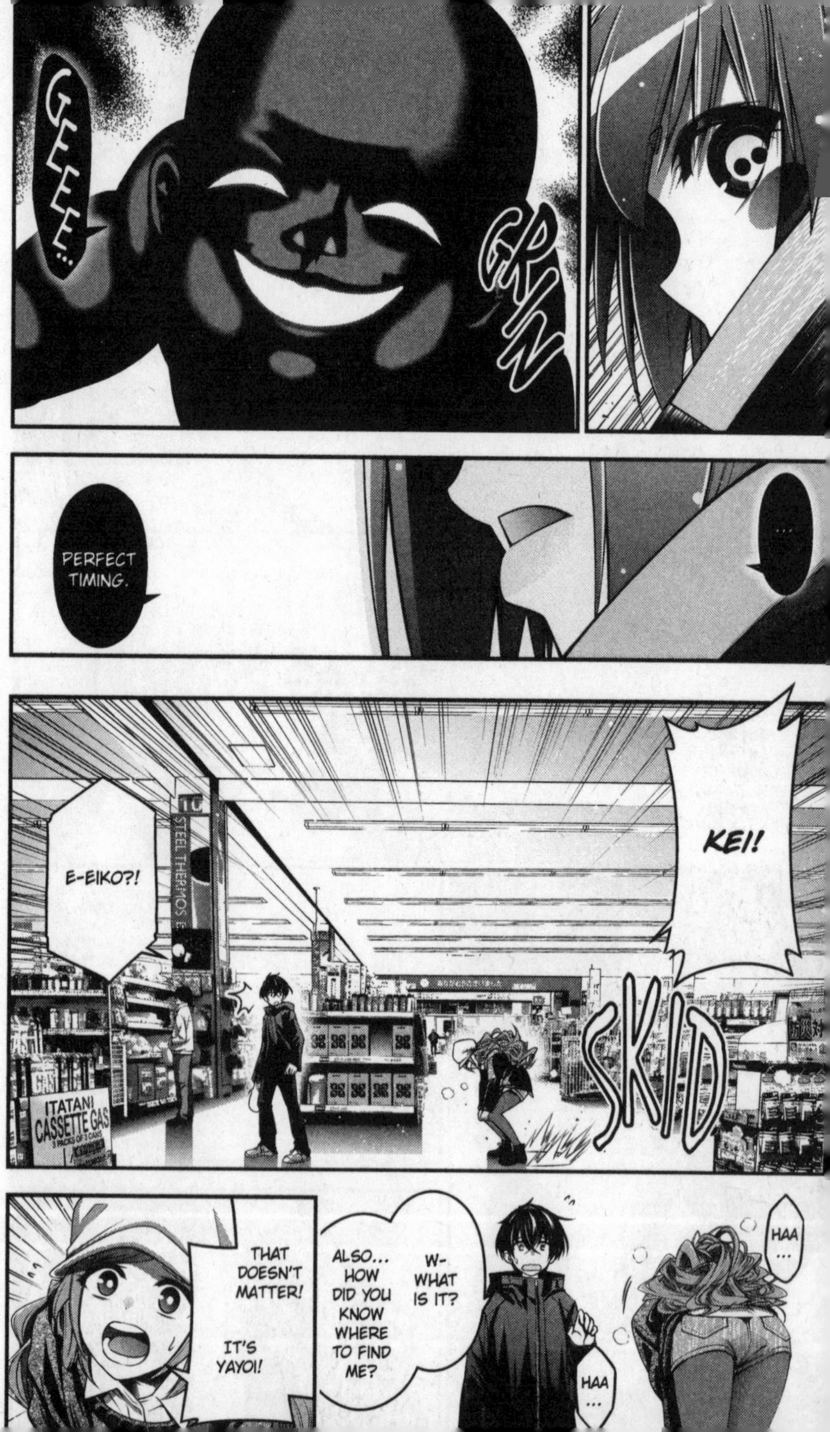
GEEEE...
GRIN
...
PERFECT TIMING.
KEI!
SKID
E-EIKO?!
STEEL THERMOS
ITATANI CASSETTE GAS
3 PACKS OF 3 CANS
HAA...
HAA...
W-WHAT IS IT?
ALSO... HOW DID YOU KNOW WHERE TO FIND ME?
THAT DOESN'T MATTER!
IT'S YAYOI!

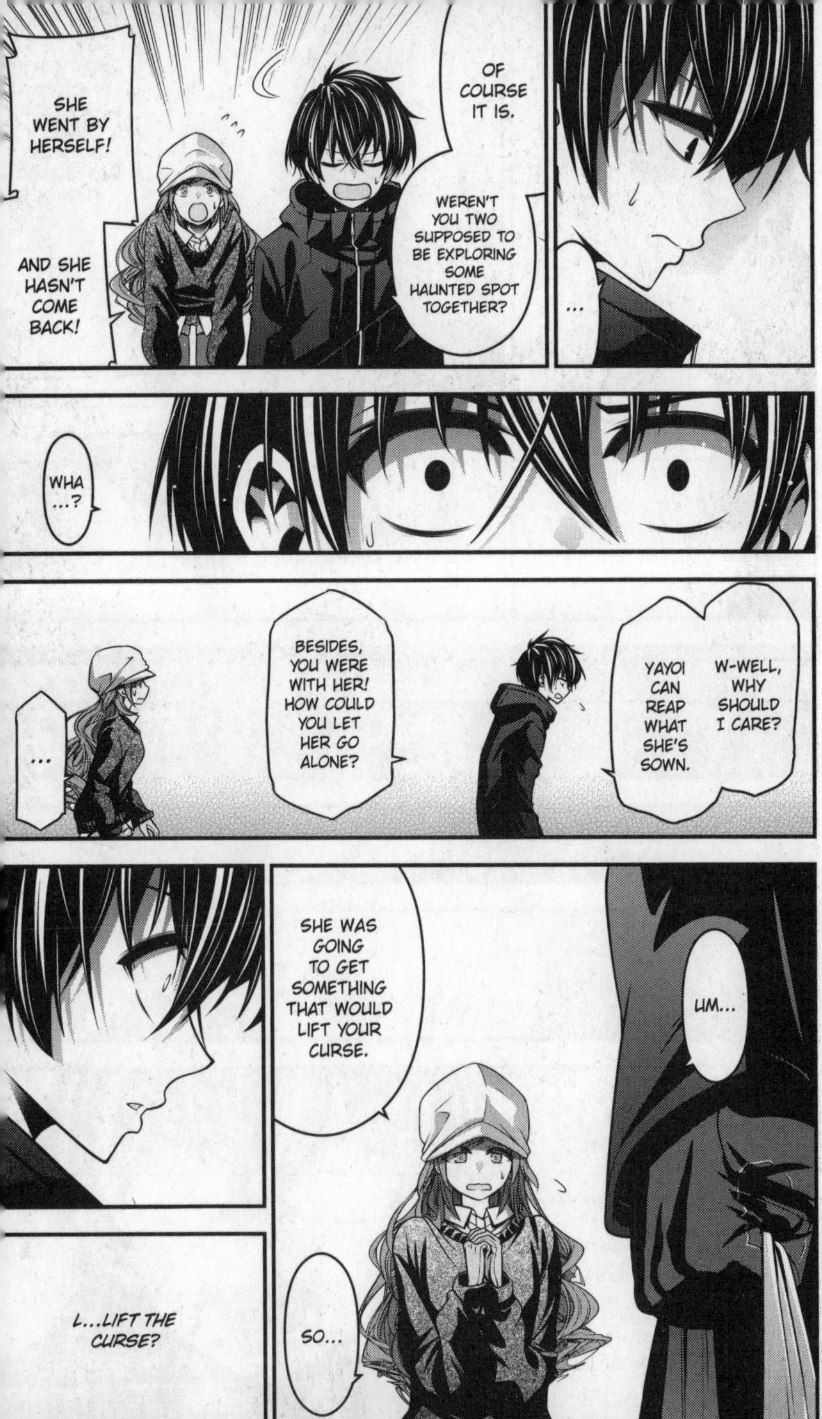
...
OF COURSE IT IS.
WEREN'T YOU TWO SUPPOSED TO BE EXPLORING SOME HAUNTED SPOT TOGETHER?
SHE WENT BY HERSELF!
AND SHE HASN'T COME BACK!
WHA...?
W-WELL, WHY SHOULD I CARE?
YAYOI CAN REAP WHAT SHE'S SOWN.
BESIDES, YOU WERE WITH HER! HOW COULD YOU LET HER GO ALONE?
...
UM...
SHE WAS GOING TO GET SOMETHING THAT WOULD LIFT YOUR CURSE.
SO...
L...LIFT THE CURSE?

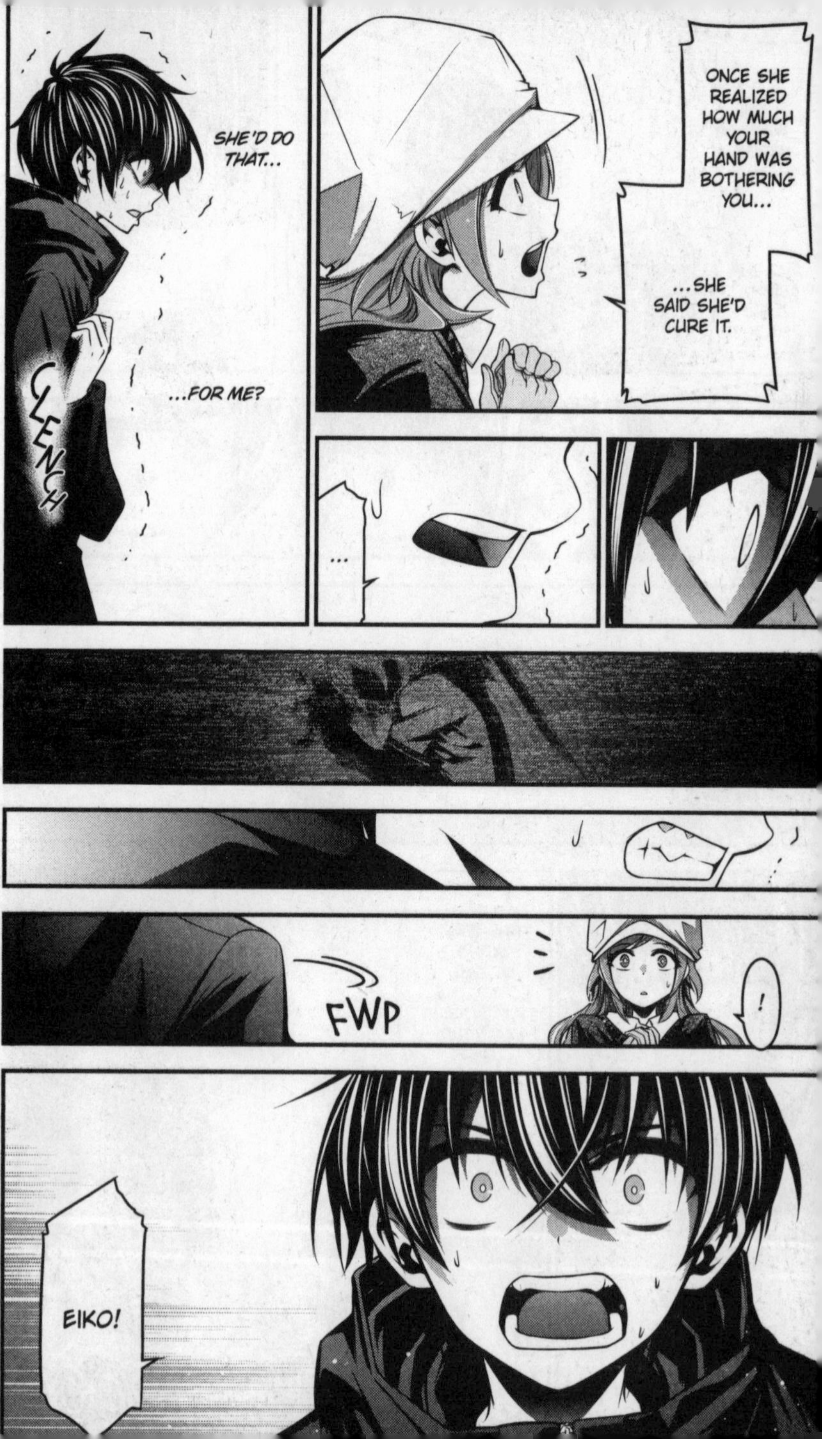
ONCE SHE REALIZED HOW MUCH YOUR HAND WAS BOTHERING YOU...
...SHE SAID SHE'D CURE IT.
...
SHE'D DO THAT...
...FOR ME?
CLENCH
!
FWP
EIKO!

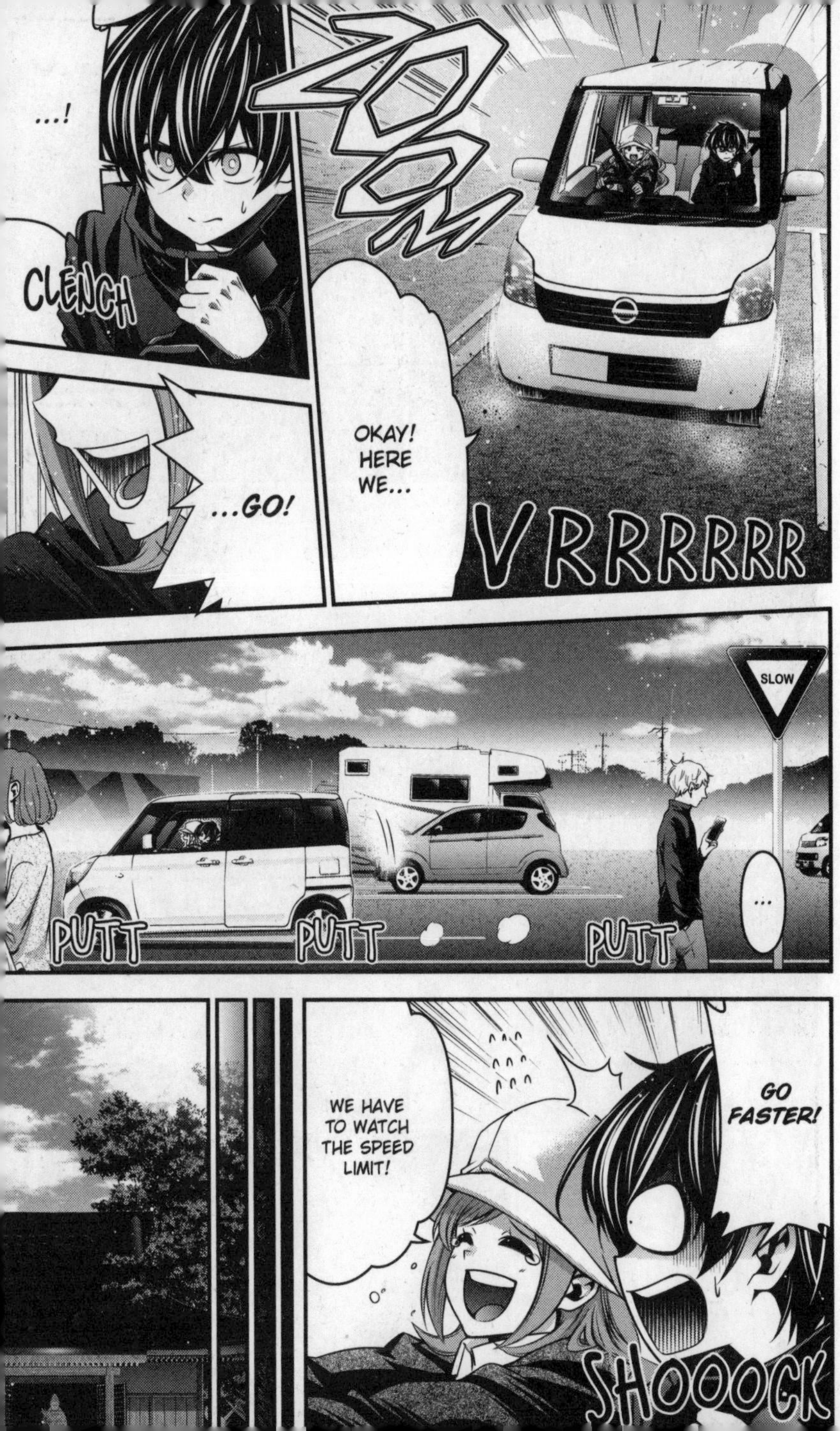
ZOOM
OKAY! HERE WE...
VRRRRRR
...!
CLENCH
...GO!
SLOW
...
PUTT
PUTT
PUTT
GO FASTER!
WE HAVE TO WATCH THE SPEED LIMIT!
SHOOOCK

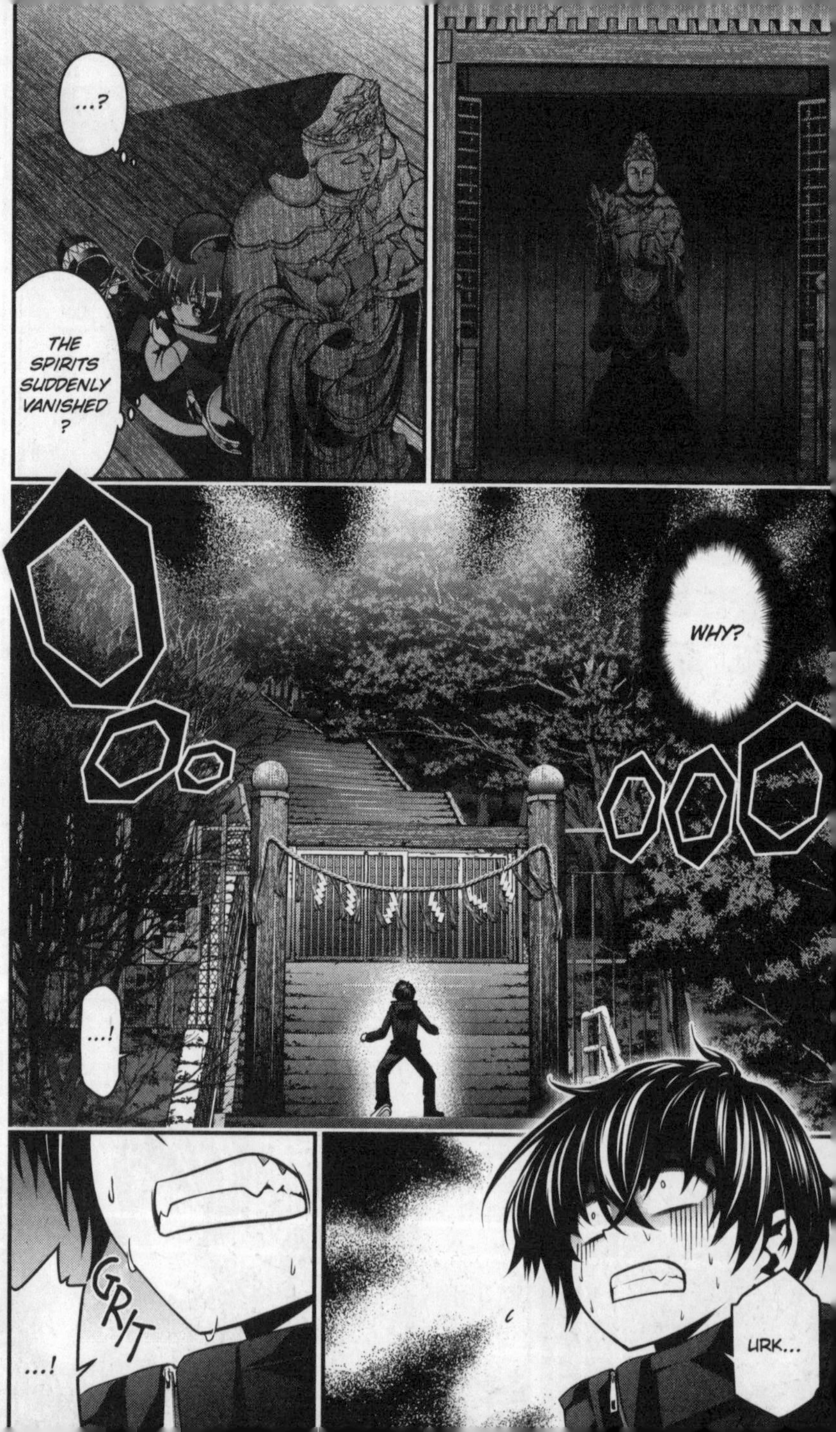
...?
THE SPIRITS SUDDENLY VANISHED ?
WHY?
...!
URK...
GRIT
...!

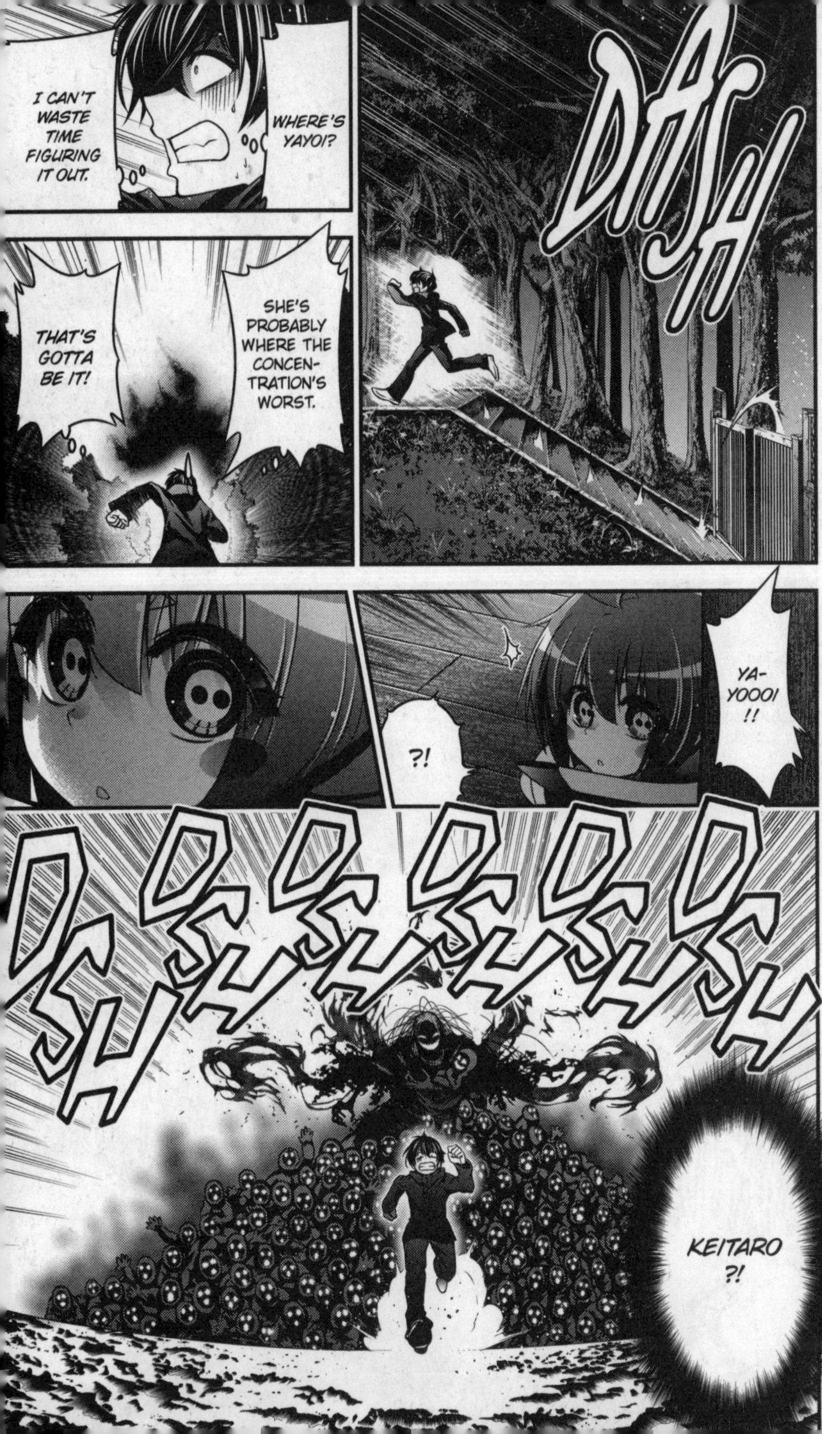
DASH
WHERE'S YAYOI?
I CAN'T WASTE TIME FIGURING IT OUT.
SHE'S PROBABLY WHERE THE CONCEN-TRATION'S WORST.
THAT'S GOTTA BE IT!
YA-YOOOI!!
?!
DASH DASH DASH DASH DASH
KEITARO?!

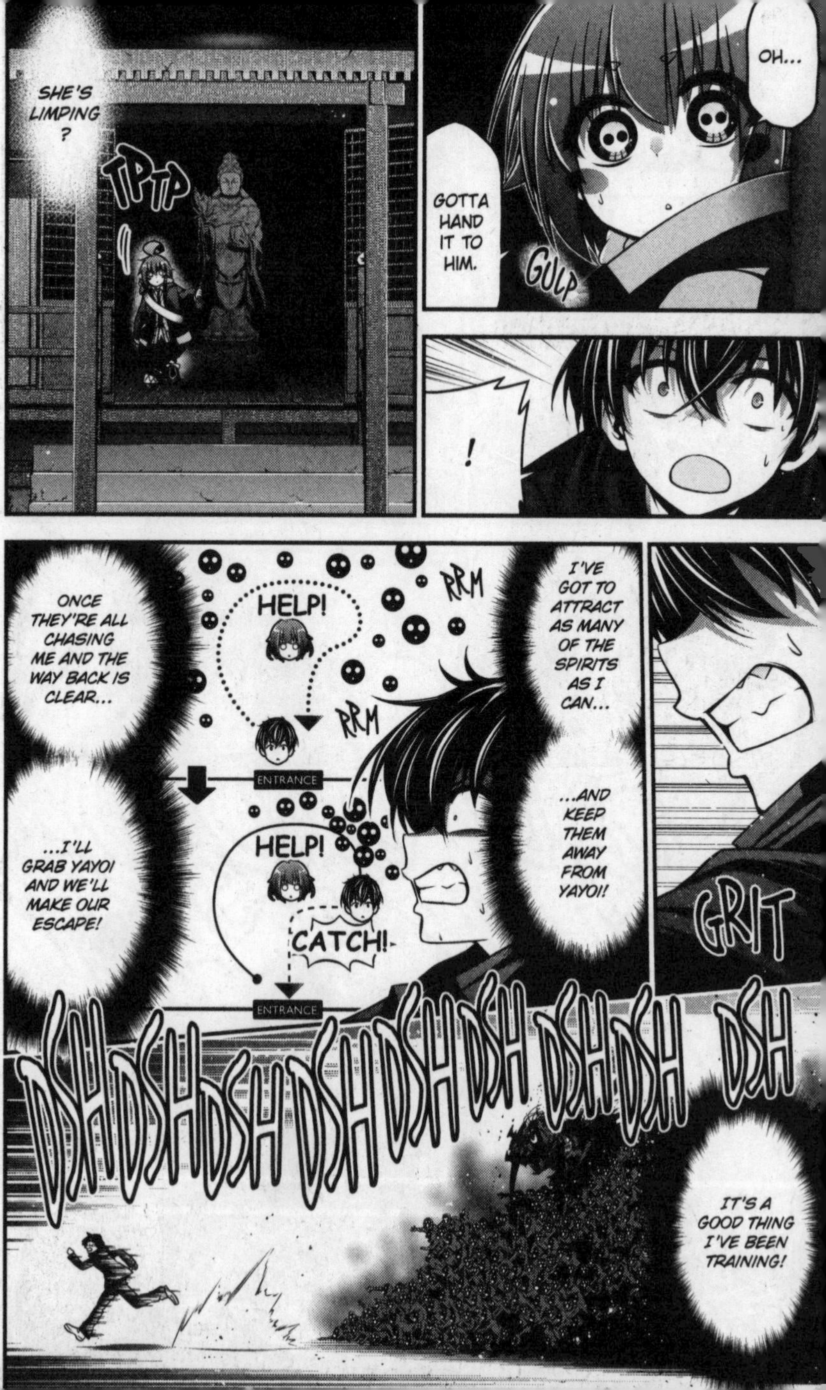
OH...
GOTTA HAND IT TO HIM.
GULP
!
SHE'S LIMPING ?
TPTP
GRIT
I'VE GOT TO ATTRACT AS MANY OF THE SPIRITS AS I CAN...
...AND KEEP THEM AWAY FROM YAYOI!
ONCE THEY'RE ALL CHASING ME AND THE WAY BACK IS CLEAR...
...I'LL GRAB YAYOI AND WE'LL MAKE OUR ESCAPE!
RRM
HELP!
RRM
ENTRANCE
HELP!
CATCH!
ENTRANCE
DSHDSHDSH DSH DSH DSH DSH DSH DSH
IT'S A GOOD THING I'VE BEEN TRAINING!

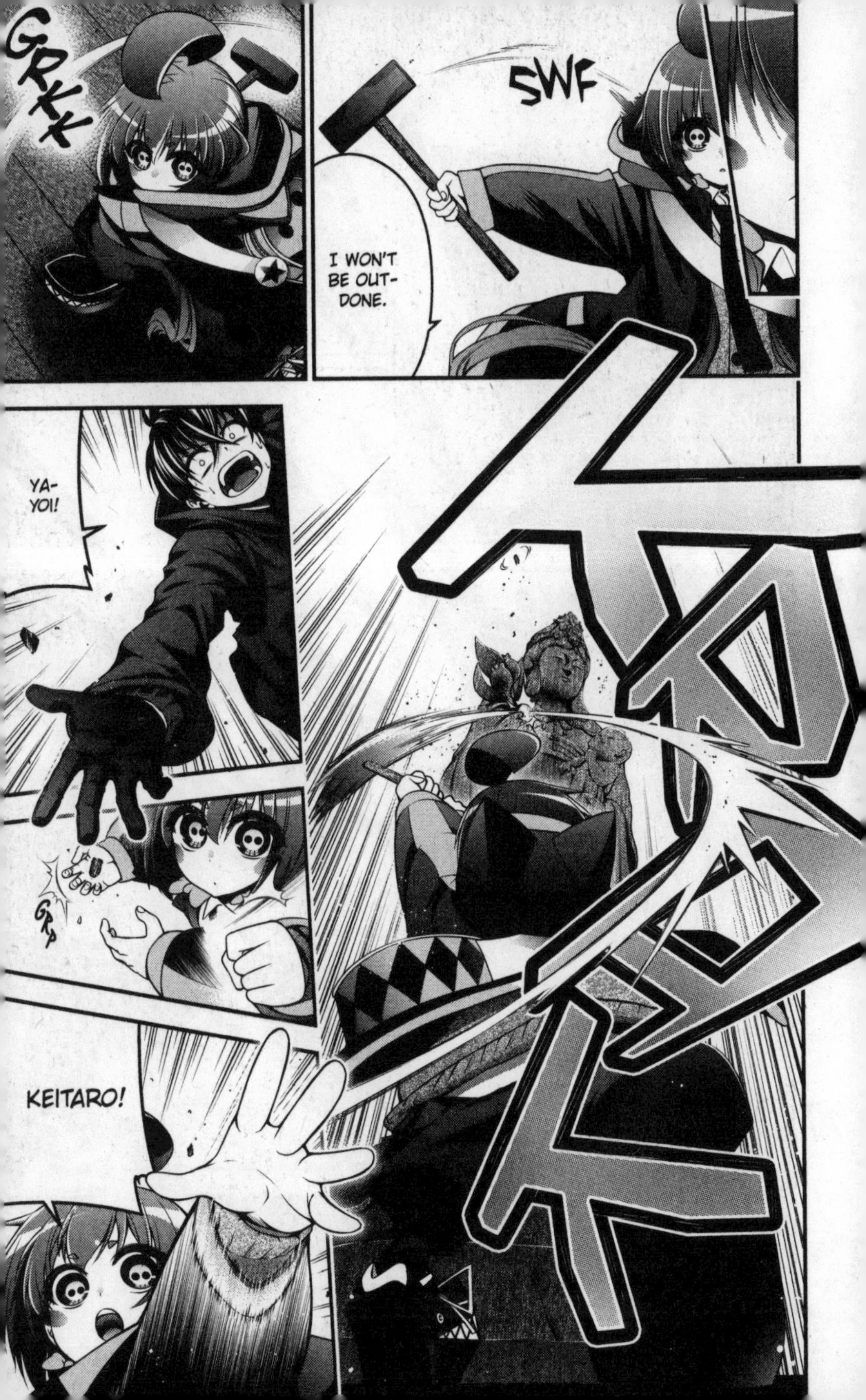
SWF
I WON'T BE OUT-DONE.
GRKK
YA-YOI!
GRP
KEITARO!

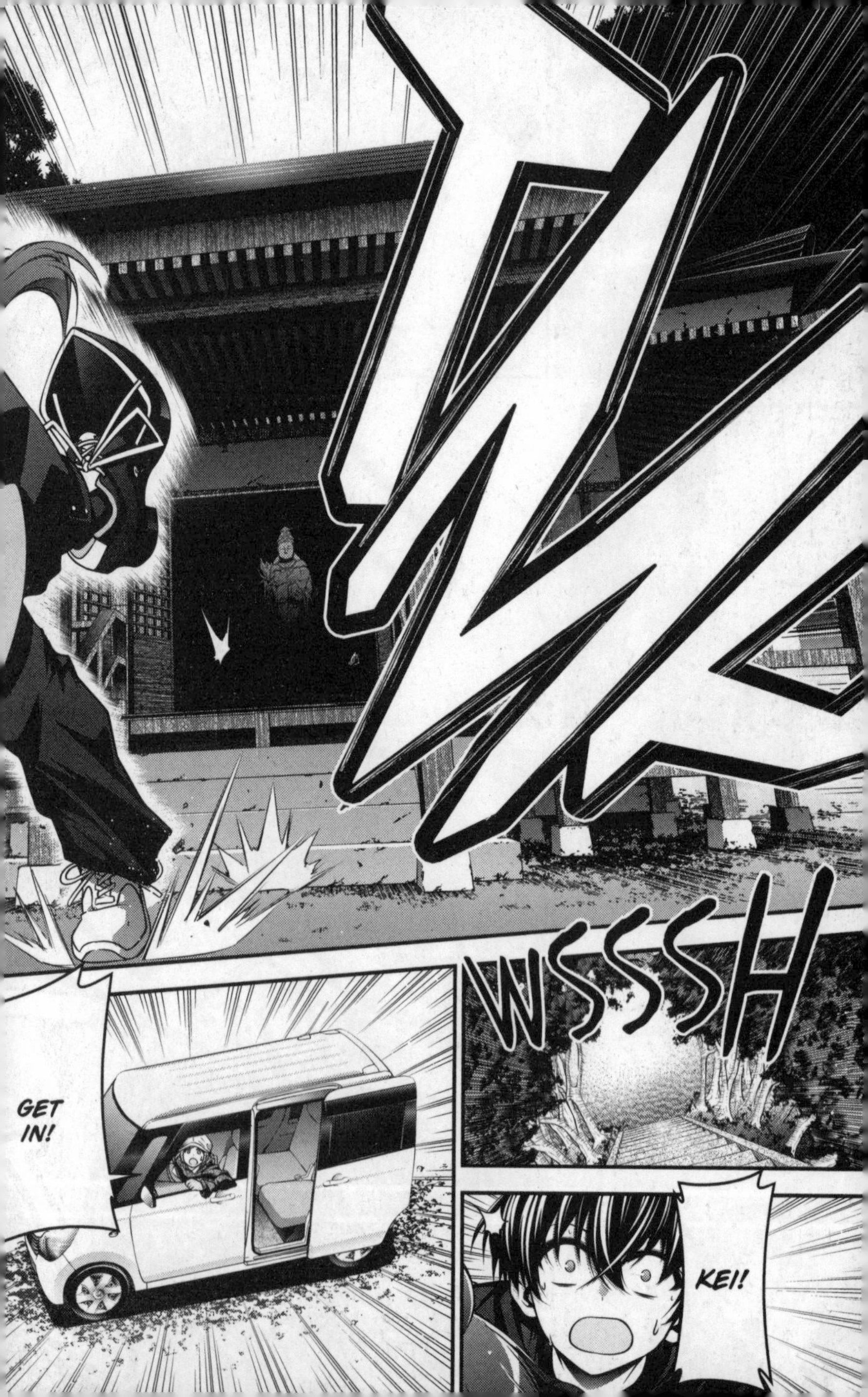
WSSSH
KEI!
GET IN!

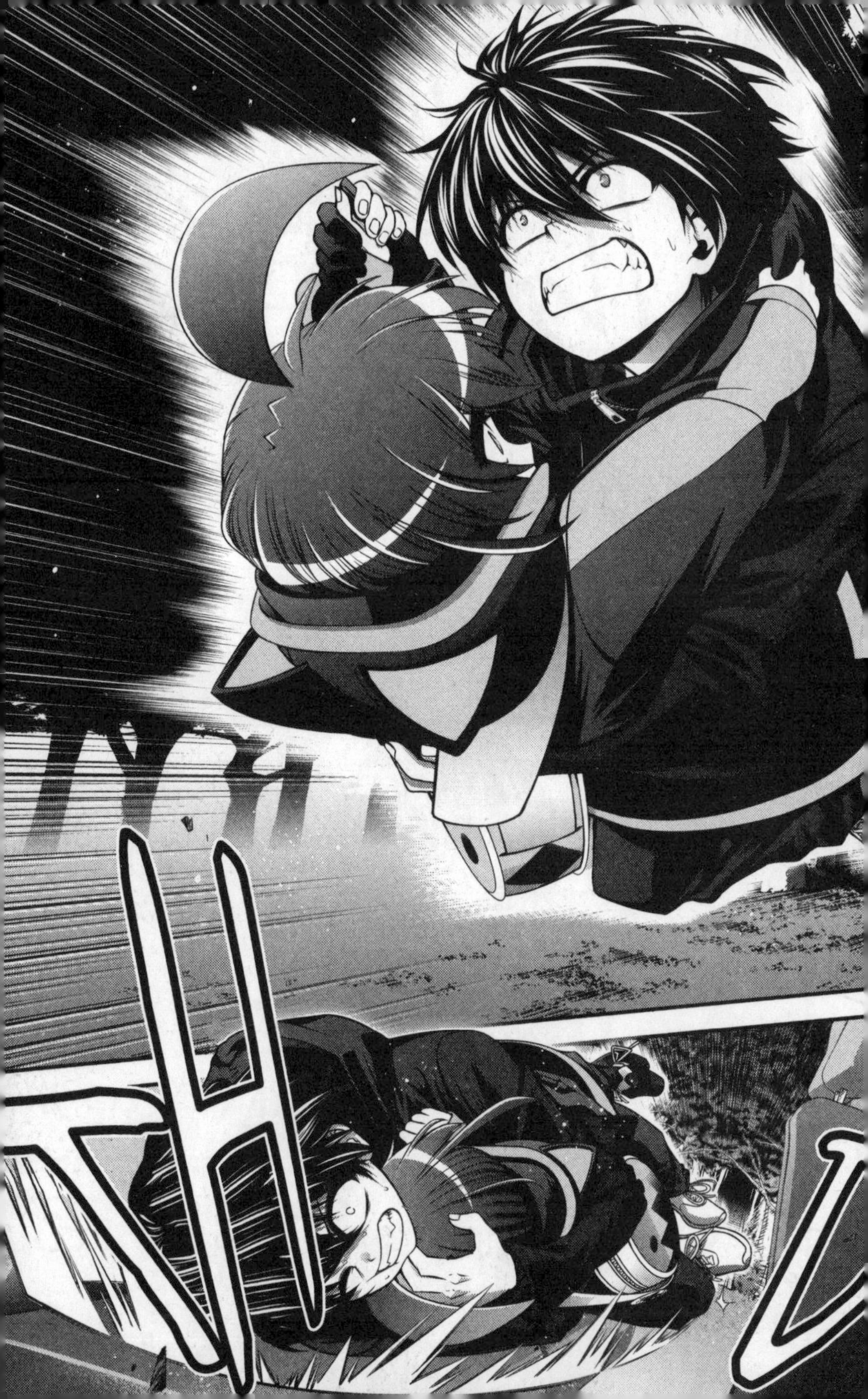

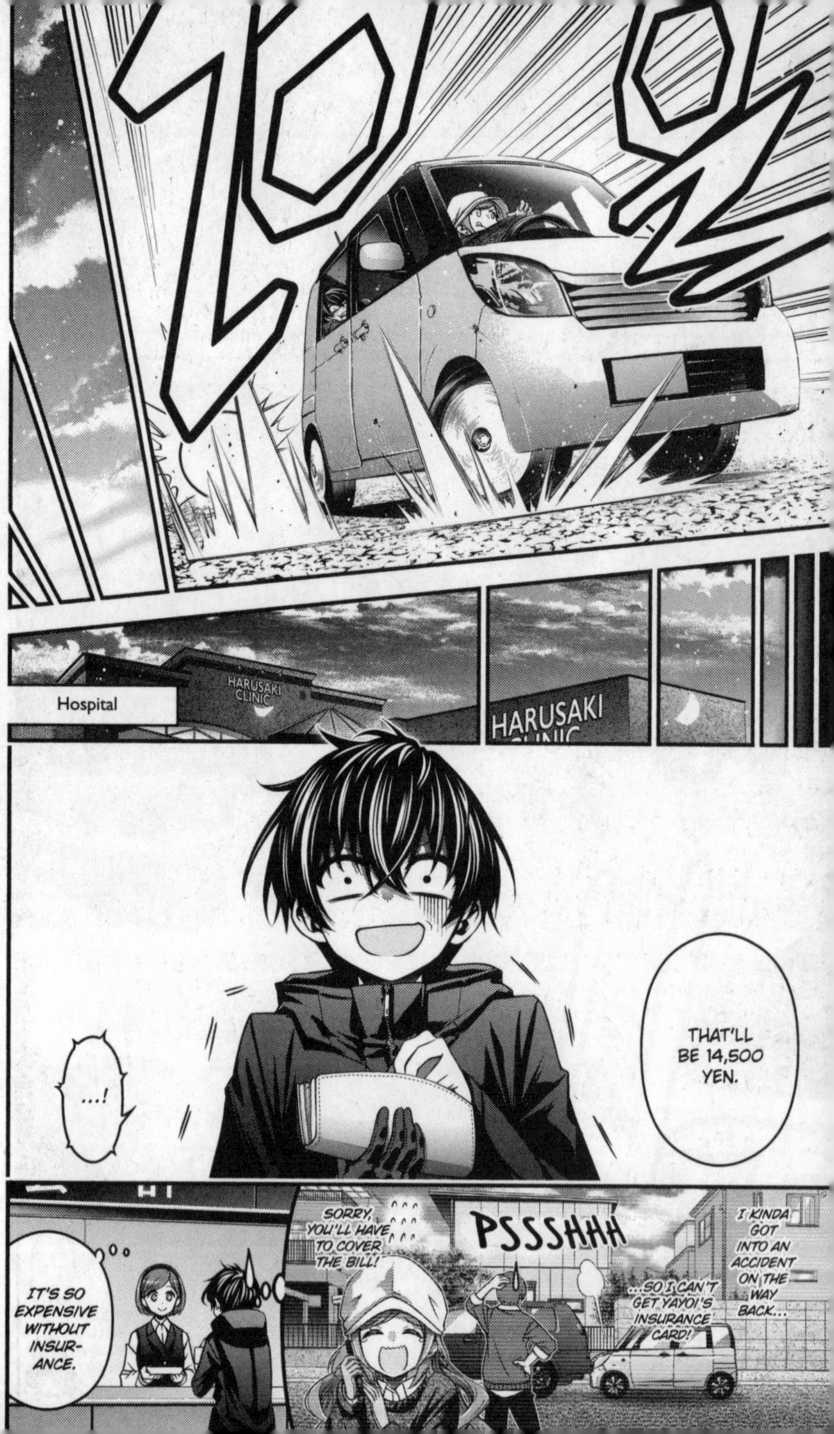
HARUSAKI CLINIC
Hospital
HARUSAKI CLINIC
THAT'LL BE 14,500 YEN.
...!
I KINDA GOT INTO AN ACCIDENT ON THE WAY BACK...
...SO I CAN'T GET YAYOI'S INSURANCE CARD!
PSSSHHH
SORRY, YOU'LL HAVE TO COVER THE BILL!
IT'S SO EXPENSIVE WITHOUT INSUR-ANCE.

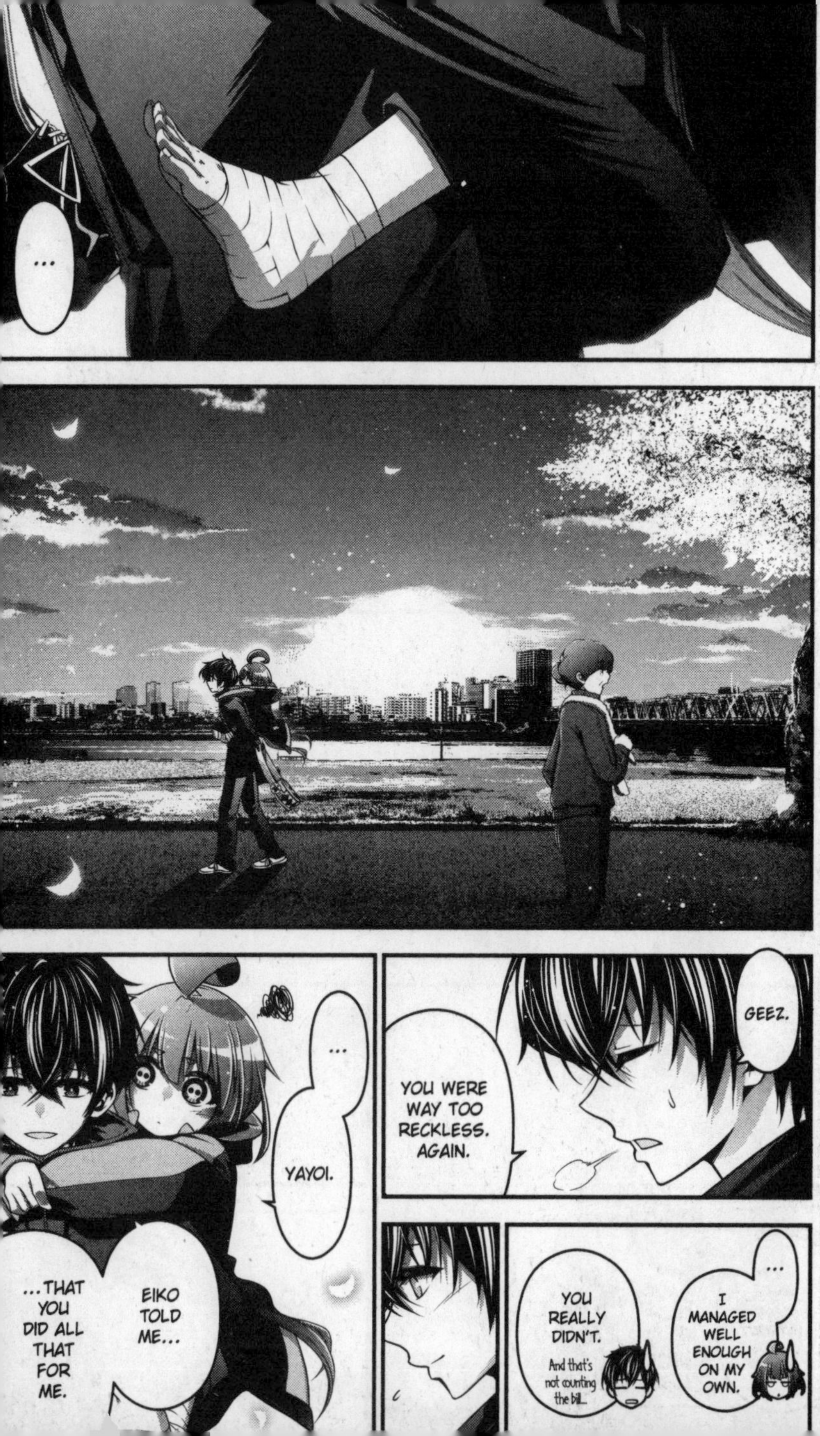
...
GEEZ.
YOU WERE WAY TOO RECKLESS. AGAIN.
...
I MANAGED WELL ENOUGH ON MY OWN.
YOU REALLY DIDN'T.
And that's not counting the bill...
...
YAYOI.
EIKO TOLD ME...
...THAT YOU DID ALL THAT FOR ME.

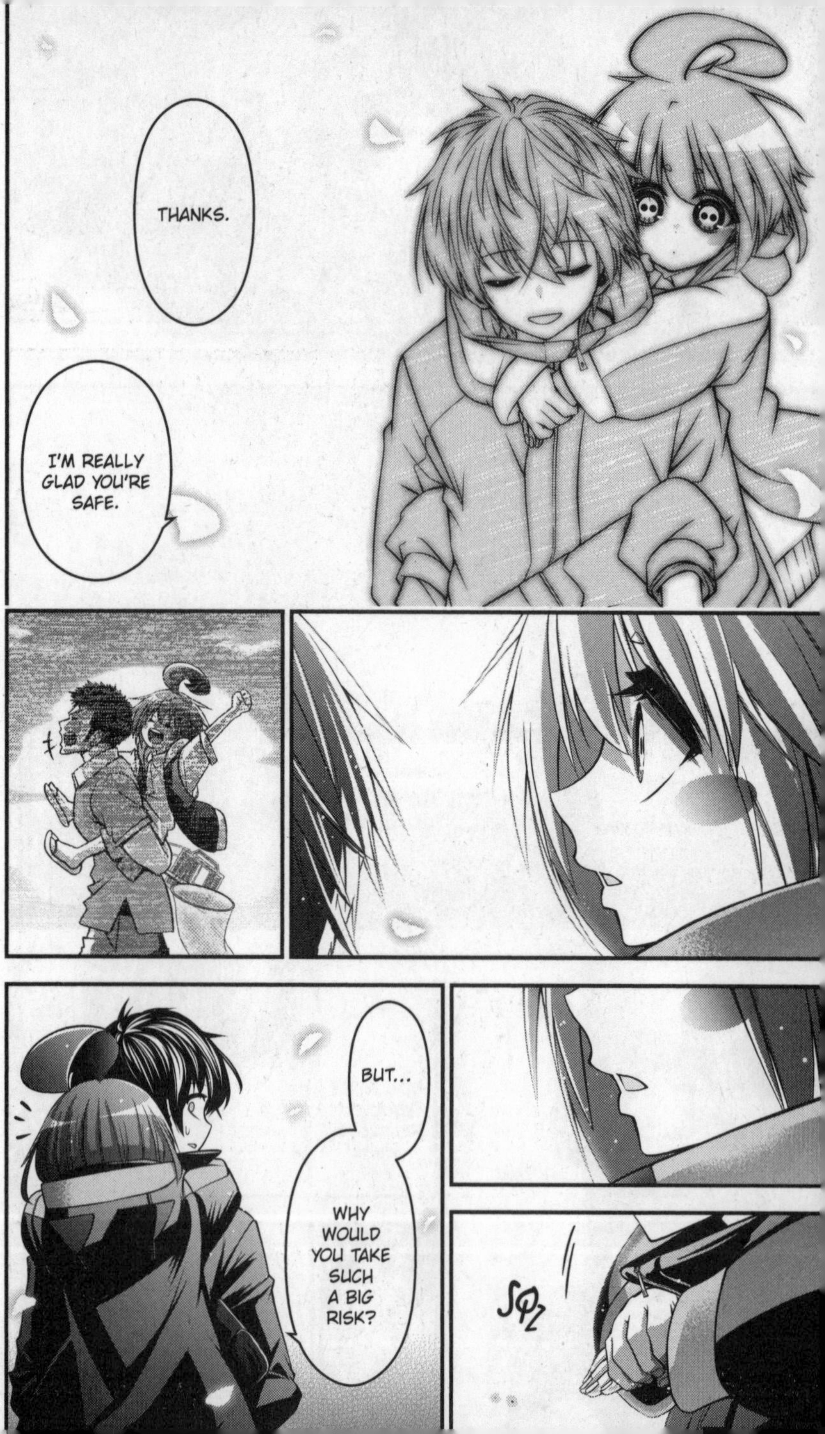
THANKS.
I'M REALLY GLAD YOU'RE SAFE.
SQZ
BUT...
WHY WOULD YOU TAKE SUCH A BIG RISK?

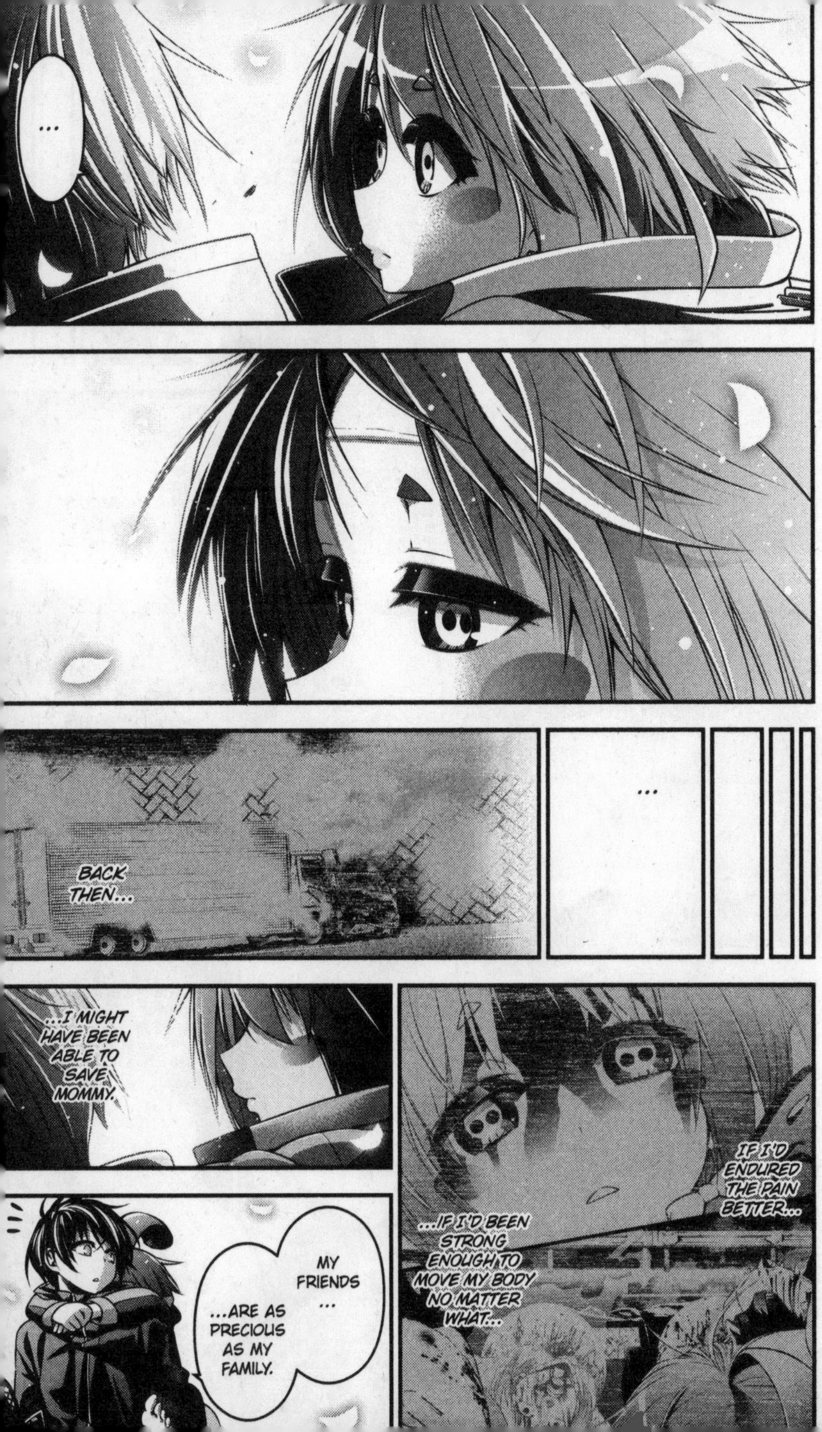
...
...
BACK THEN...
IF I'D ENDURED THE PAIN BETTER...
...IF I'D BEEN STRONG ENOUGH TO MOVE MY BODY NO MATTER WHAT...
...I MIGHT HAVE BEEN ABLE TO SAVE MOMMY.
MY FRIENDS ...
...ARE AS PRECIOUS AS MY FAMILY.

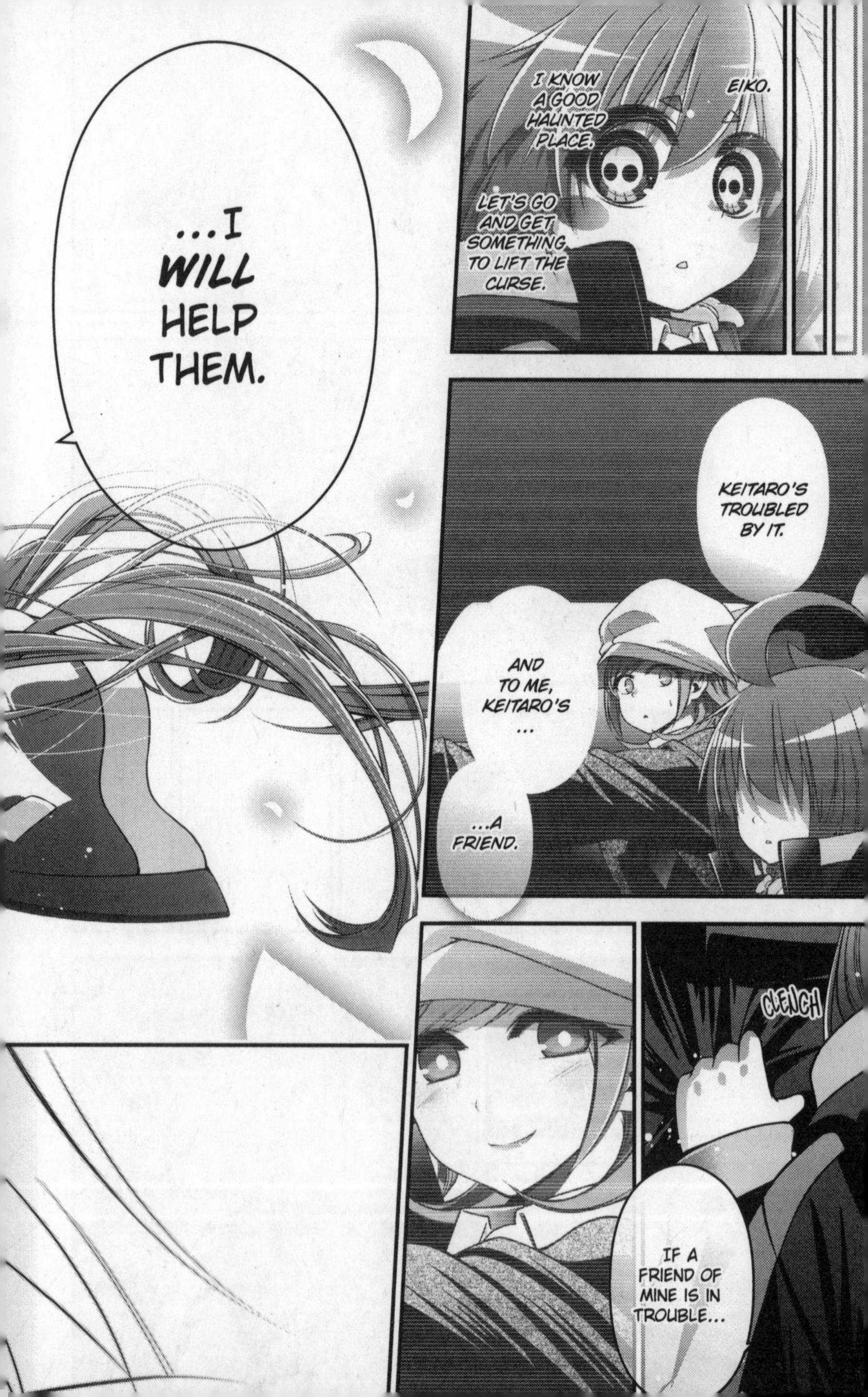
EIKO.
I KNOW A GOOD HAUNTED PLACE.
LET'S GO AND GET SOMETHING TO LIFT THE CURSE.
KEITARO'S TROUBLED BY IT.
AND TO ME, KEITARO'S ...
...A FRIEND.
CLENCH
IF A FRIEND OF MINE IS IN TROUBLE...
...I WILL HELP THEM.

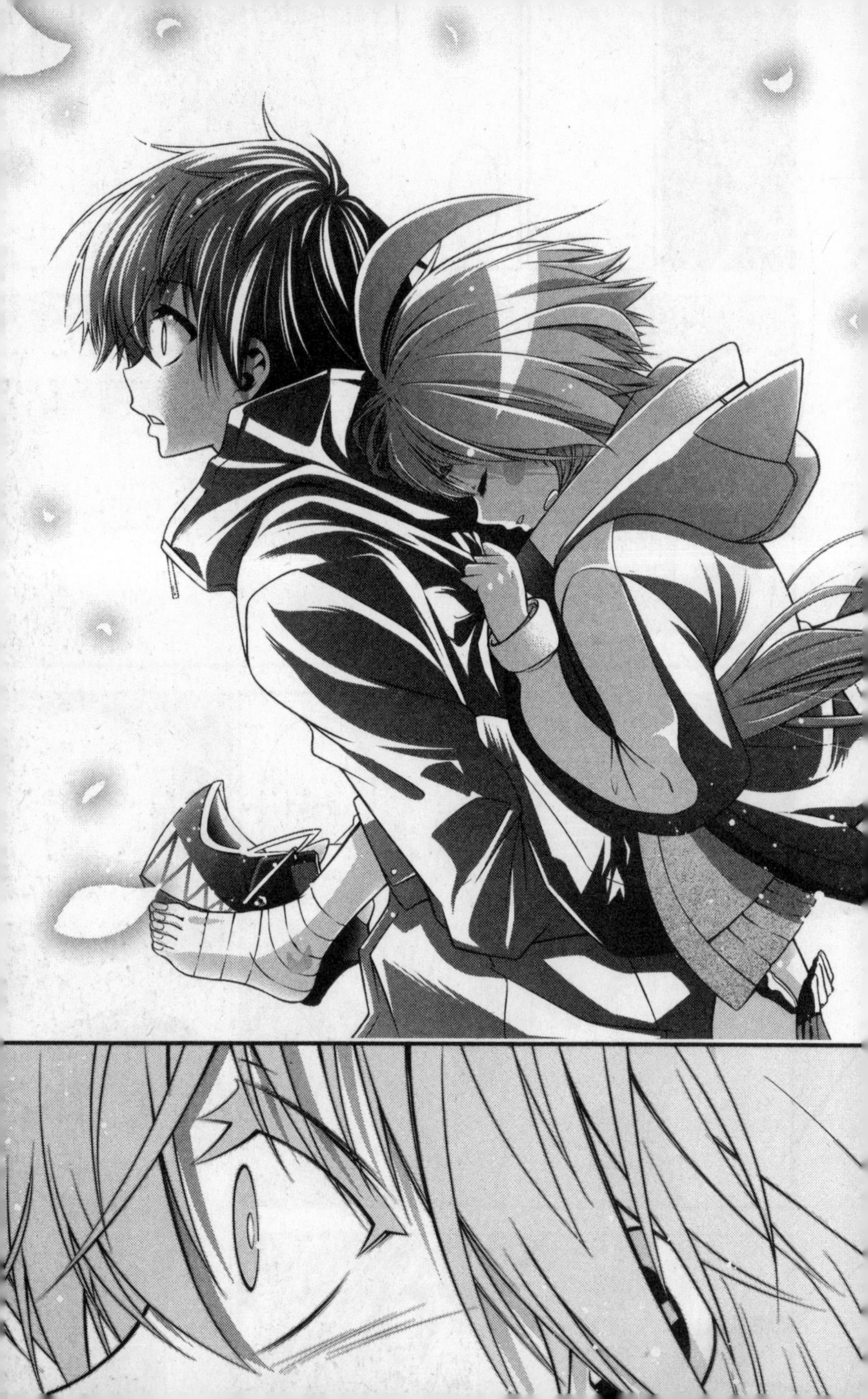

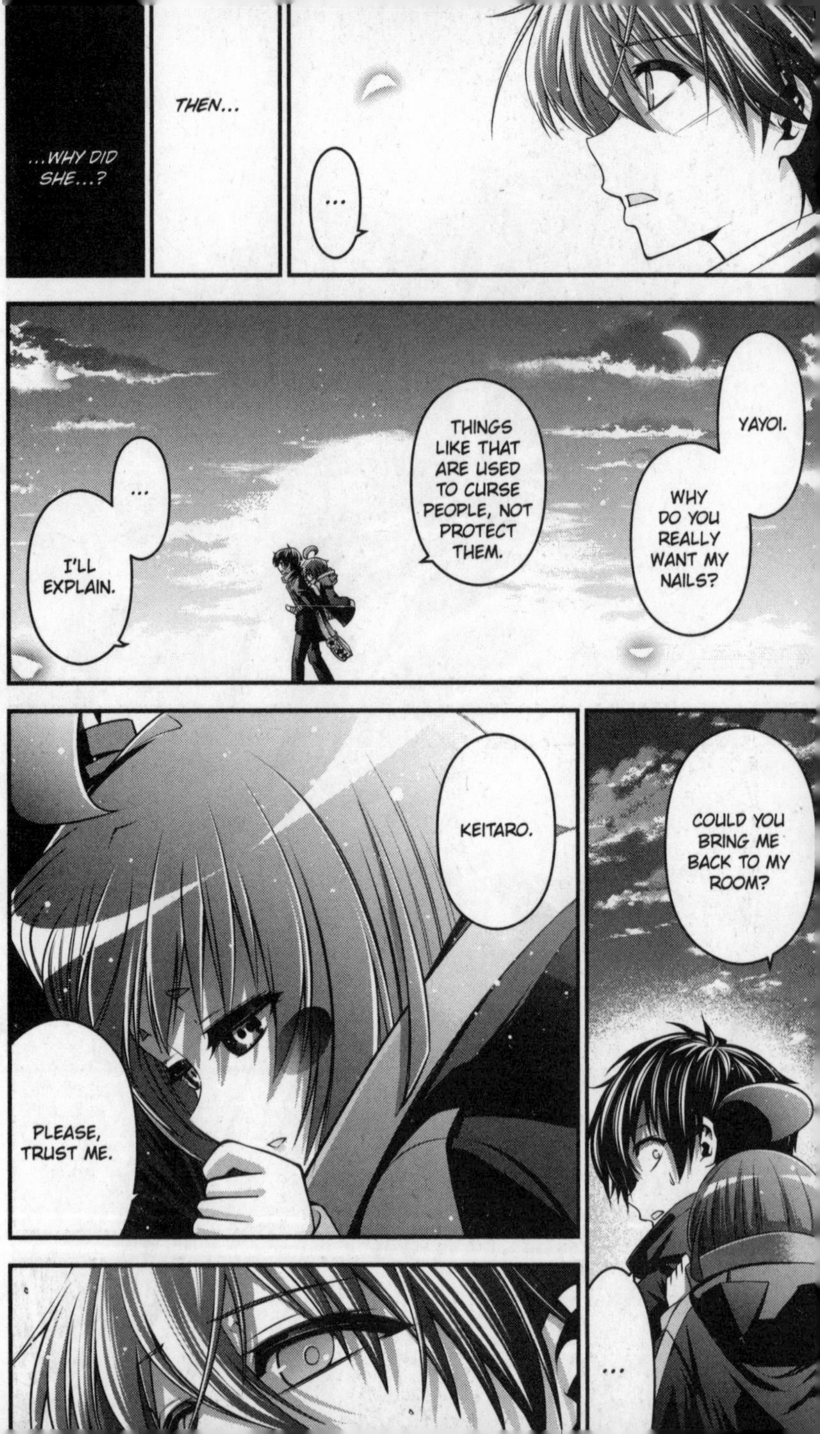
...
THEN...
...WHY DID SHE...?
YAYOI.
WHY DO YOU REALLY WANT MY NAILS?
THINGS LIKE THAT ARE USED TO CURSE PEOPLE, NOT PROTECT THEM.
...
I'LL EXPLAIN.
COULD YOU BRING ME BACK TO MY ROOM?
...
KEITARO.
PLEASE, TRUST ME.

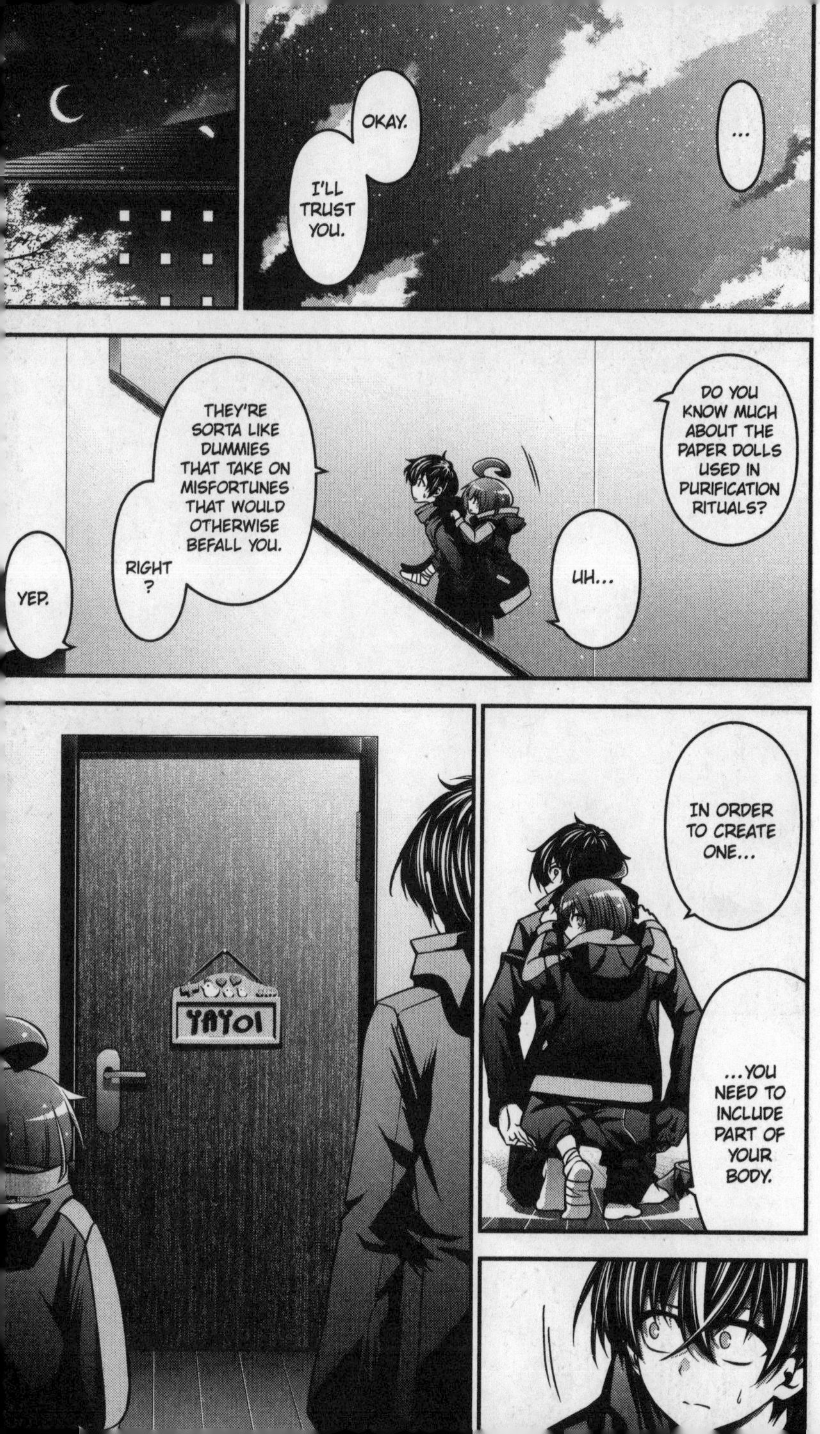
...
OKAY.
I'LL TRUST YOU.
DO YOU KNOW MUCH ABOUT THE PAPER DOLLS USED IN PURIFICATION RITUALS?
UH...
THEY'RE SORTA LIKE DUMMIES THAT TAKE ON MISFORTUNES THAT WOULD OTHERWISE BEFALL YOU.
RIGHT?
YEP.
IN ORDER TO CREATE ONE...
...YOU NEED TO INCLUDE PART OF YOUR BODY.
YAYOI

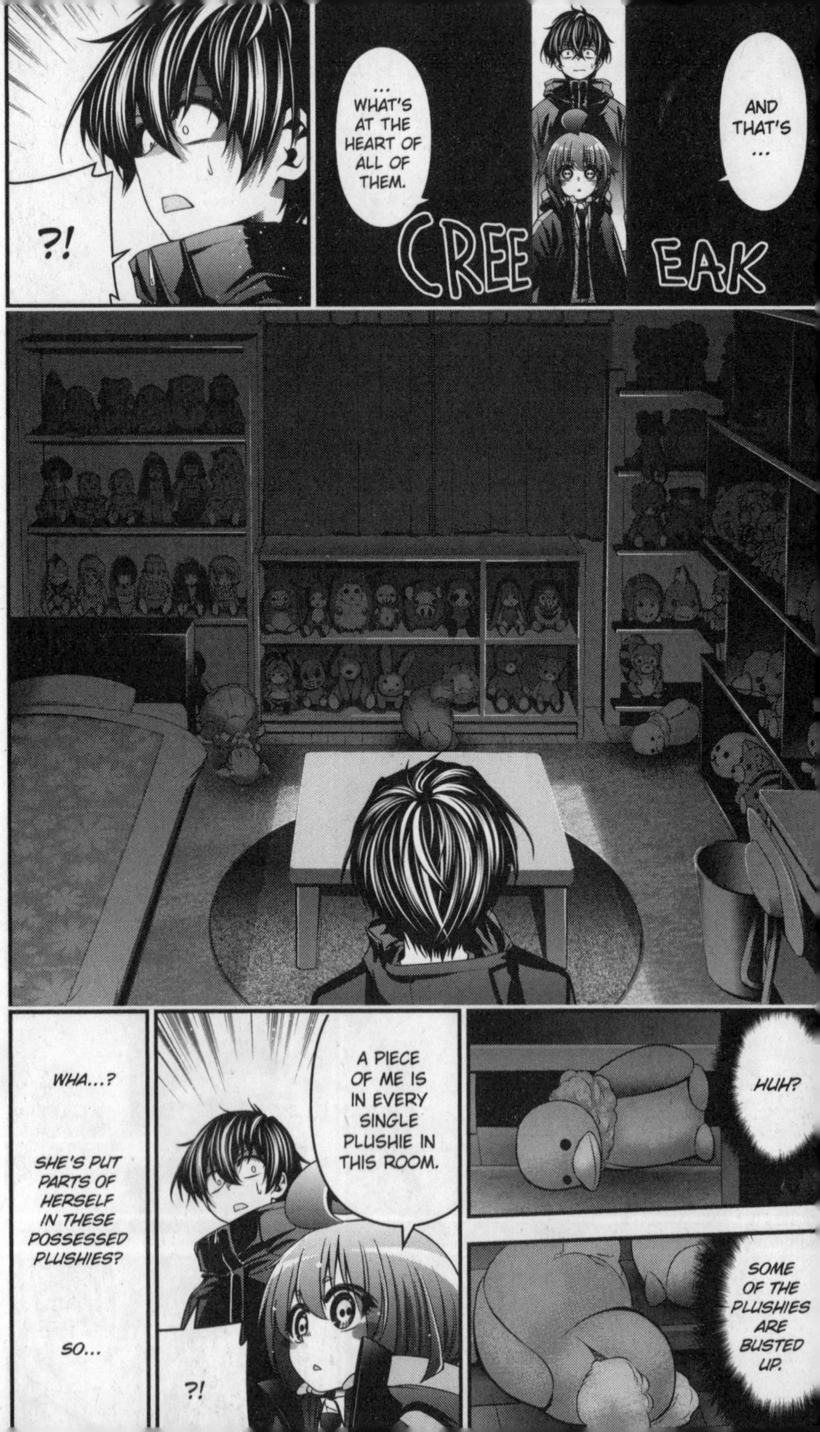
AND THAT'S ...
... WHAT'S AT THE HEART OF ALL OF THEM.
CREE EAK
?!
HUH?
SOME OF THE PLUSHIES ARE BUSTED UP.
A PIECE OF ME IS IN EVERY SINGLE PLUSHIE IN THIS ROOM.
?!
WHA...?
SHE'S PUT PARTS OF HERSELF IN THESE POSSESSED PLUSHIES?
SO...

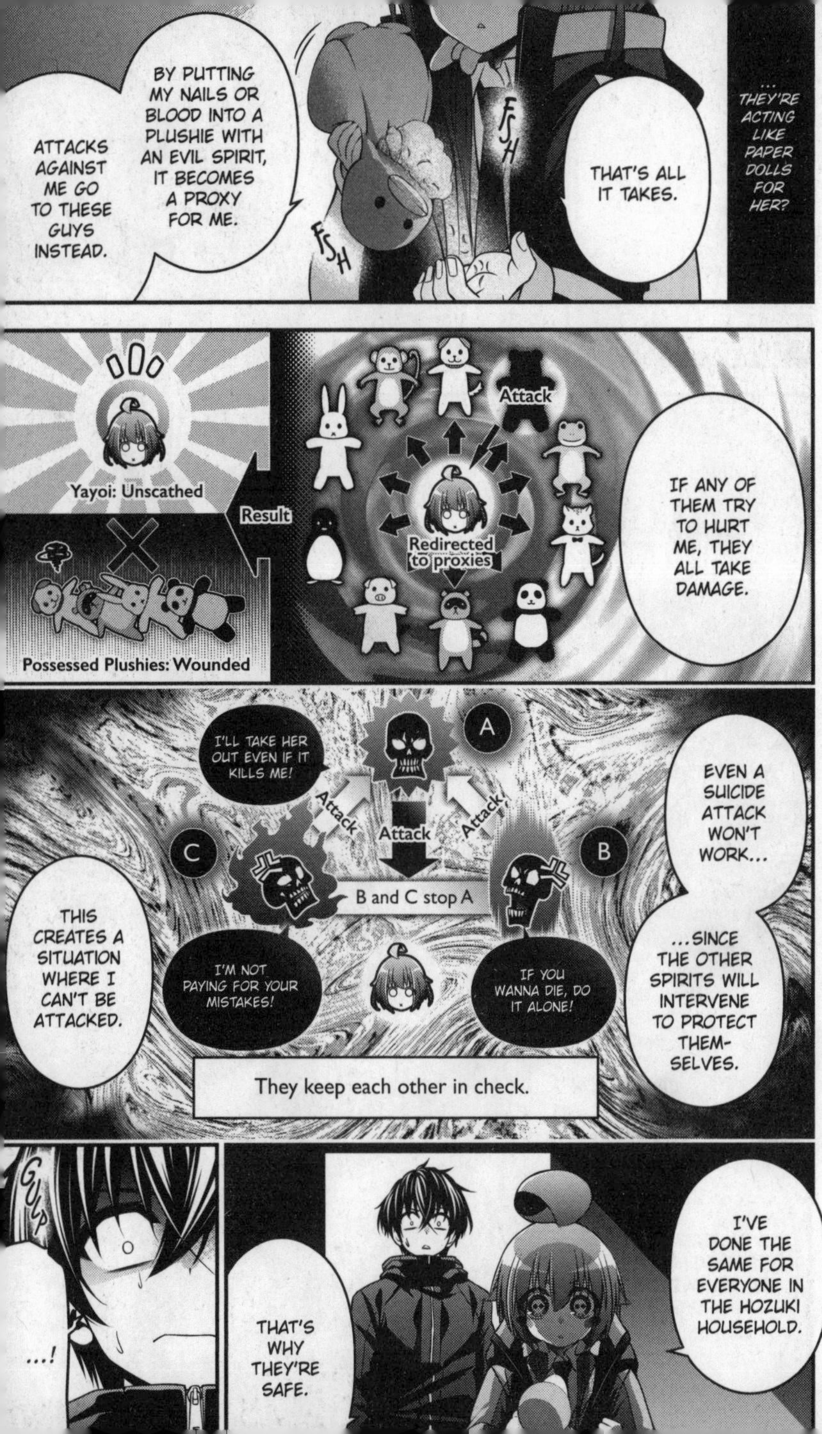
...THEY'RE ACTING LIKE PAPER DOLLS FOR HER?
THAT'S ALL IT TAKES.
FSH
BY PUTTING MY NAILS OR BLOOD INTO A PLUSHIE WITH AN EVIL SPIRIT, IT BECOMES A PROXY FOR ME.
FSH
ATTACKS AGAINST ME GO TO THESE GUYS INSTEAD.
IF ANY OF THEM TRY TO HURT ME, THEY ALL TAKE DAMAGE.
Attack
Redirected to proxies
Result
Yayoi: Unscathed
Possessed Plushies: Wounded
EVEN A SUICIDE ATTACK WON'T WORK...
...SINCE THE OTHER SPIRITS WILL INTERVENE TO PROTECT THEM-SELVES.
A
I'LL TAKE HER OUT EVEN IF IT KILLS ME!
Attack
Attack
Attack
B
C
B and C stop A
IF YOU WANNA DIE, DO IT ALONE!
I'M NOT PAYING FOR YOUR MISTAKES!
They keep each other in check.
THIS CREATES A SITUATION WHERE I CAN'T BE ATTACKED.
I'VE DONE THE SAME FOR EVERYONE IN THE HOZUKI HOUSEHOLD.
THAT'S WHY THEY'RE SAFE.
GULP
...!

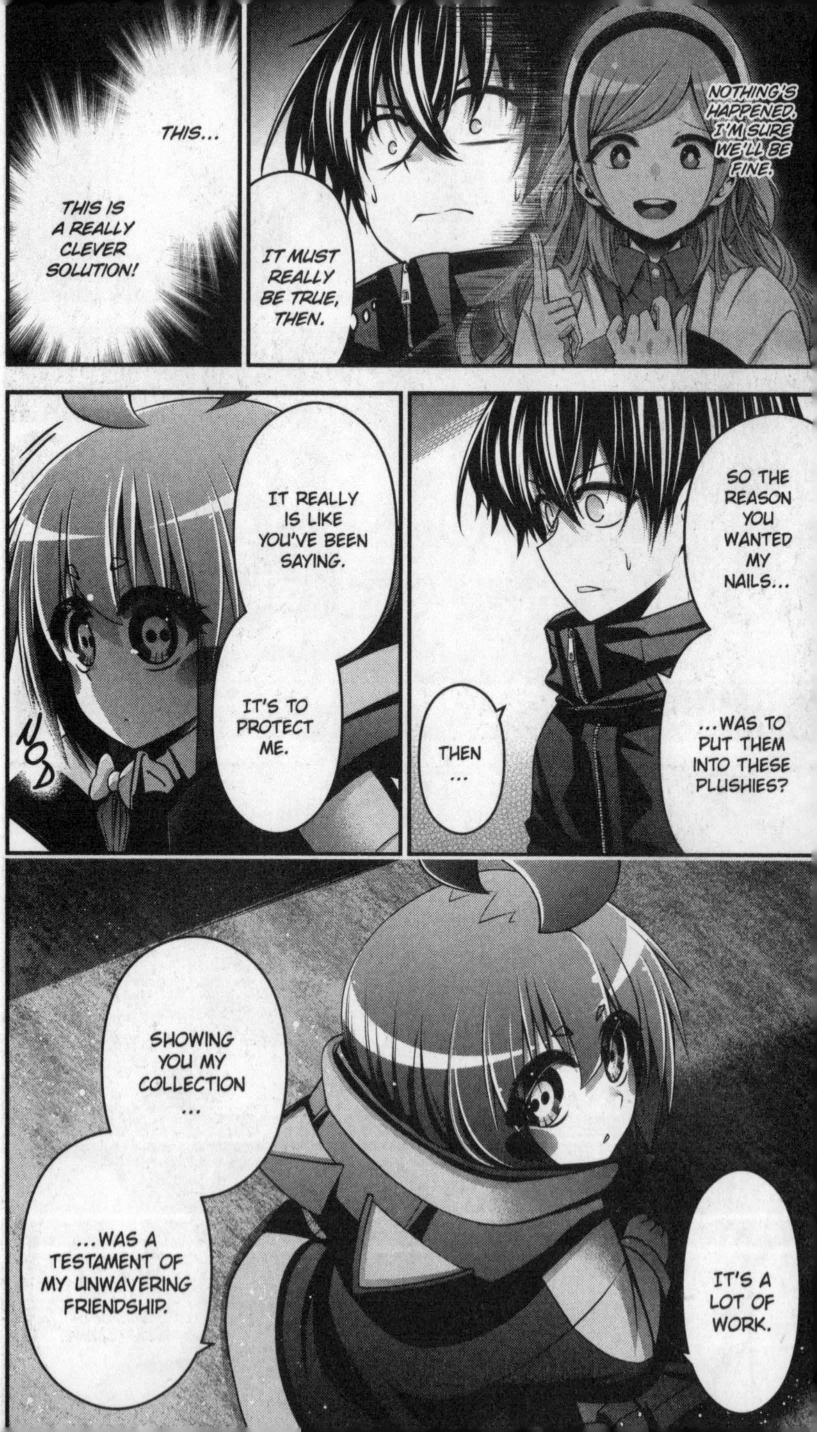
NOTHING'S HAPPENED. I'M SURE WE'LL BE FINE.
IT MUST REALLY BE TRUE, THEN.
THIS...
THIS IS A REALLY CLEVER SOLUTION!
SO THE REASON YOU WANTED MY NAILS...
...WAS TO PUT THEM INTO THESE PLUSHIES?
THEN...
IT REALLY IS LIKE YOU'VE BEEN SAYING.
IT'S TO PROTECT ME.
NOD
SHOWING YOU MY COLLECTION...
...WAS A TESTAMENT OF MY UNWAVERING FRIENDSHIP.
IT'S A LOT OF WORK.

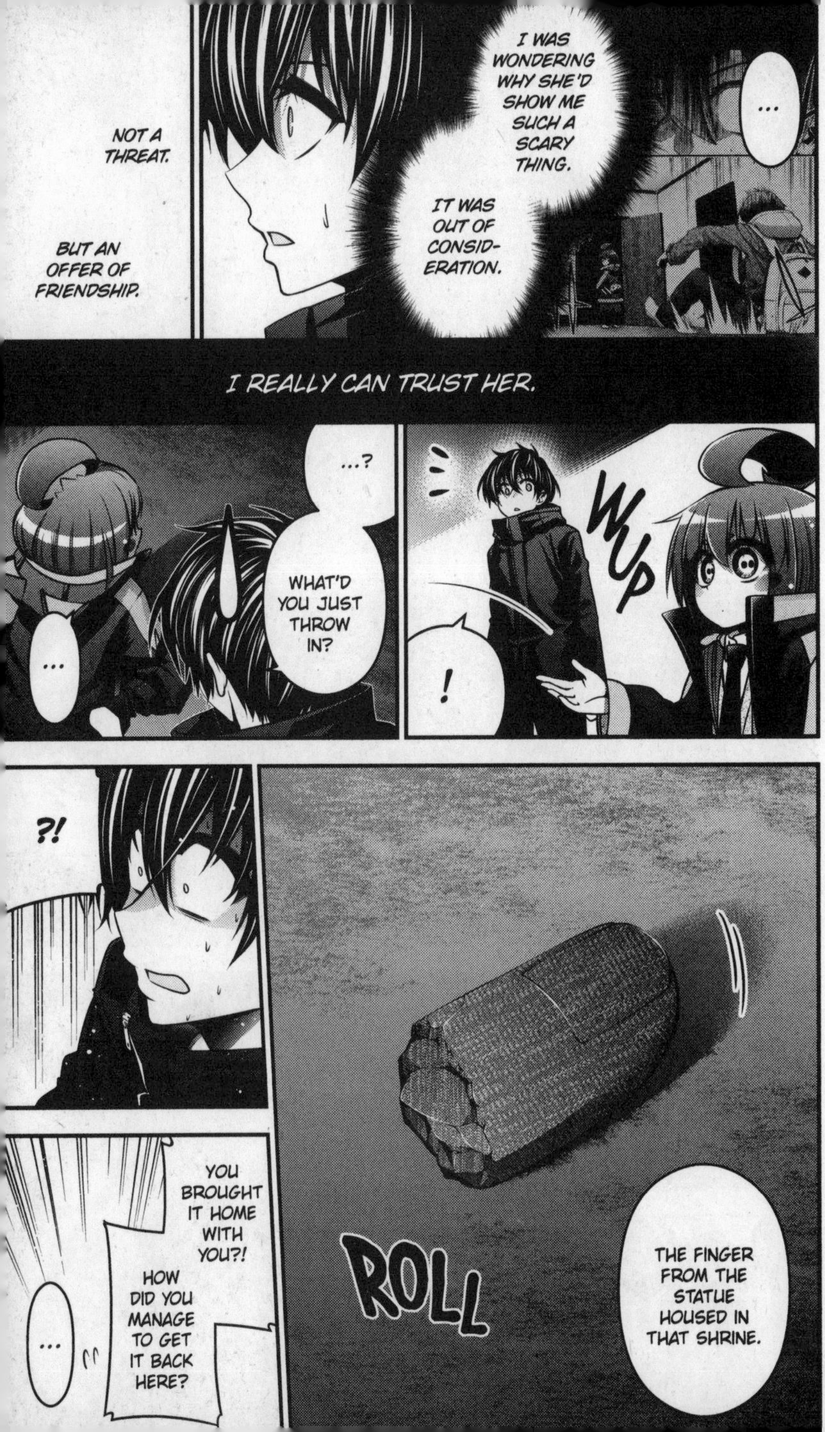
...
I WAS WONDERING WHY SHE'D SHOW ME SUCH A SCARY THING.
IT WAS OUT OF CONSID-ERATION.
NOT A THREAT.
BUT AN OFFER OF FRIENDSHIP.
I REALLY CAN TRUST HER.
WUP
!
...?
WHAT'D YOU JUST THROW IN?
...
THE FINGER FROM THE STATUE HOUSED IN THAT SHRINE.
ROLL
?!
YOU BROUGHT IT HOME WITH YOU?!
HOW DID YOU MANAGE TO GET IT BACK HERE?
...

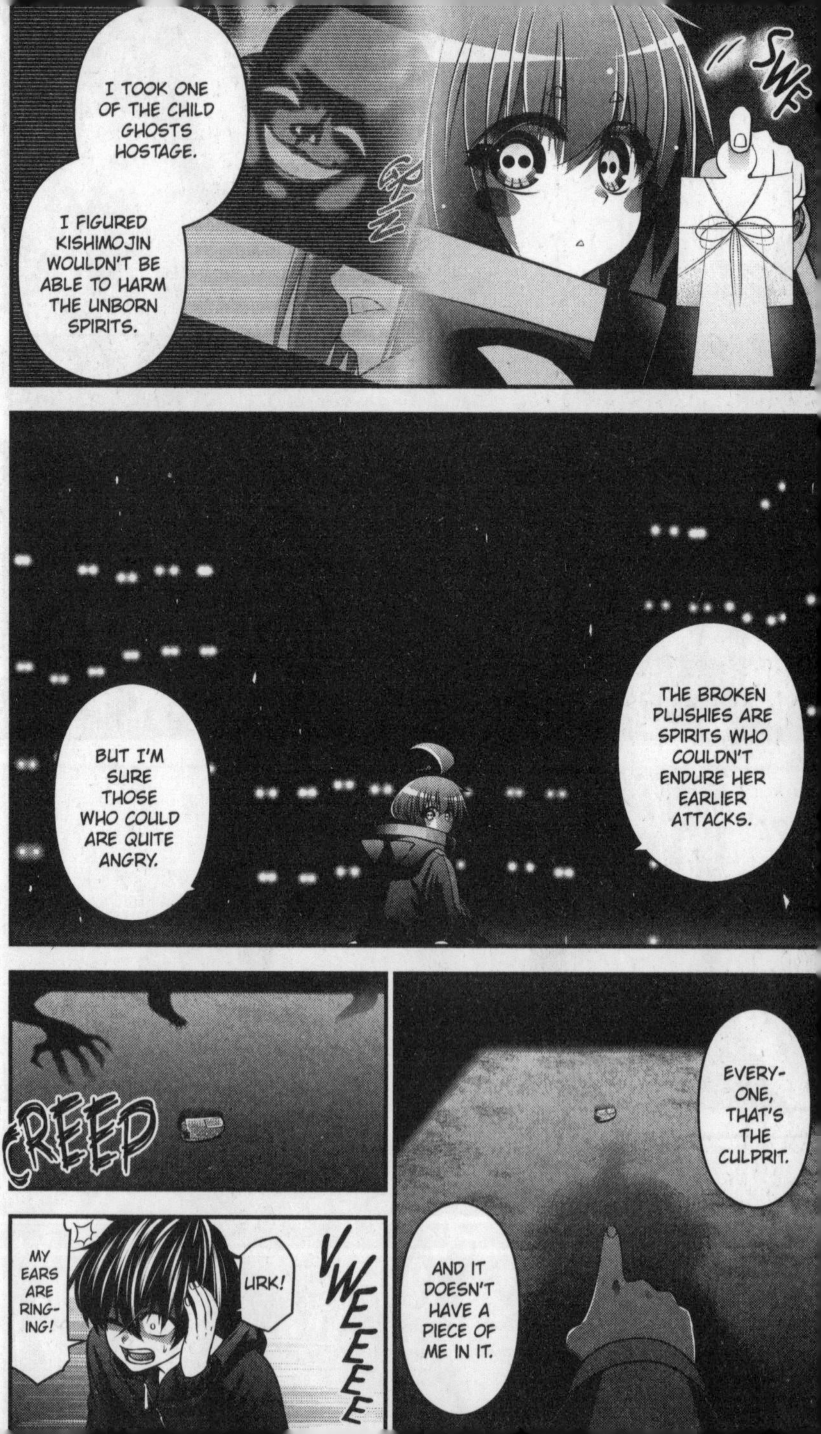
SWF
I TOOK ONE OF THE CHILD GHOSTS HOSTAGE.
GRIN
I FIGURED KISHIMOJIN WOULDN'T BE ABLE TO HARM THE UNBORN SPIRITS.
THE BROKEN PLUSHIES ARE SPIRITS WHO COULDN'T ENDURE HER EARLIER ATTACKS.
BUT I'M SURE THOSE WHO COULD ARE QUITE ANGRY.
EVERY-ONE, THAT'S THE CULPRIT.
AND IT DOESN'T HAVE A PIECE OF ME IN IT.
CREEP
VWEEEE
URK!
MY EARS ARE RING-ING!

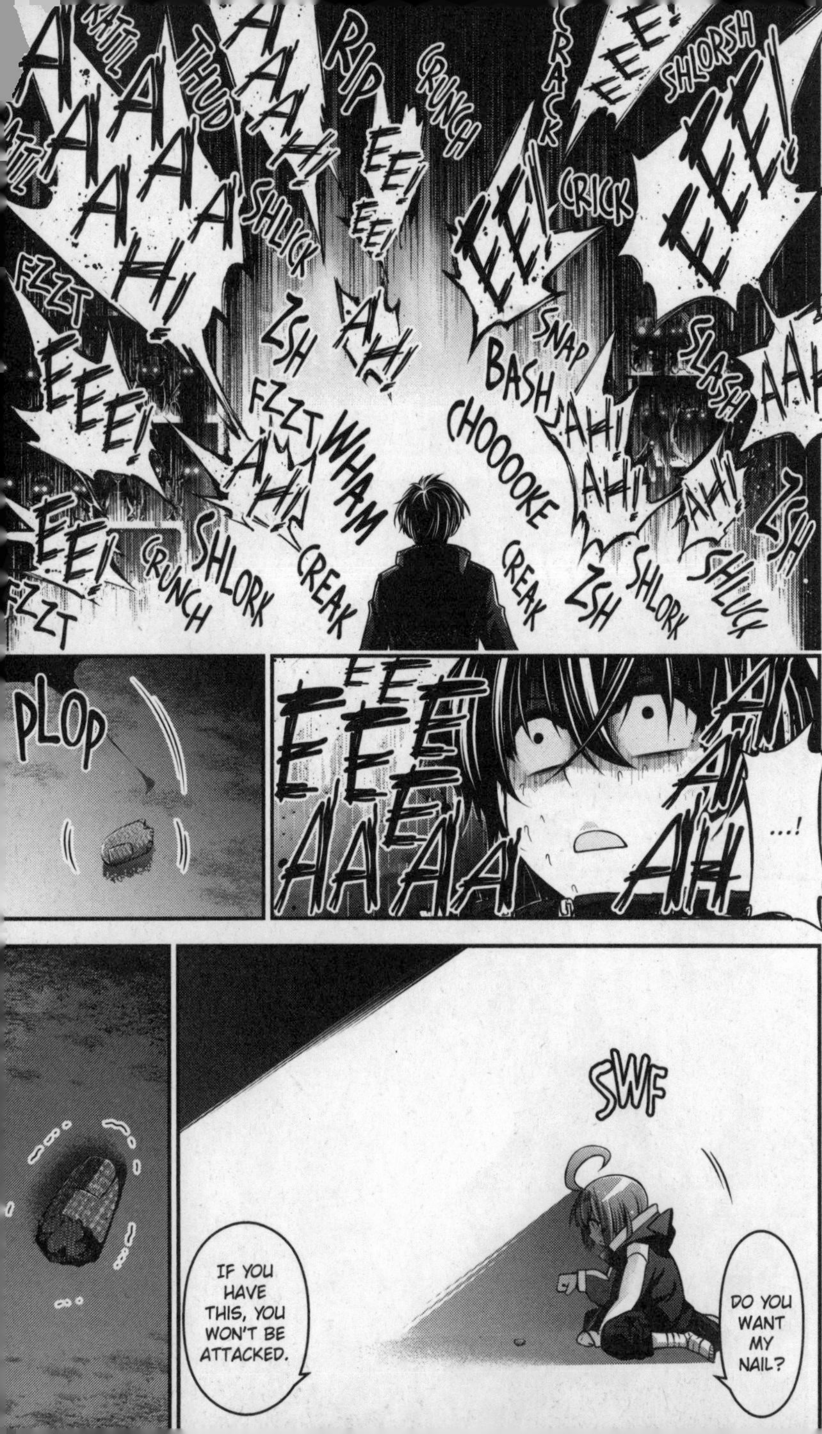
SHLORSH
EEE!
EEEE!
CRACK
CRICK
EEE!
CRUNCH
RIP
EEE!
EE!
AAH!
THUD
AAAH!
RATTLE
AAAAAH!
SLASH
AAH!
SNAP
BASH
AAH!
AAH!
AAH!
ZSH
SHLUCK
SHLORK
ZSH
CREAK
CHOOOOOKE
WHAM
CREAK
AAH!
FZZZT
ZSH
SHLICK
SHLORK
CRUNCH
EEEE!
FZZT
EEE!
FZZT
EEEEEEEAAAAAAAH
...!
PLOP
SWF
DO YOU WANT MY NAIL?
IF YOU HAVE THIS, YOU WON'T BE ATTACKED.

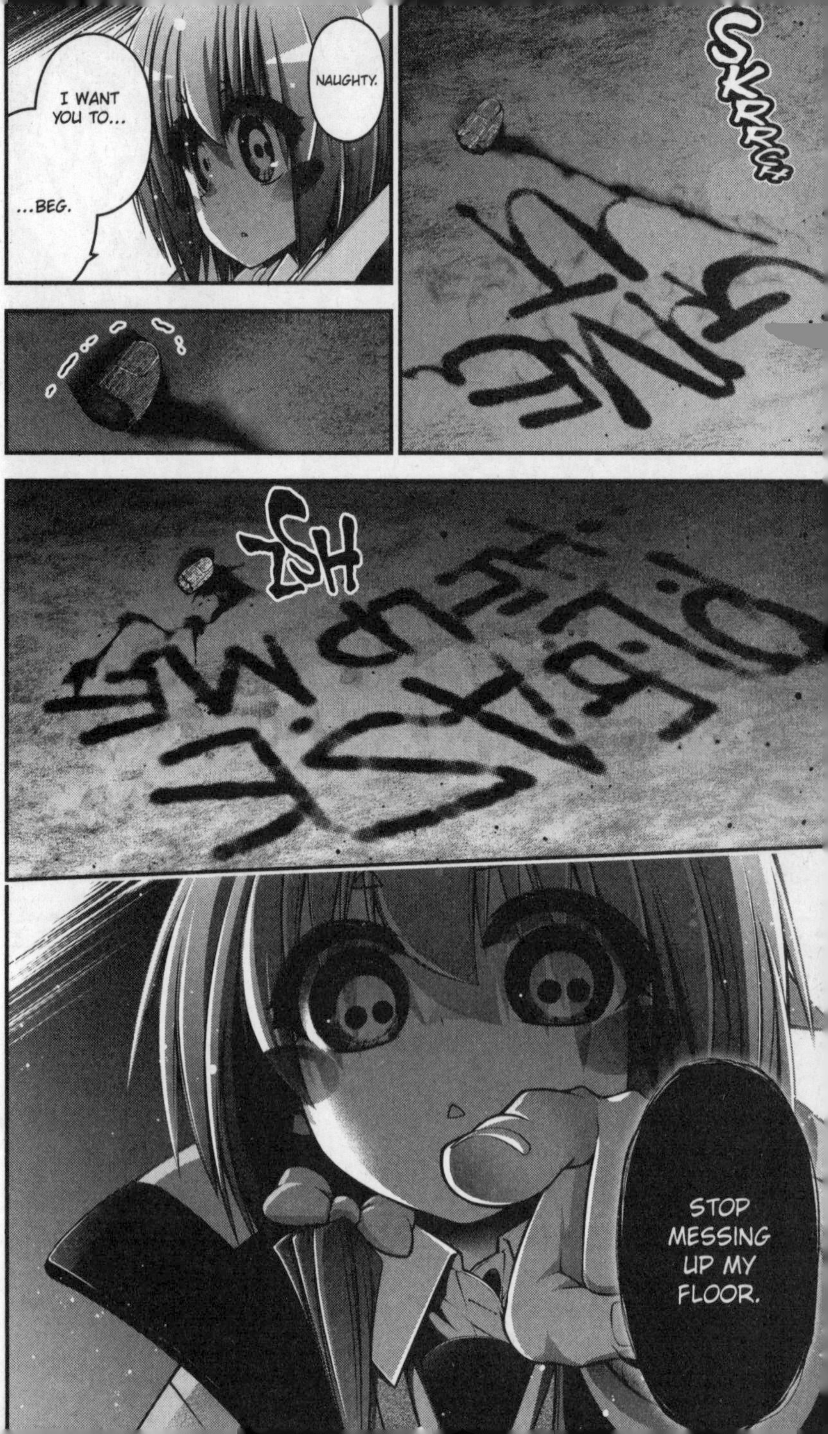
SKRRCH
NAUGHTY.
I WANT YOU TO...
...BEG.
STOP MESSING UP MY FLOOR.

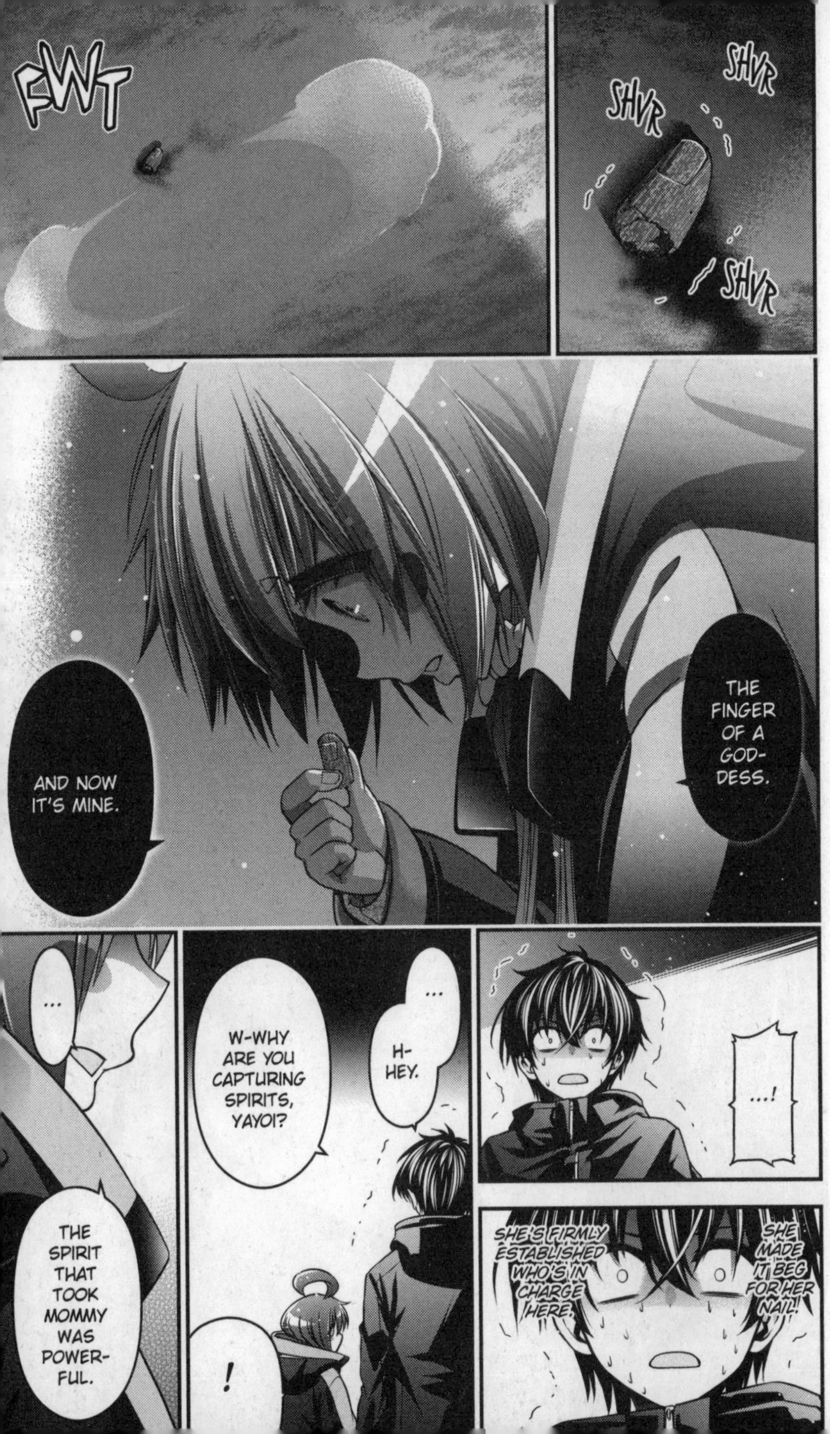
SHVR
SHVR
SHVR
FWT
THE FINGER OF A GOD-DESS.
AND NOW IT'S MINE.
...!
SHE MADE IT BEG FOR HER NAIL!
SHE'S FIRMLY ESTABLISHED WHO'S IN CHARGE HERE.
...
H-HEY.
W-WHY ARE YOU CAPTURING SPIRITS, YAYOI?
!
...
THE SPIRIT THAT TOOK MOMMY WAS POWER-FUL.

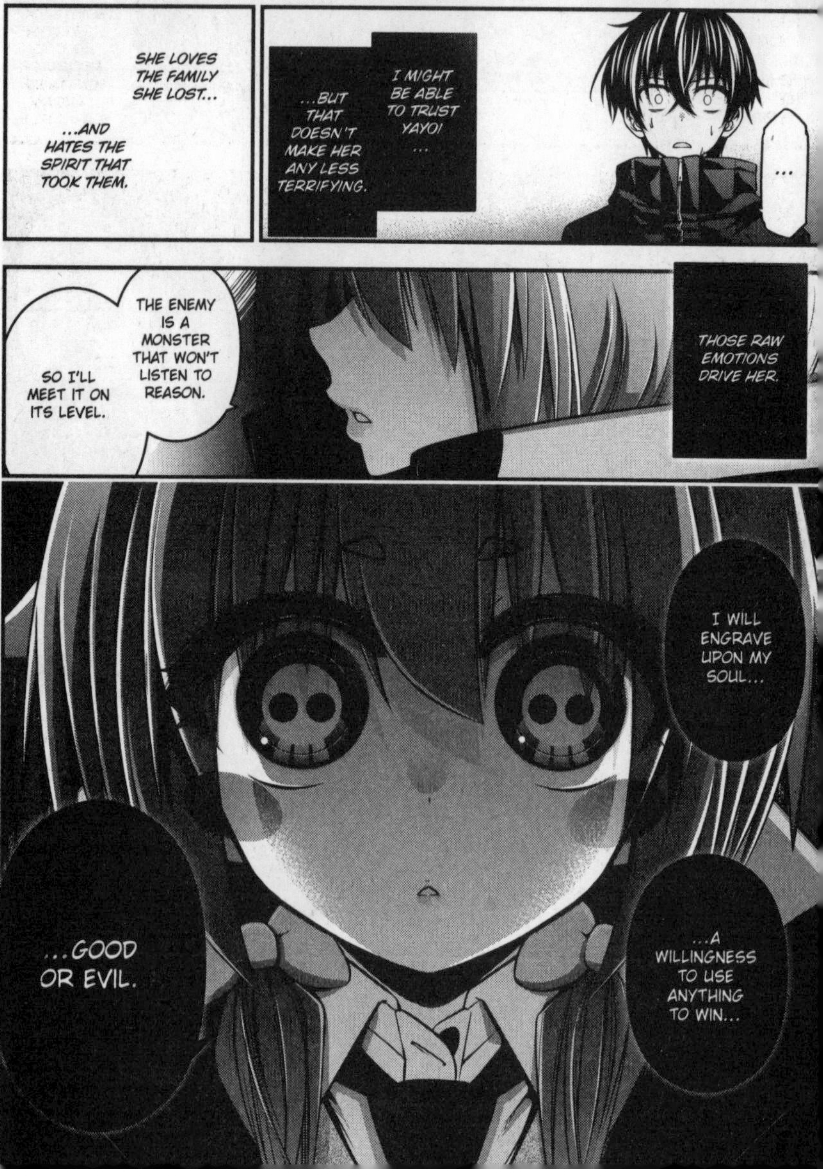
...
I MIGHT BE ABLE TO TRUST YAYOI ...
...BUT THAT DOESN'T MAKE HER ANY LESS TERRIFYING.
SHE LOVES THE FAMILY SHE LOST...
...AND HATES THE SPIRIT THAT TOOK THEM.
THOSE RAW EMOTIONS DRIVE HER.
THE ENEMY IS A MONSTER THAT WON'T LISTEN TO REASON.
SO I'LL MEET IT ON ITS LEVEL.
I WILL ENGRAVE UPON MY SOUL...
...A WILLINGNESS TO USE ANYTHING TO WIN...
...GOOD OR EVIL.

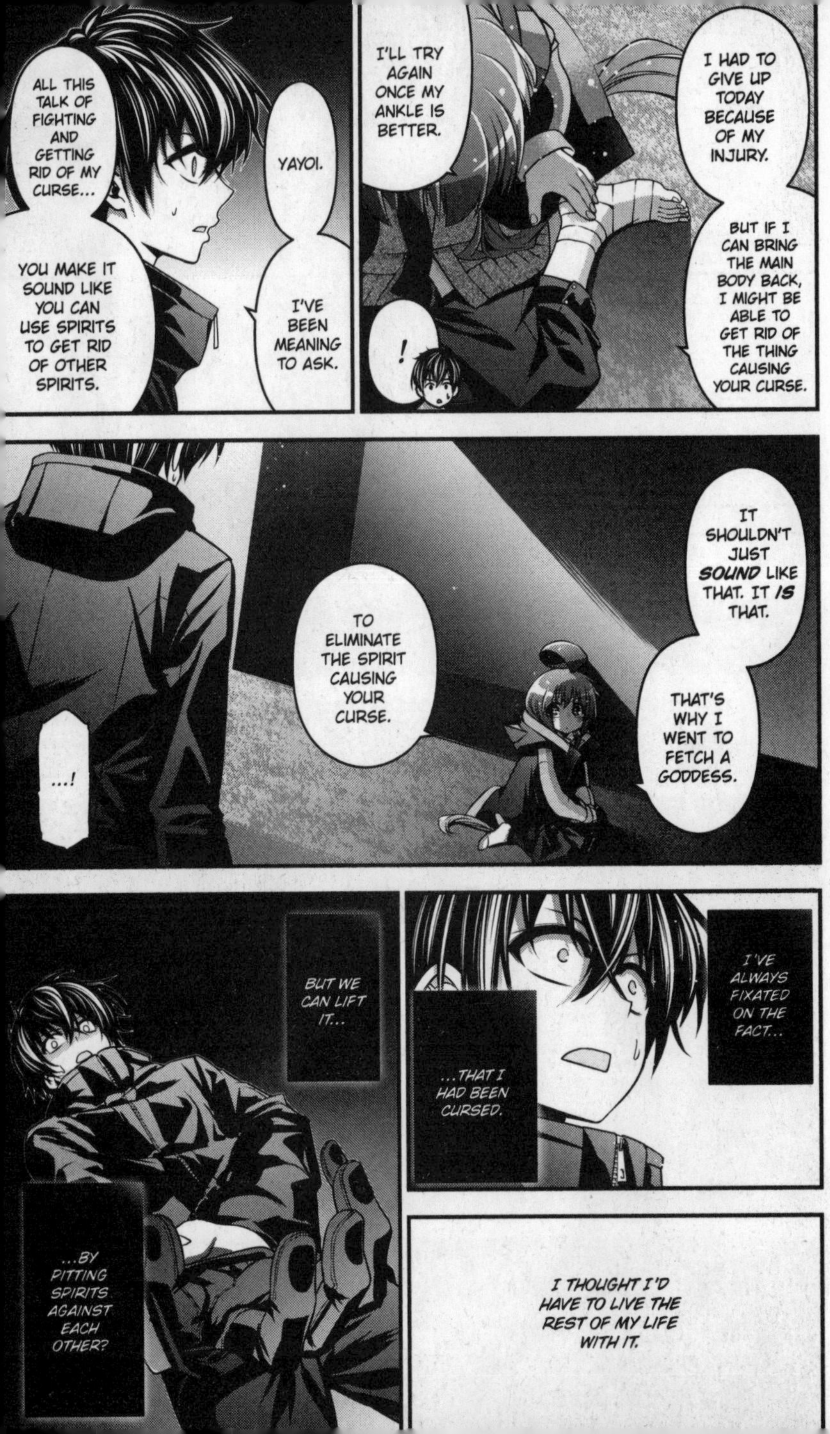
I HAD TO GIVE UP TODAY BECAUSE OF MY INJURY.
I'LL TRY AGAIN ONCE MY ANKLE IS BETTER.
BUT IF I CAN BRING THE MAIN BODY BACK, I MIGHT BE ABLE TO GET RID OF THE THING CAUSING YOUR CURSE.
!
YAYOI.
I'VE BEEN MEANING TO ASK.
ALL THIS TALK OF FIGHTING AND GETTING RID OF MY CURSE...
YOU MAKE IT SOUND LIKE YOU CAN USE SPIRITS TO GET RID OF OTHER SPIRITS.
IT SHOULDN'T JUST ***SOUND*** LIKE THAT. IT ***IS*** THAT.
THAT'S WHY I WENT TO FETCH A GODDESS.
TO ELIMINATE THE SPIRIT CAUSING YOUR CURSE.
...!
I'VE ALWAYS FIXATED ON THE FACT...
...THAT I HAD BEEN CURSED.
I THOUGHT I'D HAVE TO LIVE THE REST OF MY LIFE WITH IT.
BUT WE CAN LIFT IT...
...BY PITTING SPIRITS AGAINST EACH OTHER?

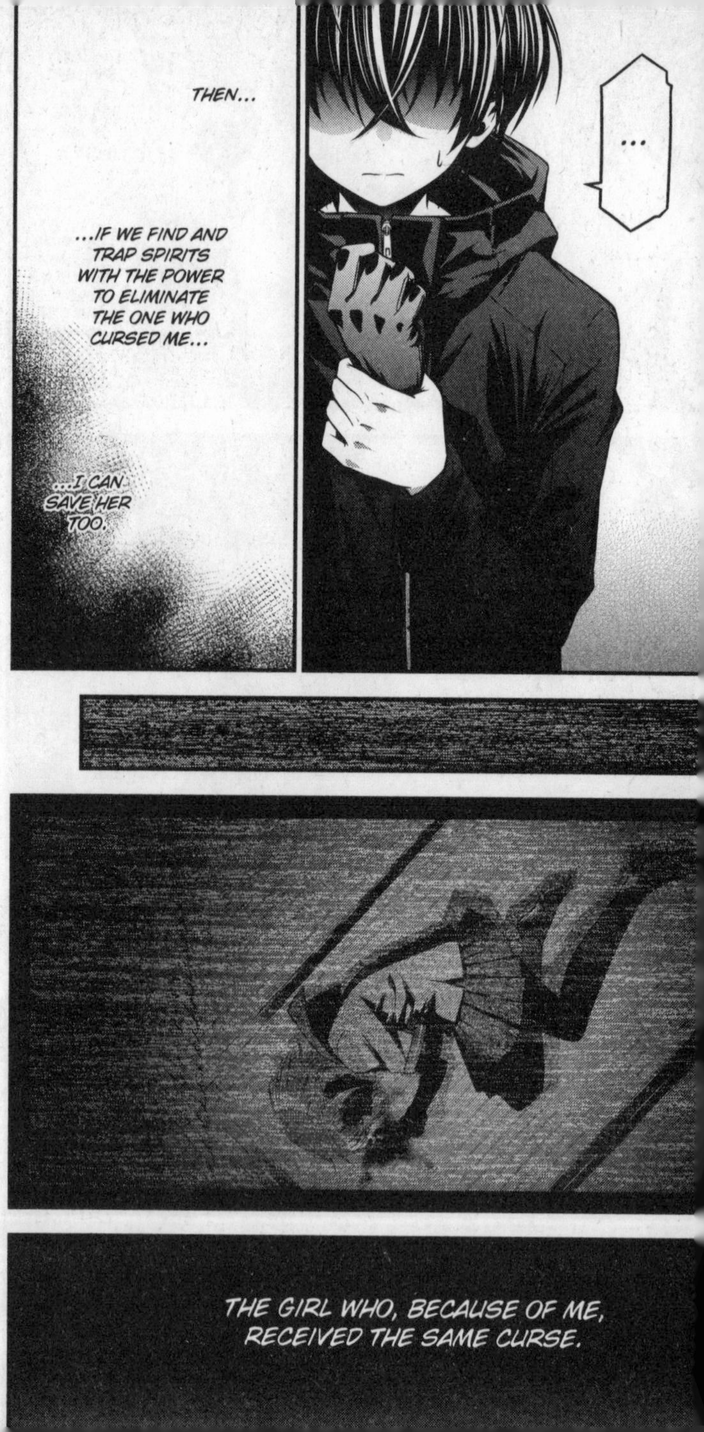
...
THEN...
...IF WE FIND AND TRAP SPIRITS WITH THE POWER TO ELIMINATE THE ONE WHO CURSED ME...
...I CAN SAVE HER TOO.
THE GIRL WHO, BECAUSE OF ME, RECEIVED THE SAME CURSE.

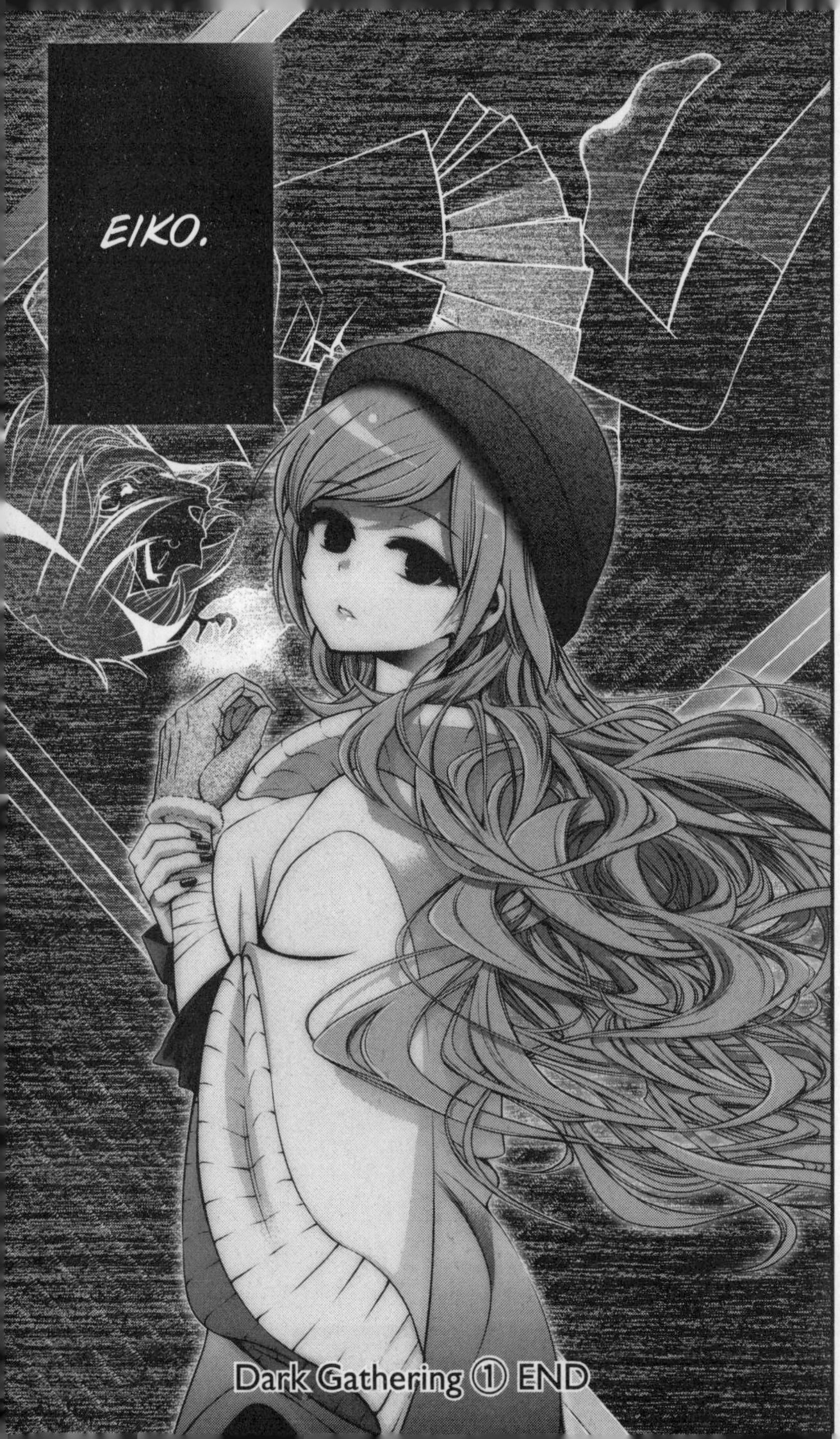
EIKO.
Dark Gathering ① END

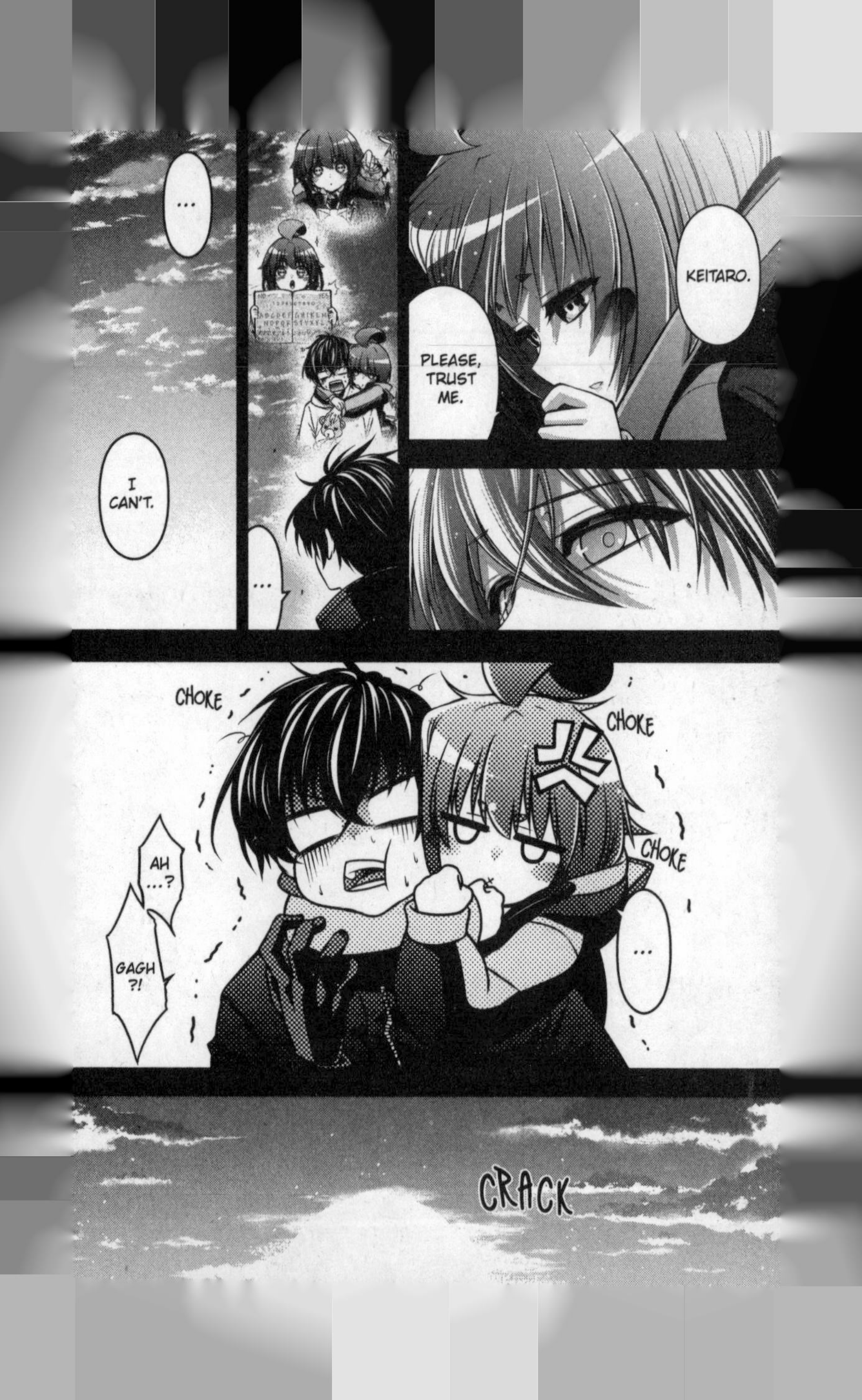
KEITARO.
PLEASE, TRUST ME.
...
...
I CAN'T.
CHOKE
CHOKE
...
CHOKE
AH ...?
GAGH ?!
CRACK

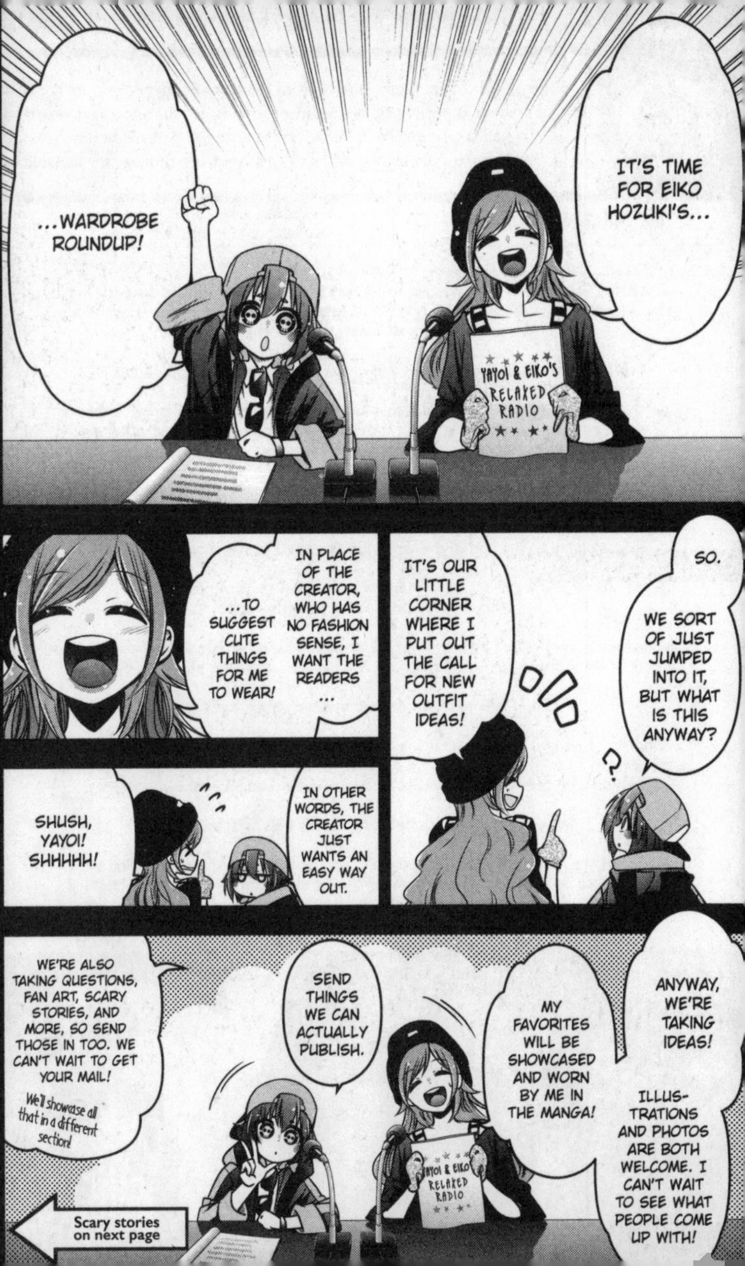
IT'S TIME FOR EIKO HOZUKI'S...
YAYOI & EIKO'S RELAXED RADIO
...WARDROBE ROUNDUP!
SO.
WE SORT OF JUST JUMPED INTO IT, BUT WHAT IS THIS ANYWAY?
IT'S OUR LITTLE CORNER WHERE I PUT OUT THE CALL FOR NEW OUTFIT IDEAS!
IN PLACE OF THE CREATOR, WHO HAS NO FASHION SENSE, I WANT THE READERS...
...TO SUGGEST CUTE THINGS FOR ME TO WEAR!
IN OTHER WORDS, THE CREATOR JUST WANTS AN EASY WAY OUT.
SHUSH, YAYOI! SHHHHH!
ANYWAY, WE'RE TAKING IDEAS!
ILLUS-TRATIONS AND PHOTOS ARE BOTH WELCOME. I CAN'T WAIT TO SEE WHAT PEOPLE COME UP WITH!
MY FAVORITES WILL BE SHOWCASED AND WORN BY ME IN THE MANGA!
YAYOI & EIKO RELAXED RADIO
SEND THINGS WE CAN ACTUALLY PUBLISH.
WE'RE ALSO TAKING QUESTIONS, FAN ART, SCARY STORIES, AND MORE, SO SEND THOSE IN TOO. WE CAN'T WAIT TO GET YOUR MAIL!
We'll showcase all that in a different section!
Scary stories on next page

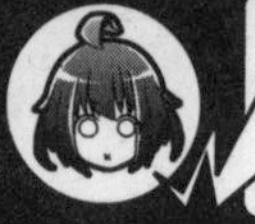

Dark Gathering is a horror manga. You know what every good horror manga needs? Scary stories! And that's what the "Tale Gathering" corner is all about.

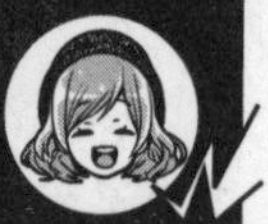

Here we collect scary stories from readers and Yayoi presents them! Personal experiences, stories from friends, or rumors you've heard are all fair game! We'll be sharing the stories that made the staff shudder! To start things off, here's a story from the creator himself!

Tale Gathering I – "Cat"

A personal account by Kenichi Kondo (creator), currently living in Saitama Prefecture

This story happened when I was in elementary school. I was playing in the park with some friends and we found the body of a cat. Another group of boys was there with us and we were all looking at the corpse.

One of them said, "I don't feel bad for this thing. It got what it deserved."

I didn't like hearing that so I replied, "How can you say that? The poor thing." However, there's a legend that says one shouldn't show sympathy for a dead animal, otherwise its spirit will come and haunt you.

At the time, I wasn't familiar with that story. And I'm not very spiritually aware, so I probably wouldn't have even noticed if I got haunted.

So, to jump to the end of the story, I got haunted by the ghost of that cat.

How, you might ask, could someone as oblivious as me realize this?
It took only a few words from my mom.

When I got home, I didn't tell my mom about what I'd seen or done. I just went to bed and the next morning she asked me, "Did you happen to see the body of a dead cat?"

She'd figured it out despite me not saying anything.

Shocked, I wanted to know how she knew. She explained that, long ago, her family had owned a cat (we couldn't own a cat because of my allergies, but that's not really relevant). The cat would sometimes walk across her bed while she was sleeping.

"Last night, I felt a cat walk across my bed," she told me.

After that, my mom sprinkled purifying salts on me. I couldn't see it, so I didn't know what else to do about it. I just remember the eerie realization that I felt something there on my skin for just a moment.

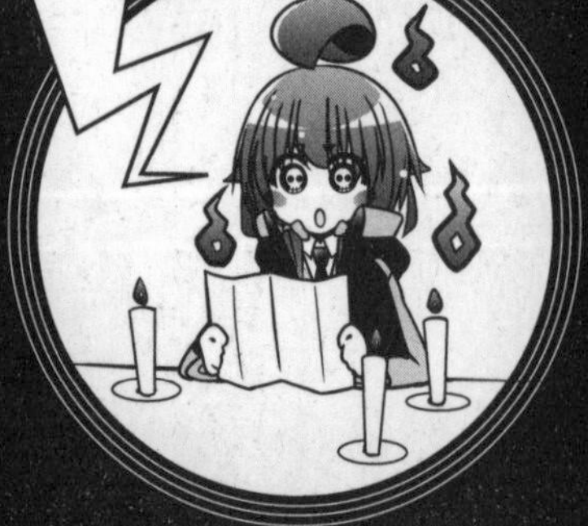

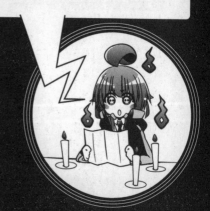

Dark Gathering Special Thanks

❀ Staff
Kinoshita-san
Furukawa-san
Areki-san
Taiki Shudo-san
Keita Nishishima-san

❀ Editor
Takuya Ogawa-san

❀ Graphic Novel Editor
Ryusuke Kuroki-san

❀ Graphic Novel Design
Daiju Asami-san

+

❀ All my readers

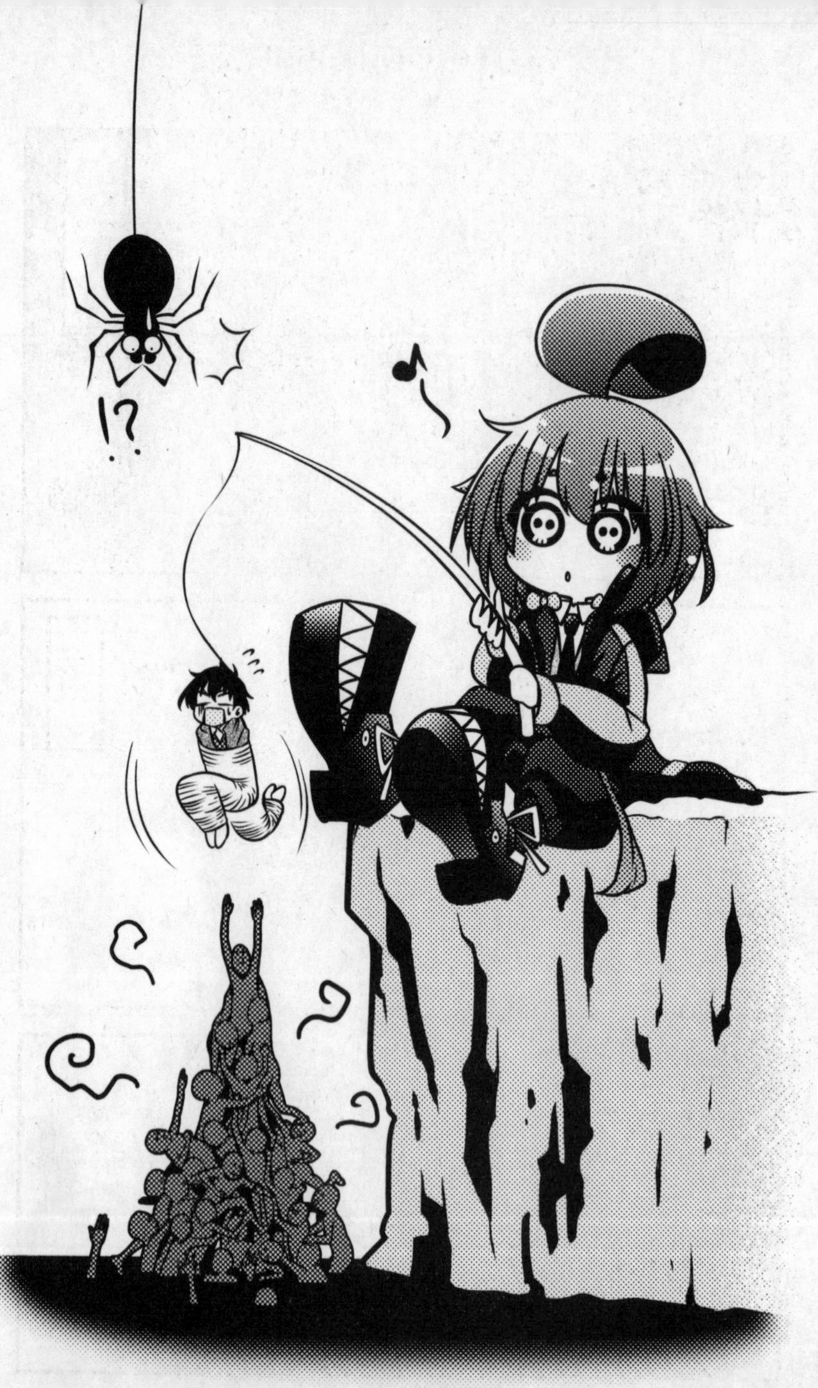
!?

THE TRUTH BEHIND THE HANDPRINTS ON THE CREDITS

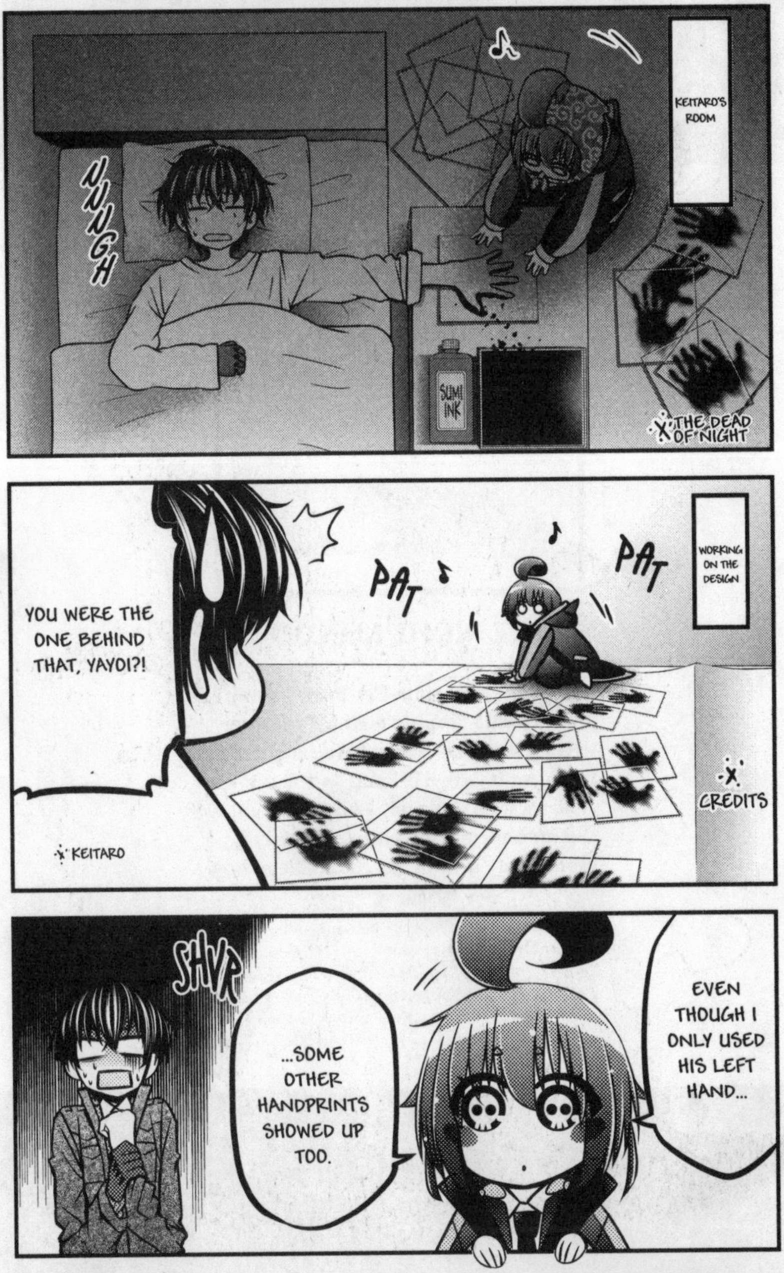
KEITARO'S ROOM
NNNGH
SUMI INK
THE DEAD OF NIGHT
WORKING ON THE DESIGN
PAT
PAT
CREDITS
YOU WERE THE ONE BEHIND THAT, YAYOI?!
KEITARO
EVEN THOUGH I ONLY USED HIS LEFT HAND...
...SOME OTHER HANDPRINTS SHOWED UP TOO.
SHVR

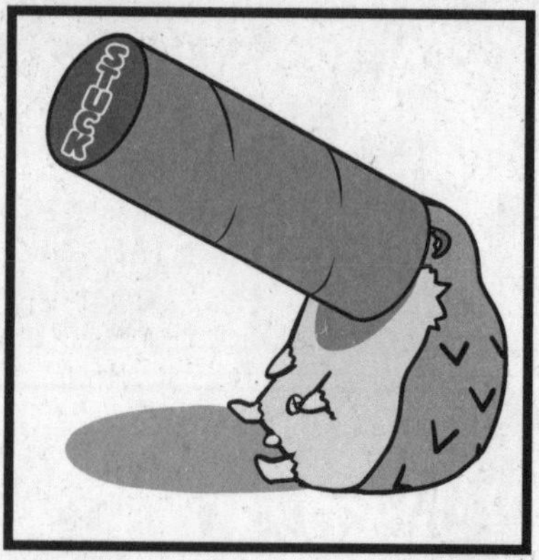
STUCK

KENICHI KONDO

This is the first time I've both written and drawn a graphic novel. I've never written scary stories before, only read them, so let's see if I can spook my readers with this one! I hope you enjoy the paranormal adventures of this elementary school girl and college boy.

Kenichi Kondo got his start working as an assistant for Katsura Hoshino on *D.Gray-man*. In 2016 he released *Cheer Danshi!! -GO BREAKERS-*, a serialized manga adaptation of Ryo Asai's novel *Cheer Danshi!!* His next project, *Dark Gathering*, began its serialization in *Jump SQ.* in 2019.

DARK GATHERING

Volume 1
Shonen Jump Edition

Story and Art by
Kenichi Kondo

Translation and Adaptation / Christine Dashiell
Touch-Up Art & Lettering / Evan Waldinger
Design / Kam Li
Editor / Andrew Kuhre Bartosh

First published in Japan in 2019 by SHUEISHA Inc., Tokyo.
English translation rights arranged by SHUEISHA Inc.

Printed in Canada

Published by VIZ Media, LLC
P.O. Box 77010
San Francisco, CA 94107

10 9 8 7 6 5 4 3 2 1
First printing, May 2023

ratings.viz.com RATED T+ OLDER TEEN

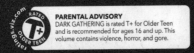

PARENTAL ADVISORY
DARK GATHERING is rated T+ for Older Teen and is recommended for ages 16 and up. This volume contains violence, horror, and gore.

VIZ MEDIA
viz.com

SHONEN JUMP

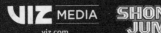

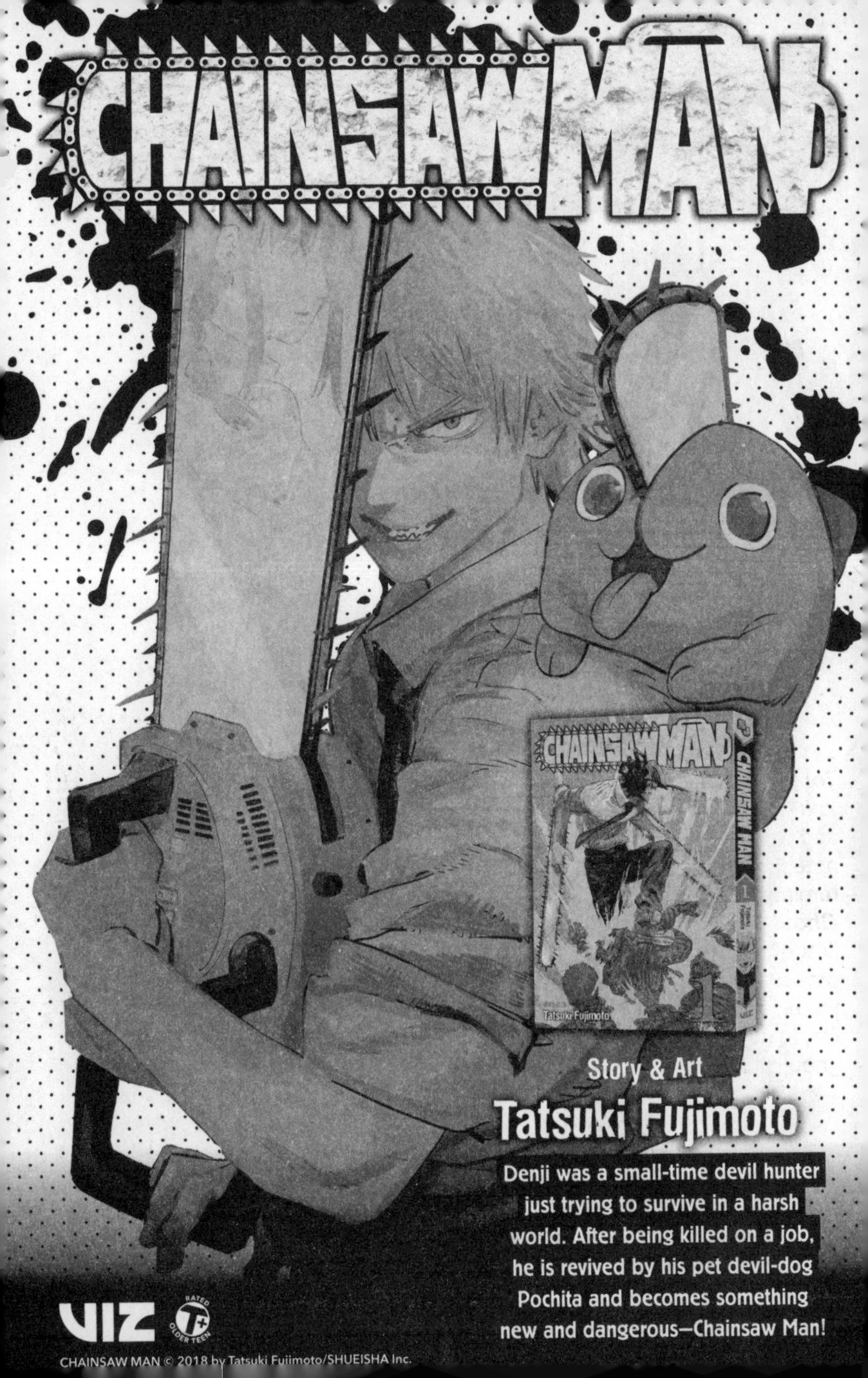

CHAINSAW MAN

Story & Art
Tatsuki Fujimoto

Denji was a small-time devil hunter
just trying to survive in a harsh
world. After being killed on a job,
he is revived by his pet devil-dog
Pochita and becomes something
new and dangerous—Chainsaw Man!

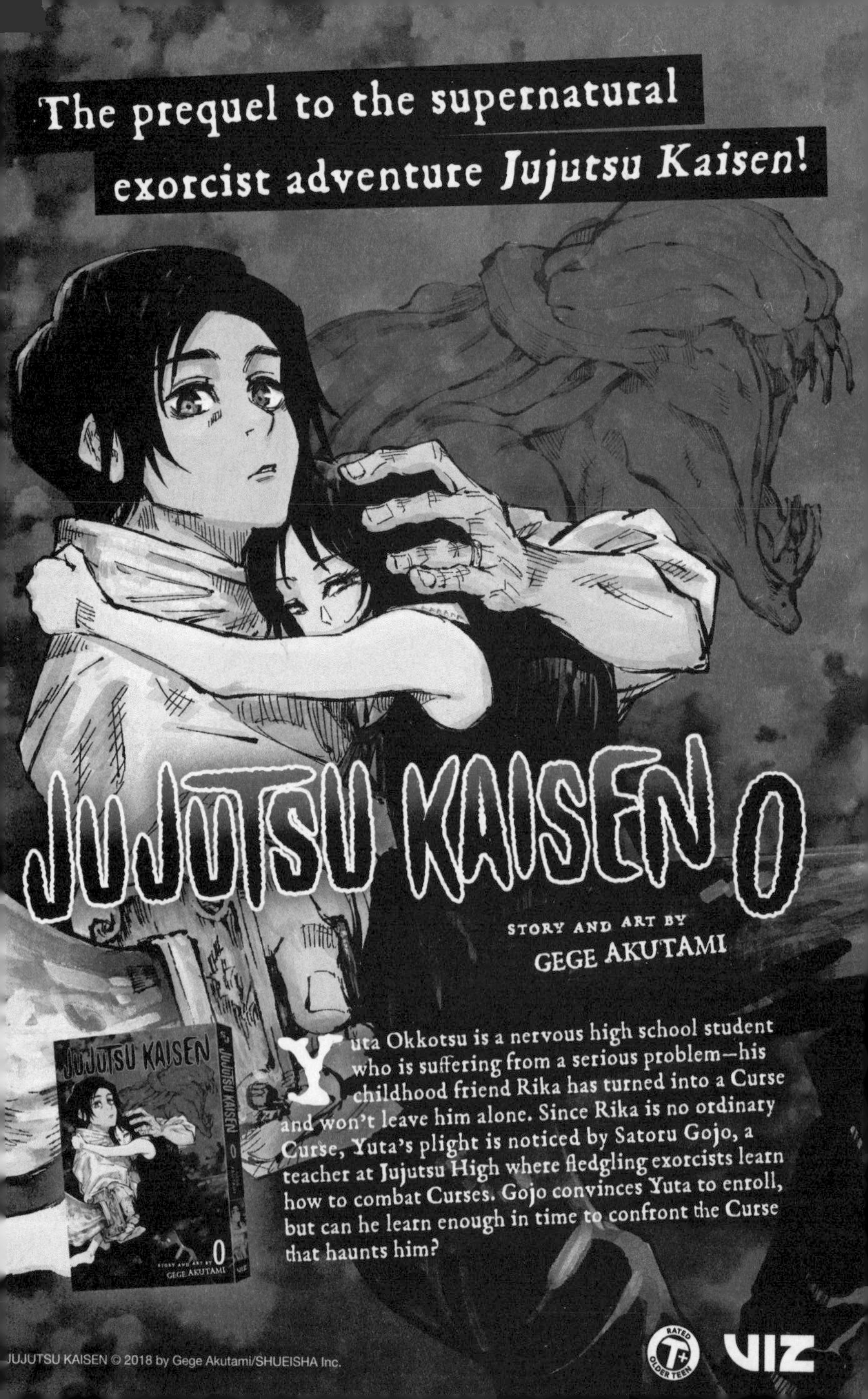
The prequel to the supernatural exorcist adventure *Jujutsu Kaisen*!
JUJUTSU KAISEN 0
STORY AND ART BY
GEGE AKUTAMI
Yuta Okkotsu is a nervous high school student who is suffering from a serious problem—his childhood friend Rika has turned into a Curse and won't leave him alone. Since Rika is no ordinary Curse, Yuta's plight is noticed by Satoru Gojo, a teacher at Jujutsu High where fledgling exorcists learn how to combat Curses. Gojo convinces Yuta to enroll, but can he learn enough in time to confront the Curse that haunts him?
JUJUTSU KAISEN
JUJUTSU KAISEN
0
STORY AND ART BY
GEGE AKUTAMI
VIZ
RATED T+ OLDER TEEN
VIZ
JUJUTSU KAISEN © 2018 by Gege Akutami/SHUEISHA Inc.